CW01654791

THE GREAT ARTISTS

Da Vinci

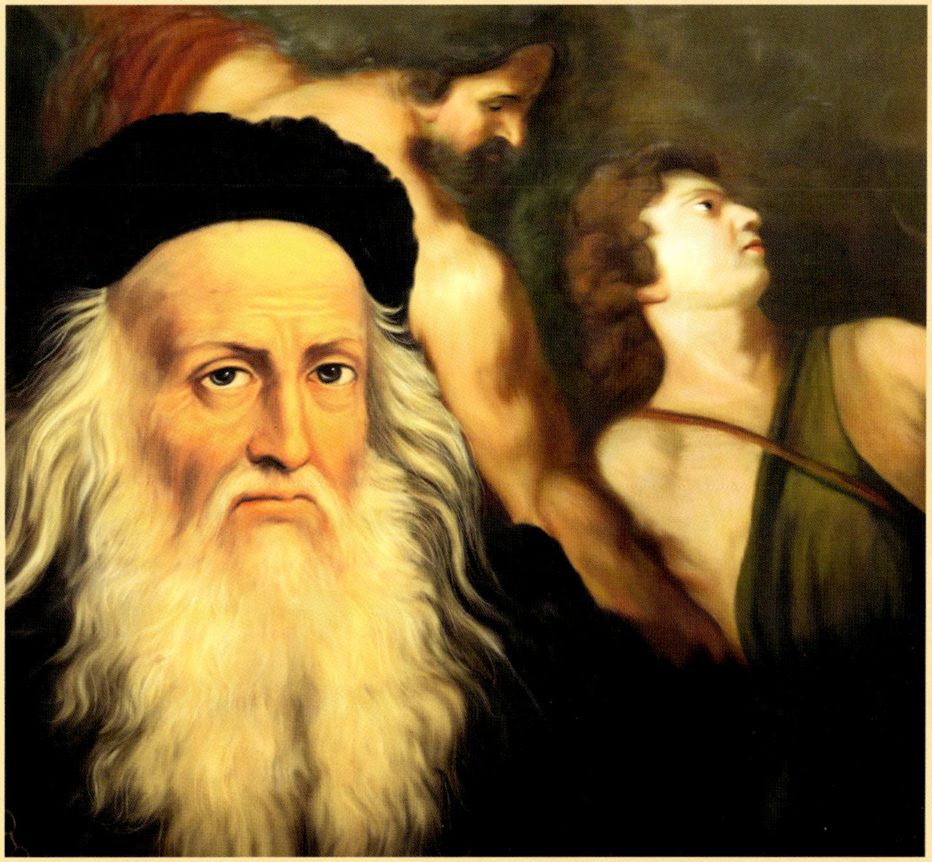

Om KIDZ
An imprint of Om Books International

Leonardo di ser Piero da Vinci was born on 15 April, 1452, in Vinci, the Republic of Florence (modern-day Italy). His father was a respected Florentine notary and his mother was a peasant. At the age of 5, he went to live with his uncle and grandparents.

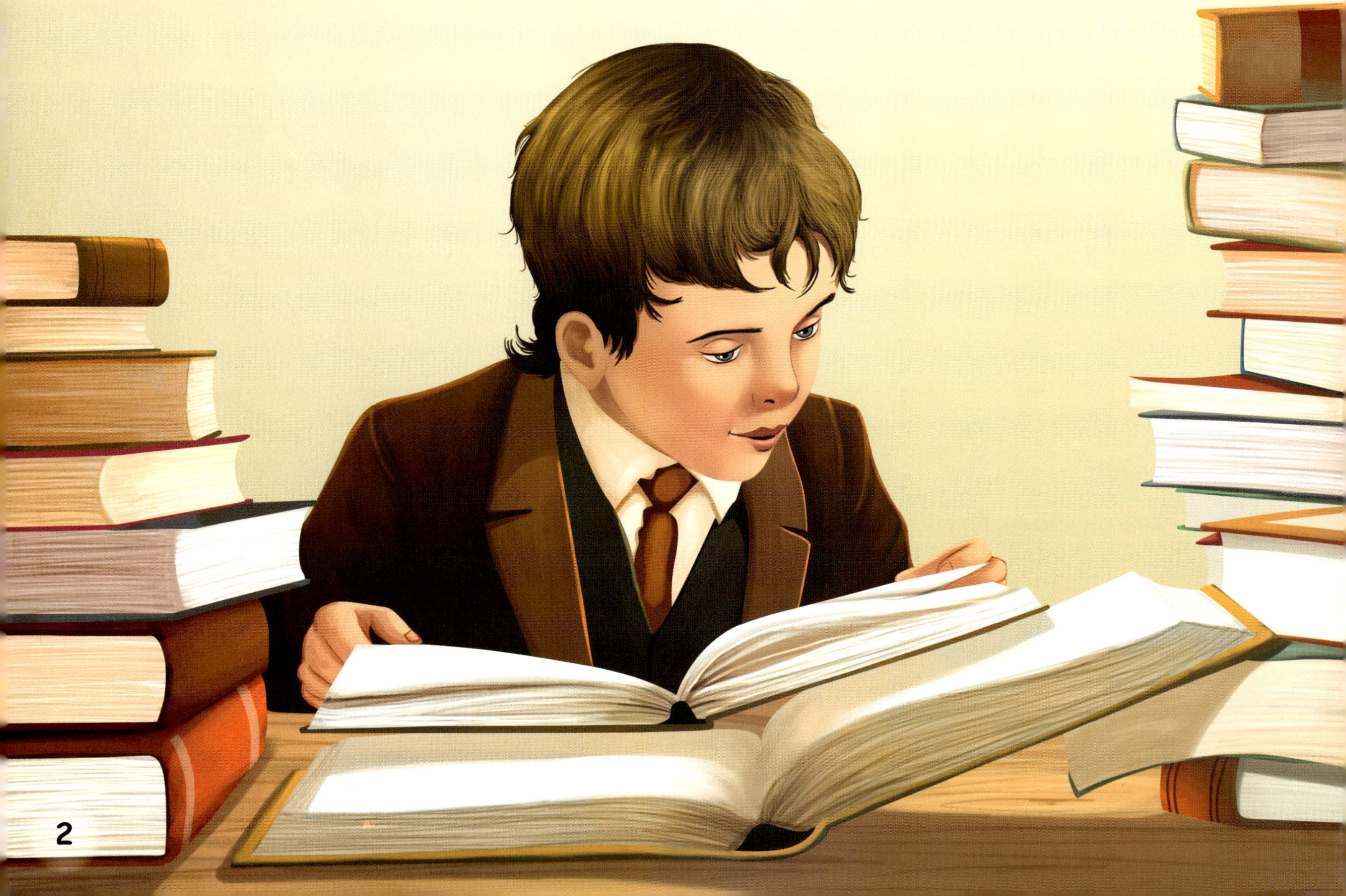

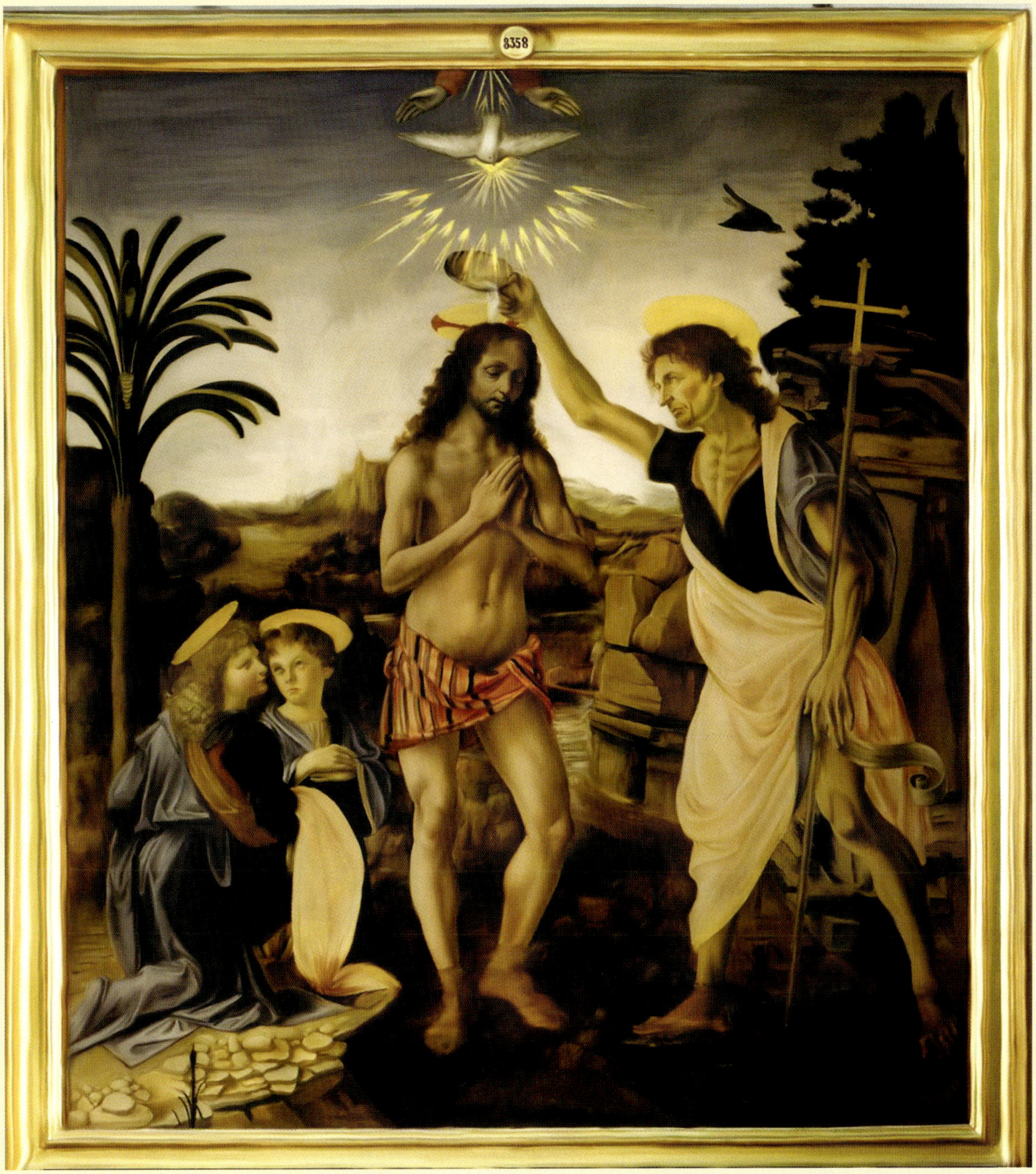

At the age of 14, Leonardo learned many skills including metalworking, leather arts, carpentry, drawing, painting and sculpting while working as an apprentice to the famous artist, Andrea del Verrocchio. It is claimed that Leonardo helped Andrea complete *The Baptism of Christ* by painting parts of the background and one of the angels.

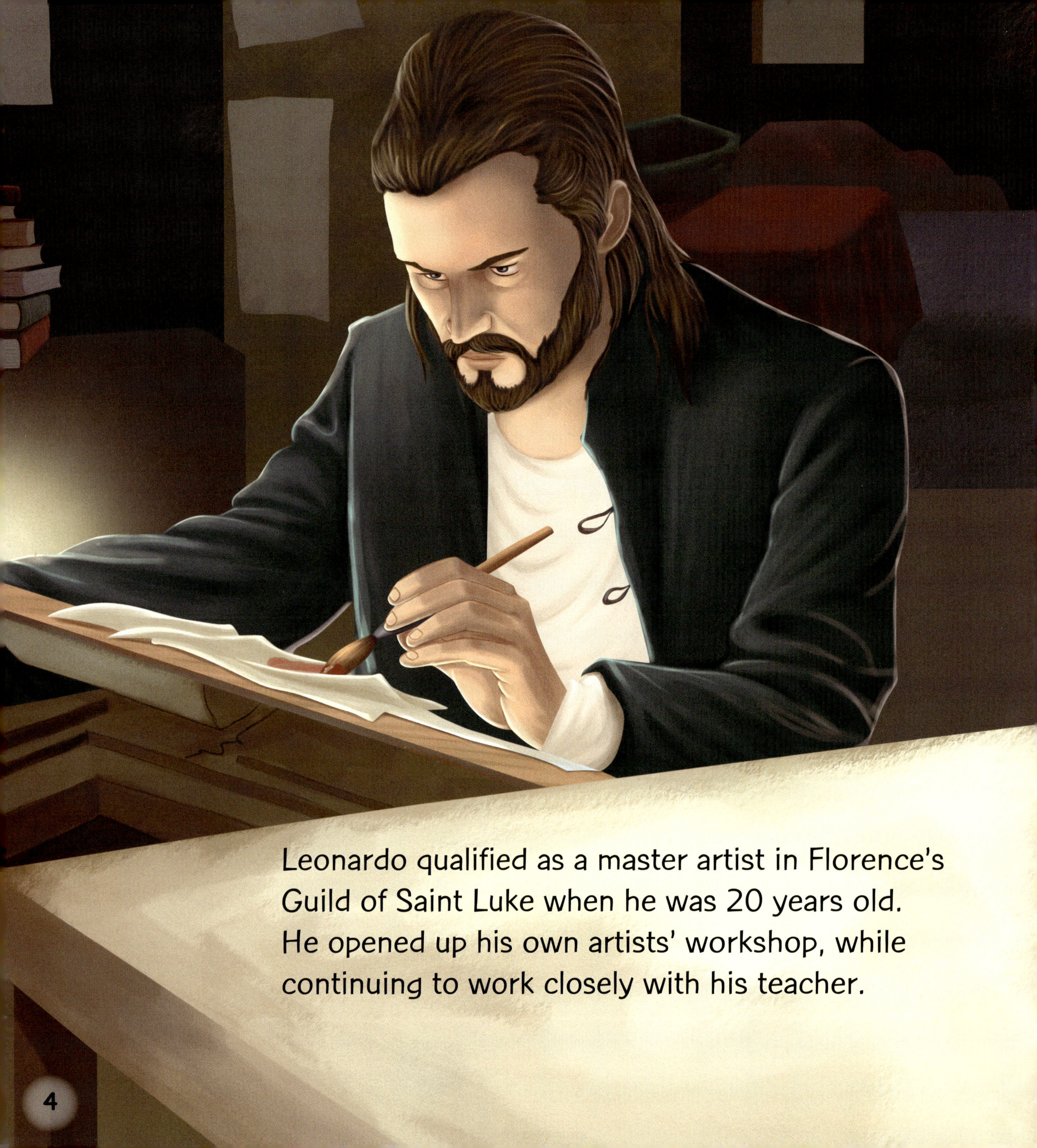

Leonardo qualified as a master artist in Florence's Guild of Saint Luke when he was 20 years old. He opened up his own artists' workshop, while continuing to work closely with his teacher.

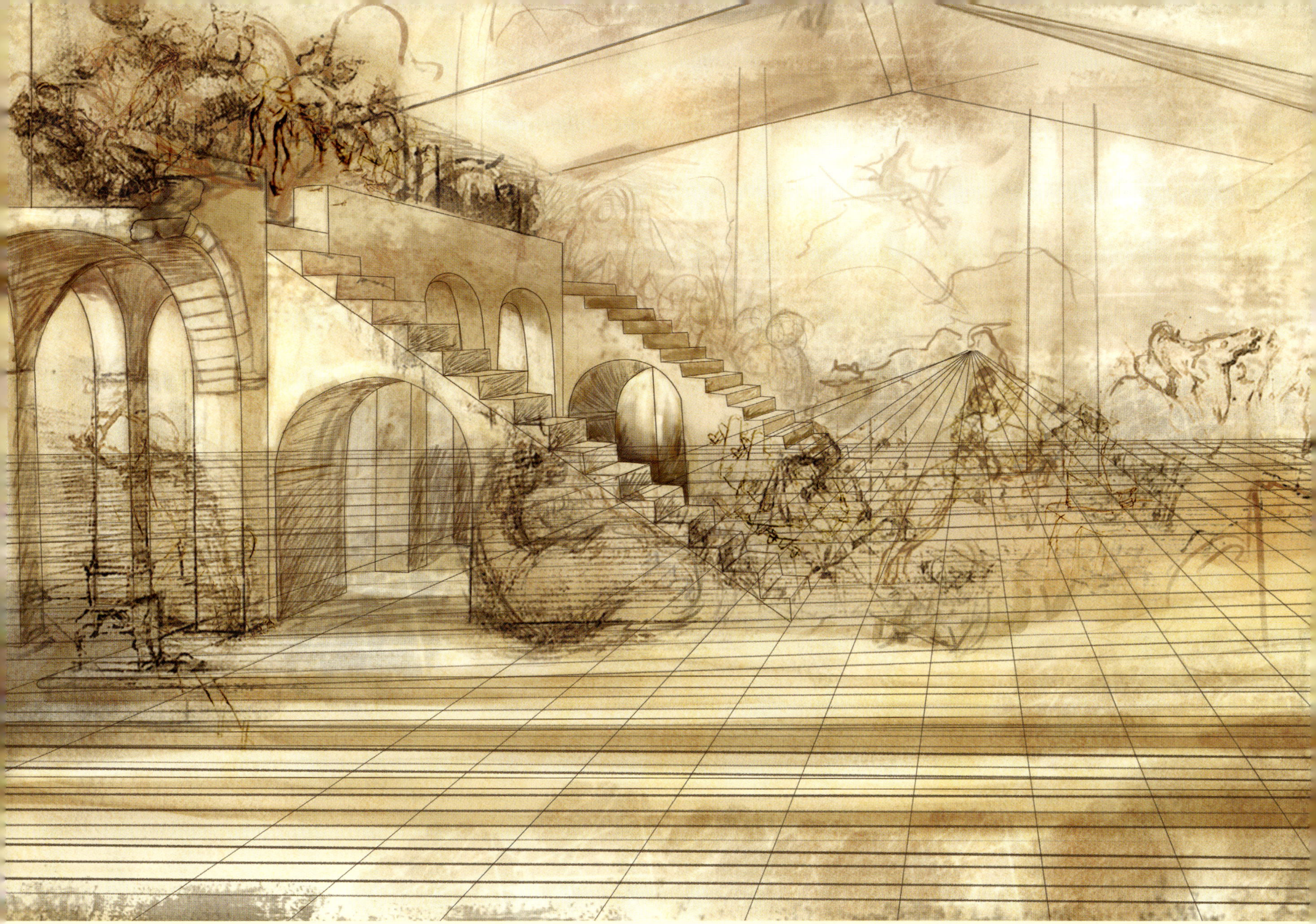

In 1481, Leonardo compiled a detailed study of *The Adoration of Magi*, which remained unfinished. A year later, he received another commission from Lorenzo de' Medici, the Florentine ruler, to create a silver flute for Ludovico Sforza, the ruler of Milan.

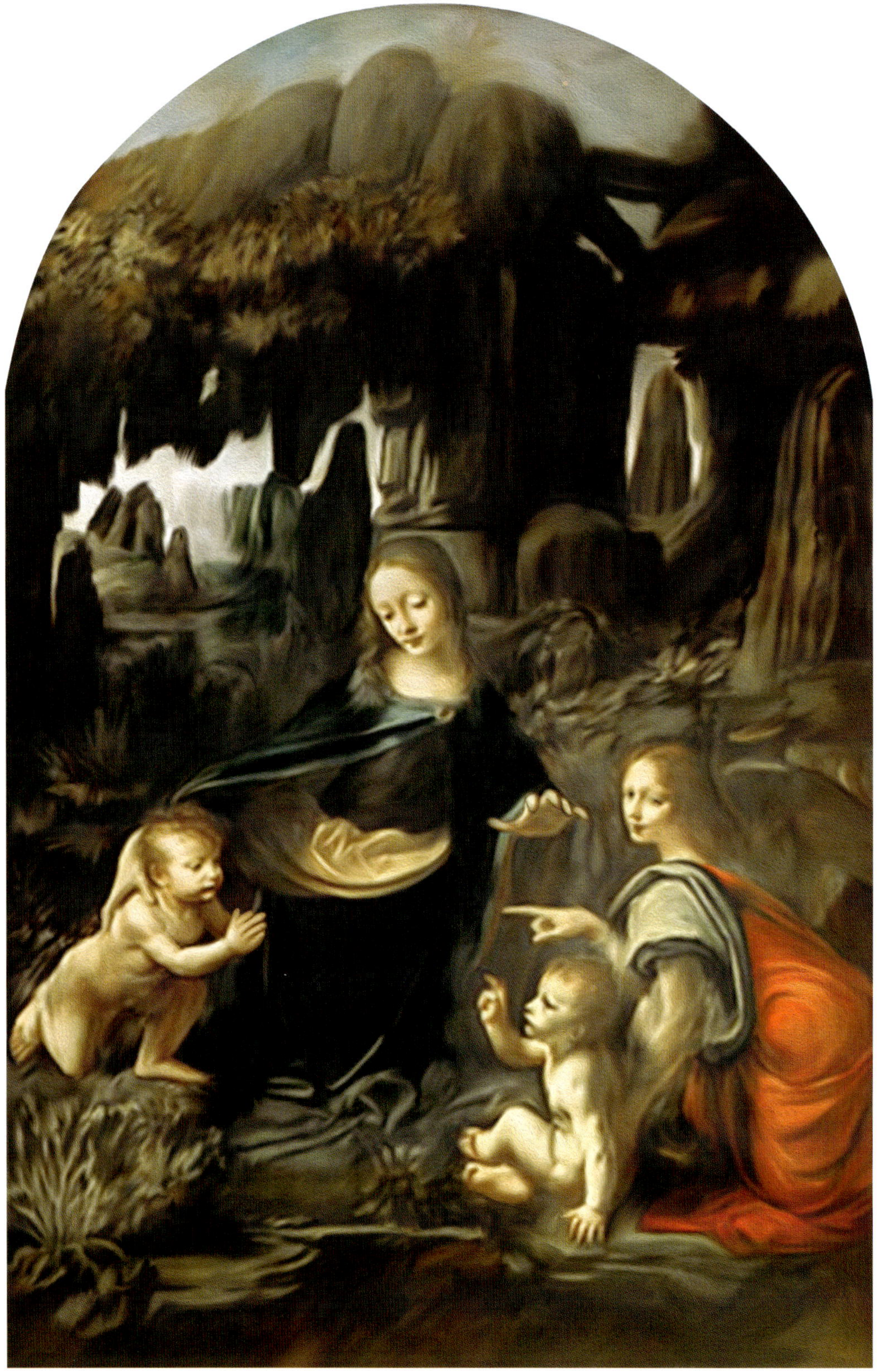

Leonardo moved to Milan for the next 17 years and completed many works, including *The Virgin of the Rocks*. He used the effects of light and dark brilliantly.

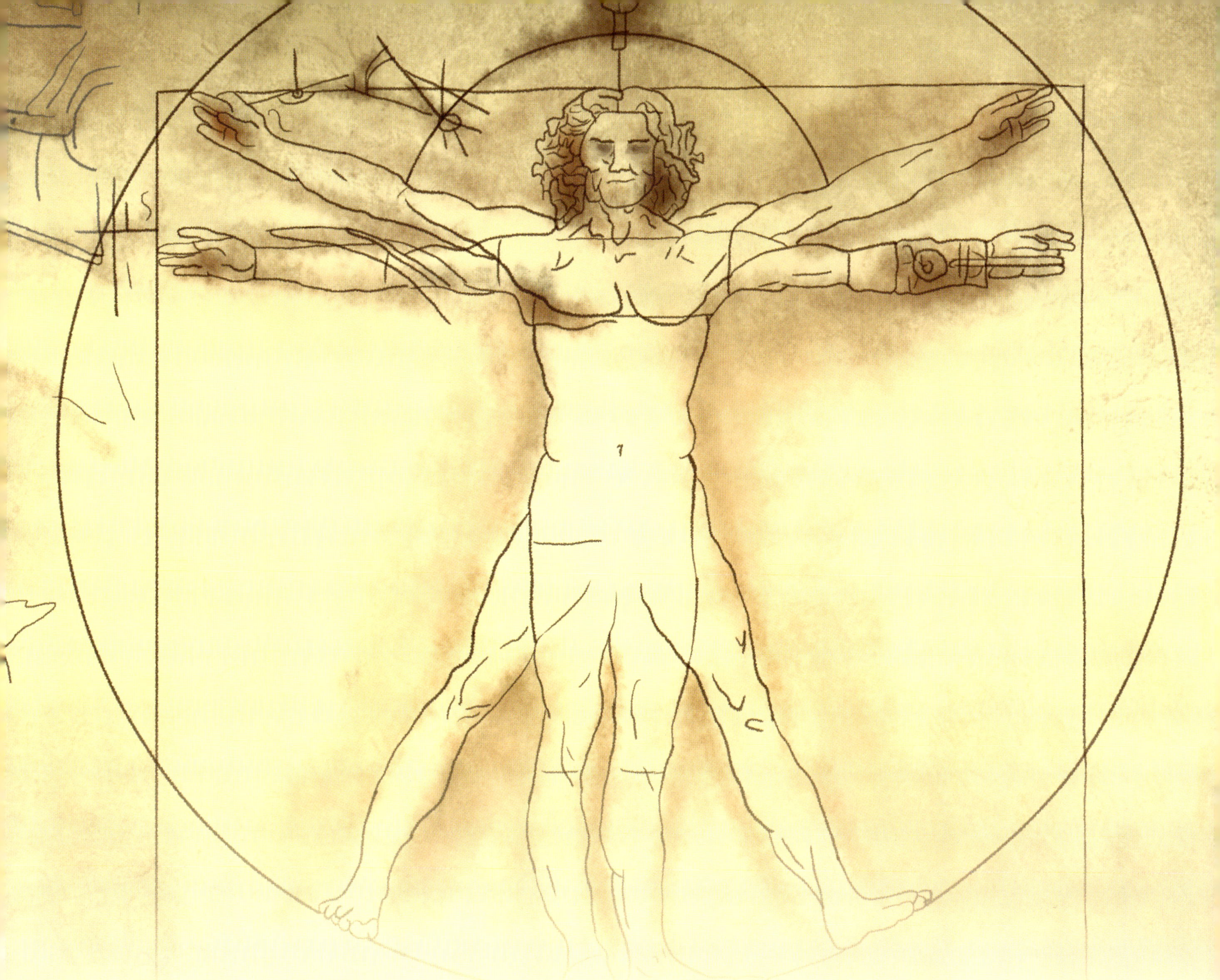

Leonardo studied the human anatomy and did not differentiate between art and science. He believed that science only enhanced the abilities of an artist. *The Vitruvian Man* is one of his most famous studies of the human body.

Leonardo's masterpiece, *The Last Supper*, was a painting for the back wall of the dining hall inside the monastery of Milan's Santa Maria delle Grazie. He completed it in about three years, but it soon became flaky as he had used tempera and oil paints on dry plaster. The painting has now been stabilised with the help of modern techniques.

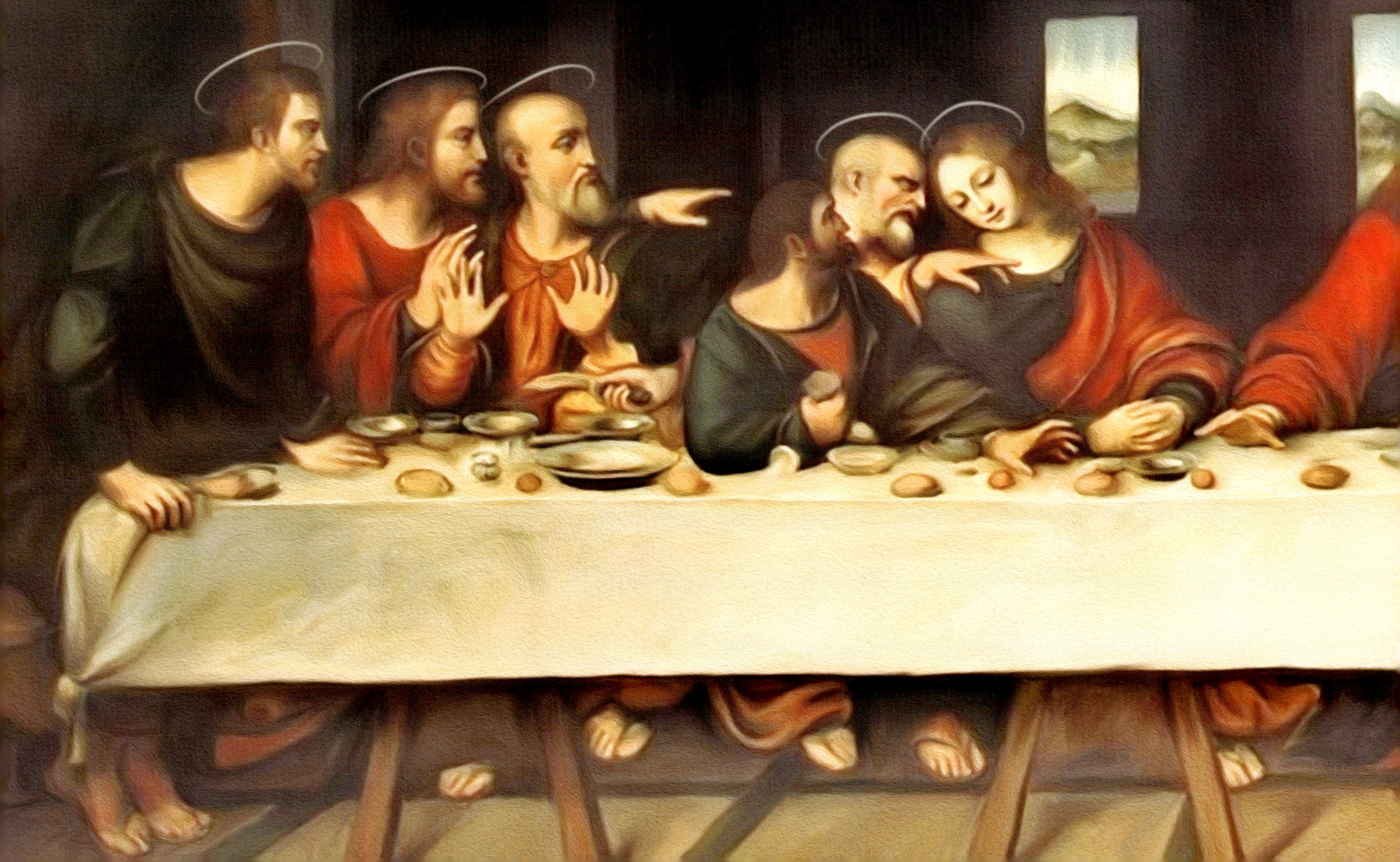

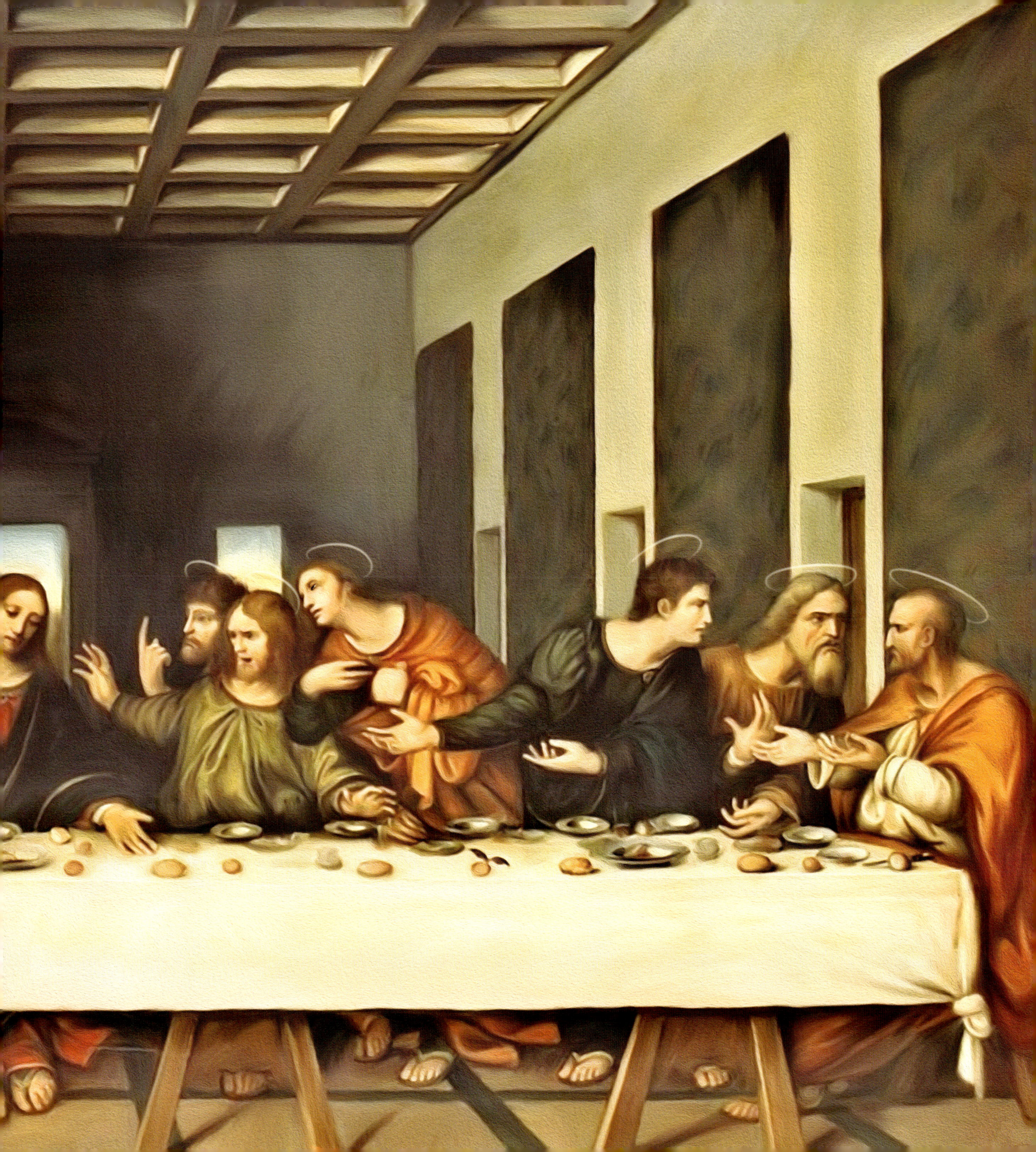

Leonardo returned to Florence, where he continued to work on military projects for powerful personnel.

He started working on a mural called *The Battle of Anghiari*, which was supposed to be twice the size of *The Last Supper*. However, this project was abandoned because the painting started flaking, even as Leonardo worked on it.

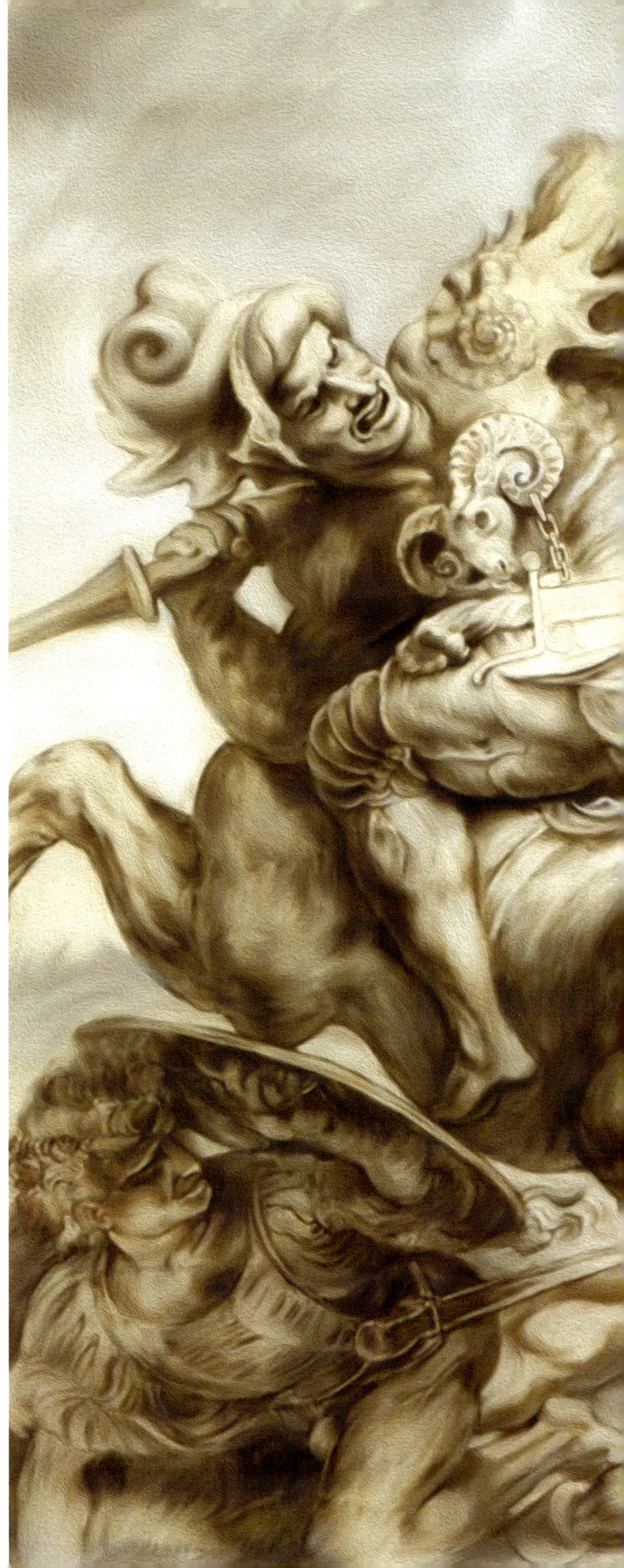

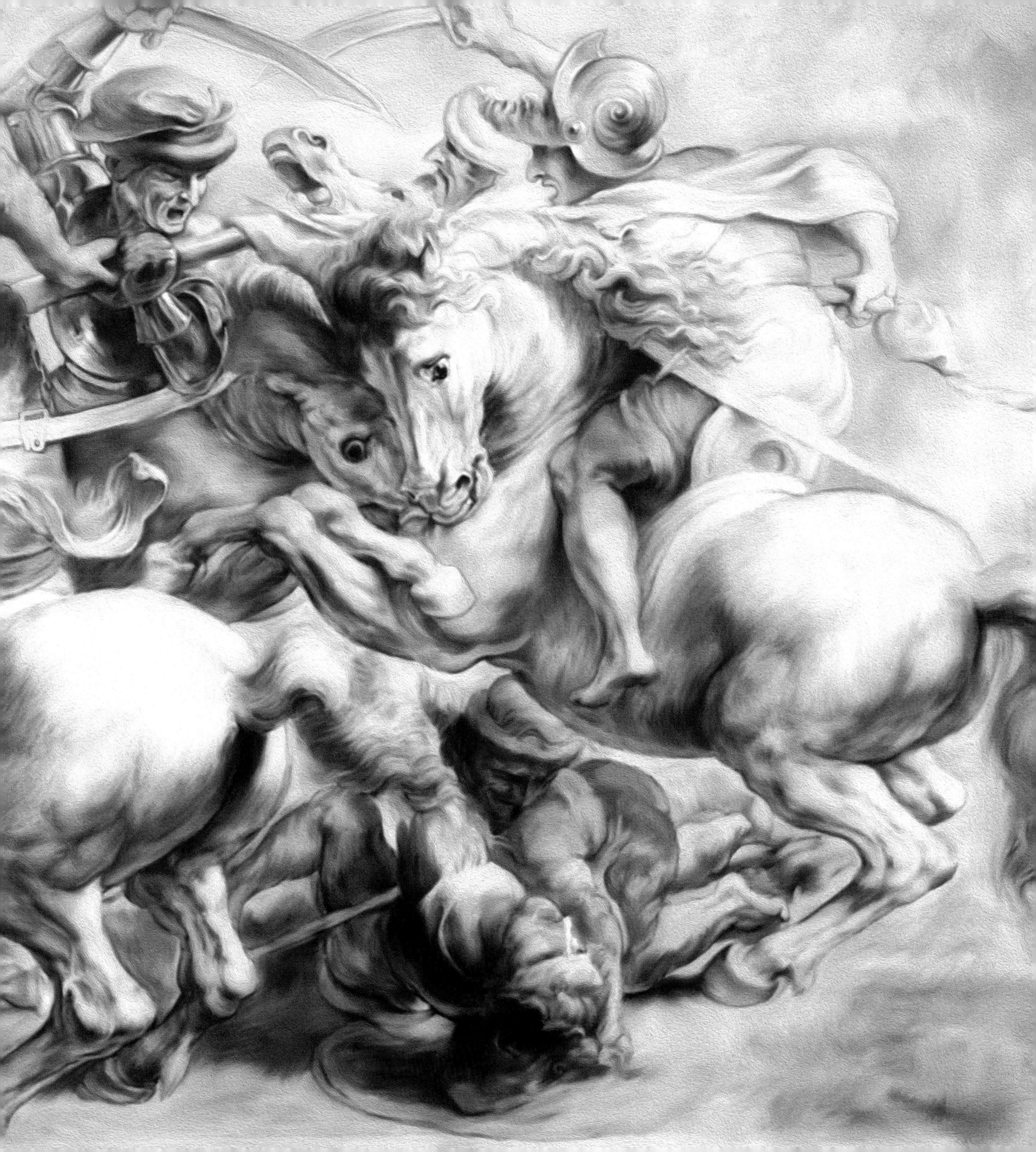

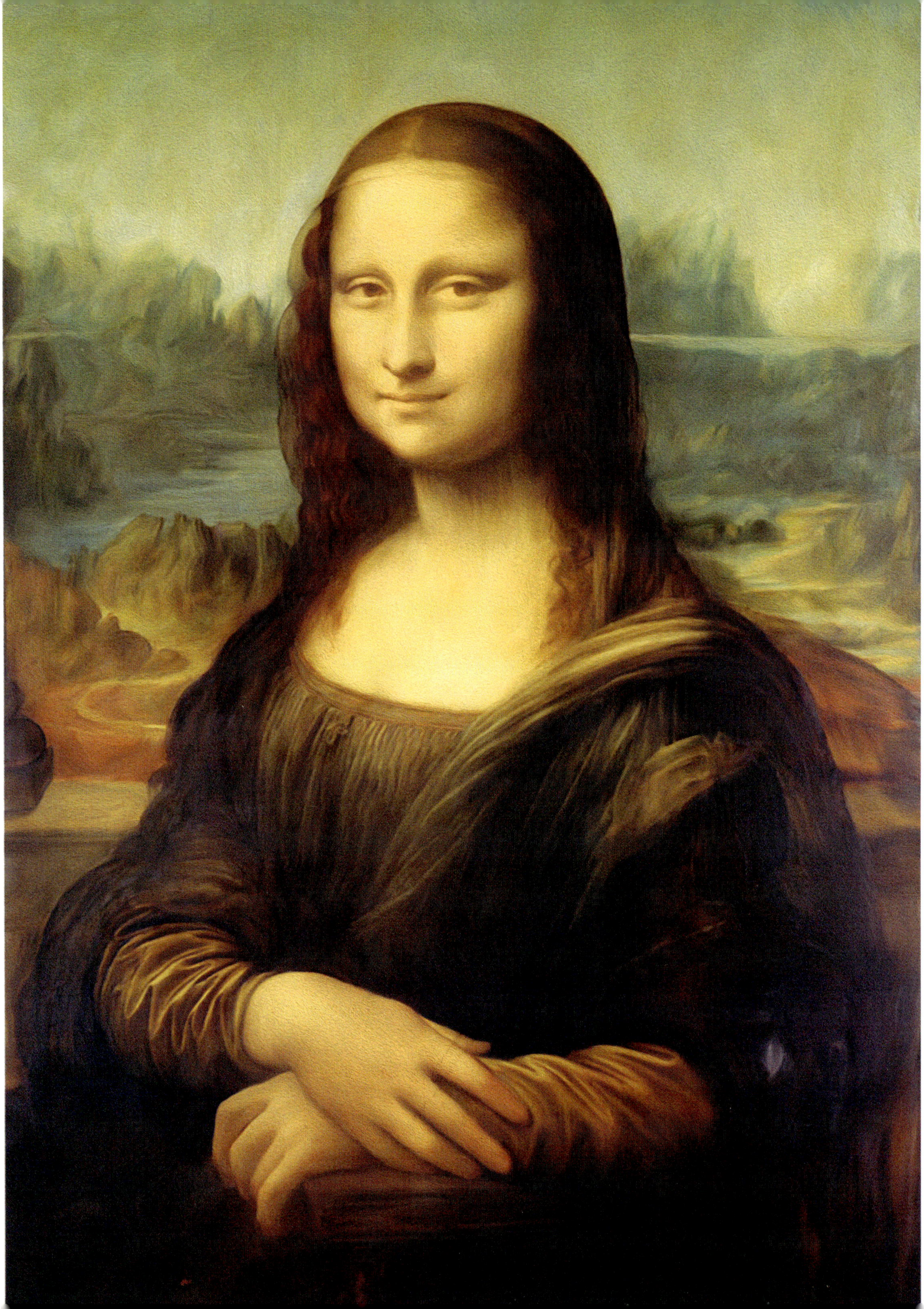

At around the same time, Leonardo started painting the *Mona Lisa*, which is arguably the most iconic painting in the world. Apart from the mysterious smile and the style that was used, the painting is also famous because the identity of the woman in it is unknown.

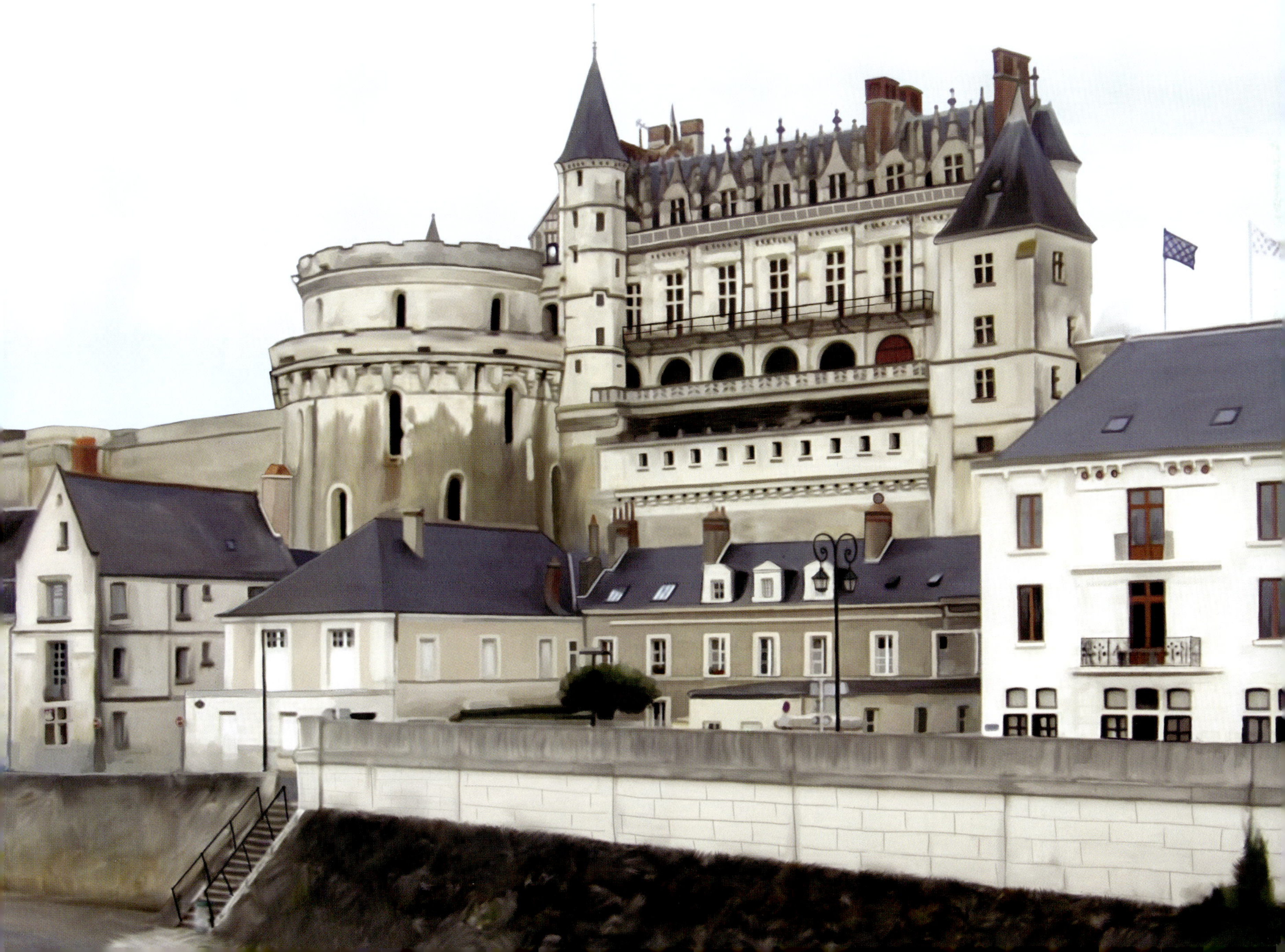

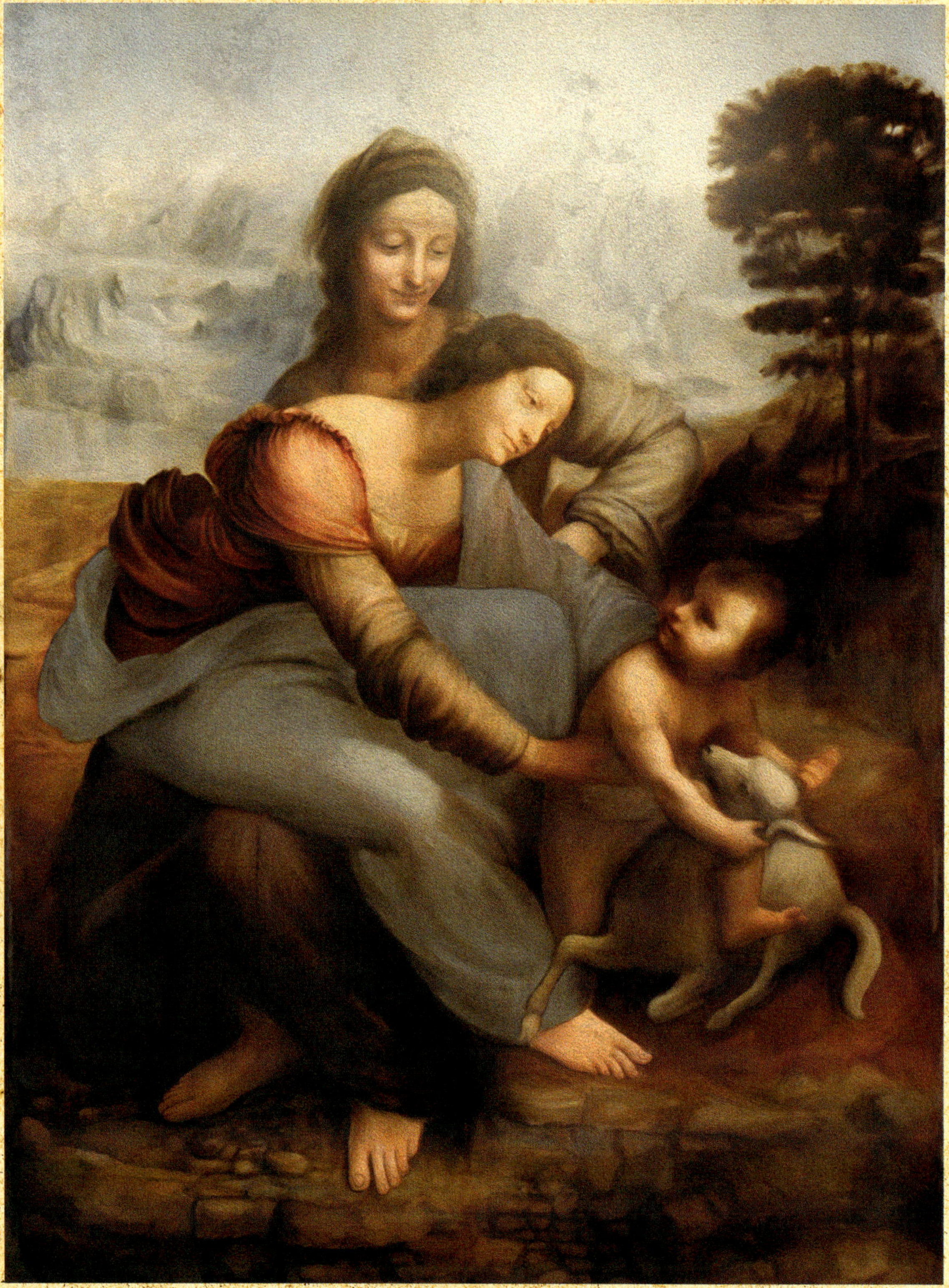

Leonardo returned to Milan, this time to work for the French. He focused more on his scientific studies and painted less and less.

Leonardo made notes in loose sheets and carried them around, tucked in his belt. He made thousands of theoretical observations, which he divided into the broad categories of painting, architecture, mechanics and human anatomy.

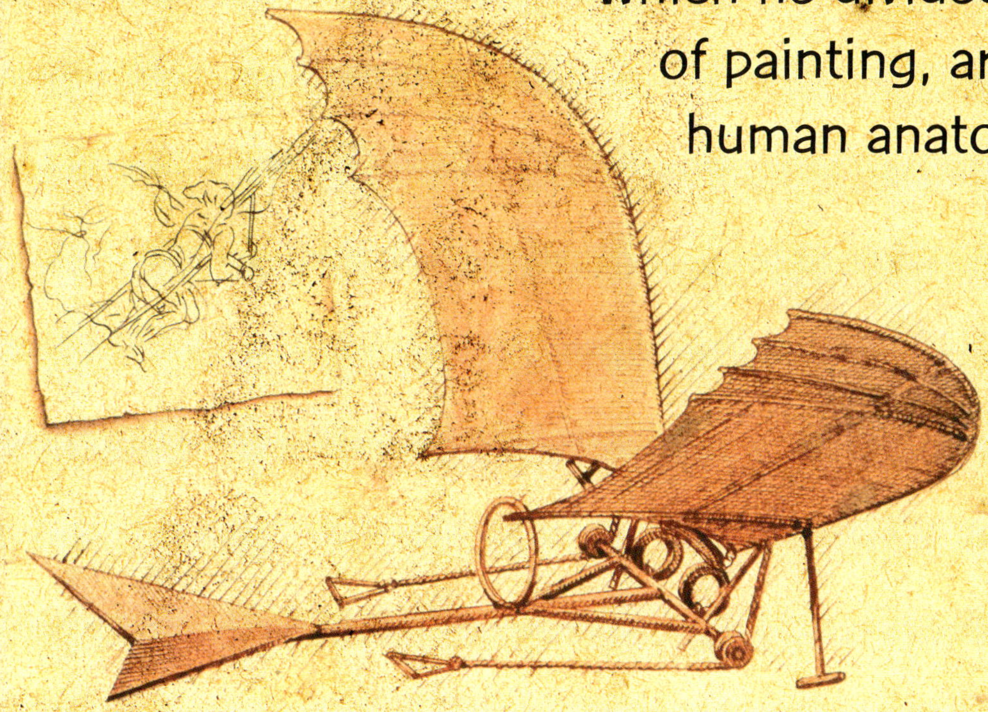

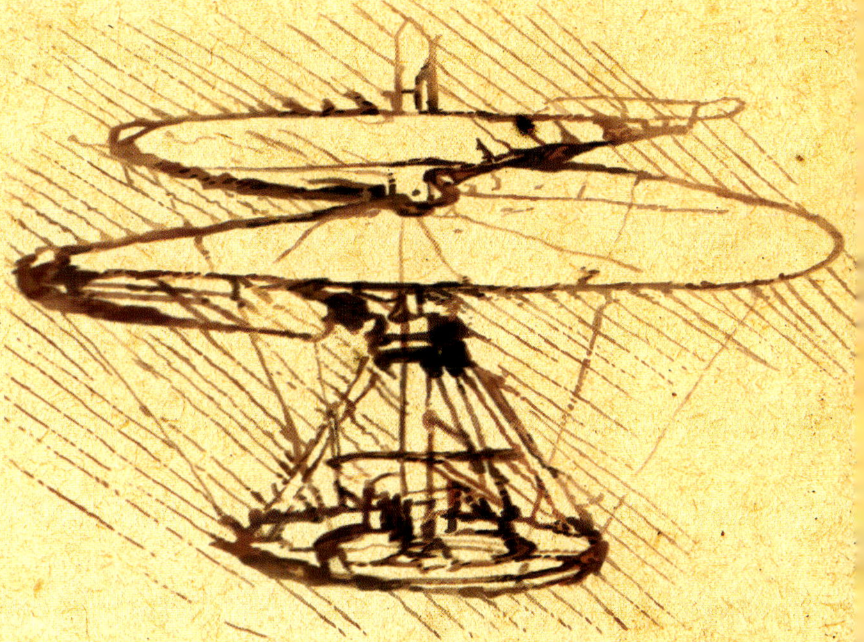

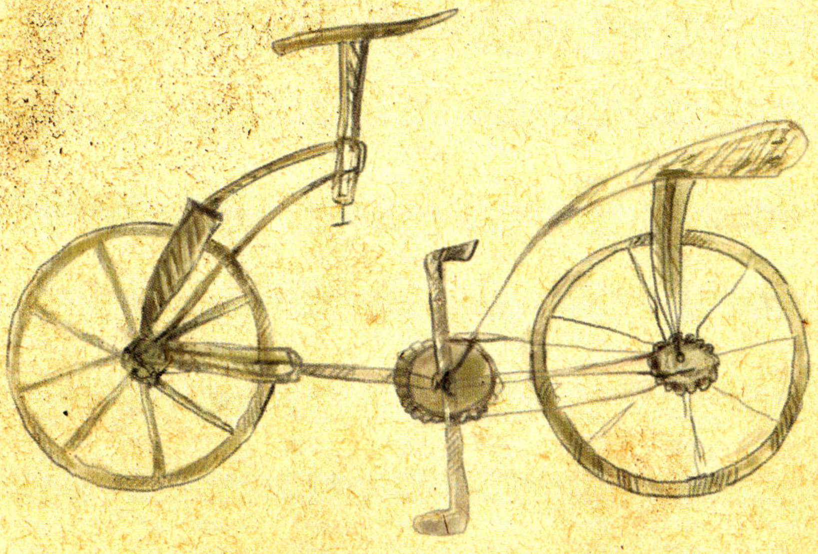

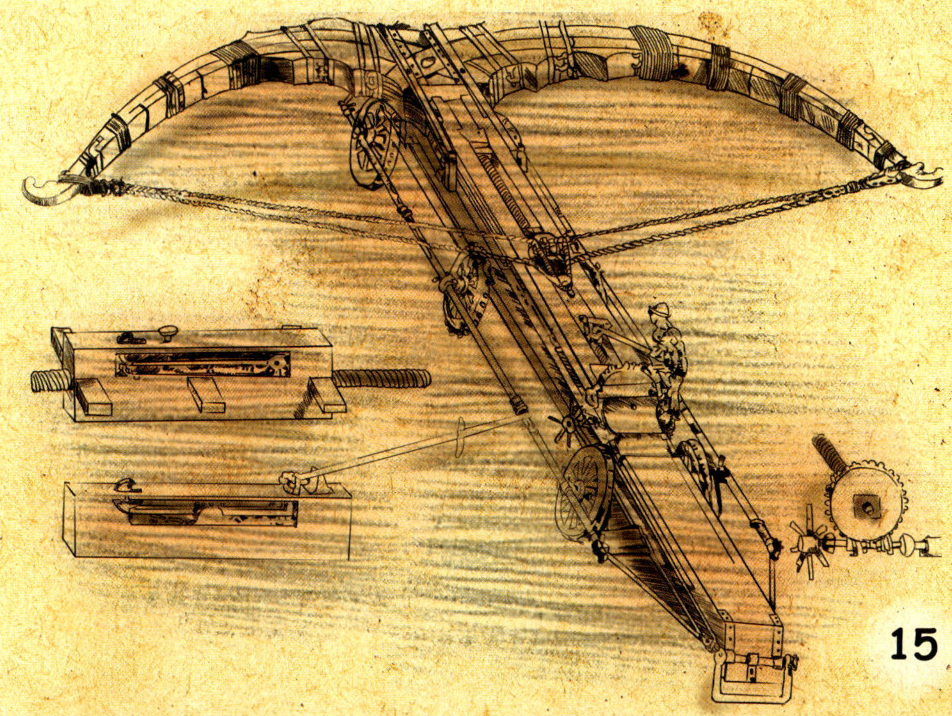

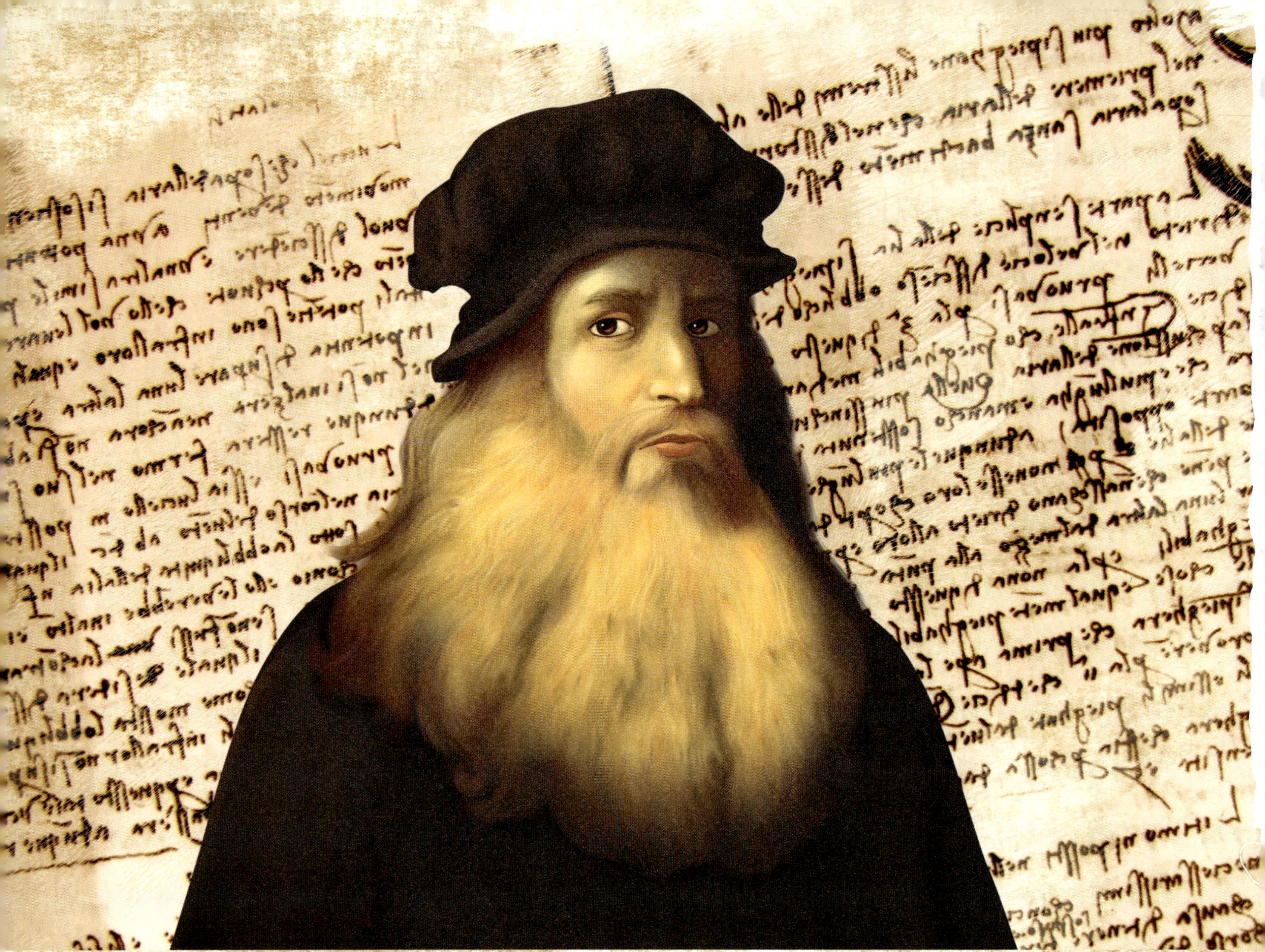

Leonardo da Vinci was an artist, scientist and inventor. He is considered to be one of the most talented and intelligent artists of all time.

He died at the age of 67 on 2 May, 1519.

The Colours of the Merseyside Area

Michael Eyre

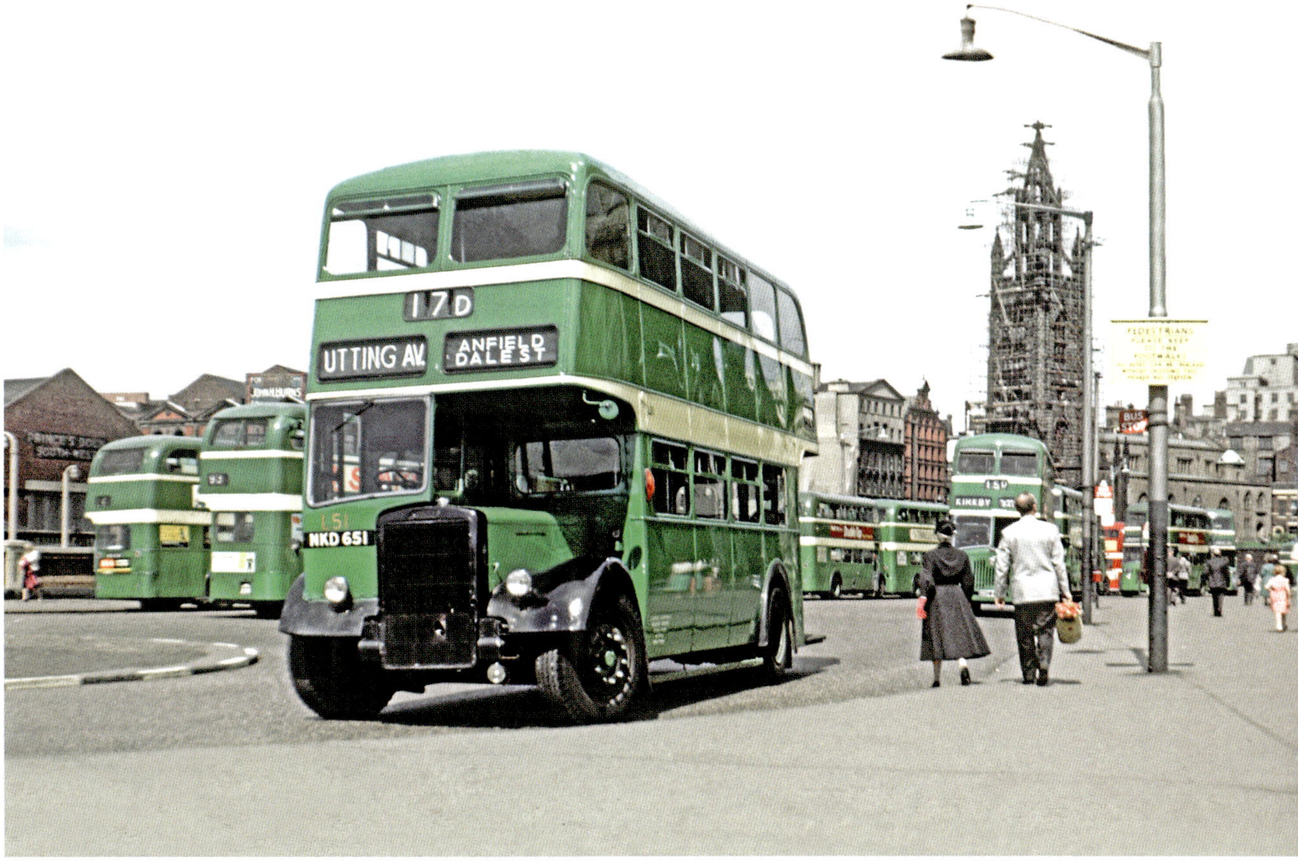

Capital Transport

Acknowledgements

As ever, this book is a team effort. The principal thanks are to the photographers who, many years ago, went out and took the photographs, often at a time when colour photography was expensive. Image restoration work has been necessary on some but there is no artificial colour in any. We have tried to ensure that each image is correctly attributed to its photographer – our apologies in advance if any are incorrect.

Peter Greaves and Ken Swallow have answered what must have seemed to them interminable questions of detail and have kindly read through the proofs. Some initial work on picture selection and text was done by Martin Jenkins and Charles Roberts but pressure of business caused a halt. The records of the Omnibus Society and the more recent publications of the PSV Circle have been invaluable as have the masterly five-volume history of Liverpool's transport by John Horne and Bruce Maund, Bruce Maund's other books on the area's bus fleets, Duncan Roberts' history of Crosville and John Robinson's Warrington history. Richard Morant, who now cares for the Geoffrey Morant images, has done sterling work cataloguing and dating images. The inevitable mistakes are the author's.

The authors' fees and the majority of the image reproduction fees for this book have either been waived or donated to the Image Archive of the Omnibus Society and the Online Transport Archive to further their work in the preservation and restoration of road transport images.

Frontispiece St Nicholas Place, alongside the north edge of the Liver Building at Pier Head, was the terminus for Liverpool and some Ribble services whilst the site for the new bus station was decided upon. In this 1962 picture Leyland Titan PD2/12 fleet number L51's paintwork shines in the sunlight. The bus was new in 1953, its Weymann body built to the Transport Department's drawings and specification. The church in the background is The Church of Our Lady and St Nicholas, the Anglican parish church of Liverpool – not to be confused with the city's modern Anglican and Roman Catholic cathedrals. *Peter Roberts*

Front cover Birkenhead was Massey's biggest client, a relationship which went back to 1931. Fleet number 143, shown here leaving Woodside Ferry terminus, was one of a batch of fifteen Leyland PD2/37 that were Birkenhead's last new rear-platform buses. In the background, across the River Mersey, is the Liver Building at Liverpool's Pier Head – an icon of the city. *March 1968, Roy Marshall*

Back cover From 1953 until they were no longer available, Chester's double-deckers were Gardner-engined Guy Arabs, almost all with Massey bodies – a durable, reliable and high quality choice which well reflected the city's proud heritage and unique character. In November 1967 the first of those postwar Guy Arabs turns from Bridge Street into White Friars on the two-mile journey to Cliveden Road, Lache, in the south west of the city. *Geoffrey Morant*

First published 2013

ISBN 978-1-85414-361-7

Published by Capital Transport Publishing Ltd
www.capitaltransport.com

Printed by 1010 Printing International Ltd

Contents

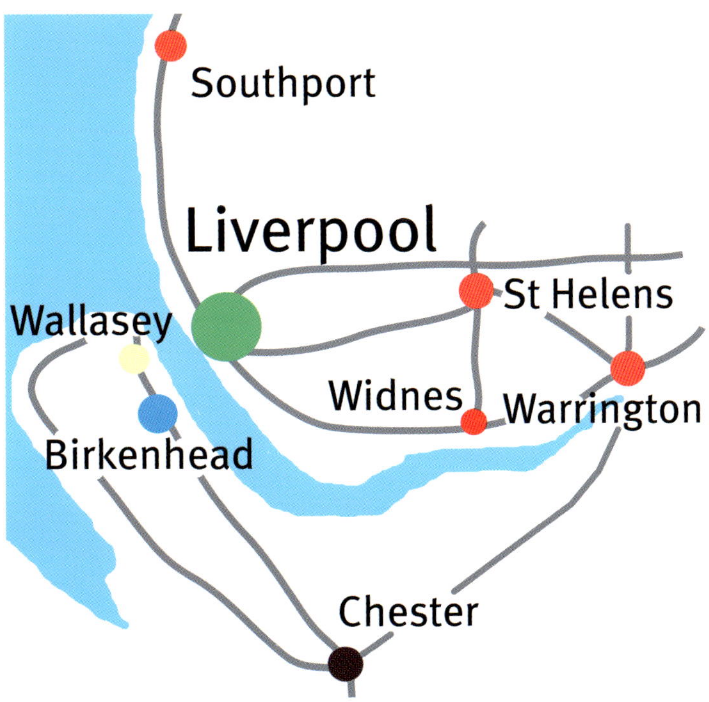

Southport
Liverpool
St Helens
Wallasey
Widnes
Warrington
Birkenhead
Chester

Introduction

This book of colour images from the 1950s, 1960s and early 1970s remembers the bus fleets of the Merseyside area. In addition to Merseyside itself, the book's scope continues a little further up the River Mersey to Widnes and Warrington and extends the Wirral beyond the Domesday Book's boundary of 'two arrowfalls from the city walls' so as to include the city of Chester.

Many hoped that the municipal transport departments' existence would follow the words of the Beatles 1969/70 hit *'Let It Be'* but central government politics is stronger than local feeling and in December of 1969 the newly formed Merseyside Passenger Transport Executive acquired and merged the Liverpool, Birkenhead and Wallasey undertakings. Local Government reorganisation of April 1974 created the Metropolitan County of Merseyside which brought St Helens and Southport into the Merseyside PTE. At the same time, Chester, Warrington and Widnes were reconstituted as new larger individual authorities, in the case of Widnes with a new name of Halton, and the book ends at these events.

Liverpool has a long history of social and commercial innovation and success – the port, the docks, the civic and commercial buildings, two modern cathedrals, the Pier Head, the world famous 'Merseybeat' sound, the Beatles and more. Its transport heritage includes early electric railways, the overhead railway, a splendid tramway system and the road and rail tunnels under the river.

Liverpudlians' famous sense of humour was never more needed than in the Second World War when the city suffered the worst bombing blitz outside London. The trams kept the city going but at great cost to their maintenance and the decision was taken to replace them with buses. The transport department's staff had firm ideas on what was wanted, especially in bodywork, and by 1958 had a fleet of over 1,100 buses, all but seven of which were double-deckers, principally AEC Regents and Leyland PD2s with bodies to the department's own practical design.

By the time the trams were gone the bus industry was suffering from a new rival – the private car. In 1963 the Ford Motor Company opened a new plant at Halewood, Liverpool where it produced the Anglia, the styling of which influenced Liverpool's striking design for the body on its fleet of 380 Leyland Atlanteans.

Across the Mersey, on the Wirral peninsula, the largest borough was Birkenhead, home to the famous Cammell Laird shipyards. Jointly with Vickers, Cammell Laird owned bus body builder Metropolitan Cammell. A little way up the Mersey was the works of Lever Brothers, later Unilever – home of such famous products as Persil washing powder, Sunlight soap and Stork margarine. Birkenhead's smart blue and cream bus fleet – mainly Leylands with Massey bodies – reflected the town's prosperity and civic pride.

Wallasey was principally residential but included the seaside resort of New Brighton, to which people flocked – until the jet engine opened new horizons. The bus fleet was durable Metro Cammell-bodied Leylands bought in big batches, not least thirty Atlanteans more or less off the drawing board. In the 1960s the need to combat falling traffic brought several innovations, including the first municipal minibus service.

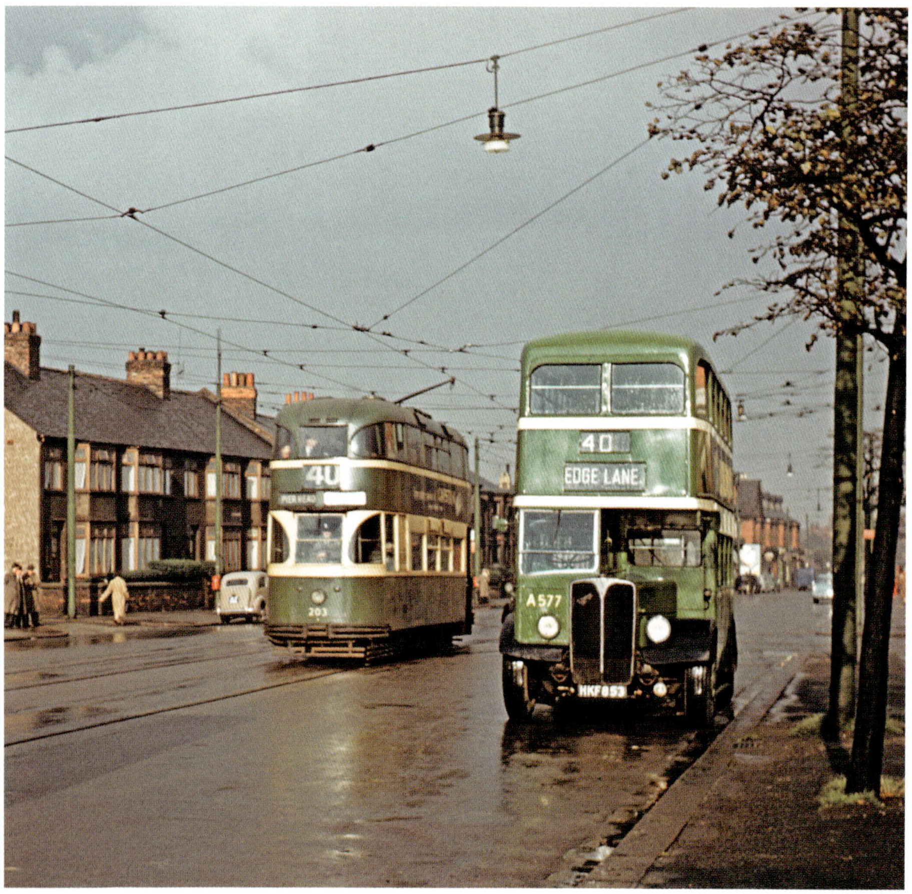

Outside Liverpool's Edge Lane Works where it was built, 1938 Baby Grand tram 203 bound for Pier Head passes 1948 AEC Regent A577 – its Weymann body also finished in the works. The specially posed picture was taken during the final week of the trams in September 1957. When the final procession of trams left Pier Head as the Liver Building clock struck six-o-clock on the evening of the 14th, the Transport Department band played 'Wish me luck as you wave me goodbye' – the Beatles weren't around in 1957. *Phil Tatt*

North of Liverpool, Southport was wealthy and up-market. Although a seaside resort, it was home to the business magnates of Liverpool and Manchester and many a Southport house had a Rolls Royce or Daimler in the garage. The appropriately immaculate bus fleet was mainly Leylands but it also had the most unusual bus service in the country – buses which were 4x4s and ran on the sands, often with the sea lapping at their wheel hubs.

St Helens' bus fleet worked hard serving a largely working-class population. Its services were unconstrained by civic boundaries and St Helens buses could be seen in Liverpool, Southport, Warrington, Widnes and Wigan. It also ran trolleybuses, the long route through Haydock and Hindley to Atherton jointly operated with Lancashire United's trolleybus subsidiary South Lancashire Transport. Most interesting of all its buses were 40 'London Transport' RTs bought brand new in 1950-1952.

Chester, county town of Cheshire, was and still is a fine walled city which dates back to Roman times, with wonderful old buildings including the famous 'Rows'. It was both the commercial and shopping centre for miles around and also a major attraction for visitors. The smart bus fleet – mainly Guys with Massey bodies – mirrored this proud history.

Warrington was something of a mixture – plenty of industry but a town centre with a cramped mediaeval street pattern. Its transport department was a stepping stone for ambitious transport managers and the frequent changes of general manager affected the bus fleet – though principally Leylands, there were also Fodens, Guys, Bristols, Daimlers and an Albion. One thing that was constant was East Lancashire Coachbuilders bodywork.

For years Widnes was the home of the country's chemical industry and the price it paid was pollution. Its modest fleet, mainly Leylands, worked a tight and efficient network of frequent services. The buses were well cared for and Widnes got a long life from them although, until the Clean Air Act changed things, no paintwork, however carefully applied and maintained, could withstand the atmospheric pollution.

With the exception of Birkenhead and Wallasey, the distance between these towns was such that inter-town services were provided by Ribble and Crosville, with Lancashire United and North Western on the eastern edge. Ribble and Crosville each had something like one quarter of their fleets on Merseyside and the revenue and profits they generated were extremely important to both companies. The municipalities resisted and then tolerated the companies' presence and sometimes extracted a heavy price for access to key terminals so that, although all had working agreements, cooperation was not always harmonious. Ribble's knack of finding a way of working with anyone maybe eventually made it more welcome than Crosville, which had few joint services. The book includes brief coverage of the vehicles they ran in the area along with glimpses of the other operators that worked in on joint services – Lancashire United, North Western and the Corporations of Wigan and Leigh.

St Helens was a busy industrial town with a wide variety of industries and its bright red and cream fleet provided a bright splash of colour. The fleet worked hard for its living and vehicles were not always able to be as nicely turned out as in this 1971 picture of East Lancs-bodied Leyland PD2A 177 passing the Sefton Arms on Baldwin Street outbound on the 16 service to Parr. *David Powell*

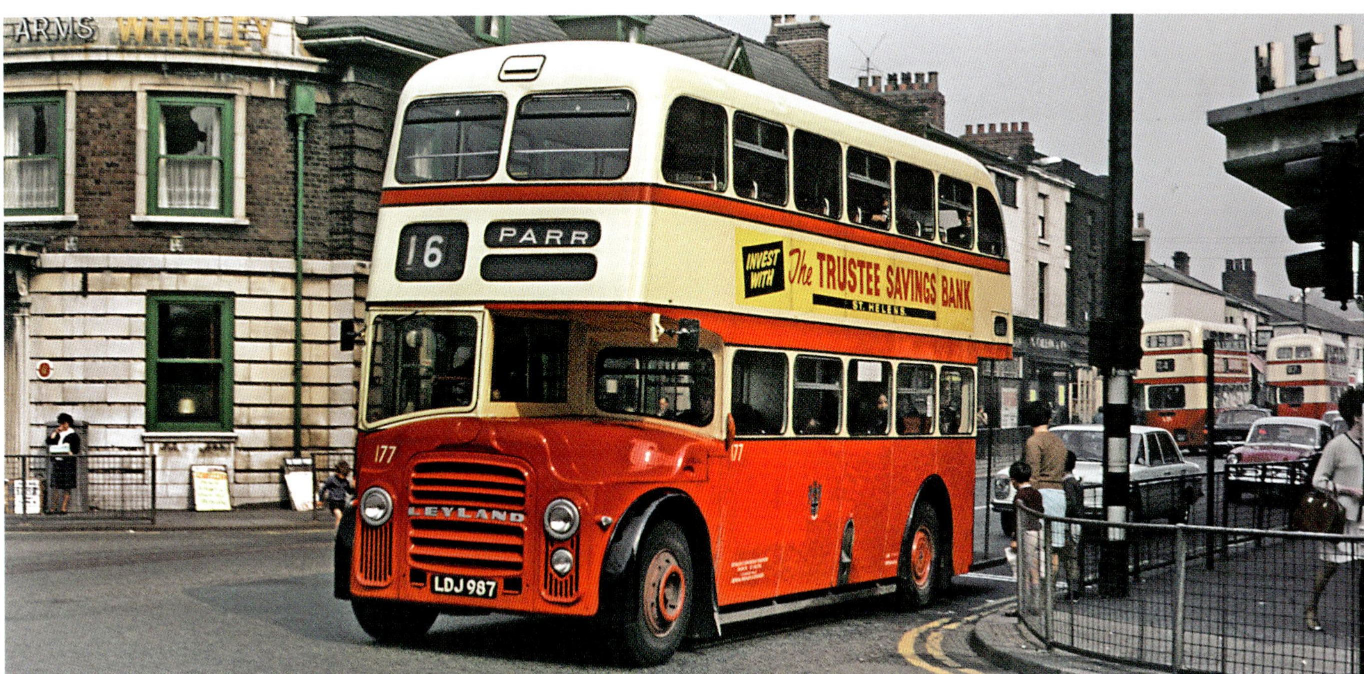

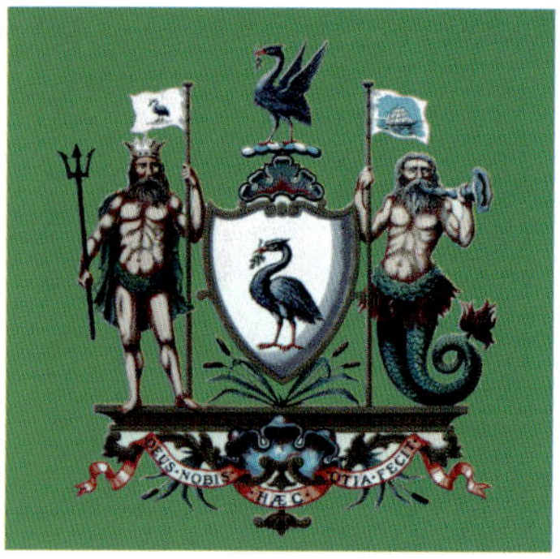

Liverpool

Until the late 1940s Liverpool was predominantly a tram city so much so that it had no 'modern' buses until 1935 when it bought a fleet of AEC Regents. The fine tramway system served the city well with its fleet of modern streamline cars and reserved tracks to outlying suburbs. For decades, the network's focal point was the Pier Head where thousands employed in the city crossed the river on ferry services operated by Birkenhead and Wallasey Corporations.

The city suffered badly during the war and whilst its tram system kept going and indeed was extended up to 1944, it could not have the care and attention it needed and in 1945 the financial case for replacing the trams was overwhelming. General Manager W G Marks, who had overseen the tramway expansion of the 1930s and also the introduction of the undertaking's first modern buses in 1935, retired in 1948 and it fell to his successor, Wilfrid Martin (known as 'Bill') Hall, to manage the tramway abandonment, which took until 1957, and the purchase of hundreds of new buses.

The bus fleet was mainly AEC and Leyland, with Daimlers and Crossleys bought in the late 1940s when delivery times dictated. The principal vehicle interest in the fleet was bodywork. Liverpool's engineers had firm 'no frills' views on design, maintenance and ease of repair and the fleet was large enough for Weymann, Crossley, Metro Cammell, Duple and Alexander to produce custom designs very different from their standard products. Many bodies were supplied as 'shells' for completion at Liverpool's extensive Edge Lane Works, described by one respected writer as 'one of the cathedrals of the bus industry'.

Perhaps the most striking and ground breaking design was the Metro Cammell body for its Atlanteans. An innovative and fashionable style at a time when most builders' offerings were bland and lacking character, it caused a rethink across the industry.

From 1966, rather than one-man high capacity double-deckers, Liverpool at first chose the high-capacity, one-man single-decker. Over 100 were bought and then many of the existing fleet of two-man operated Atlanteans were converted to one-man shortly before the fleet of just over 1000 vehicles was absorbed into the newly-created Merseyside PTE on 1st December 1969.

Lord Street is one of the oldest streets in the city. Laid out in the 17th century to connect the Castle, which was at the far end in this view, with a bridge across the Pool from which the city took its name. The bridge was at the road junction in the foreground, the Pool running along the line of the crossing street just ahead of the bollards. This picture was taken from Church Street and the buildings on the south (left in the picture) side are post-war reconstruction after the blitz. Coming towards the camera is a 1953 Crossley-bodied AEC Regent with Liverpool's own design of 'new look' front. The two young ladies in the foreground, one wearing a Beatles-patterned skirt, are a reminder of the other sort of 'Liver Birds' – girls featured in the popular 1960s television series of that name. *Ian Stewart*

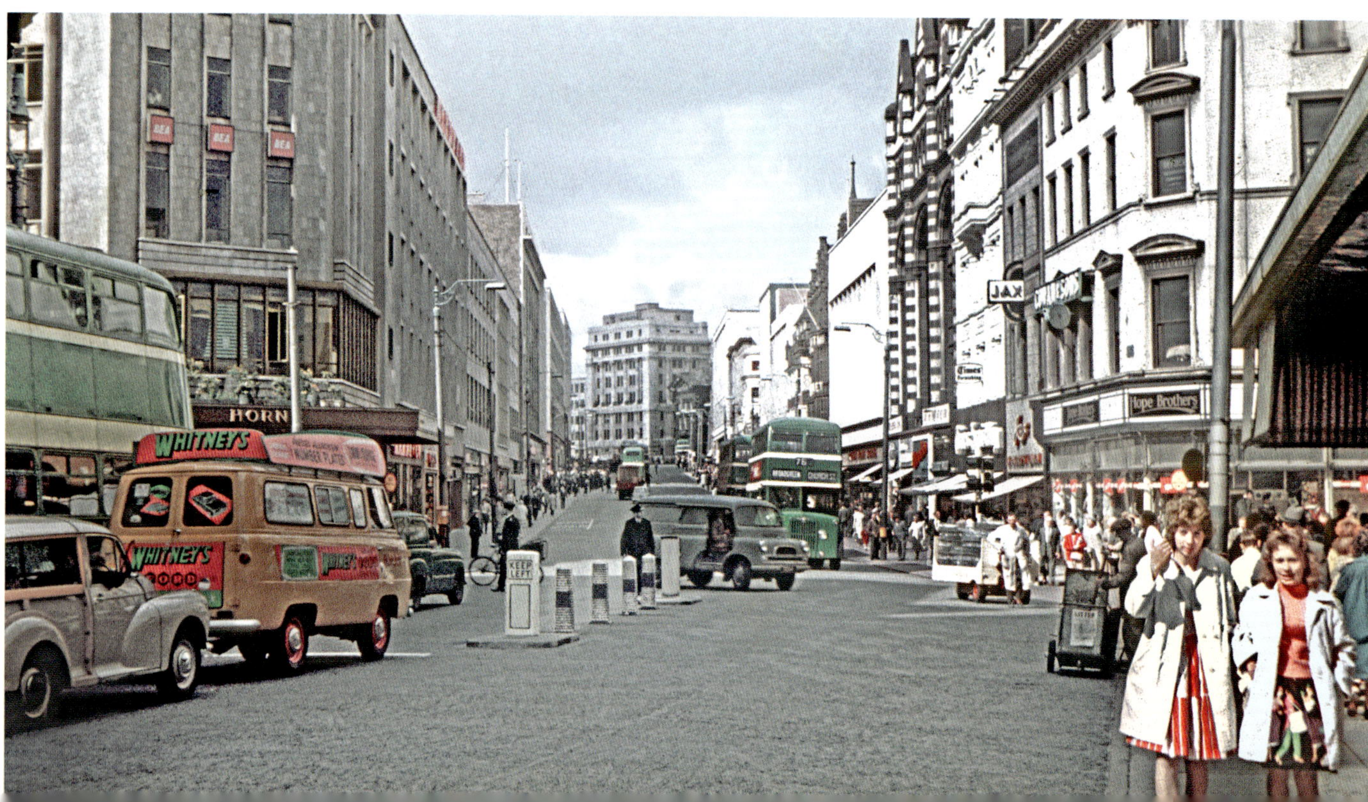

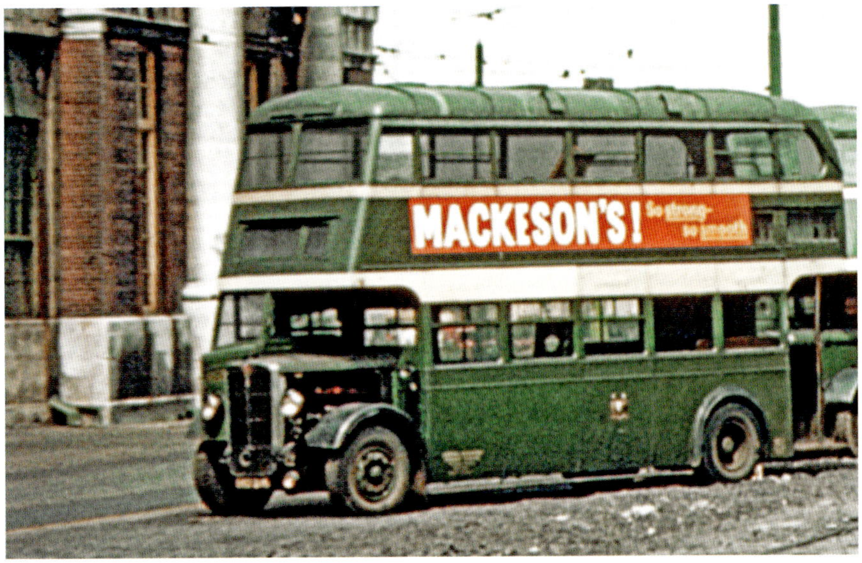

With its fine tramway system, it was not until 1935 that Liverpool acquired its first 'modern' buses. The 192 pre-war double-deckers (A1-A172, A179-A198) were AEC Regents with Weymann bodies of that firm's standard design. Some were supplied as what were termed 'body shells' – frames with floors and curved panels such as domes, for completion, trimming and painting by Edge Lane, something which would continue until 1958. All the pre-war Regents were gone by 1959 and this picture is the only colour one which has been found – it is a small corner from a 1955 picture whose main subject was a tram in the yard at Edge Lane works and the inclusion of A128, ready to be collected by a scrap dealer, was accidental. *Online Transport Archive*

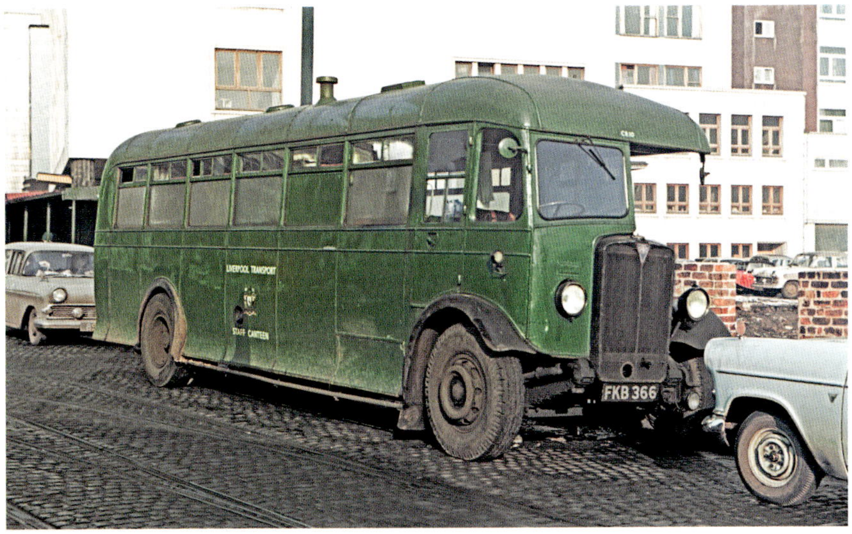

In addition to the pre-war AEC Regents, there were six single-deck AEC Regals (A173-178) also Weymann-bodied. New in November 1939, A178 was withdrawn in 1957 and converted to a mobile canteen. It passed to the PTE but was sold shortly afterwards. *Brian Faragher/Online Transport Archive*

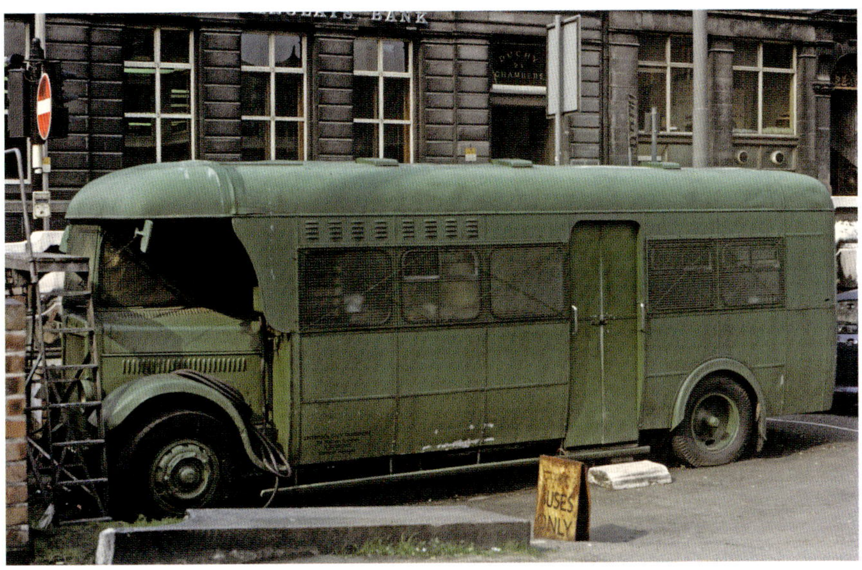

During the war the city's strategic importance with its seven miles of docks and labour-intensive wartime establishments, not least being the Royal Ordnance Factory at Kirkby, required more buses than the corporation's modest fleet of AECs. Commencing in 1940, large numbers of elderly Leyland Titans, mainly TD1s, were either hired or purchased from dealer Millburn Motors, some surviving for a few years after the war. One that survived longer than most was KJ 2578, a TD1 new in 1931 to Redcar, Tunbridge Wells, it then passed to Maidstone and District in 1935 and to London Transport (TD193) later that year, before coming to Liverpool in 1940. Fitted with a Gardner 5LW engine in 1943, it was later used as a driver training bus, was then converted to a stores van and finally, in 1951, was rebuilt as a canteen. The veteran survived and passed to the Merseyside PTE – and without doubt was the only Leyland TD1 owned by a PTE. The PTE finally sold it in 1980 – a remarkable record. May 1973 *Roy Marshall*

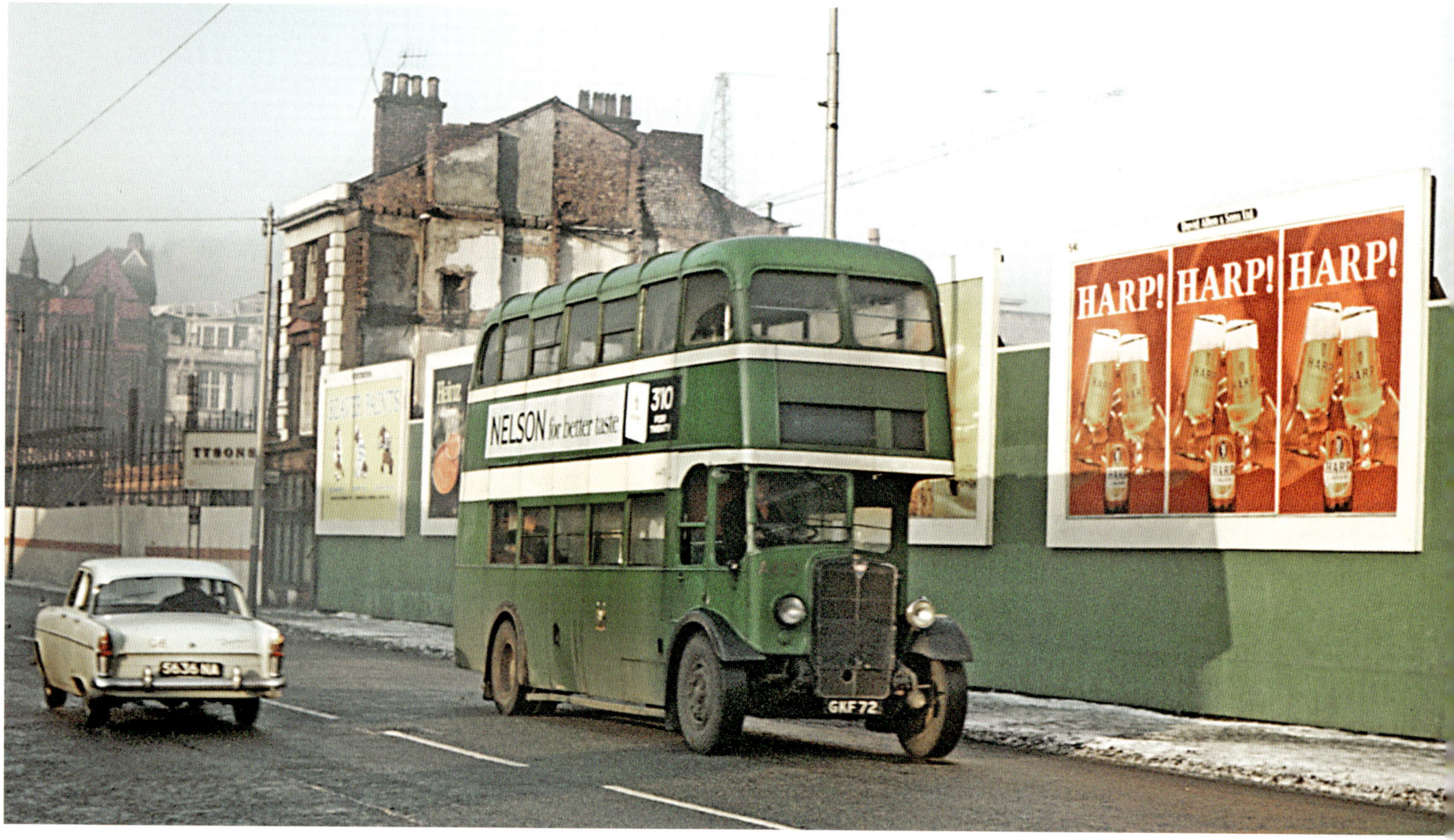
HARP! HARP! HARP!
NELSON for better taste
310
5636 NA
GKF 72

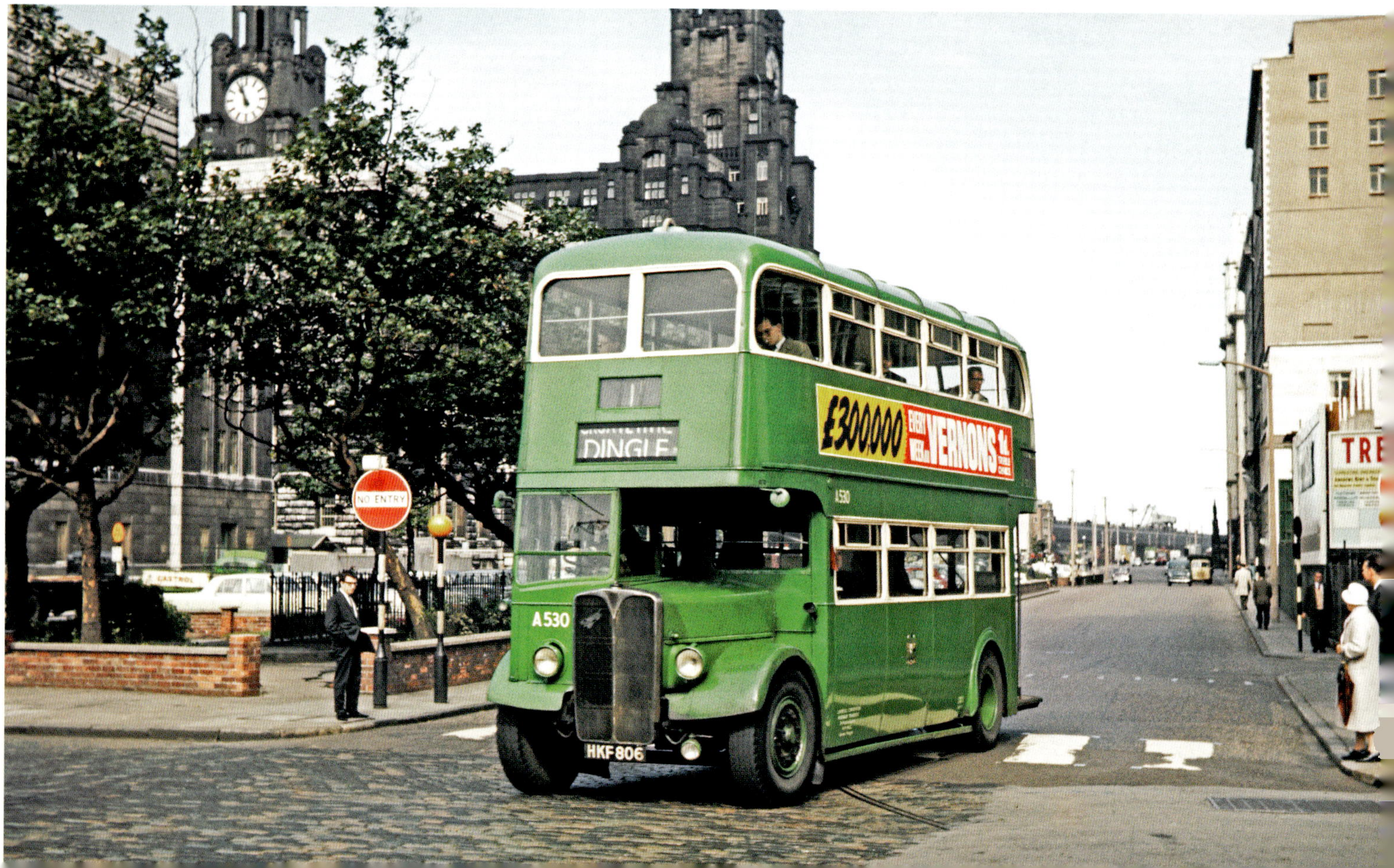
DINGLE
£300000
VERNONS
NO ENTRY
A530
HKF 806
CASTROL

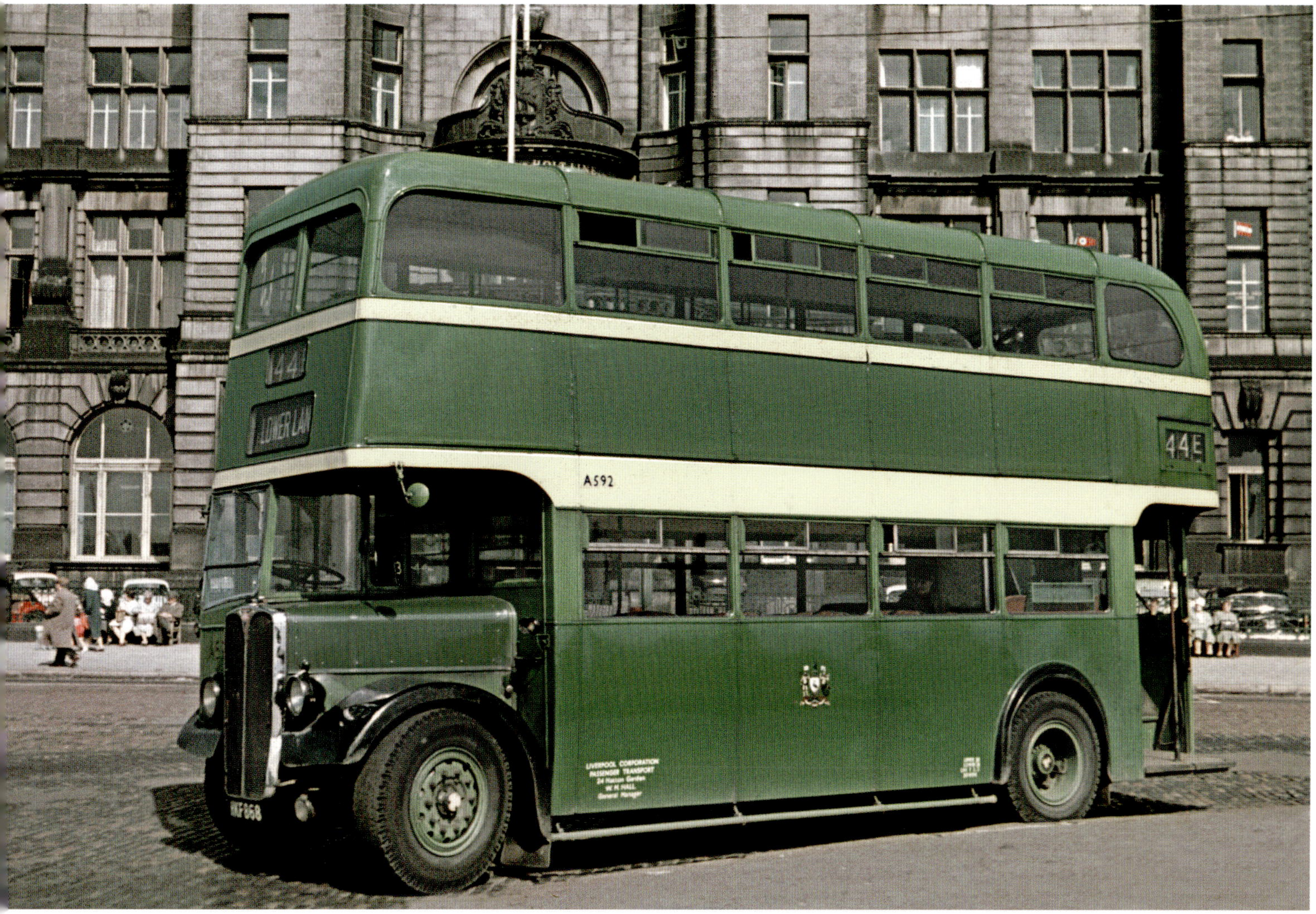

Opposite top In 1942 a provisional order was placed for 100 AEC Regents with Weymann bodies. The government authorised their build in 1945/46 and they were delivered in batches of 16, 42 and a further 42 (A225-324) in 1946/47. On a snowy day, a pale winter sun shines thinly on A473, previously A273 – the AECs had 200 added to their numbers when the later A-series reached the 200s. From 1946 to 1953 new vehicles were numbered in a single chronological sequence with a prefix letter to indicate the make – A for AEC, C for Crossley, D for Daimler and L for Leyland. *Brian Faragher/Online Transport Archive*

Above In its original livery is A592 (formerly A392), one of the 75 with 7.7-litre engines. The two pictures illustrate clearly the simple, no frills lines of Liverpool's body. The interiors were similarly plain. 1962 *Ian Stewart*

Opposite bottom The first tram replacement buses were 100 AEC Regent IIIs (A325-424) with Weymann shells completed at Edge Lane. The first 25 had 9.6 litre engines and preselector gearboxes; the other 75 were the 7.7 litre-engined, crash gearbox 6811A model. It was the largest order for the latter model from anywhere. Liverpool subsequently standardised on the larger engine but with the synchromesh gearbox. The department's engineers also decided upon a simpler body design with as few curved panels as was reasonable and none of what they considered to be unnecessary frills with their consequent cost in weight and fuel consumption. All the usual curvature at the front end of these Weymann bodies was removed giving them a severe, upright profile. The results were not altogether harmonious and when they entered service in 1948/49 the crews nicknamed them 'coffins'. Features which became standard for future Liverpool buses were the 4-bay body frame and sliding cab door. A530, originally A330, was one of the 25 with the larger engine. It is pictured towards the end of its life in the spray paint livery with green mudguards. It is heading south along The Strand on route 1, the direct replacement for the Liverpool Overhead Railway which closed in 1956 and ran along the line of the docks from Dingle in the south to Seaforth in the north. The elevated structure once ran along the left of this scene. *Bill Ryan*

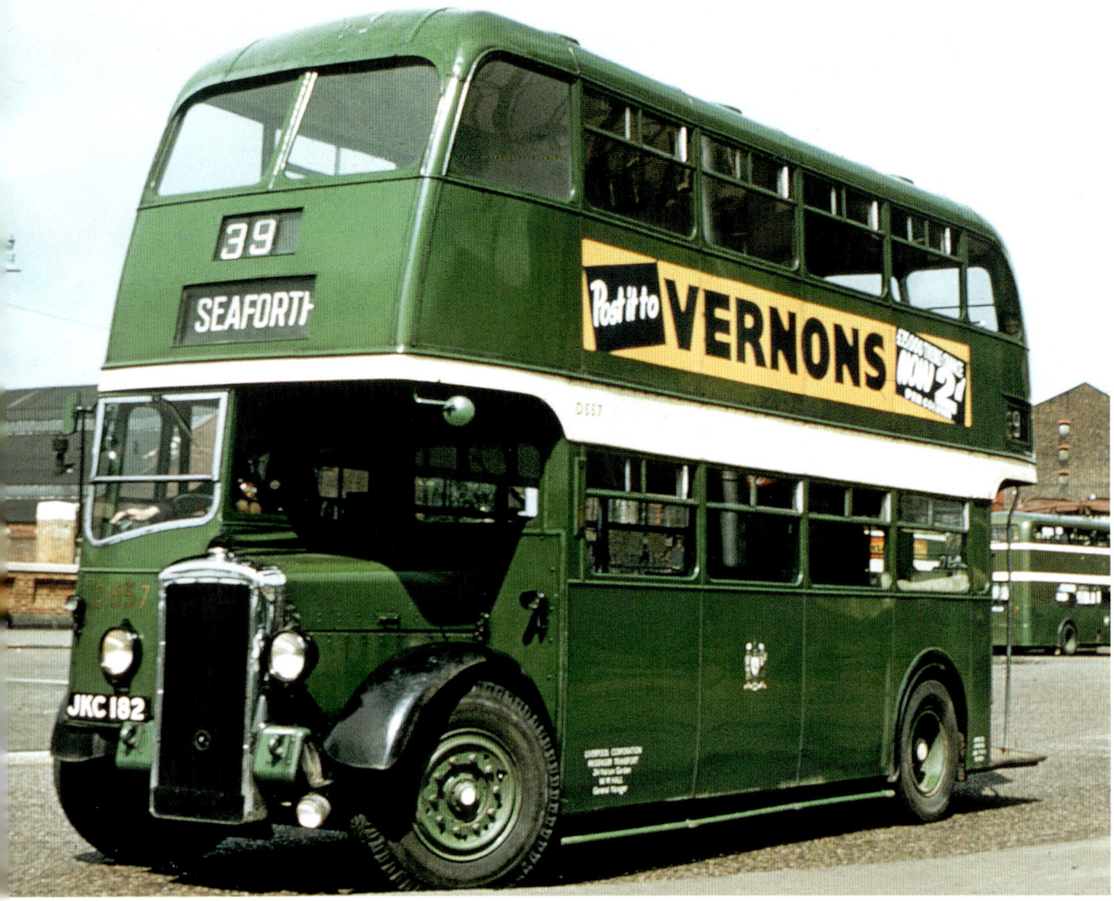

In 1947, 290 double-deckers were ordered for the 1948-1951 stages of the tramway conversion programme. To secure timely deliveries the orders were placed with several manufacturers – 100 AEC, 50 Crossley, 90 Daimler and 50 Leyland chassis – Leyland supplied an additional 10 to help relieve the effects of the Green Lane depot fire which destroyed many trams. The chassis of the first of the AECs, A656, was the prototype built for development of the 7.7-litre 6811; the rest were the 9.6-litre engined 9612E. The body order was similarly spread – 10 Leyland (taking advantage of a cancelled order) and 50 Roberts bodies for the Leylands, 50 of the Daimlers had Northern Counties bodies and the Crossleys had Crossley bodies. The remainder had Weymann shells finished at Edge Lane. Daimlers D516-565 had Northern Counties bodies – they had that firm's first four-bay frames but otherwise were to its usual rounded design. Ten, D541-549/65, were CVD6 with Daimler engines and the others CVA6 with the same 7.7-litre AEC engine as A350-424. In this 1962 picture D557 is in a short-lived livery which omitted the top cream band but retained the darker green. *Roy Marshall*

Left Delivered in 1948, Leyland PD2/1s L435-484 were bodied by the Wakefield firm of Charles Roberts which modified its standard 4-bay body to meet Liverpool's specification. This is L471. Fleet numbers L485-L495 were allocated to some of the surviving Leyland TD1s acquired in 1940/41 and D496-515 were elderly Daimler COG5 acquired from Birmingham to bridge the gap until delivery of new vehicles; all were gone long before the era of colour photography. *Online Transport Archive*

Right Daimler CVA6s D566-605 had Weymann shells finished at Edge Lane Works – such bodies were usually referred to as 'Weymann/LCPT'. *Peter Roberts*

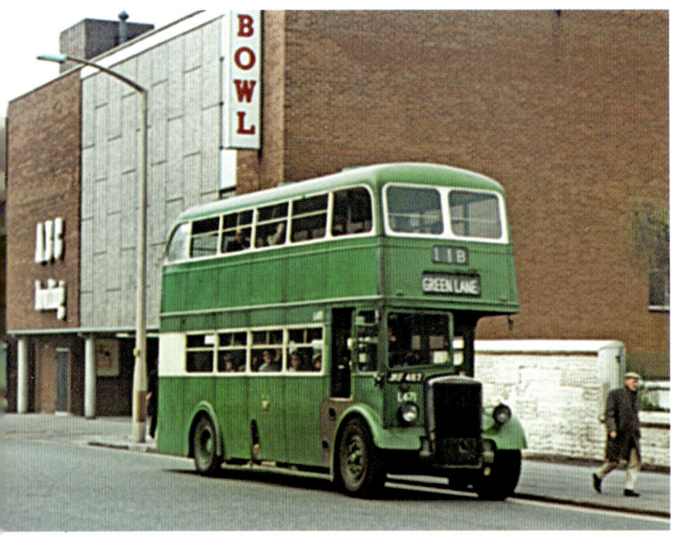

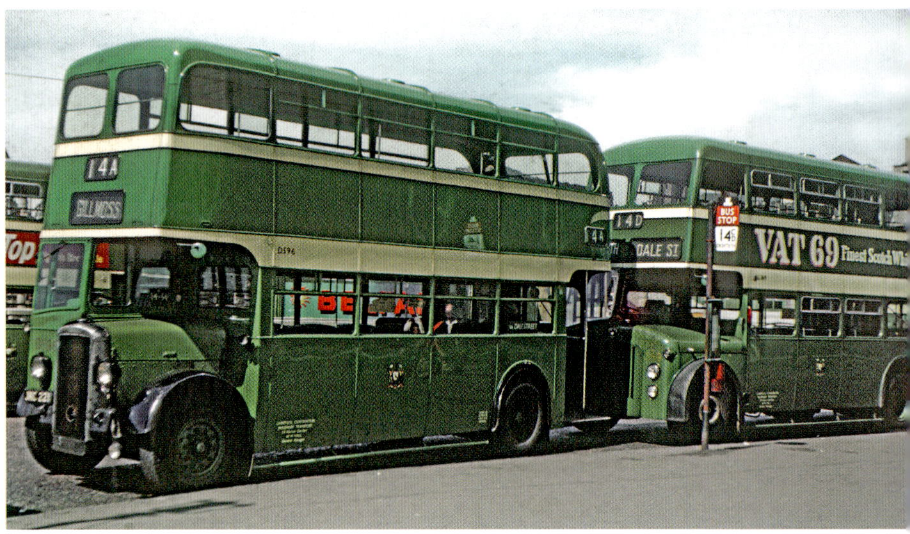

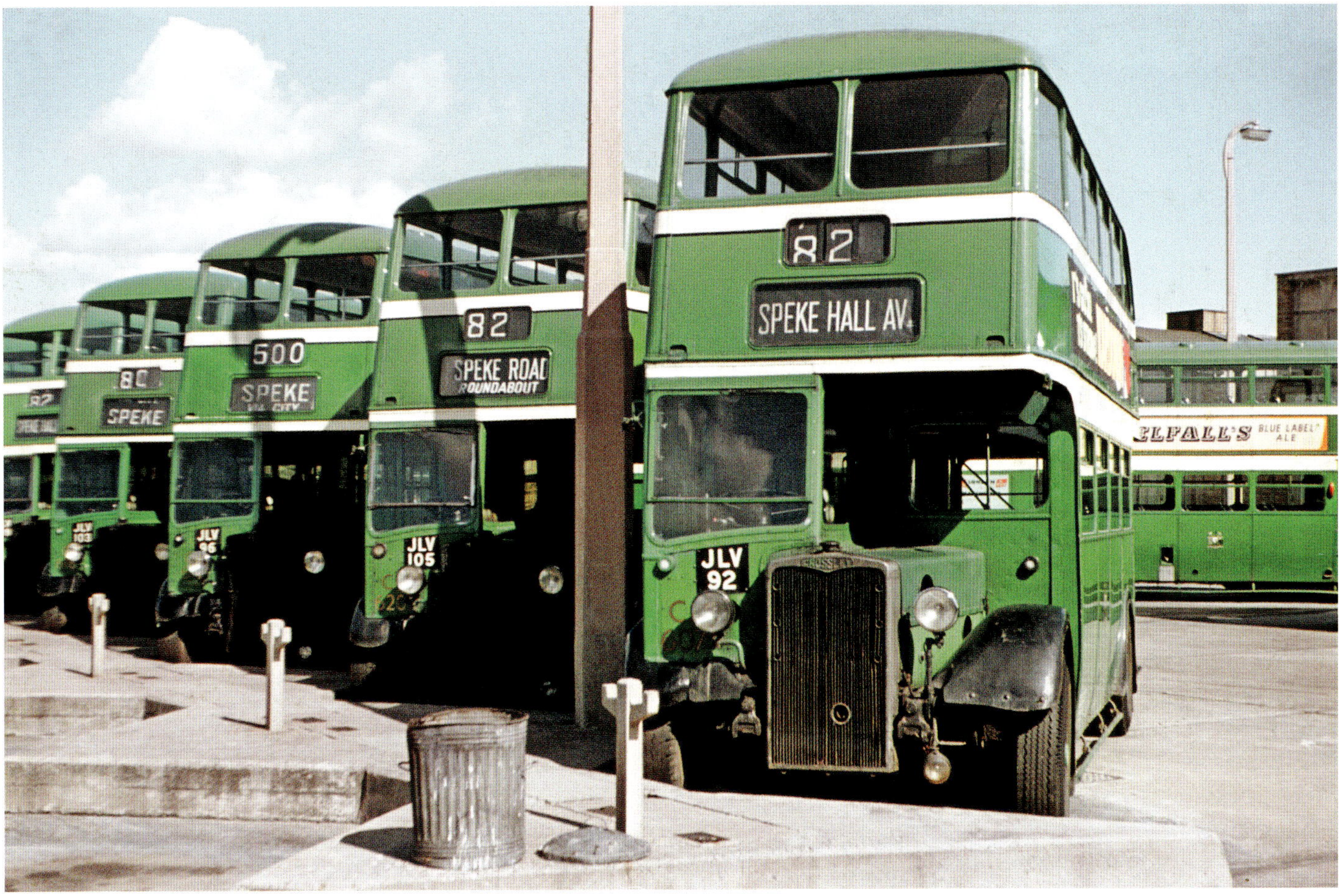

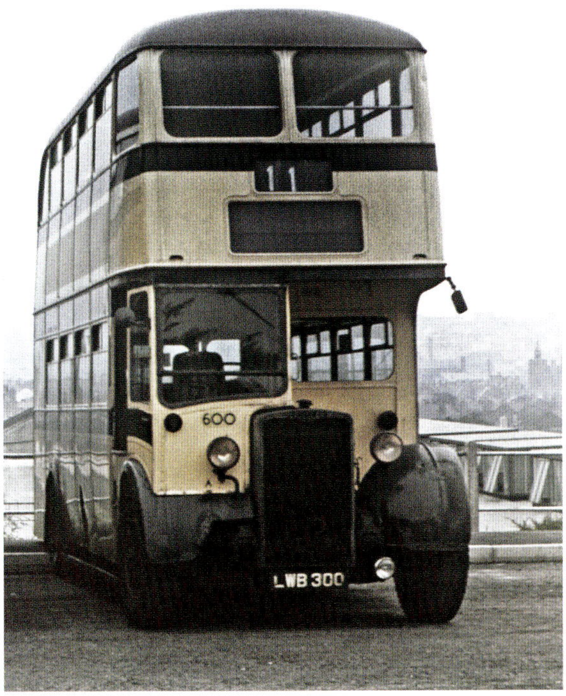

Above The fifty Crossley DD42s had a 4-bay version of Crossley's standard 5-bay body. It incorporated some Liverpool features, such as a flat-in-plan-view front and sliding cab door but was otherwise to Crossley's normal styling. Delivered in 1948/49, C606-655 spent their entire working life in the south of the city. Initially allocated to Garston depot, most later moved to Speke, where C607, 620, 611, 618 and others were photographed in 1962. Many had their engines modified to the improved and more reliable 'downdraught' version but AEC's decision to end manufacture of Crossley spares contributed to their early withdrawal and all were gone by the end of 1963. Modifications their engines may have needed; not so their bodies and Crossley would become Liverpool's preferred supplier of bus bodies, supplying a further 346 bodies or shells. *Peter Roberts*

Left The second half of the Liverpool order was delayed by six months – the reasons are unclear and formal records give different reasons, although the root cause appears to be that Liverpool wanted them to be fitted with Fraser hydraulic clutches. Fraser arranged for Rubery Owen to make them and the latter spent some months trying without success to reproduce the working prototype. Meanwhile many of the chassis and bodies were already complete and rather than store them Crossley fitted standard transmissions and opportunistically sold 22 to other operators who wanted buses on quick delivery. Sheffield took 4, Rotherham 12 and Sunderland 6 – this is Sheffield 600. As the picture shows, even the indicator boxes were left unchanged. The Fraser device was then abandoned and the balance of the Liverpool order was supplied with normal clutches and gearboxes. *Michael Eyre*

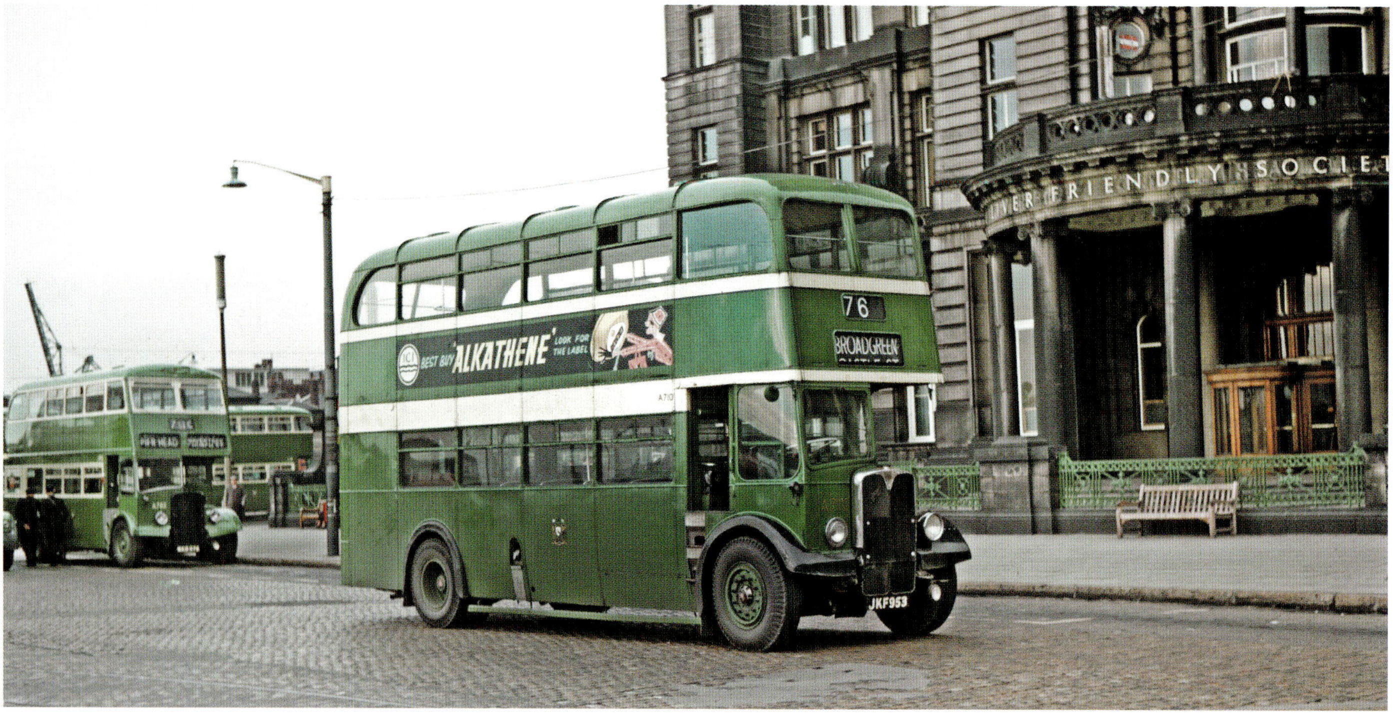

The intention was that AEC Regents A657-A756 should have Weymann/ LCPT bodies. However, Edge Lane was busy with tramcar repairs and some had to be passed to outside contractors. The initial plan was for Saunders-Roe (Anglesey) to do twenty and Withnell, Shotton, ten but the city council required the work to be given to competent local firms and the orders went to Davidson & Co in Church Road (which did 10 – not that well it seems), J Blake & Co, Kirkby (10 increased to 21), Pearson's, Smithdown Lane (9) and Martin Hearn's company Aero and Engineering (Merseyside) Ltd, Hooton (20). The results all looked much the same as the Edge Lane-finished ones. This picture is of one of the latter, A710 at Pier Head in November 1962. *Roy Marshall*

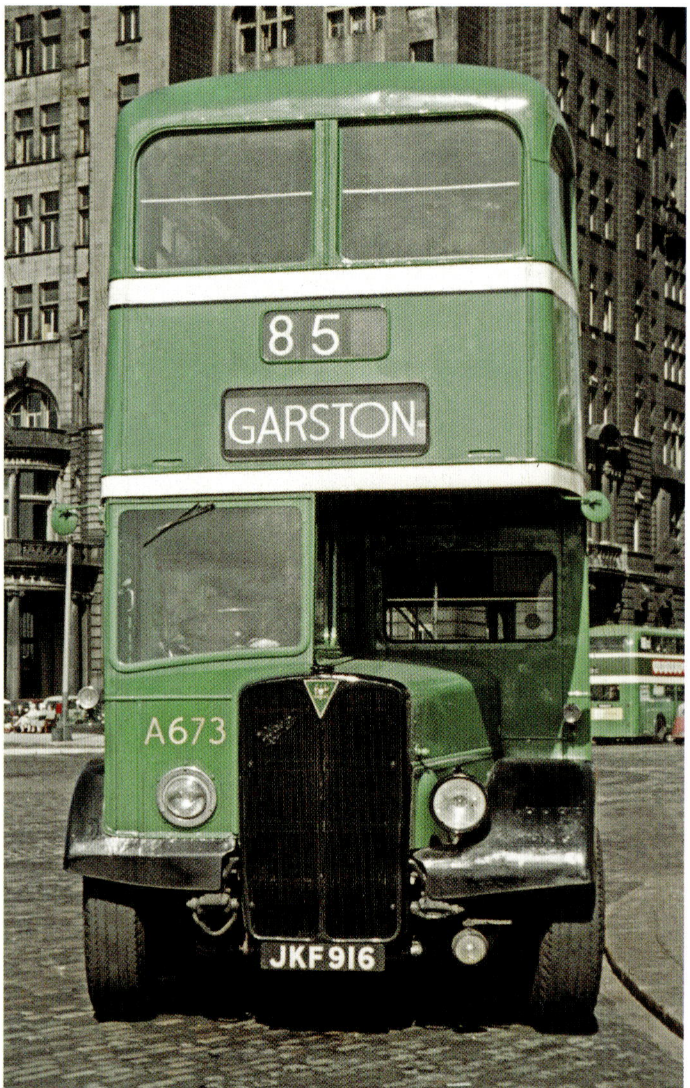

As shown in this 1962 picture of A673, the typical Weymann styling was more apparent when viewed front-on. *Ian Stewart*

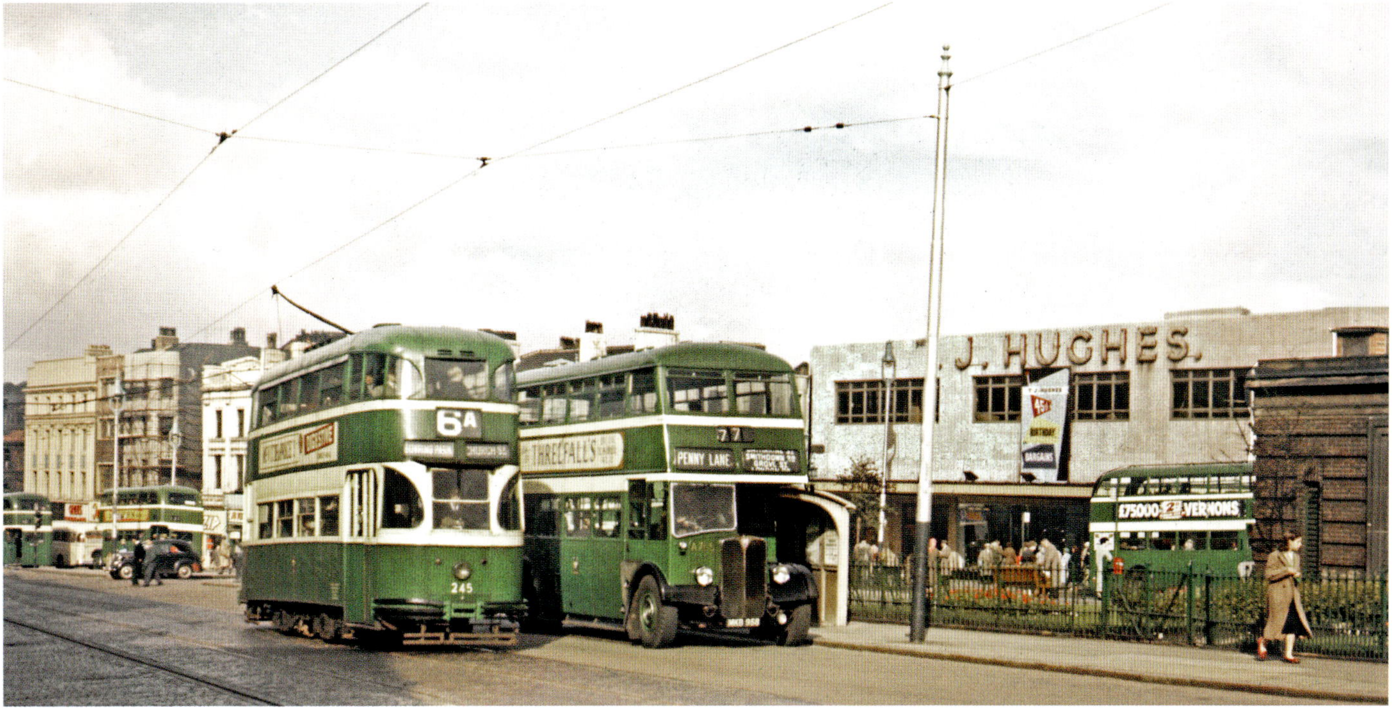

As the postwar demand for new buses eased, Liverpool was able to choose its suppliers and for the next decade, AEC and Leyland would share the chassis orders more or less equally, with Crossley and Weymann usually getting the body orders. The order for the next phase of tram conversion was 50 AEC Regent III with Crossley bodies and 60 Leyland PD2/12 with Weymann bodies. The department's first 8ft wide buses, their increased width allowed for addition of an intermediate route indicator. The Regents were A757-A806 and this picture of Monument Place nicely captures the days of tram conversions with one of the last 'Baby Grand' trams, 245, alongside A765 on route 77 to Penny Lane.

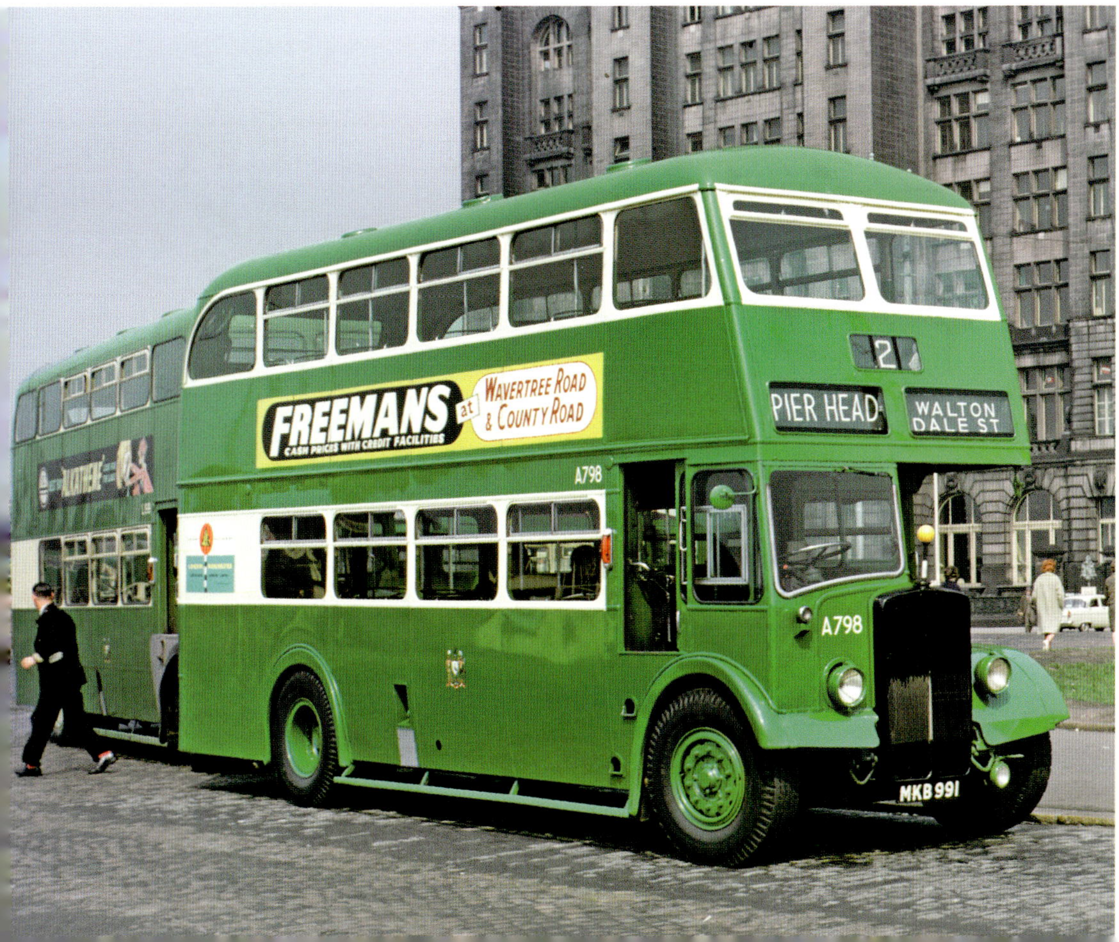

Fresh out of Edge Lane's new spray paint shop, its blind not yet set for the journey to Aintree, this picture shows A798 at Pier Head in September 1962. The off-white areas were reduced to save paint shop time by use of large, standard masks in the spray booth. Whilst it saved money, the result looked awkward. Most one-coat hot spray paint quickly lost its gloss, further detracting from the general appearance. The small disc just ahead of the fleet number near the cab door and the similar one towards the rear were covers for the body lifting sockets which were fitted to all Liverpool-design bodies of the period – the initial step in the major overhaul process at Edge Lane required the body to be taken off the chassis. *Geoffrey Morant*

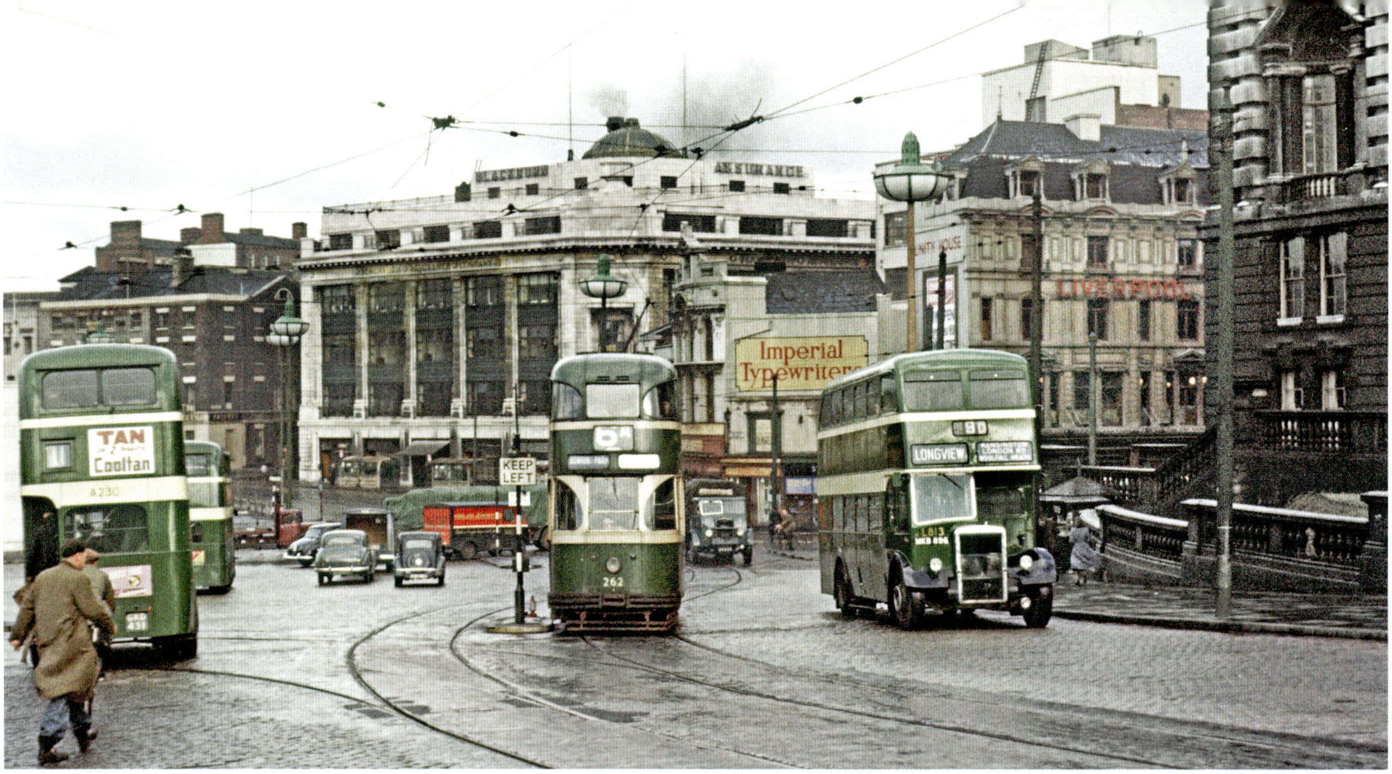

Having settled on the design of the Crossley body, the drawing office then produced a revised design for other suppliers. It had a flat sloping front profile rather than the gentle curve of the Crossley. Weymann built the first examples on the sixty Leyland PD2s, L807-866. The upper picture again shows the days of tram conversion. Brand new and advert-free L813 climbs granite sett paved William Brown Street, working service 9D, part of March 1955 conversion of Prescot Road routes, the 'D' indicating that it will run via Dale Street in the city centre – a C suffix indicated via Church Street and many services served the two alternately. Tram 262 is on route 6A to Bowring Park; the tracks to left led to the Old Haymarket terminus. The three tall lighting standards with green shades and large glass half globes were a special feature of the entrance and approaches to the first of the two Mersey road tunnels, Queensway, opened in 1934. The second, Kingsway, opened in 1971. Both were predated by the rail tunnel of 1886. *Online Transport Archive*

The next order continued the buying pattern – 100 AEC Regents and 90 Leyland PD2s. Fleet numbering recommenced at 1 with separate sequences for AECs (A-prefix) and Leylands (L-prefix) and L1-60 of 1954 were similar to L807-866. In this picture at St Nicholas Place, L32 is on route 15D Kirkby – part of the November 1955 tram conversion. A feature of the Liverpool fleet was the duty running board for the day's running (55-13 in this case); carried in the driver's cab it stayed with the bus rather than the crew. Timetable cases were provided at major stops, their contents were drafted in the Publicity Department at the head office at Hatton Garden and then individually typed in the typing pool. Across the road, on the other side of the wall, is the cutting for the floating roadway for vehicles to access the Pier Head landing stage. September 1962 *Roy Marshall*

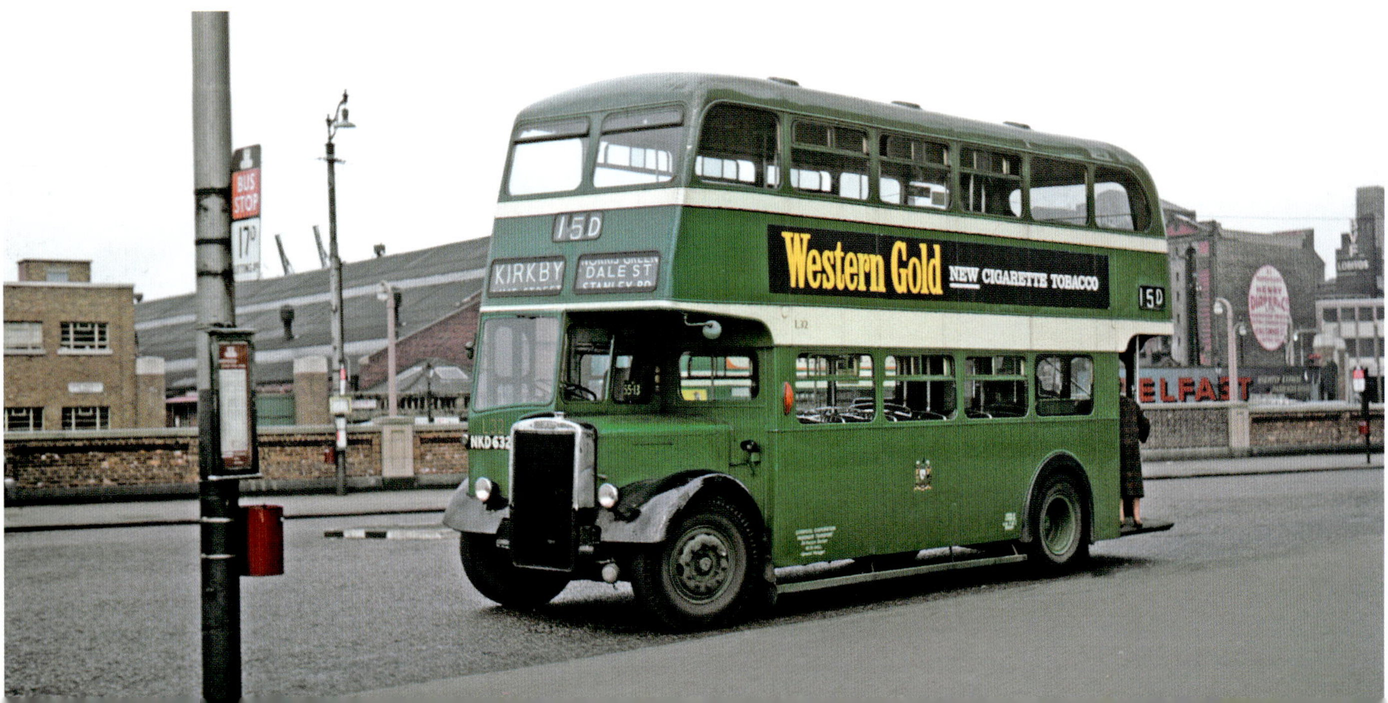

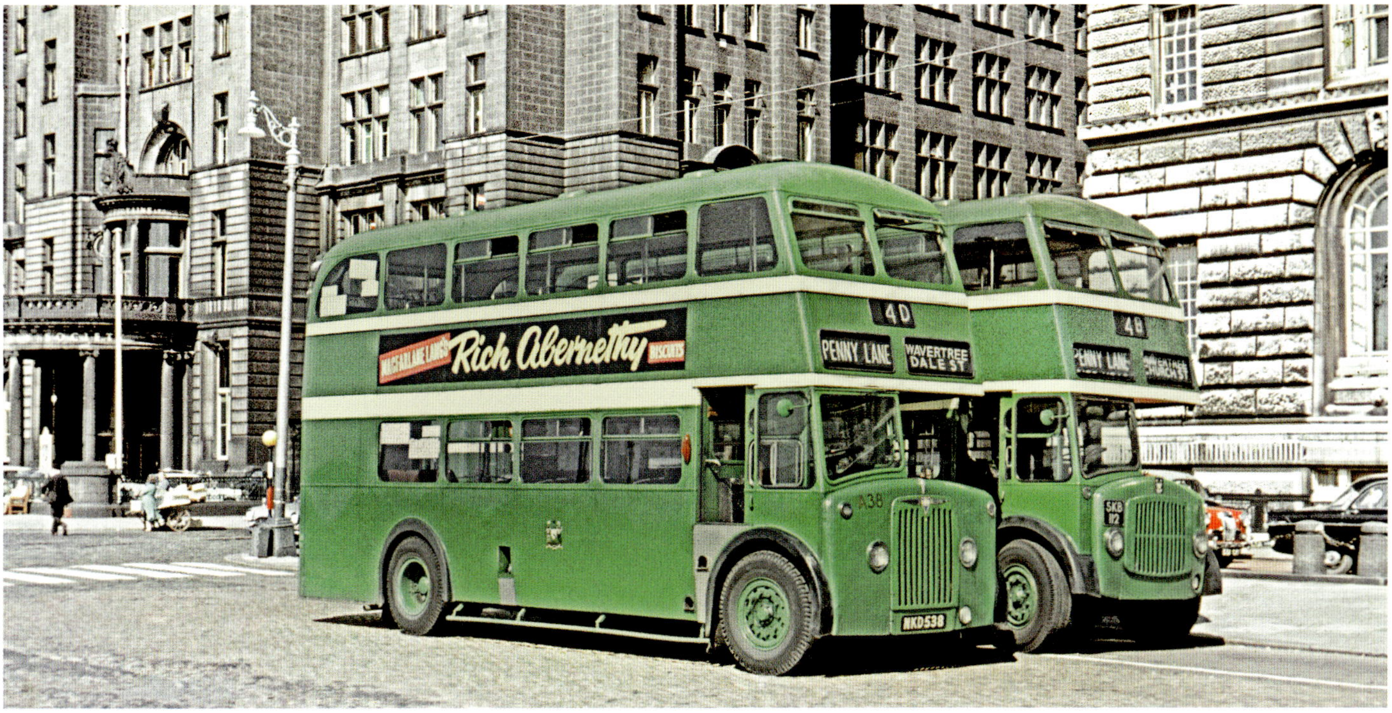

The 100 Regents (A1-100) had another Liverpool innovation – its version of the so-called 'new look' front – a cowl extending the full width of the bus. A1-38 had Crossley bodies and A41-100 Crossley shells completed at Edge Lane. The sheet steel cowl was made by Crossley and the first completed bus (A1) appeared at the 1952 Commercial Motor Show badged as a Crossley – it was fitted with AEC insignia before delivery. Standing at the terminus of service 4 in front of the Cunard building in 1963 with the Royal Liver Building to the left are A38 and 1955 Regent V A112 – side by side parking in front of the three waterfront buildings was common. *Ian Stewart*

New in 1954, A39 and A40 had lightweight aluminium-framed bodies by Beaumaris, Anglesey based Saunders-Roe. About 1 ton lighter than the Crossley body, on A40 the aluminium panels were left unpainted, the idea being to reduce the cost of repainting. The steel parts, such as the bonnet assembly, were painted aluminium to match. The bodies proved durable but no more were built. A40 was only 10 months old and still shone in the sun when this picture was taken at Pier Head in September 1955. *Bruce Jenkins*

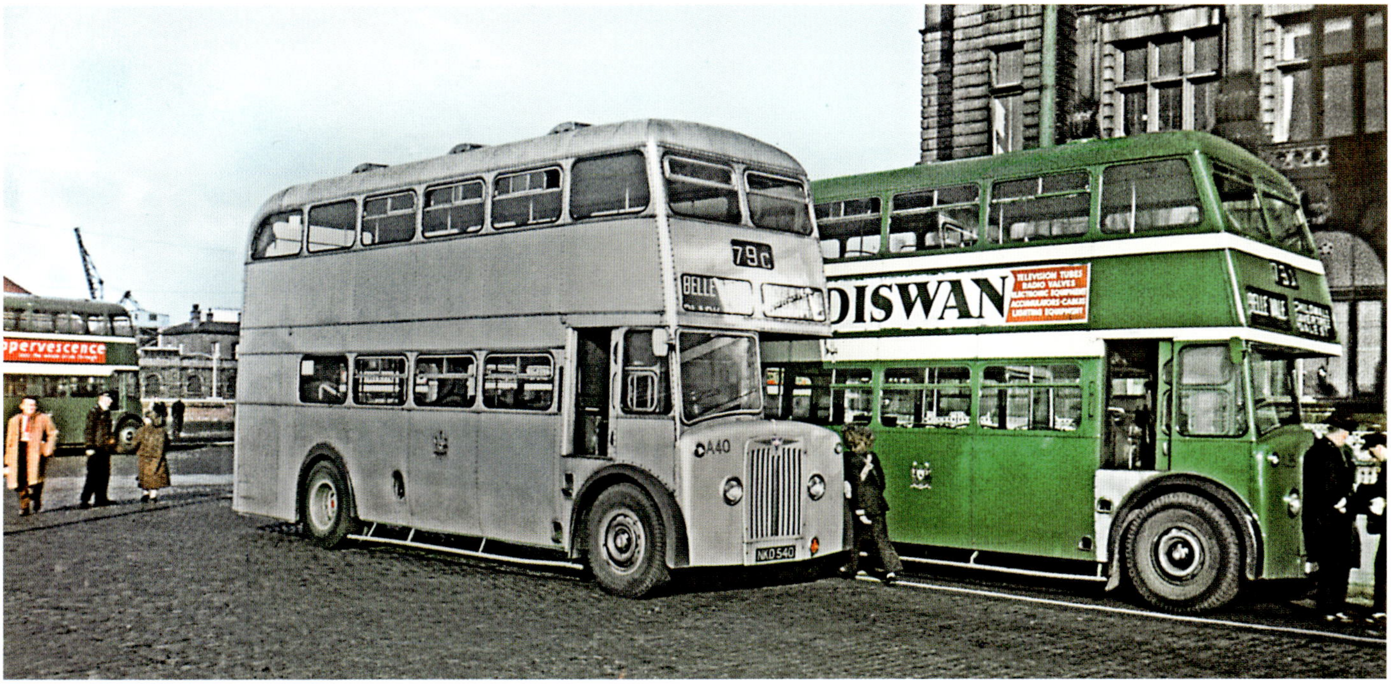

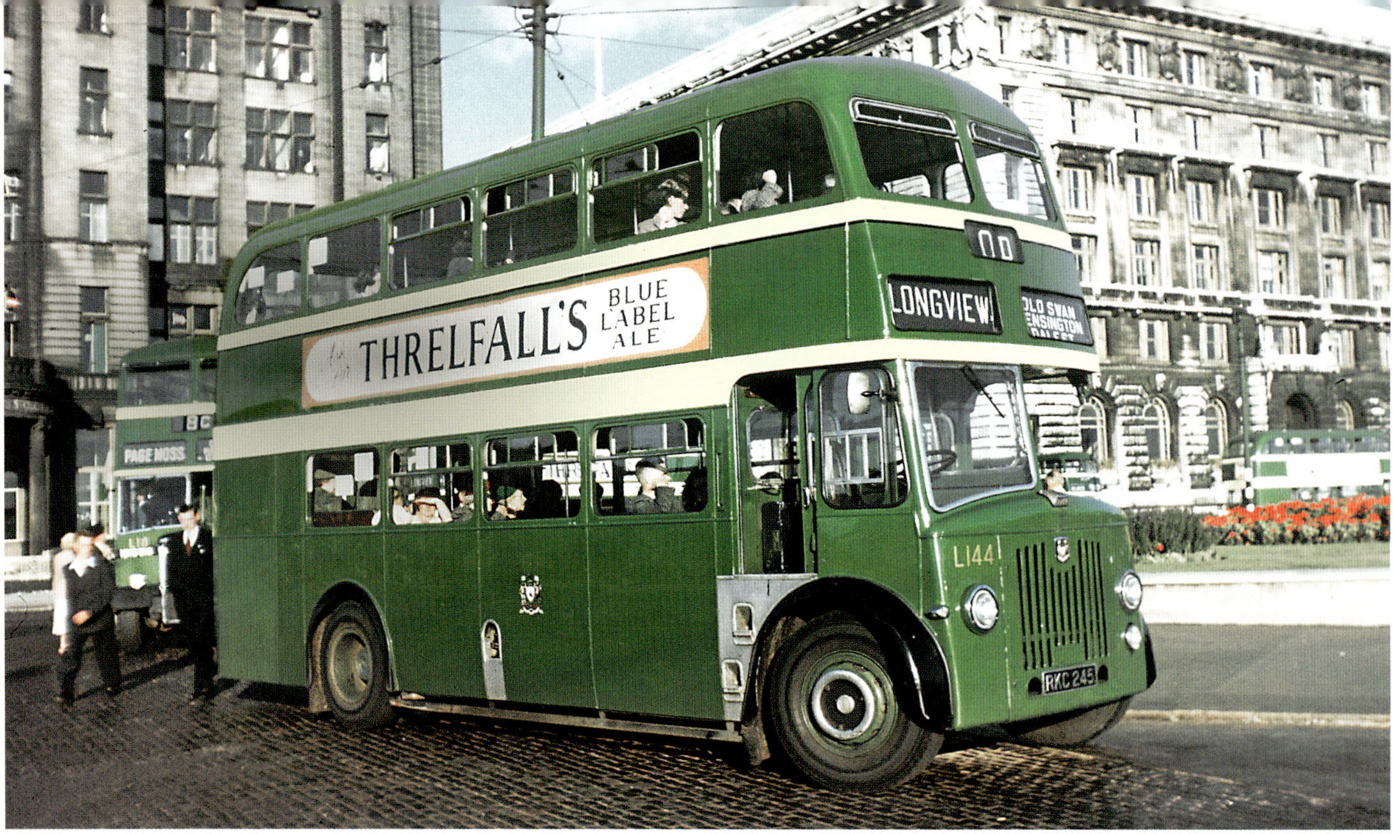

Leyland PD2s L61-90 had Leyland's 'new look' front and winning the order for their bodies was a breakthrough for Falkirk, Scotland, based Alexander which had not sold bodies to English operators for many years. It won the order in part because it was prepared to build to Liverpool's drawings and received a further order for 30 more (L141-170); all were delivered in 1954. This is two-year old L144 at Pier Head in October 1956. *Bruce Jenkins*

The choice of body maker for the other 50 Leyland PD2/20s of the 1953 order (which Leyland won from AEC on price) was also unusual. Although the country's principal builder of coaches, Duple produced few double-deck bodies. It had planned to break into the double-deck bus market but, due to management changes within Duple, Liverpool's 50 would be the last. L91-140 were built to Liverpool's drawings and, at first glance, looked much the same at the Alexander-bodied ones. The majority of the batch was built at Kegworth, Leicestershire, in what had been the works of Nudd Brothers and Lockyer, a firm which Duple had acquired in 1952, although the first few were constructed at the company's main works at Hendon. Whilst consideration was being given to the long term arrangements for bus terminal facilities in the city centre, there was an interim scheme using part of St Nicholas Place as a terminus, as in this November 1962 picture of L125, until the new Pier Head bus station was built. The building on the right is the side of the Royal Liver Building. *Roy Marshall*

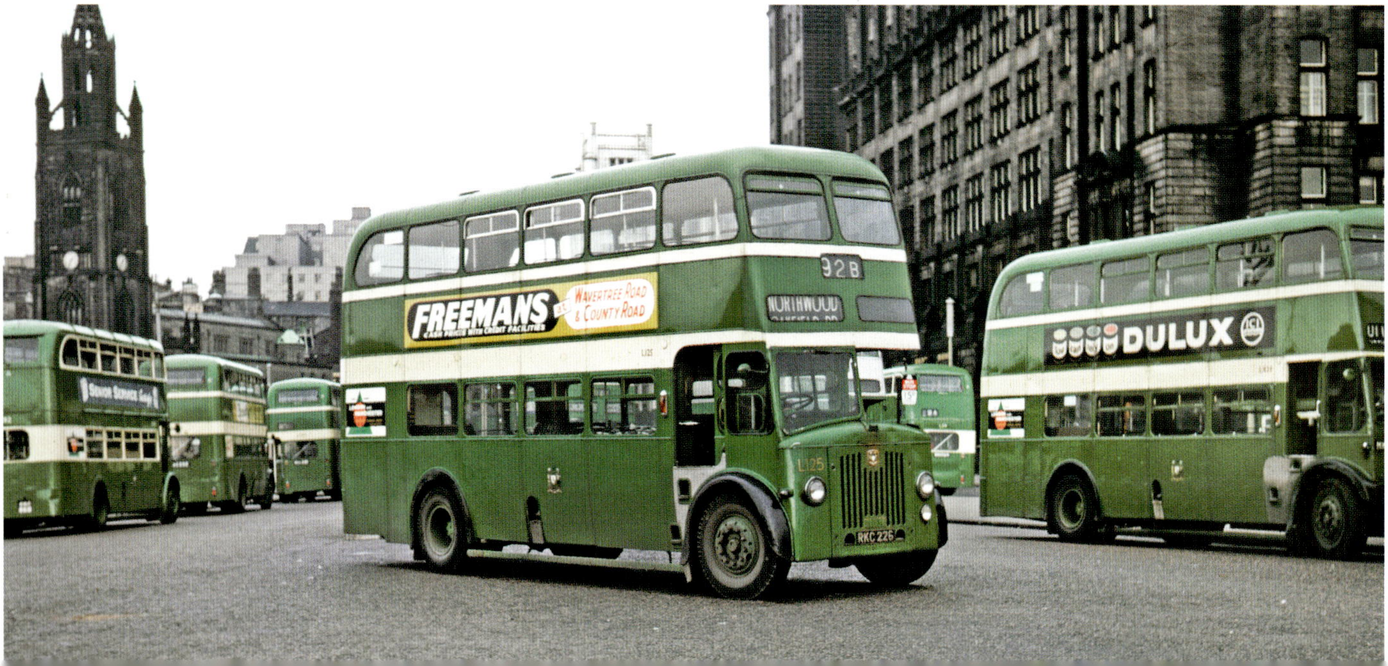

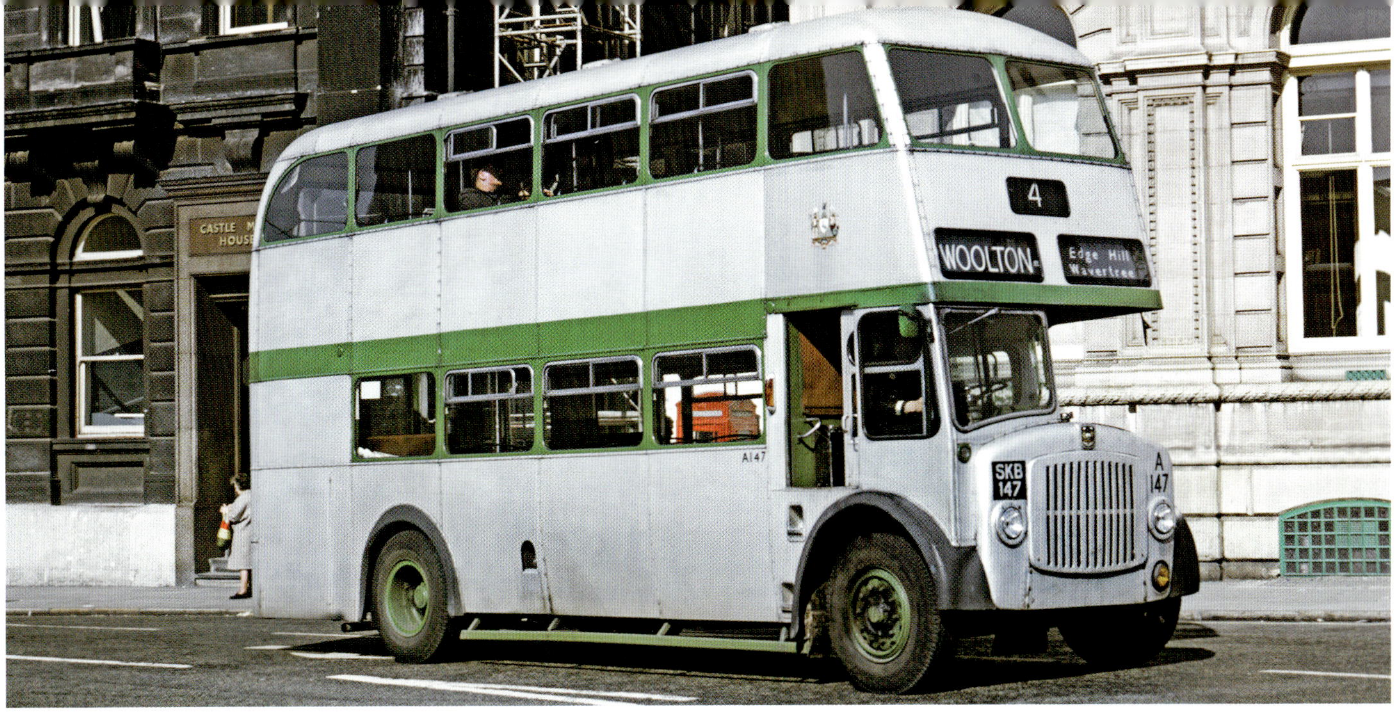

Sixty seven AEC Regent Vs came into the fleet in 1955/56. A101-127 had Crossley bodies whilst A128-167 were Crossley/LCPT. They had the standard AEC bonnet assembly but fitted with a simpler removable pressed steel radiator grille with no brightwork – a design introduced by Glasgow Corporation but modified for Liverpool to eliminate the place for a maker's emblem; instead a neat badge with the city's coat of arms was fitted above the grille. A147 was the only unpainted member of the batch and is pictured here at Derby Square on 12 September 1968 heading for the commercial heart of the city, from where it would pick up plenty of traffic for its journey to Woolton. *Roy Marshall*

The corresponding Leyland order was for 68 PD2/20. Leyland's bulky front was easy to damage and expensive-to-repair and the department's engineers decided to have something the size of the AEC cowl instead. Unique to Liverpool and used on the rest of the department's PD2s, the result was plain but certainly practical. Delivered late in 1955 the first 35 (L177-211) had Weymann 'Orion' bodies with Liverpool's required 4-bay construction rather than the Orion's more usual 5-bays. They were followed by Crossley-bodied L212-L229 and Crossley/LCPT L230-44 which were delivered over the following twelve months. This is the first of the Weymanns, L177, its front dome not completely cleaned by the garage bus washing machine. The new front, with its flat plain panel for the cab front blended well enough with the Orion but, as shown in some of the following pictures, it married up less happily to the Crossley body. July 1958 *Geoffrey Morant*

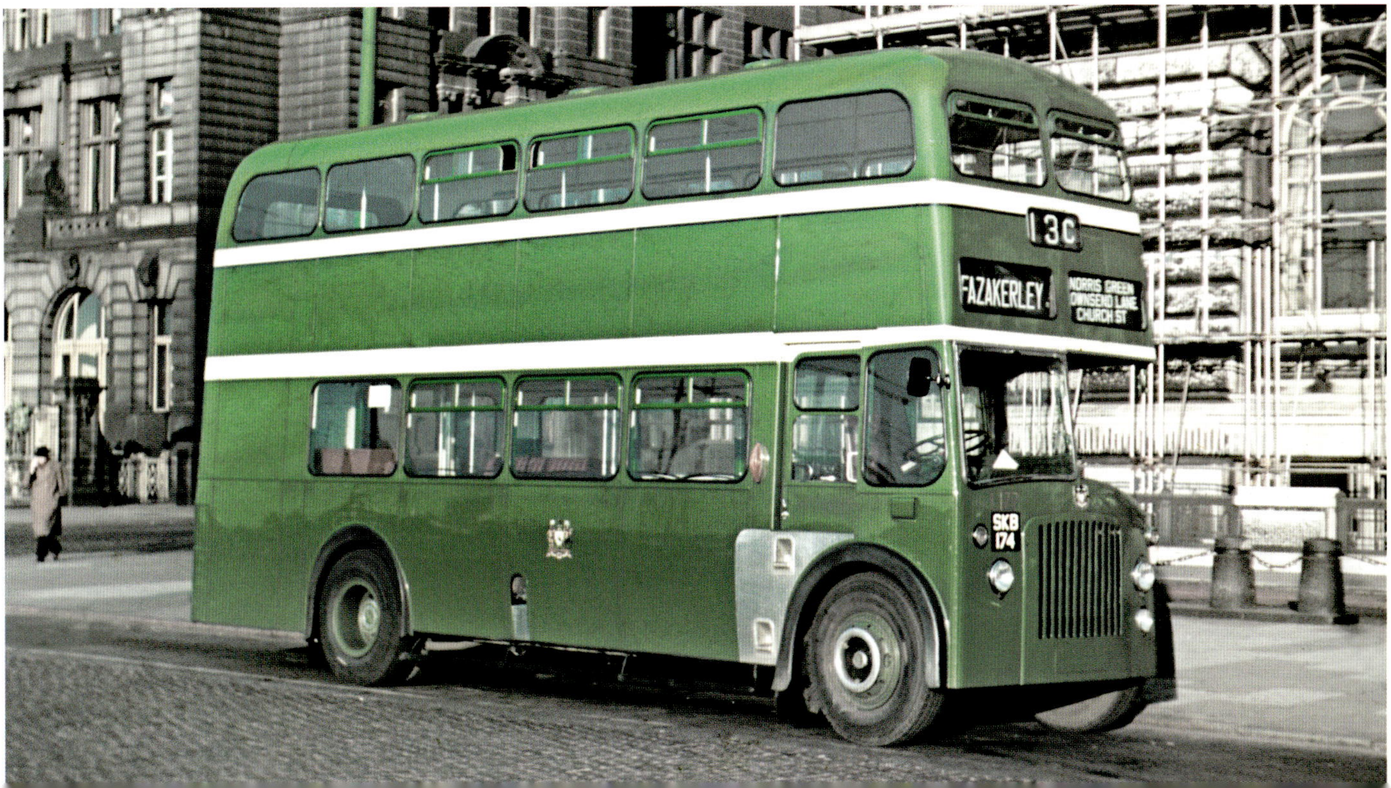

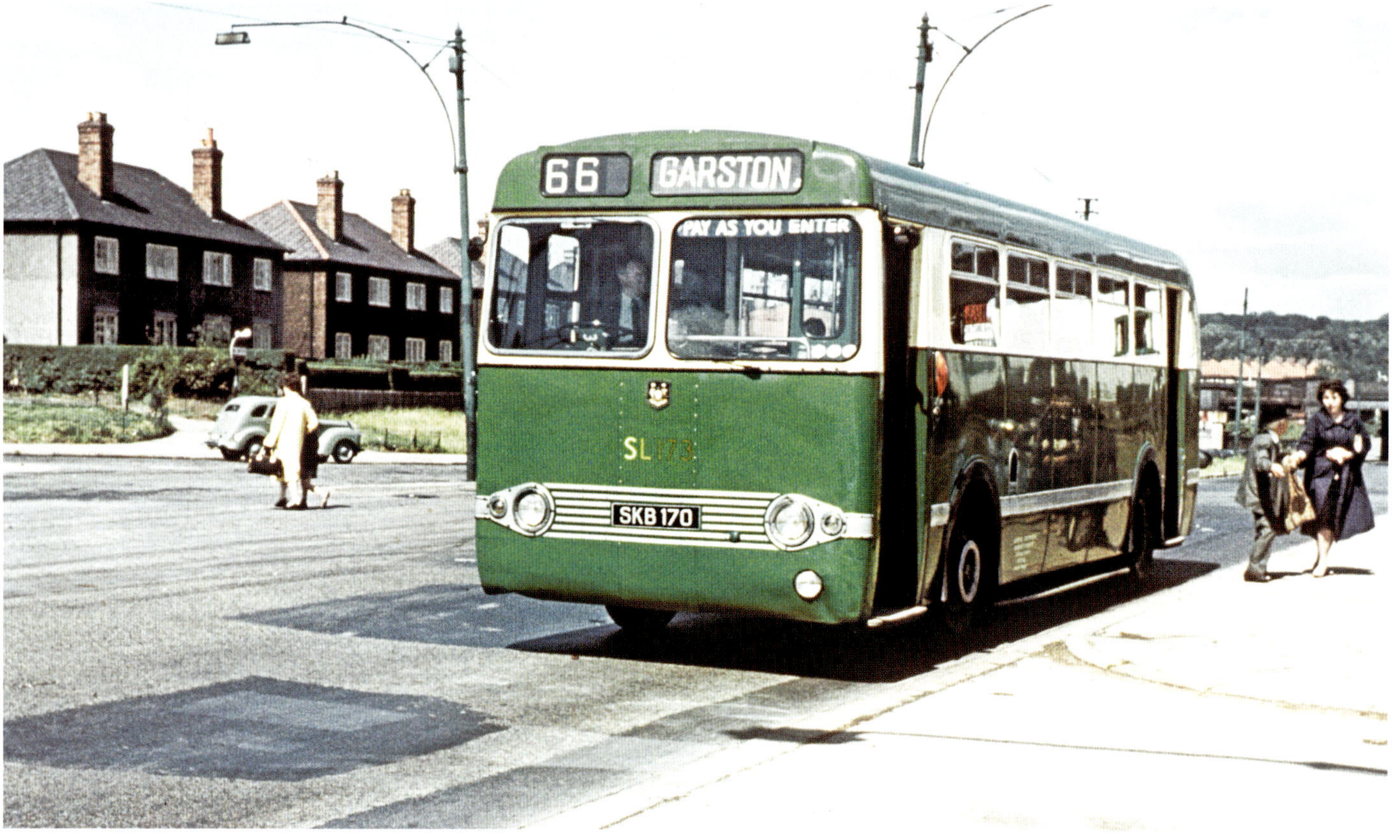
66
GARSTON
PAY AS YOU ENTER
SL173
SKB 170

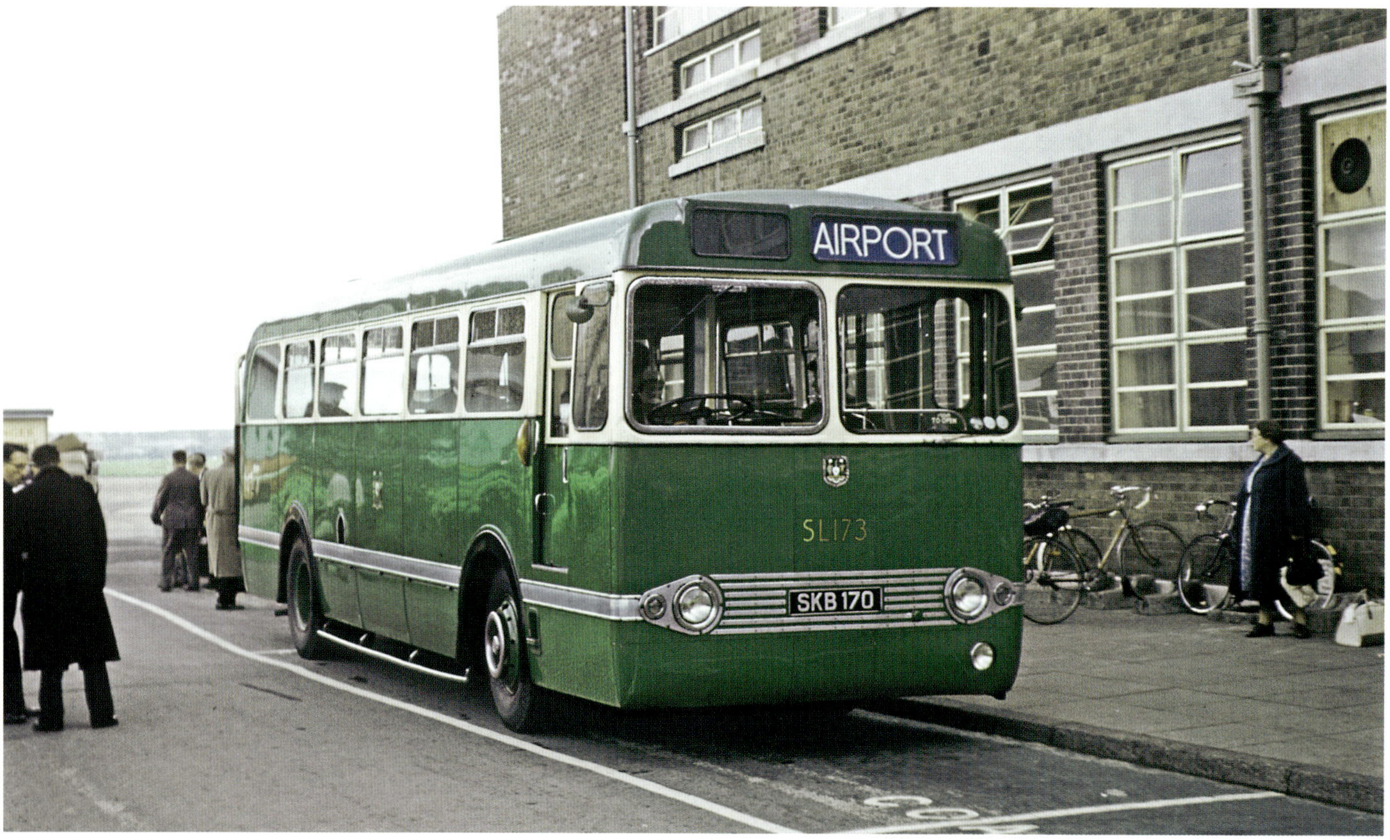
AIRPORT
SL173
SKB 170

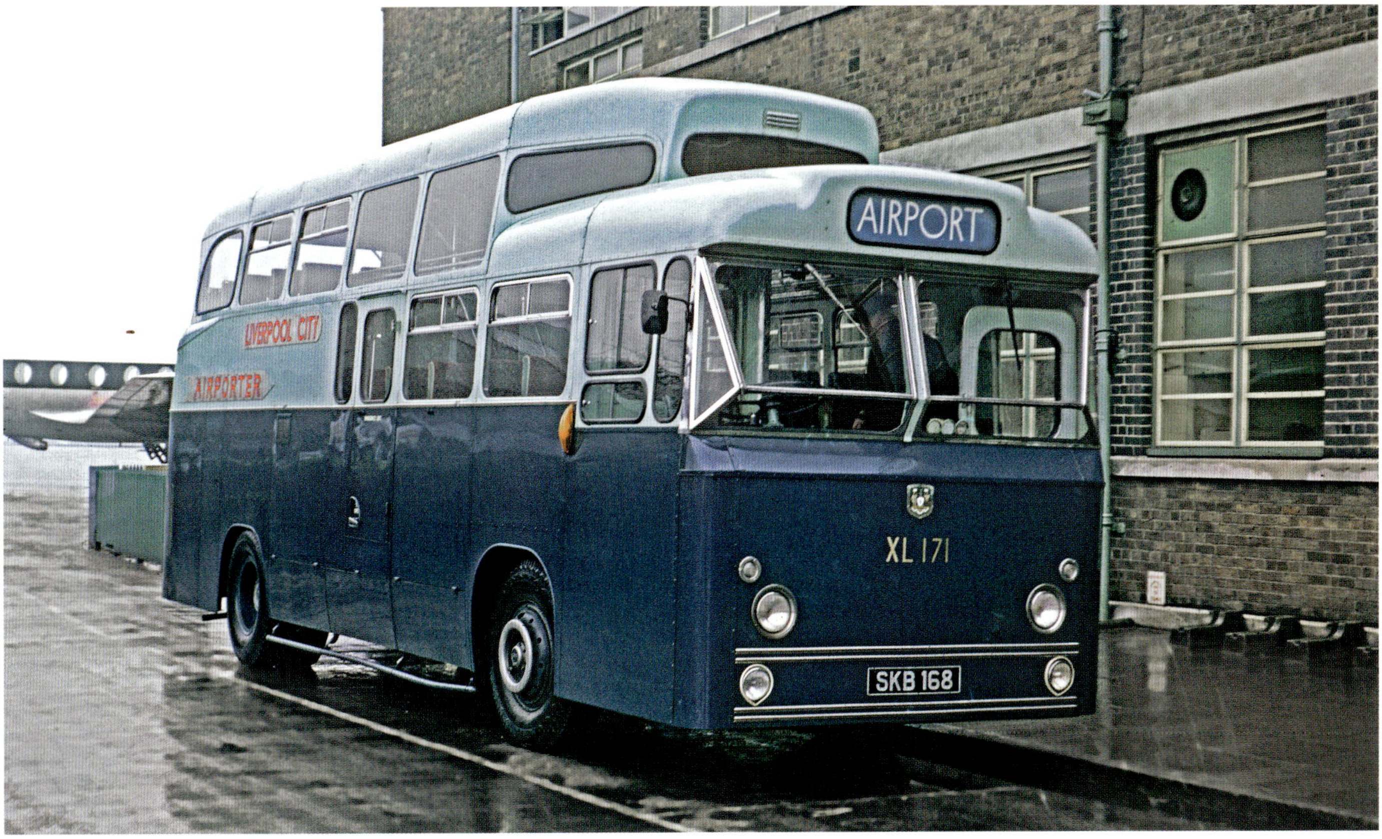

Opposite top Six Leyland Royal Tigers (SL171-176) entered service in 1956. The body order was first placed with Duple which then asked to be relieved of the contract due to lack of capacity at its works and the order was changed to Crossley shells finished at Edge Lane. The first four were fitted for one-person operation with rear exits in addition to the front entrance and automatic cash dispensers to try and speed up loading and unloading. The other two were for private hire and the Mersey Tunnel night service and had improved seats and no rear doorway. The trade unions were opposed to one-person operation but limited experiments took place on routes 66, 77 and 88. This picture shows SL173 on the 66 in Woolton Road, with Allerton station bridge just visible in the background and the former tram track, abandoned in 1953, on the left.
Photographer untraced/Online Transport Archive

Opposite bottom When the trials ended in 1960, SL172/73 were rebuilt with single front doorways for use on the Airport service replacing four Bedford OBs which the Corporation acquired when it took over the route from British European Airways in 1952. After rebuild, this is the same bus as above, at Speke Airport on the airport service in 1959. Its rear door has been opened to allow a wheelchair passenger to alight.
Geoffrey Morant

Above With the growth in airport traffic, there was a need for something with more luggage accommodation – such as the raised-roof airport coaches used by London and Manchester. The general manager is said to have noticed a picture of a contemporary American Greyhound coach in one of the trade magazines and in 1961 SL171-174 were despatched, with a set of drawings, to Metro Cammell to be rebuilt into one-and-a-half deck airport coaches. The eye catching results were renumbered XL171-174. The raised rear compartment had 21 coach seats, beneath it was a large luggage locker; the lower front section seated 23. With a BEA Vickers Viscount on the apron, 'Liverpool City Airporter' XL171 waits in pouring rain at Speke Airport to take passengers to the city centre in June 1962. The four operated the service until May 1966, when it was replaced by route 586 using specially adapted Atlanteans, and were then used on the shuttle service between Lime Street station and the Isle of Man Ferry. It is difficult to believe that XL171 once looked exactly the same as SL173 in the previous pictures. *Geoffrey Morant*

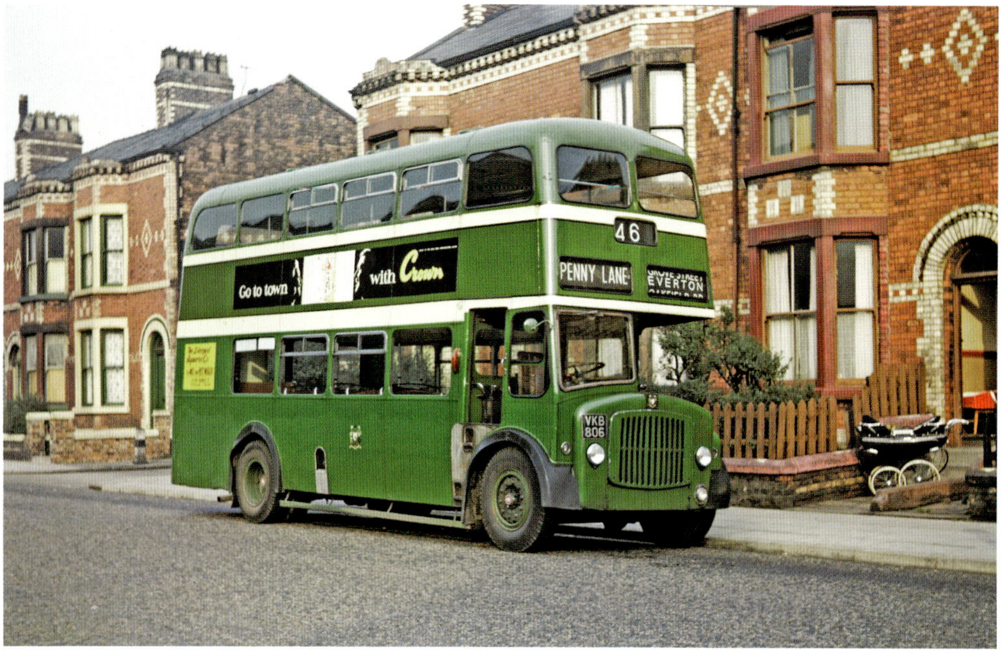

The next order continued the half AEC, half Leyland pattern, initially for 64 of each, both orders were increased to 100. A168-A267 were AEC Regent V, this time with Metro Cammell (rather than Weymann) Orion bodies built to Liverpool specifications – noticeable items being the window pans. Their delivery spanned three years – November 1956 to October 1959. This is A208 at Carisbrooke Road, Walton on 4 November 1962 on the cross-city service 46 to Penny Lane, its crew almost certainly in the depot canteen across the street. The destination 'Penny Lane' was strictly 'Smithdown Place' but the use of 'Penny Lane' for area and also for the bus and tram terminus long pre-dates the Beatles who made the bus (originally tram) shelter famous there as the 'shelter on the roundabout' in their 1967 hit song. *Roy Marshall*

Although the fashion for unpainted buses had passed, Liverpool continued to experiment and A221/28-32 were thus. This is A221, still unpainted in September 1968. At one stage there was a plan to allocate the unpainted buses to limited stop services but it was never implemented. *Roy Marshall*

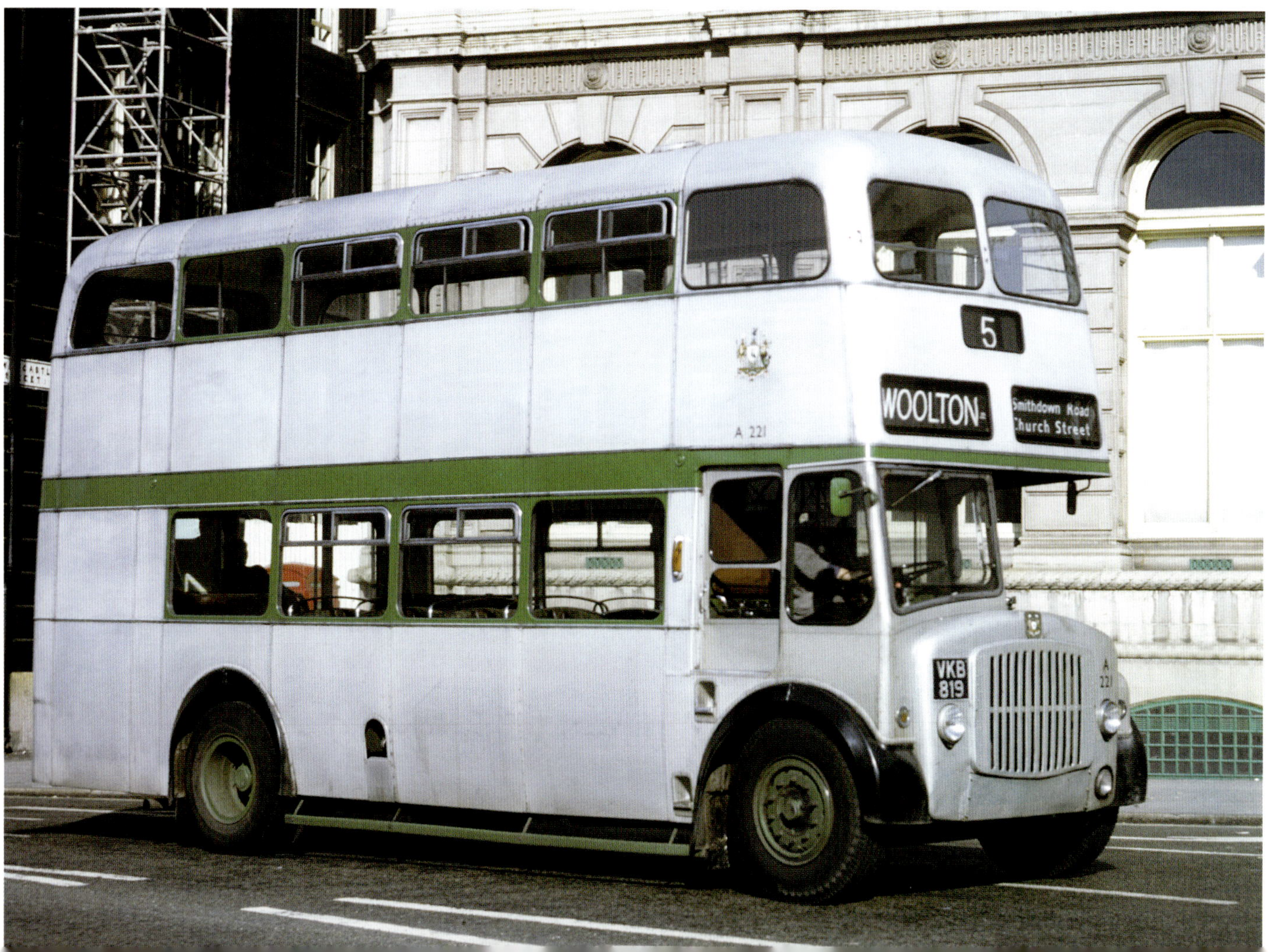

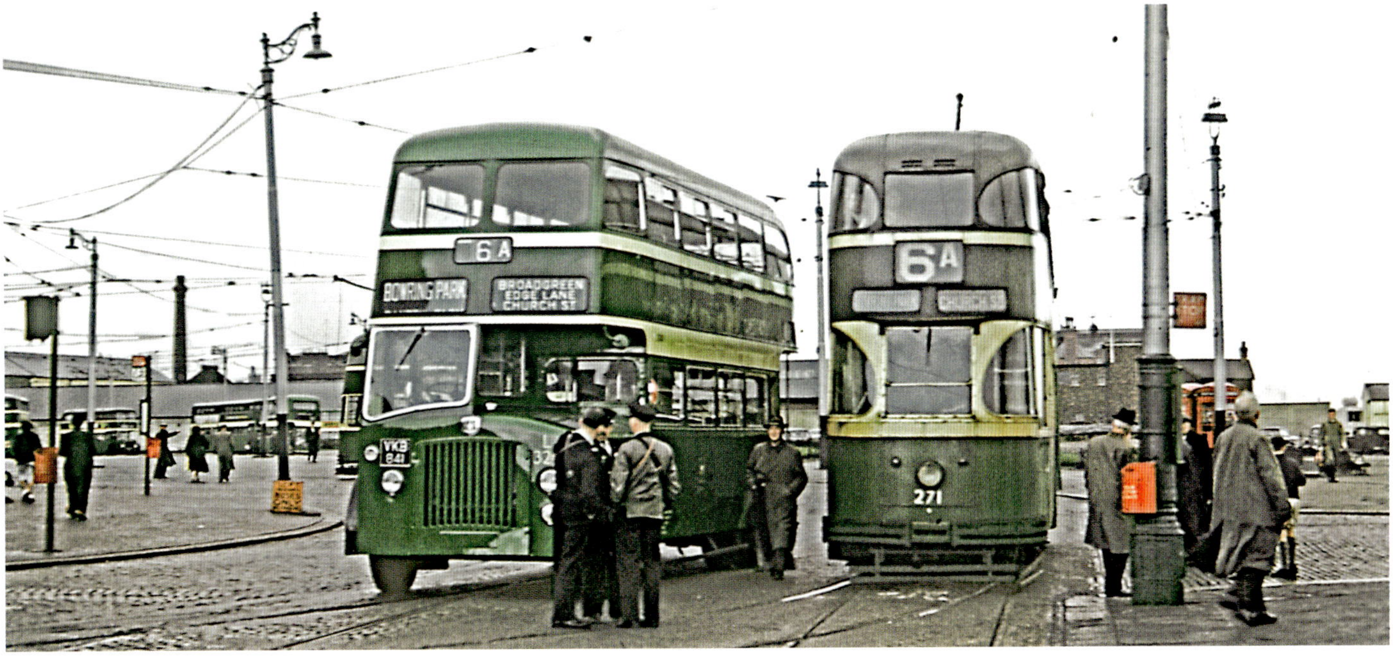

The balance of the order was 100 Crossley or Crossley/LCPT-bodied Leyland PD2/20s and they had Liverpool's simplified bonnet/radiator cowl. The delivery – and build – of L245-344 was complicated. L245-279 and L310-344 were all-Crossley and went into service over the period November 1956 to February 1958, a change in Leyland model numbers resulting in L340-44 being PD2/30s. The chassis of L280-309 were also PD2/30 and their bodies were Crossley shells intended to be finished at Edge Lane – but this did not happen. Firstly Edge Lane was busy with overhaul work; a review of vehicle needs then showed that there would be a surplus of buses and the untouched chassis/shells were put into store at Edge Lane where they stayed until 1961 when, Crossley having closed in 1958, they were sent to Metro Cammell for completion.

Above The changeover to buses on the last day of the tram services took place gradually during the afternoon of Saturday 14th September 1957 until by tea-time the former tram routes 6A and 40 were being operated by buses observing the tram timetables and stops. They included some of the new PD2s which then took over the services with new timetables on the Sunday. In this picture of the south loop terminus at Pier Head, the conductors of tram 271 and brand new L320 chat with the controlling inspector. *J B McCann*

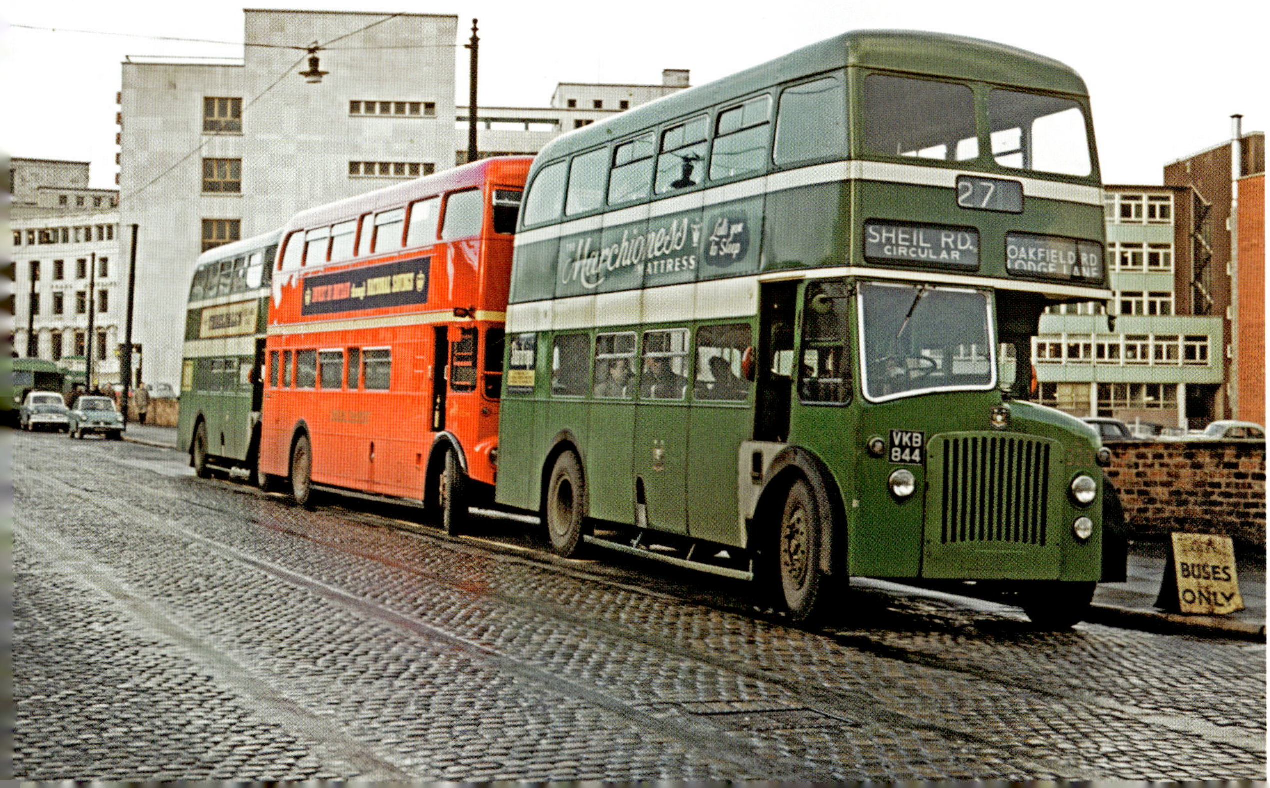

Left This is Crossley/Metro Cammell-bodied L323 in South Castle Street in November 1962. The heavily-used 26/27 Sheil Road Circulars were the first tram to bus conversions in June 1948. Behind is London Transport's AEC Routemaster RMF 1254 on loan from AEC – its brief stay was part of Liverpool's evaluation programme for future orders. The AEC Regal canteen can be seen in the background.
G D Smith

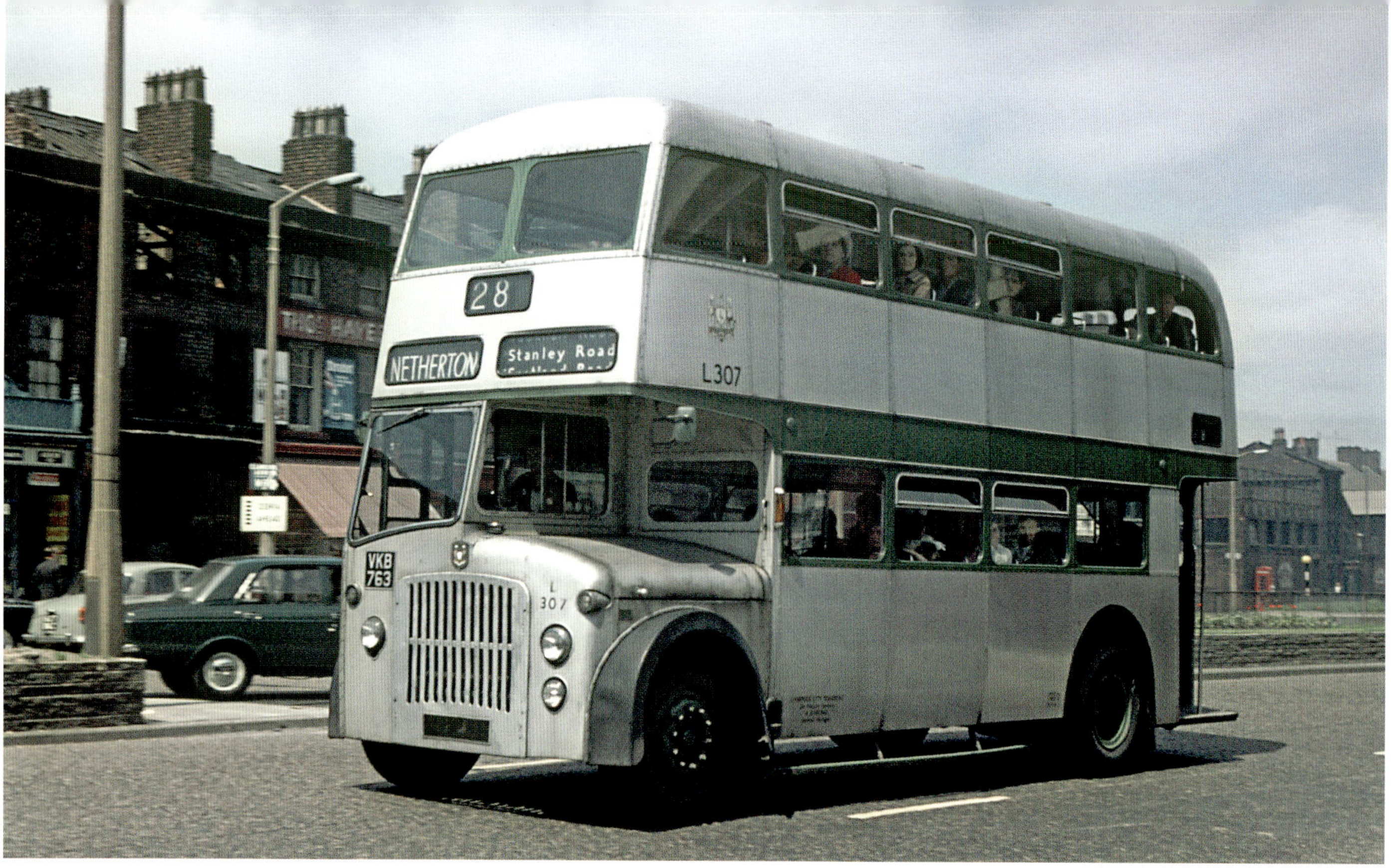

As mentioned previously, matching the revised bonnet/grille to the standard Crossley body required the windscreen to be raked outwards at a sharper angle than the rest of the front and it looked really inelegant. Still persisting with the experiments, Crossley/Metro Cammell L294/5, 300/03-09 were delivered unpainted in 1961. Replaced panels were all too obvious. *Alan Murray-Rust*

Before L280-309 were delayed, the order had been increased in 1956 by a further 25 Leylands and 25 AECs to cover the planned closure of the Liverpool Overhead Railway. Metro Cammell-bodied AEC Regent V A268-292 came first, in late 1957 and early 1958, followed by the Crossley-bodied Leyland PD2/30s L345-369. They were the department's last Crossley bodies – AEC closed Crossley Motors in 1958 and there is speculation that, due to staff leaving Crossley's in the run up to closure, L360-369 and the shells of L295-302 were assembled or finished at other ACV group works. Four year-old L348 is waiting to leave the Pier Head on the 48-minute run to the Northwood district of Kirkby. *Roy Marshall*

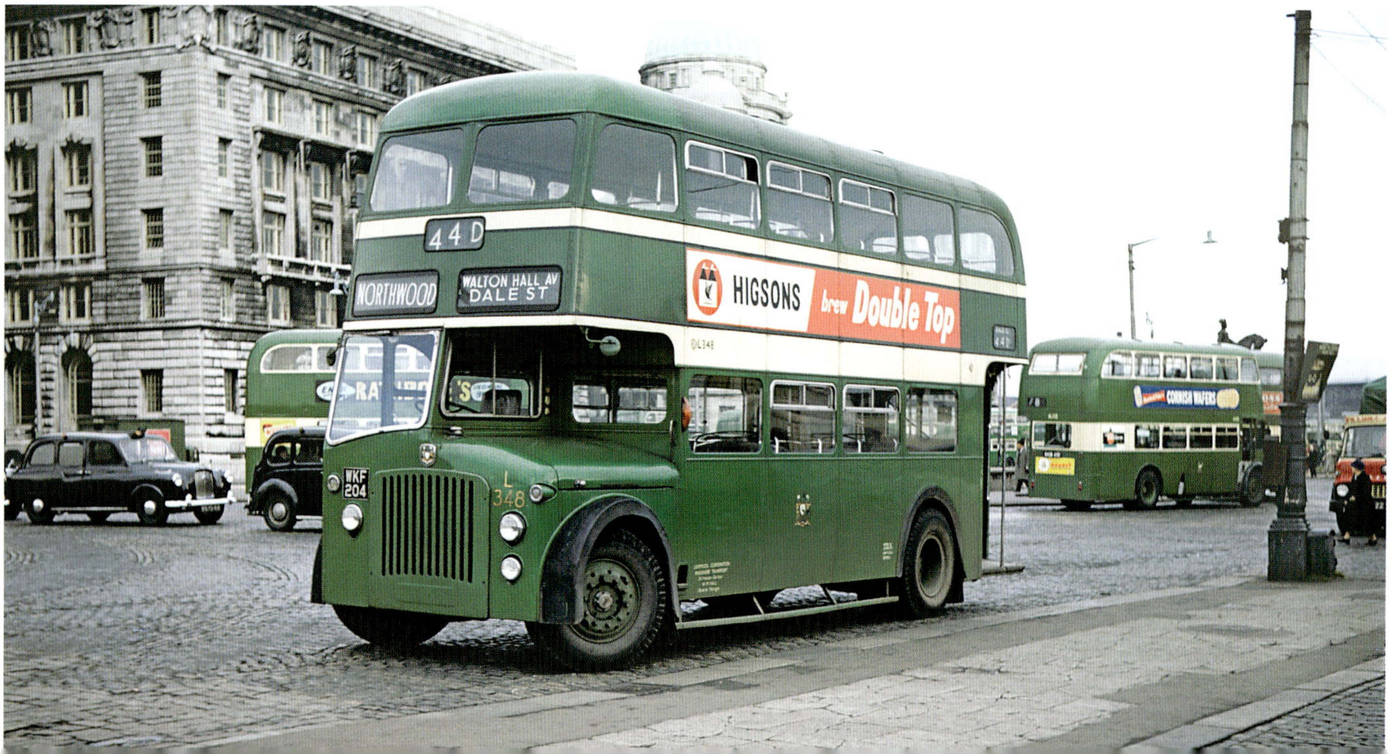

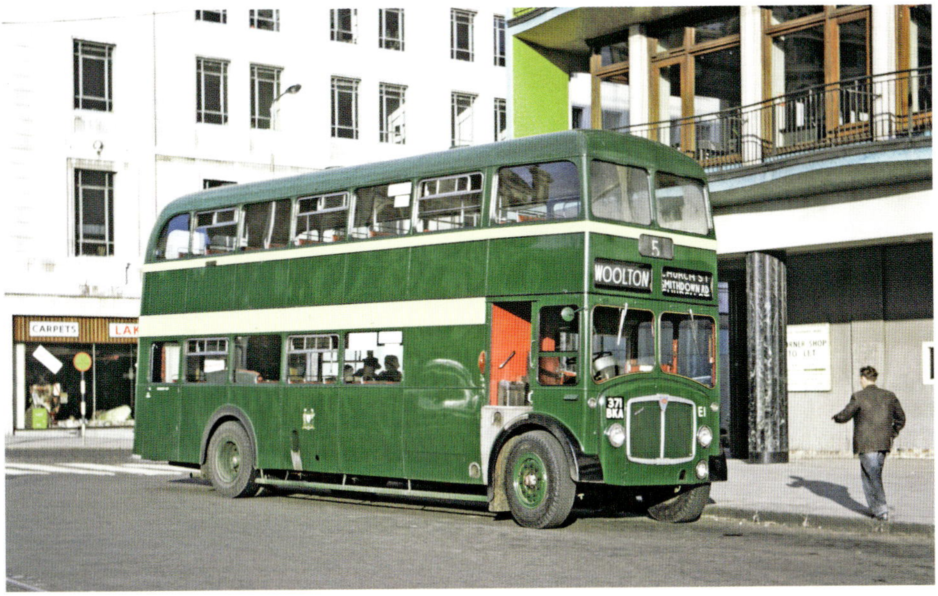

To help determine future vehicle policy, in 1959 Liverpool bought or hired three experimental buses, numbering them E1 to E3. Often allocated to the 4 and 5 services to Woolton, a 30-ft long AEC Regent V (E1) was the first to enter service in August 1959. The layout of its Park Royal body with forward entrance and sliding door was similar to the fleet of Leyland PD3s which Ribble was operating in the city. Forty similar Regents were built for the East Kent Road Car Company but differed in many details and E1's body and sales numbers together with other evidence suggests it had been built by AEC as a speculative venture, possibly as the pilot for the East Kents. November 1962, *Roy Marshall*

E2 was a Leyland Atlantean with Metro Cammell's standard body. When this picture was taken in 1964, the body had been modified in several details one of which was the seating, which was altered to back-to-back pairs over the rear wheel arches – a feature which was to become standard on Liverpool and Merseyside PTE buses for many years and which was adopted by other operators. *Bryan Pyne*

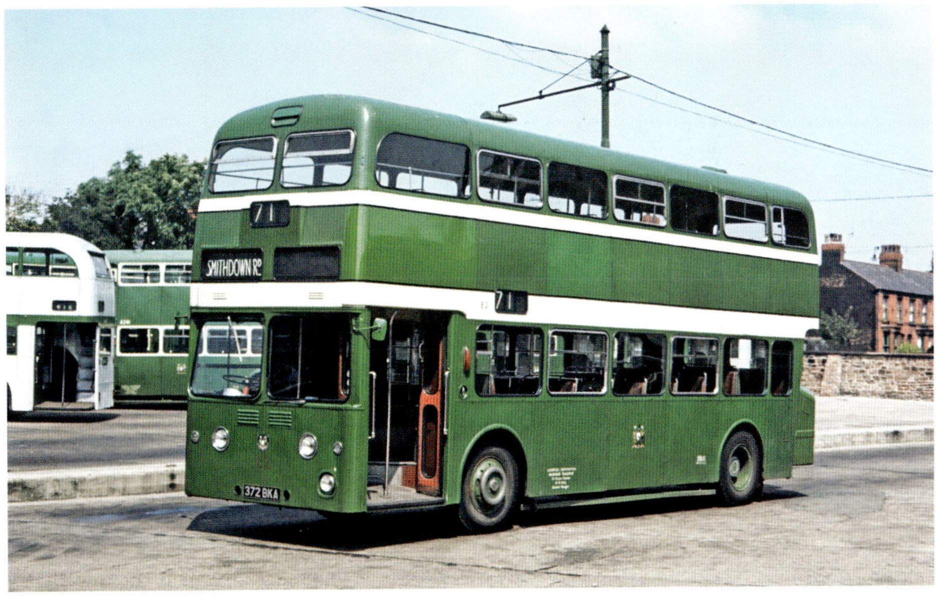

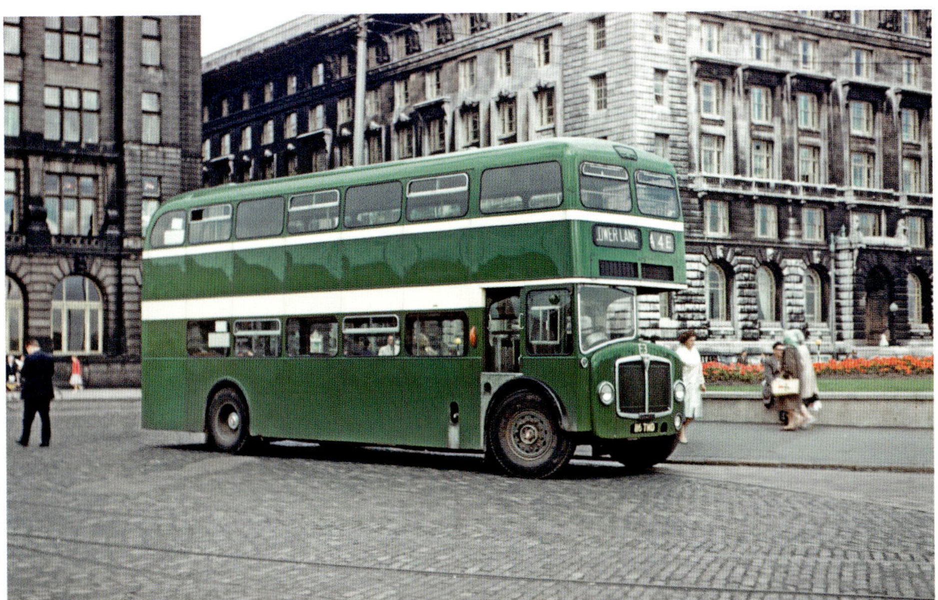

The third experimental vehicle was a Park Royal-bodied AEC Bridgemaster on loan from its makers and painted in Liverpool colours. Registered 116 TMD it arrived in January 1959 but ran for only two days before being blacked by the union. AEC then used it to demonstrate elsewhere whilst the union problem was resolved. It returned in October, received the fleet number E3 and the council agreed to buy it in December 1960. With its half-cab and open rear platform, the integrally-constructed Bridgemaster's principal feature was its low overall height – of little value in Liverpool which had no significant low bridges. The heater intake grilles on the front of the body vehicle meant there was insufficient room for a three piece indicator display. 1962 *Roy Marshall*

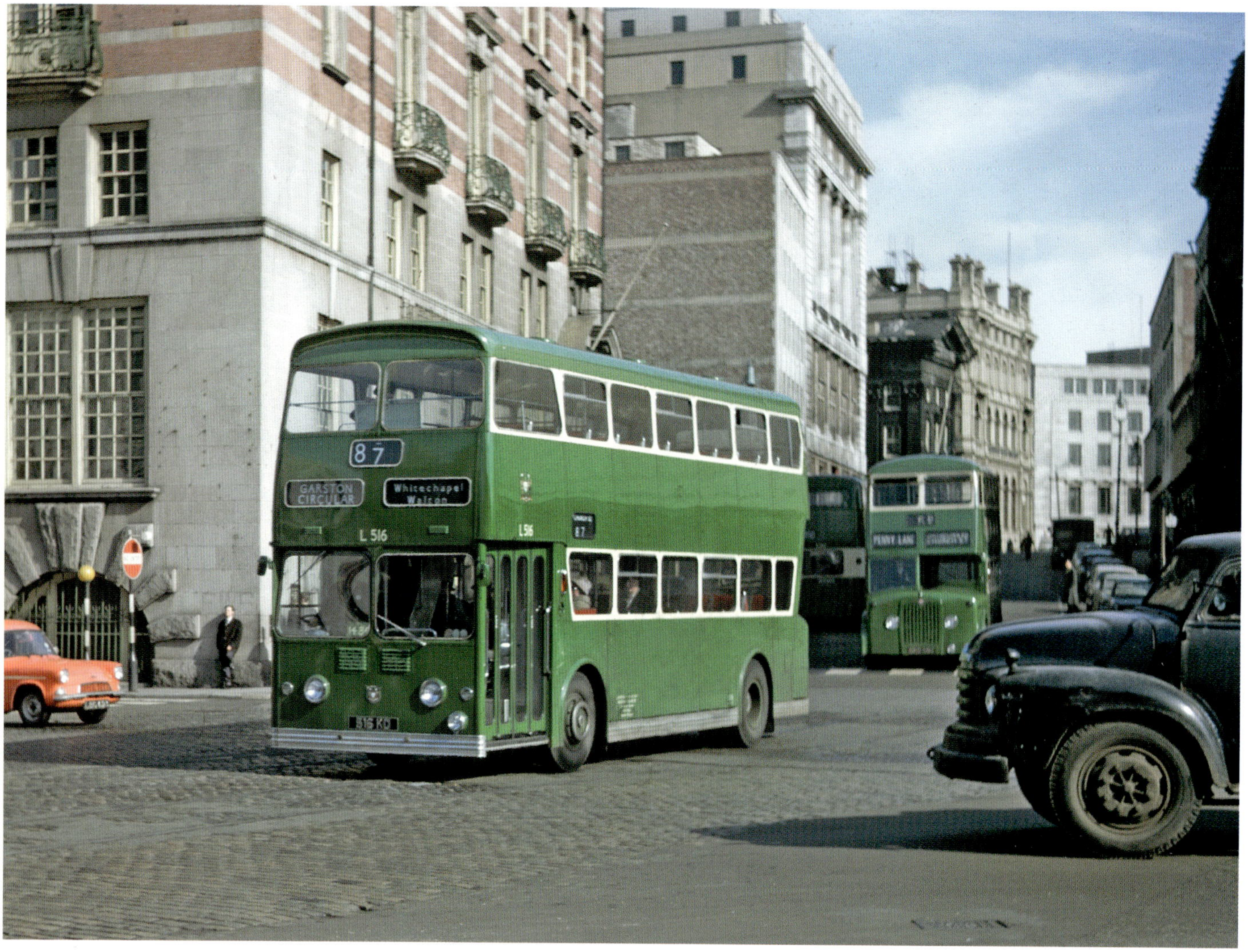

The department's choice was, perhaps unsurprisingly, the Leyland Atlantean. Equally unsurprisingly, the department's engineers had views on the body design and they produced something really stylish and very different from the bland and undistinguished standard offerings from Metro Cammell and others. Liverpool's business was sufficiently valuable that Metro Cammell, which won the body order, was willing to build exactly what Liverpool wanted. The most striking features were the peaks in the front and rear domes, which started an industry fashion, and the reverse slope above the engine bustle, said to have been inspired by the rear window of the Ford Anglia then in production at the new Ford plant in nearby Halewood. The first order was for 200. Numbered L500-L699 in a new series, L500 and L501 entered service late in 1962 but, as elsewhere, their general introduction was delayed for some months whilst agreements for operating higher-capacity vehicles were negotiated with the union. Regular service began on the Garston Circular 86/87 routes in February 1963, as in this picture of L516 turning into The Strand. *Roy Marshall*

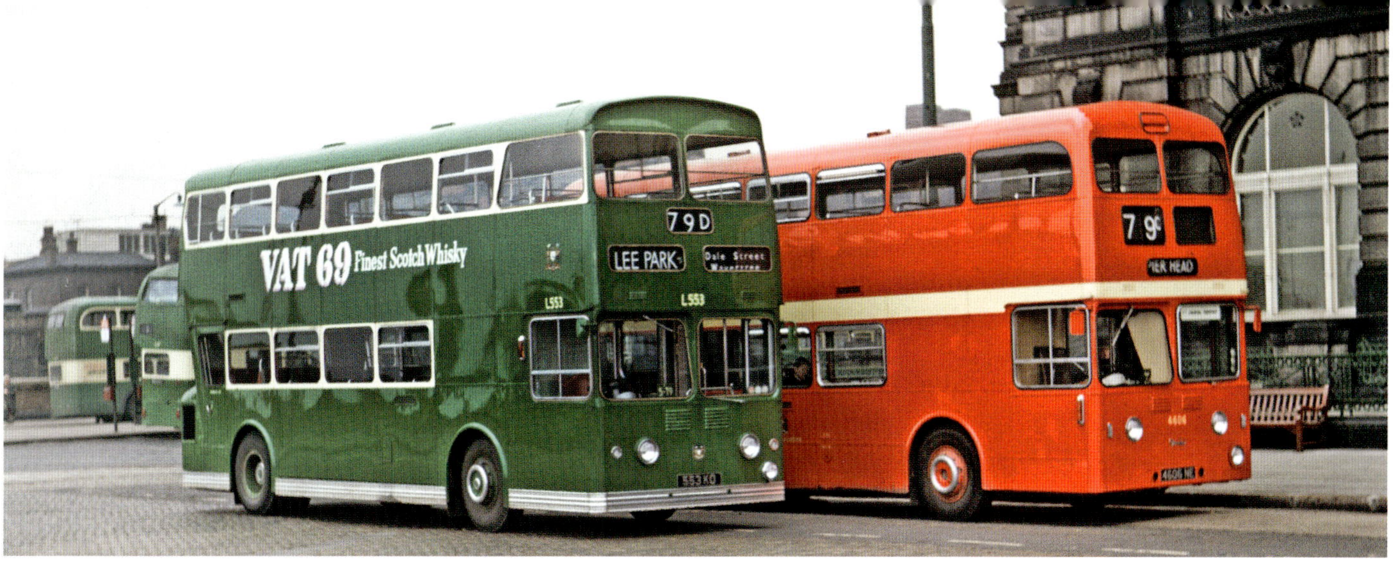

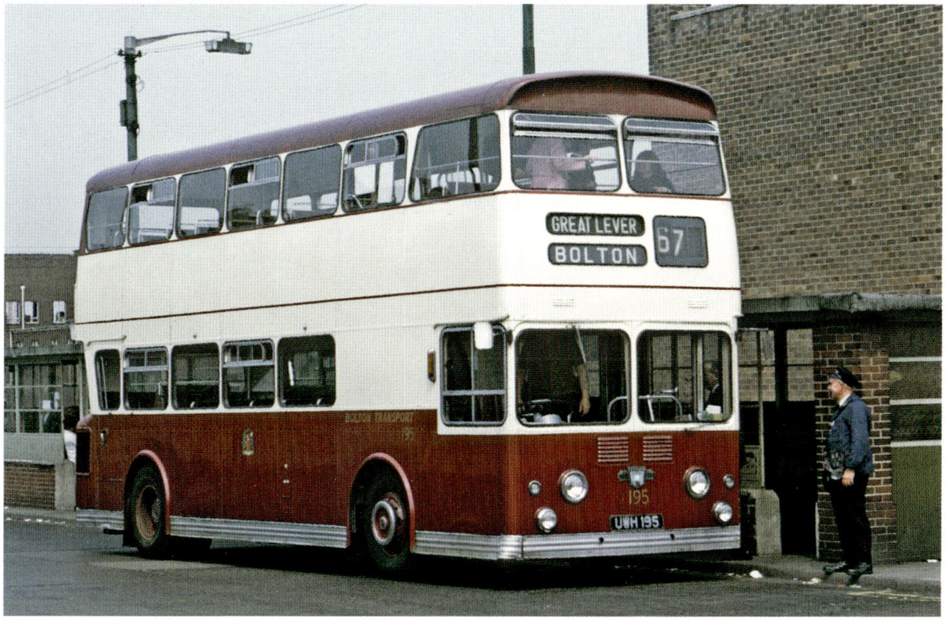

Manchester's Daimler Fleetline 4606 was borrowed in February and March of 1963 for comparison with the Atlanteans. Alongside Liverpool's brand new L553 it illustrates the bland nature of the then standard Metro Cammell offering, even though its bright red was, perhaps, more striking than Liverpool's green. *Roy Marshall*

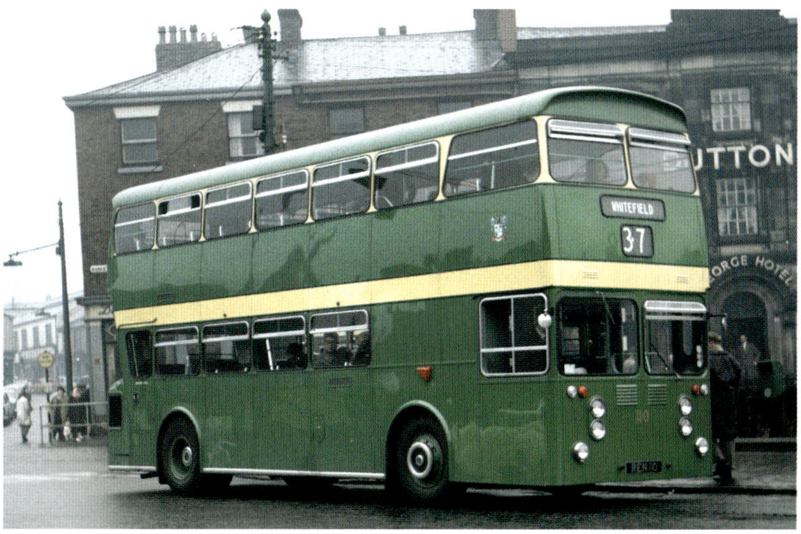

Above and left Liverpool's body for the Atlantean was a major improvement in the design of bodies for rear-engined double-deckers and although it stimulated other manufacturers, it was slightly surprising that only two other operators bought 'Liverpool' bodies. They were Bolton and Bury, the former with a style of livery then coming into fashion and the latter more traditional and with some small changes of detail. It is, of course, personal judgement which looked the most handsome but the pictures show that the style suited very different liveries – a mark of any good design. Bolton, August 1968; Bury, April 1963; *Roy Marshall*

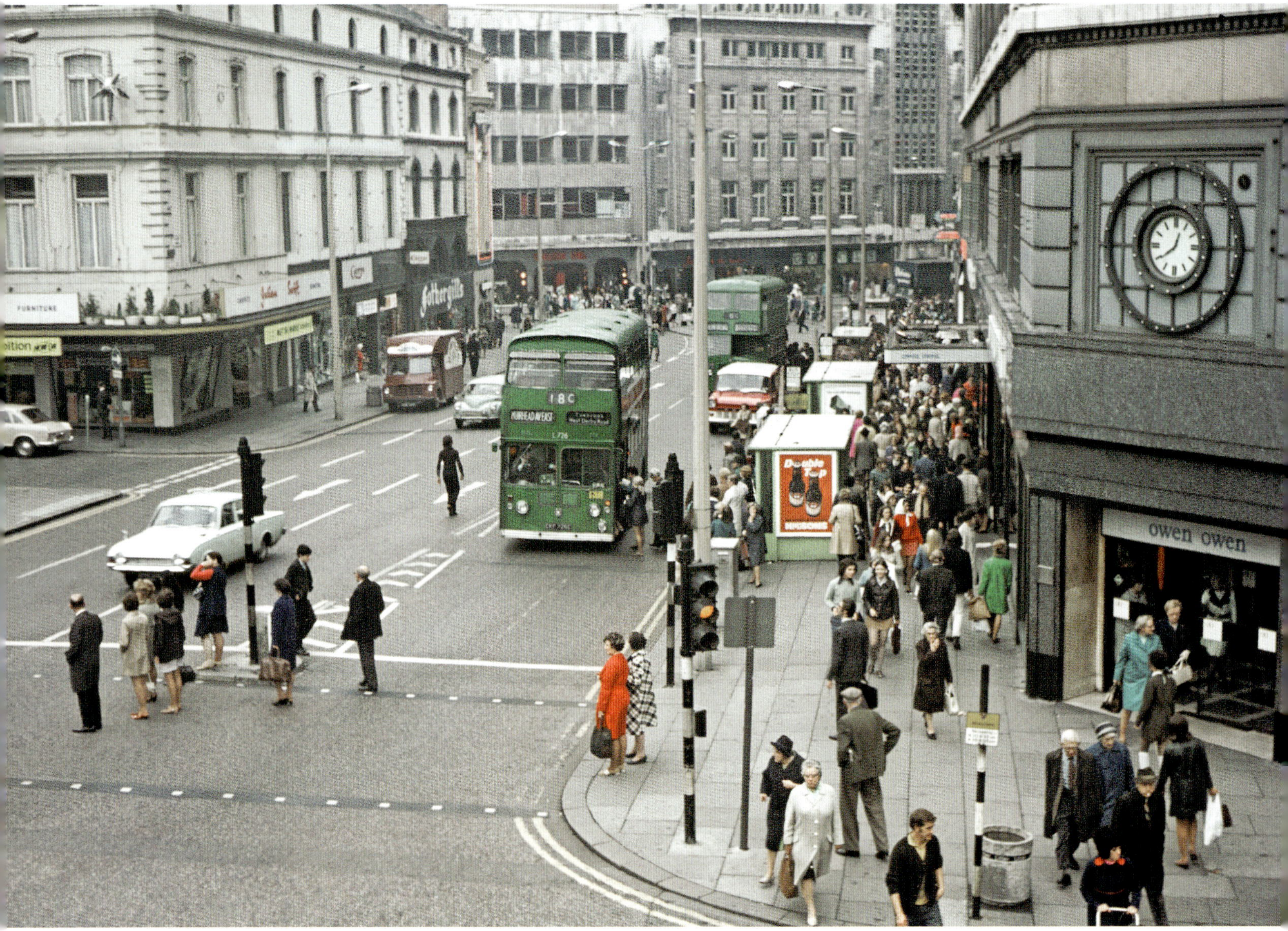

At twenty minutes to one o'clock on a Saturday in 1969 Parker Street is busy with shoppers, many of whom will have been to the famous Owen Owen department store, as L726, one of the second batch of Atlanteans, loads for Muirhead Avenue on an 18C. The yellow notice on the front panel is for 'Bus Economy Tickets' – ten-trip tickets bought off bus and cancelled on board. *Ian Stewart*

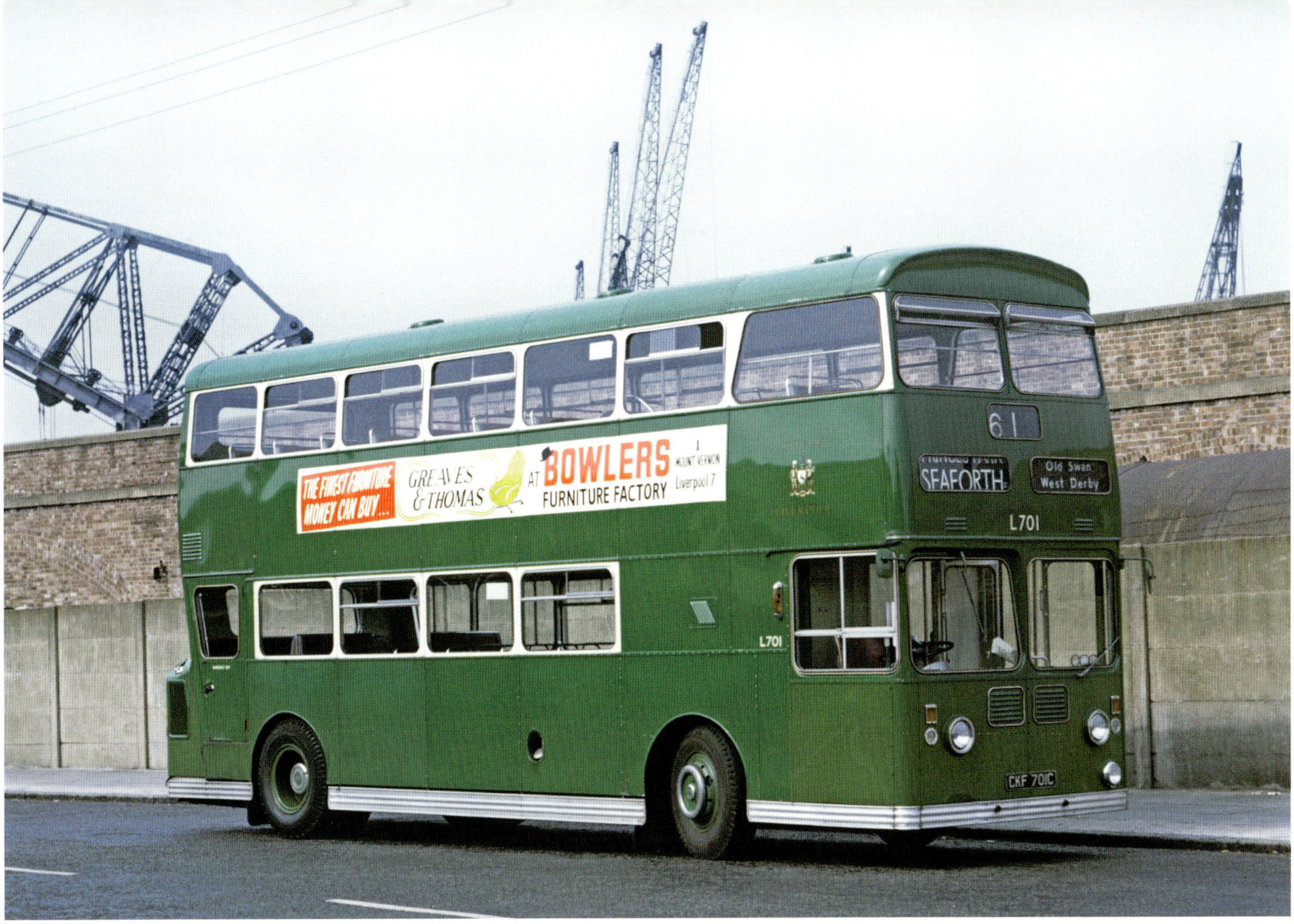

By 1967 Liverpool had 380 Atlanteans in service. Experience in use led to detail changes on the second batch. L700-879, delivered between 1965 and 1967, were nine inches longer at 30ft 9in, had a tip-up seat for the conductor, two-piece doors, opening vents above the front upper deck windows and smoothing of the reverse slope at the rear to eliminate the small 'step' at upper saloon floor height, the latter shown clearly in this August 1968 picture of L701, the first of the second type. Liverpool's shades of green were apt to vary as here on the front lower deck and rear wheelarch panels which have had accident attention. *Roy Marshall*

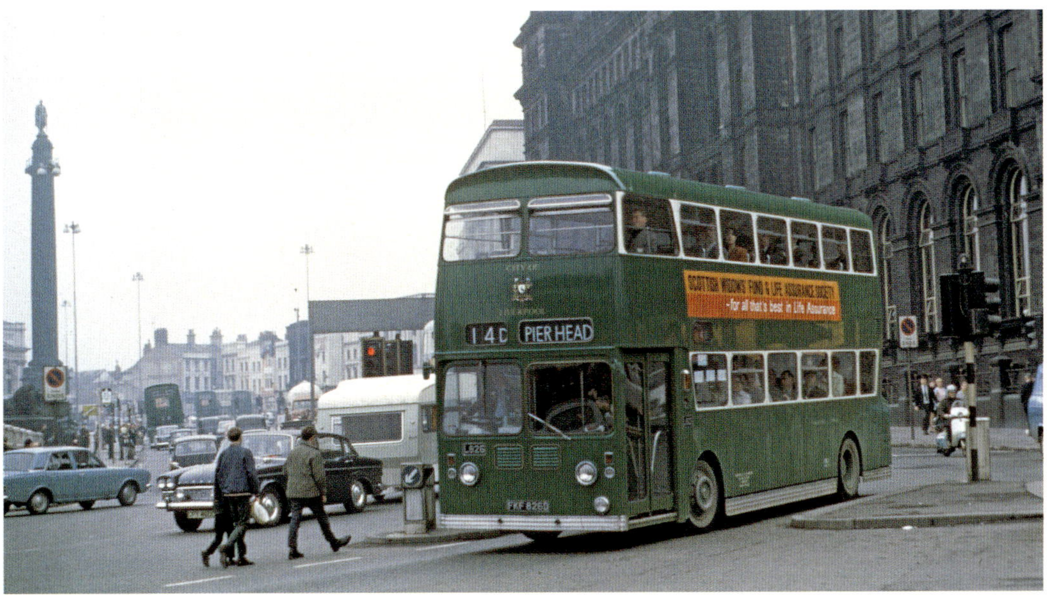

With the general industry move to one-man operation of large double-deckers, a programme to convert all the Atlanteans commenced in 1969. The most obvious change was an alteration in the destination indicators to two-piece, enabling the driver to change the blinds without leaving the cab – previously the winding gear had been accessed from inside the upper saloon. This May 1969 picture shows modified L826 turning from Lime Street into St John's Lane, bound for Pier Head via Dale Street. In the background is the Wellington Column, one of Liverpool's great statues. With L780-879 Liverpool ceased using cream fleet number transfers and moved to black on white, pressed aluminium number plates. *Roy Marshall*

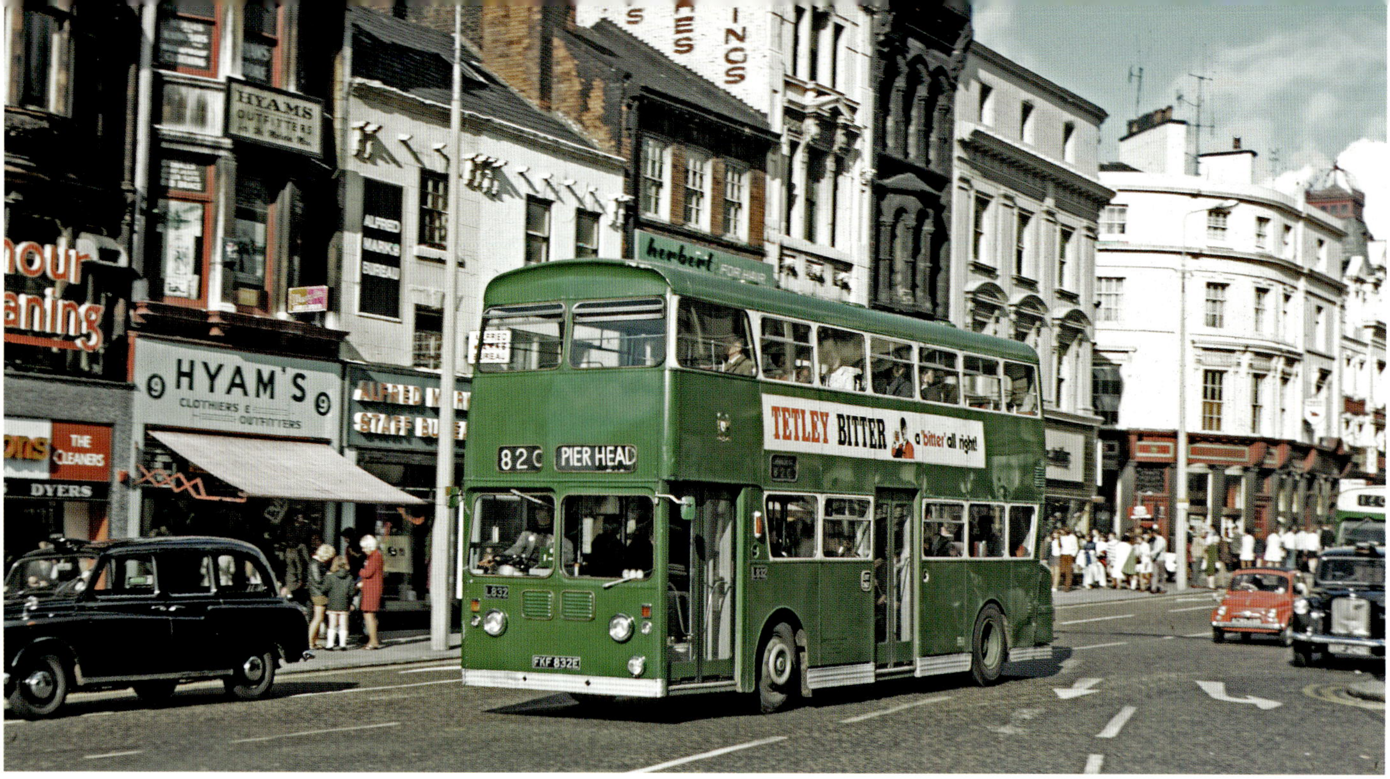

Pennine Coachcraft, the bodybuilding division of Seddon, did the work on L780-879 in May to October 1969, including a more extensive rebuild for L830-879 to dual door with a centre exit, the staircase being moved to central position and seating reduced from 78 to 71. Photographed not long after its conversion to dual door in August, L832 is on Ranelagh Street, inbound for Pier Head. *Dennis Kerrison*

Sadly, general manager 'Bill' Hall died in office in 1965 and Albert Burrows, then manager at Chesterfield, was appointed in his place. He had some experience of one-man operation and before the somewhat sudden government's authorisation of one-man operation of full-size double-deckers in 1966, had decided to proceed with large capacity one-man single-deckers. The second order for 120 'Liverpool' Atlanteans (L700-819) was already delivered or in build but he changed to single-deckers as many as he could of the third order for 130, which became 60 Atlanteans and 70 of Leyland's rear-engined 36ft-long Panther. The Panther order was then increased to 110. Delivered in 1968/69 MCW-bodied Panthers 1001-1110 were finished in the revised livery shown in this picture of 1060 in South Castle Street in April 1969. *Roy Marshall*

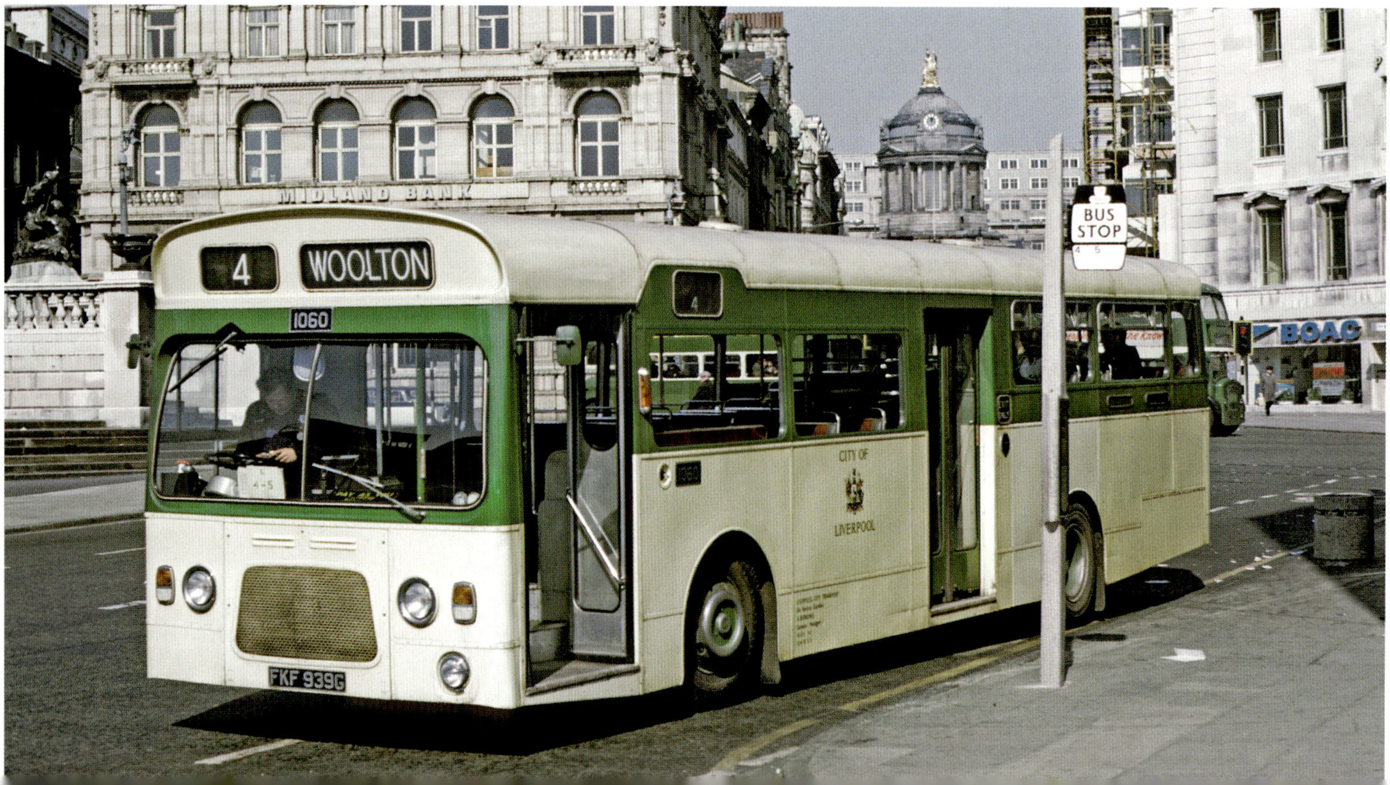

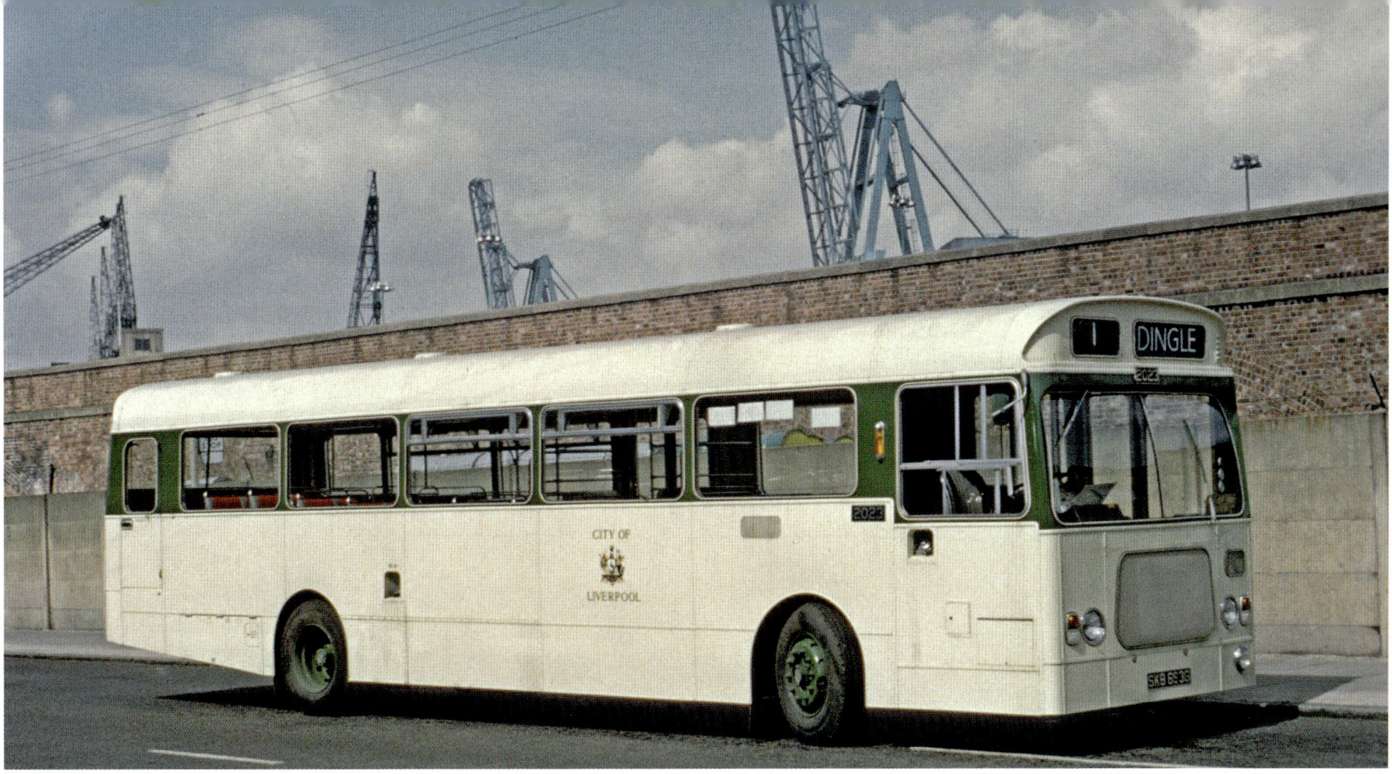

The Panther was not Leyland's most successful model and the next order was for 25 Bristol RELL with Gardner 6HLX engines and Park Royal bodies. Delivered a few months before the undertaking passed to the PTE, they were based at Litherland depot where they were usually allocated to the former Overhead Railway replacement service 1, as in this June 1969 picture of 2023 at the Regent Road, Seaforth, terminus. In the background are the cranes of Gladstone Dock. *Roy Marshall*

The authorisation of one-man double-deckers caused a rethink and orders were placed for 40 Atlanteans with Alexander bodies, 25 Bristol VRT with East Lancs bodies, then a further 85 Alexander-bodied Atlanteans and 35 more East Lancs VRTs. Alexander was by then firmly established in supplying outside of Scotland and the bodies were generally to Liverpool's standard design although the high Alexander front upper-deck windows made them look rather different. Numbered 1111-1150, the first of the Alexander Atlanteans (1111) arrived a few days before the PTE took over but did not enter service until the following month along with four other members of the class – the remainder of the orders were delivered to the PTE. This is 1131 on Lord Street – new to the PTE, it still showed Liverpool City Transport as its legal owner in the May 1971 picture. *Roy Marshall*

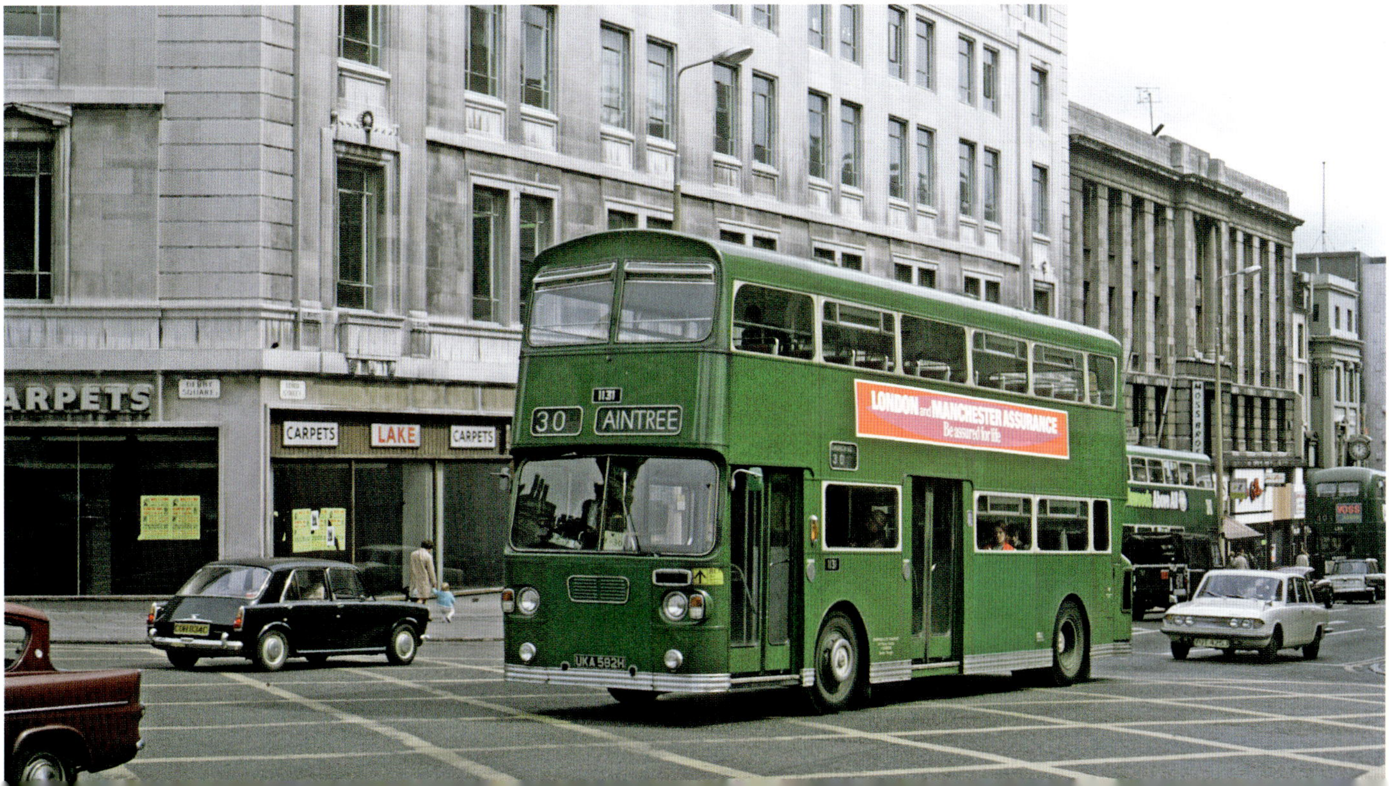

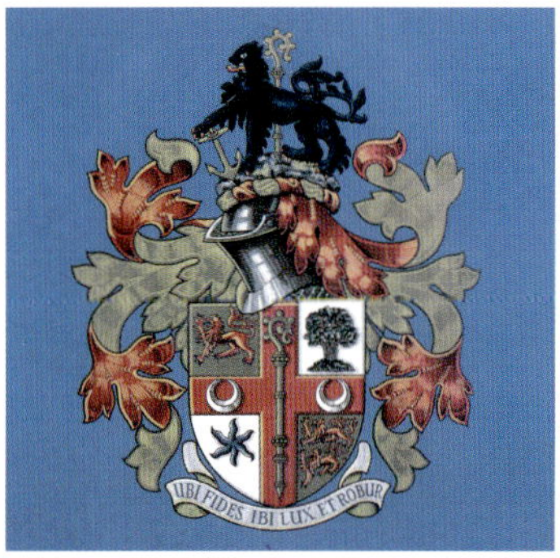

Birkenhead

Birkenhead made its first mark on public transport history in 1860 when George Francis Train opened the first street tramway in Britain. The corporation took over the horse tramways, converting them to electrical power. It bought its first buses in 1919 using them to extend operations beyond the tramway network, the last trams running in 1937.

For the greater part of its existence Birkenhead was a dedicated Leyland customer; the war brought 36 utility Guys and the reliable and economical Gardner engine made its usual impression, so that until the mid 1950s Guy shared the orders with Leyland. For bodywork, Massey was preferred supplier and Birkenhead was that firm's biggest customer. The original livery of dark maroon and white was changed in 1933 to an attractive light blue and cream which distinguished the fleet of some 230 buses until it passed to the Merseyside PTE on December 1st 1969.

The transport department did not regard the town's boundaries or company operators as some sort of limit on its operations. Although Crosville had a considerable presence, the corporation extracted a heavy price for allowing it to run to the ferry terminal at Woodside so that, in addition to serving the busy docks, Cammell Laird's shipyards and the Unilever factories, Birkenhead's services ran well beyond the town boundaries and not just to serve new housing estates – the corporation's timetable encouraged passengers to *'visit the beauty spots of the Wirral Peninsula by travelling on Corporation omnibuses to Heswall, Thurstaston, Irby, Eastham, Moreton and New Brighton'.*

The hub of the Birkenhead transport network was the busy bus/ferry/rail interchange at Woodside. This view looks down towards the Ferry terminal with the Liverpool waterfront and famous Liver Building across the Mersey. Daimler Fleetlines 107 and 109, Leyland PD2s 38, 48, 151 and one other plus a Crosville Bristol MW are on the service stands. On the left is the parking area where vehicles used at peak periods would spend their day, avoiding dead mileage to the garage. March 1968 *Roy Marshall.*

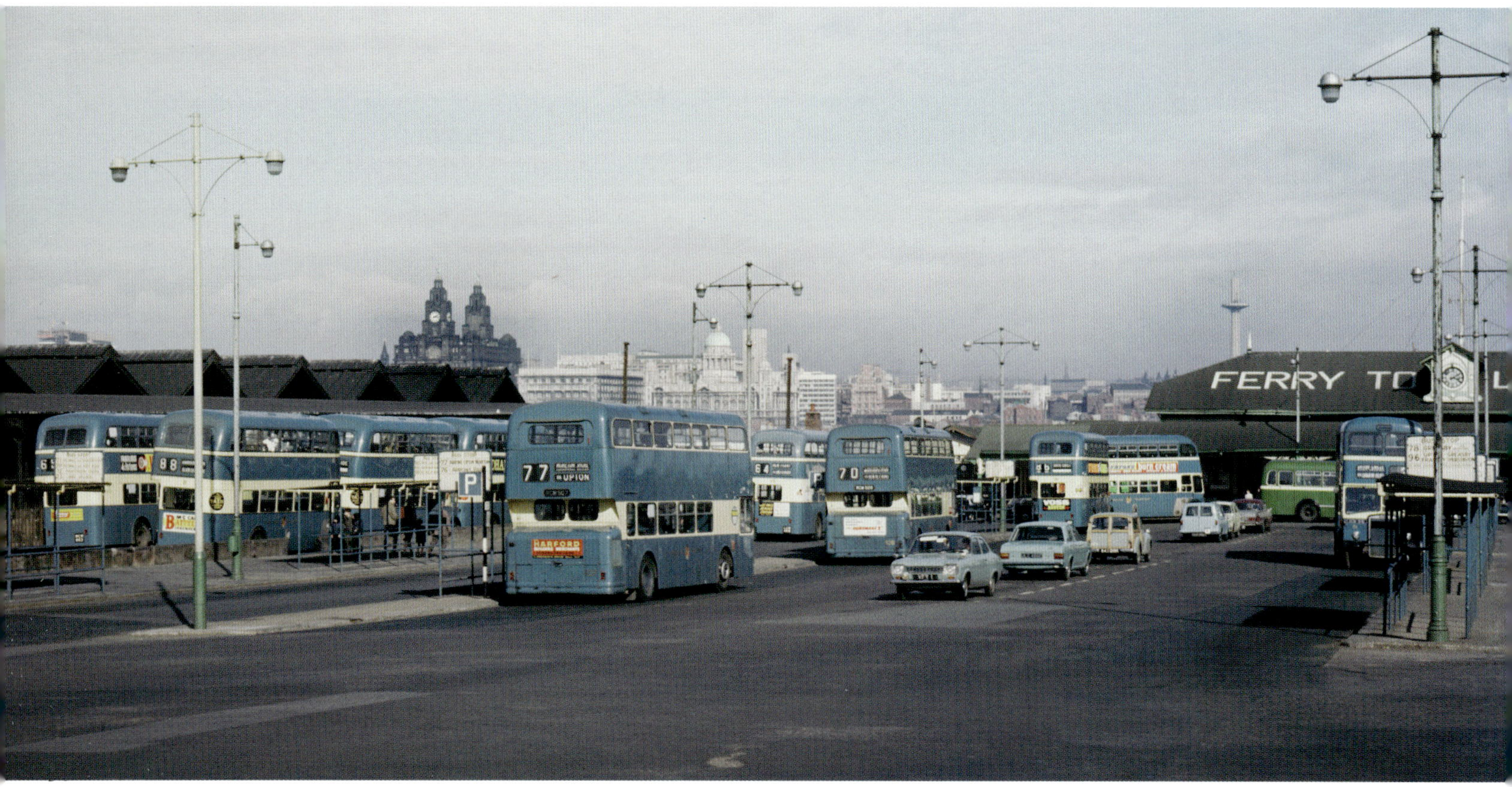

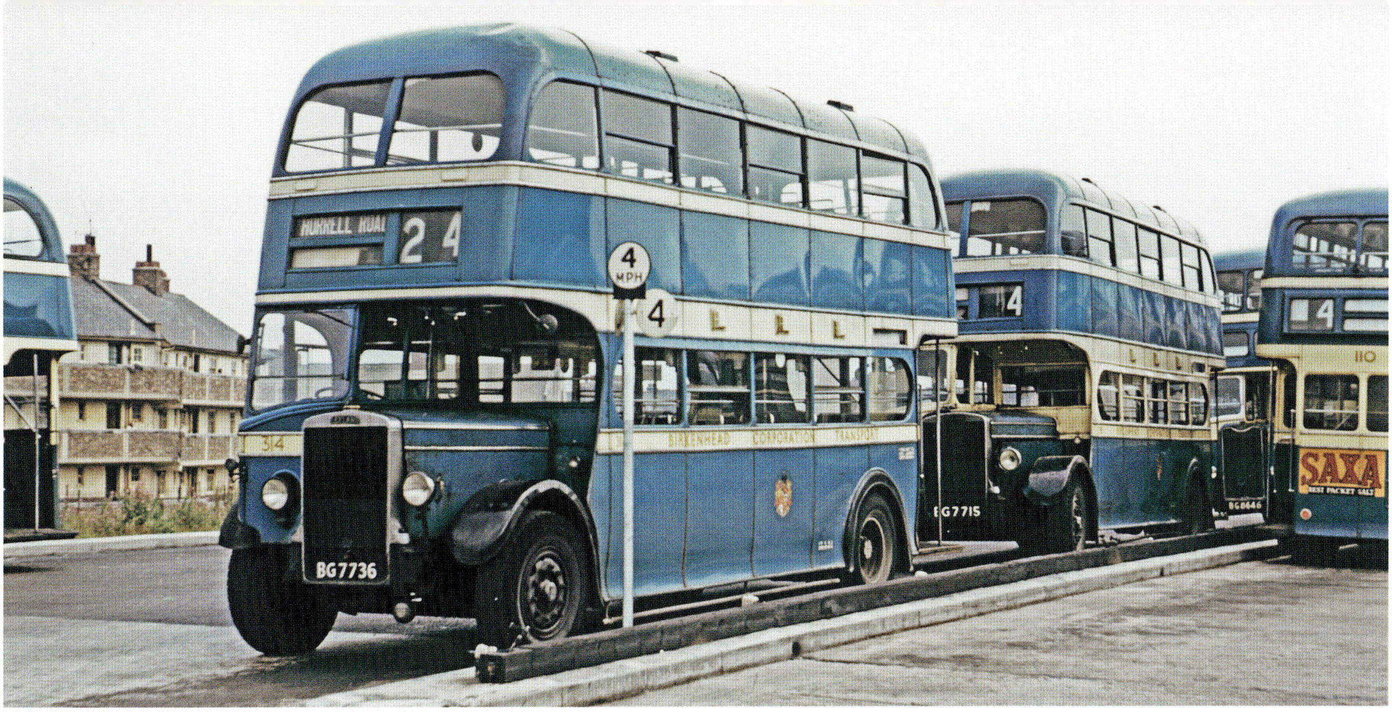

Photographed in 1955 in the large open parking area at the rear of the Laird Street garage and workshops, 314 and 293 were two of 40 Massey-bodied Leyland TD5c delivered in 1939 – their torque converters had been replaced by normal gearboxes in 1947 and 1948. Massey bodywork of this style was not the most durable and all but one were thoroughly rebuilt either by Massey or in the Corporation's own workshops. Withdrawn in 1957, 314 was one of the last pre-war vehicles in the fleet. *Dennis Kerrison*

Thirty six Guy Arabs with Gardner 5LW engines were allocated to the corporation in 1943-46, with bodies by Weymann (319-320), Massey (321-338), Park Royal (339-350) and Northern Counties (351-354). In 1953, the chassis of 323-337 were overhauled, fitted with new Gardner 6LW engines and despatched to Wigan where Massey Bros fitted new metal-framed bodies of the unusual width of 7ft 9in. Renumbered 241-255, they were virtually new vehicles and ran until 1969. On 31 July 1968 the crew of 249 smile for the photographer at the terminus of service 73 in the village of Irby. One of many peak hour or industrial workings, the 73 augmented the main 71/71A Woodside – Heswall service. *John Ryan*

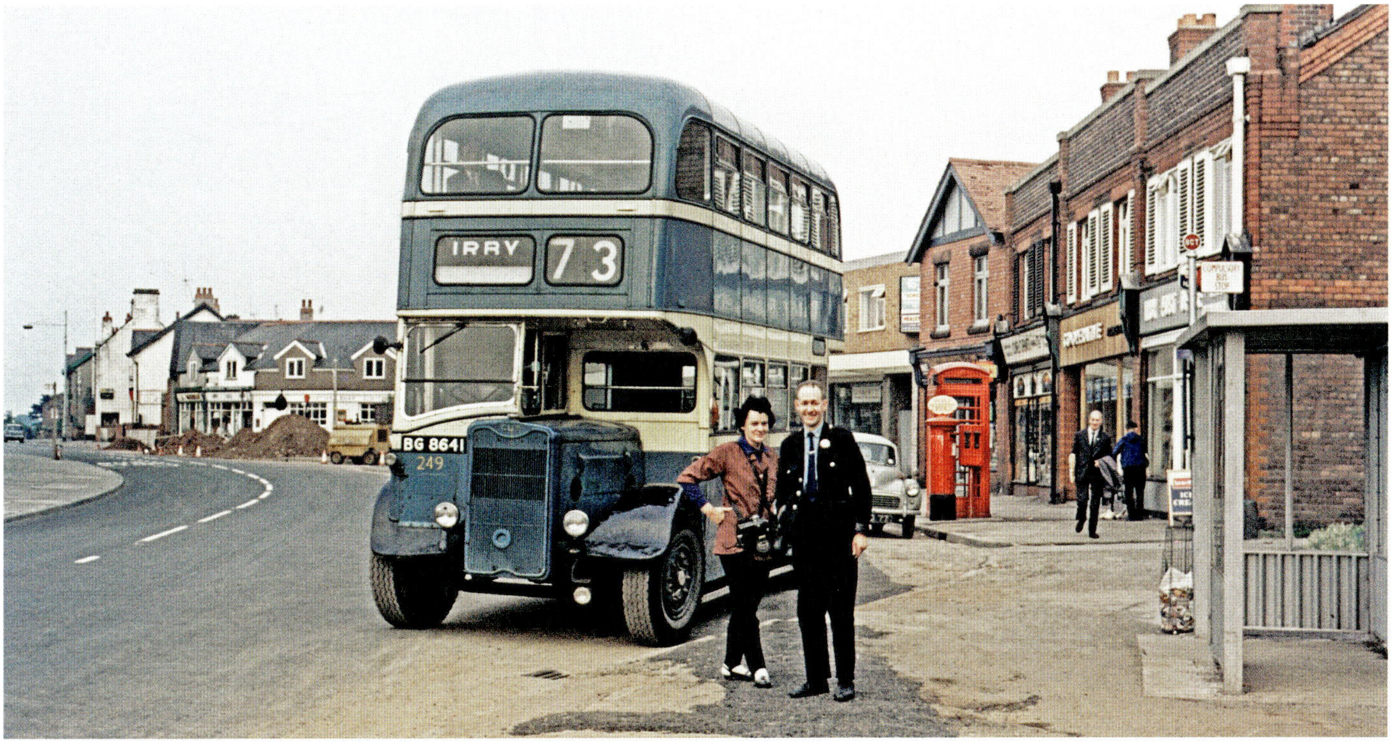

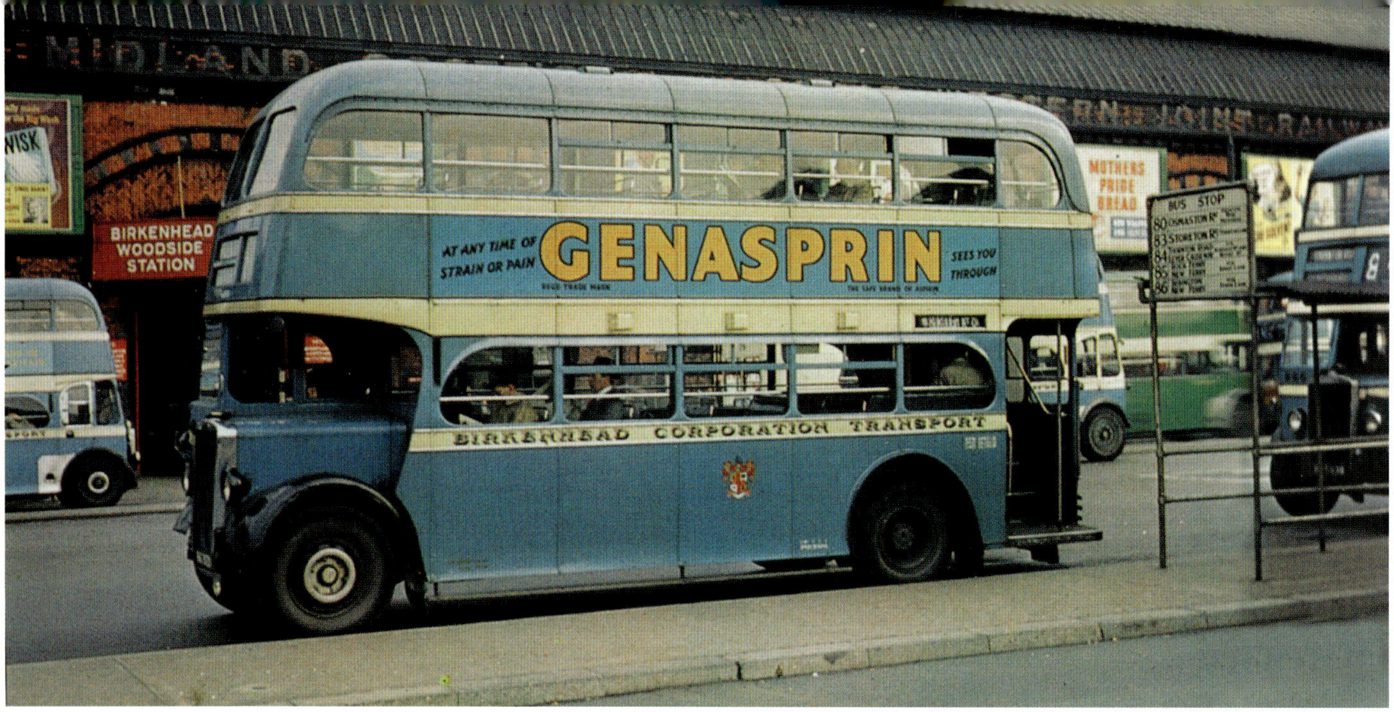

The first post-war deliveries were two batches of Massey-bodied Leyland PD1s, 101-112 in 1946 and 113-125 in 1947. Their saloon heaters received favourable comment in the local press at the time. In this 1950 picture 111 still has the three cream bands and heavily shaded fleet numbers and fleetname. Withdrawn in 1959/60/61 almost all went on to service with other operators, some being exported. Behind 111 is the front of 1937 Massey-bodied TD5 256. Withdrawn shortly after this picture was taken, it had the earlier flat-fronted style of Massey body.
C Carter

Single-deckers were required for service 44 (New Ferry to Eastham) which passed beneath the low bridge in Bromborough Road. Four Massey-bodied Leyland PS1s (97-100) joined the fleet in June 1948 and ran until 1964 when they were replaced by four Leyland Leopards. In July 1962, 98 passes the Railway Inn in the picturesque 'model village' of Port Sunlight, built by William Hesketh Lever between 1888 and 1914 for the employees of the Lever Brothers soap factory. *Geoffrey Morant*

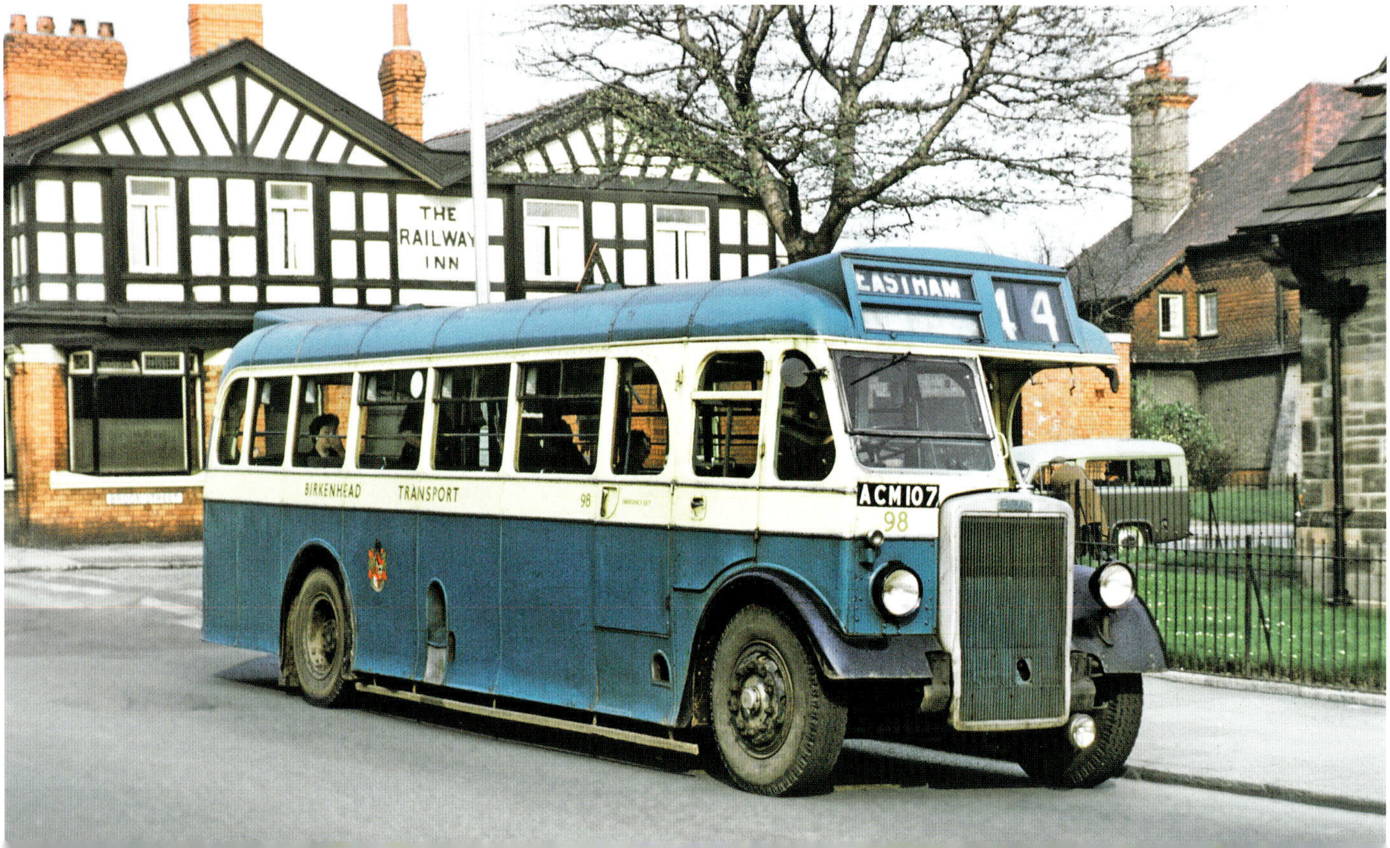

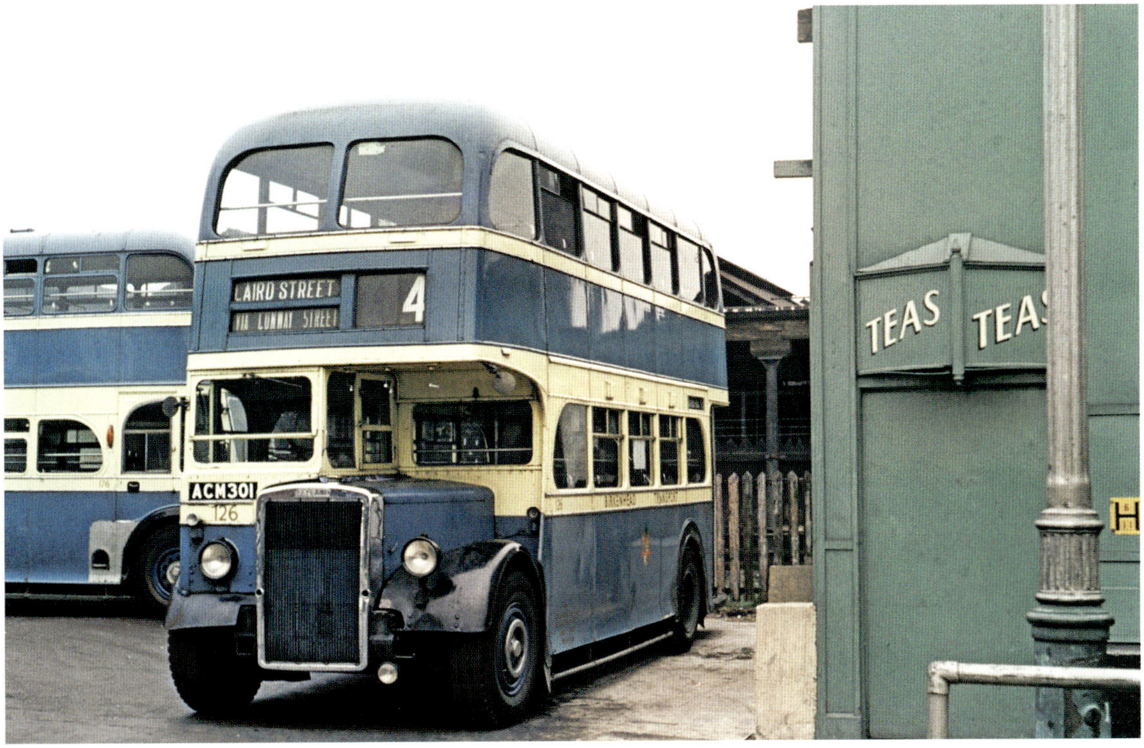

Twenty more Massey-bodied Leyland PD1s (126-145) were delivered in 1948. By 26 July 1962 only six remained, of which 126 was photographed at the east end of the large off-peak storage area at Woodside. The sans-serif lettering was used from 1950 onwards and the word 'Corporation' omitted from the fleetname from 1953. Buses taking the direct route back to Laird Street garage usually showed service number 4. *John Ryan*

With a full order book at Leyland and raw materials still under government control, many operators hedged their bets by placing orders with other manufacturers. Daimler and Guy could offer quicker delivery, although Birkenhead was fortunate to get Gardner engines for the Daimlers. Fifteen of each make were delivered in 1949 and similar quantities in 1950, all with Gardner 6LW engines and Massey bodies. Guy Arabs 146-160 were new in 1949 and 191-205 in 1950. This 1964 picture is of 152 arriving at Moreton Shore on a 22 from Woodside which ran every 30 minutes but with many duplicates on a sunny day. A popular attraction with its sand dunes, beaches and funfair, Moreton Shore was also served by Wallasey Corporation buses and electric trains to Moreton Station. *Peter Roberts*

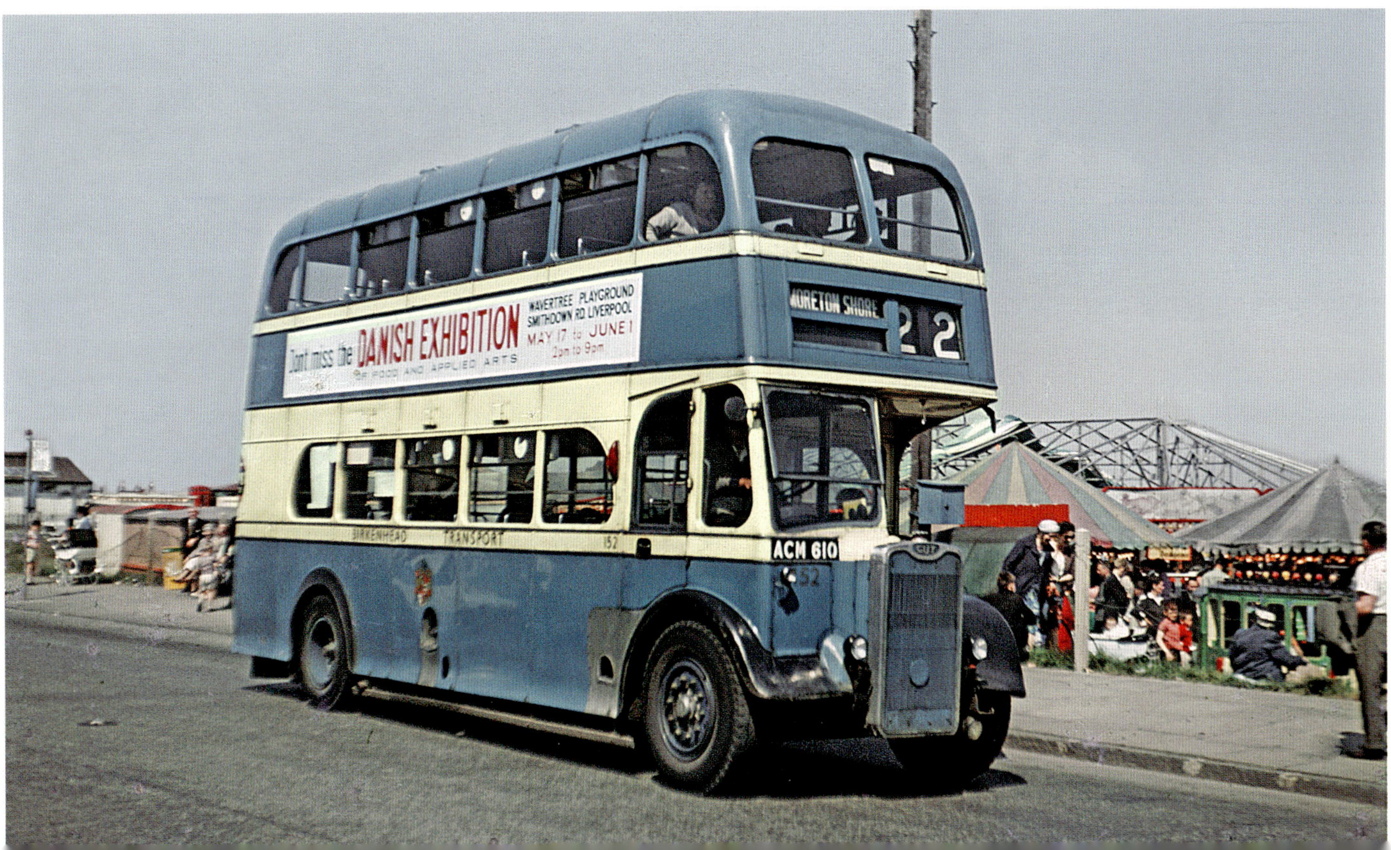

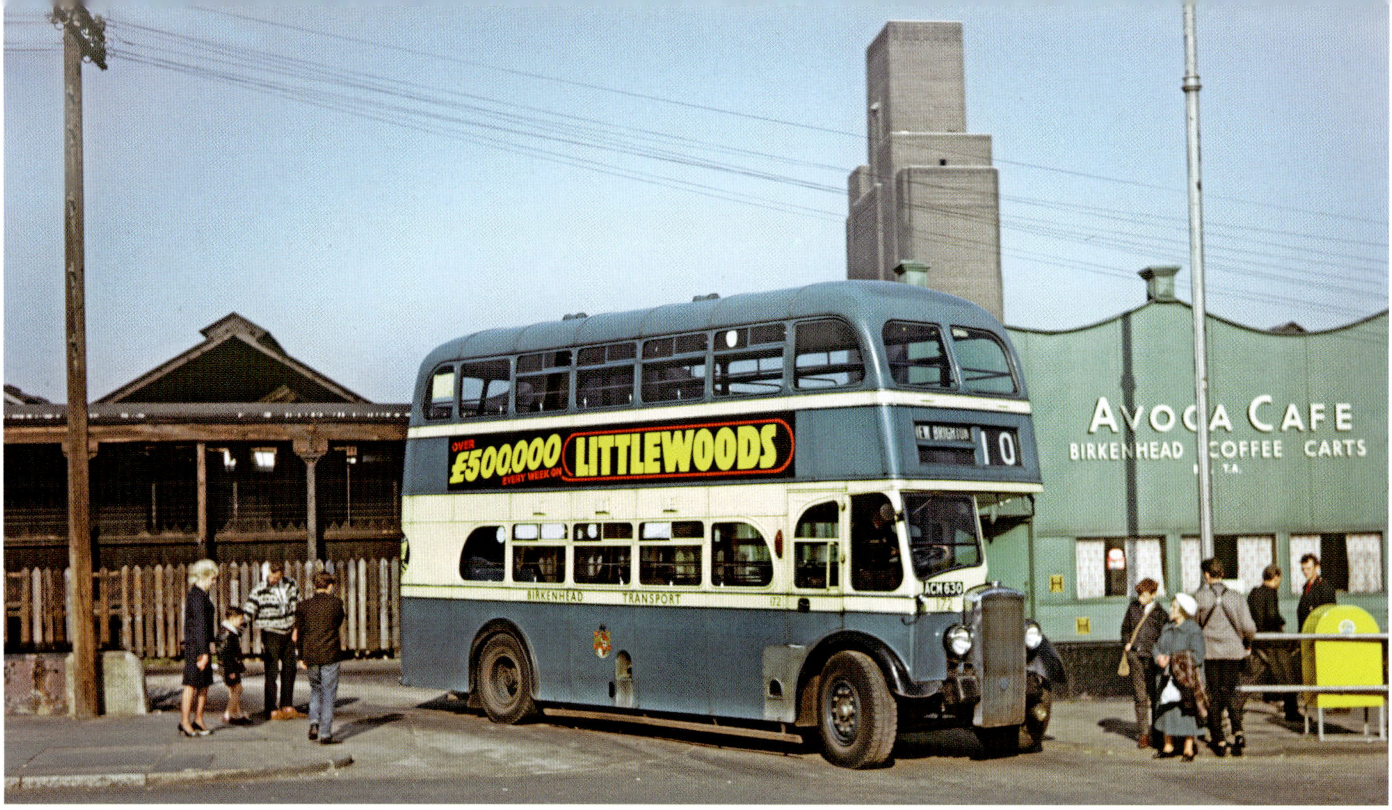

The Daimler CVG6s were numbered 161-190. 172 is turning out of the parking bays at the river end of Woodside terminus. In the left background are former cattle lairages and the site of the floating roadway which led down to the Corporation-owned landing stage used by passenger and goods vessels; on the right is the Avoca café – a source of refreshment for passengers and crews. October 1963 *Roy Marshall*

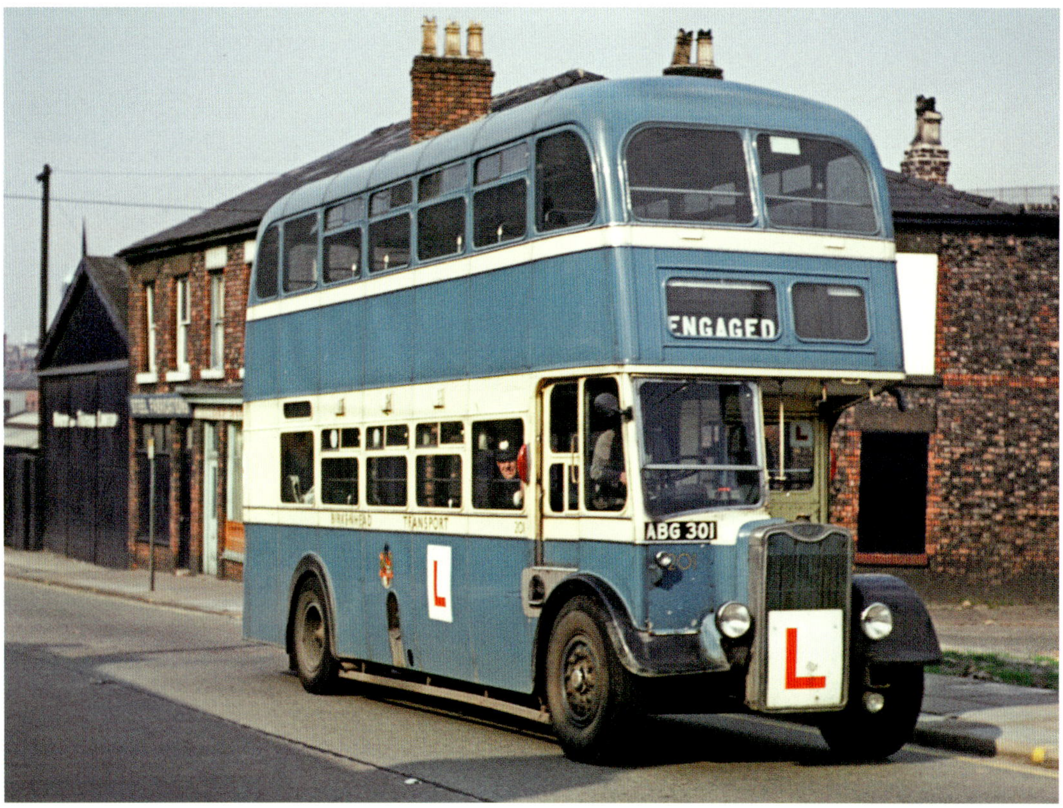

Guy Arab 201 had Massey's prototype steel-framed body. Previously the firm had determinedly stayed with timber framing, something which prompted two of its senior staff to leave in 1938 and set up East Lancashire Coachbuilders in Blackburn. Massey's new frame had a good pedigree – it was designed by Edgar Evans who joined the firm from Leyland Motors where he had worked for Colin Bailey, who was responsible for Metro Cammell's and Leyland's hugely successful metal-framed bodies. The styling was updated, eliminating the radiused end windows and flared skirt panels; 201 also had a sliding cab door which became the standard on future Birkenhead vehicles.
E V Richards

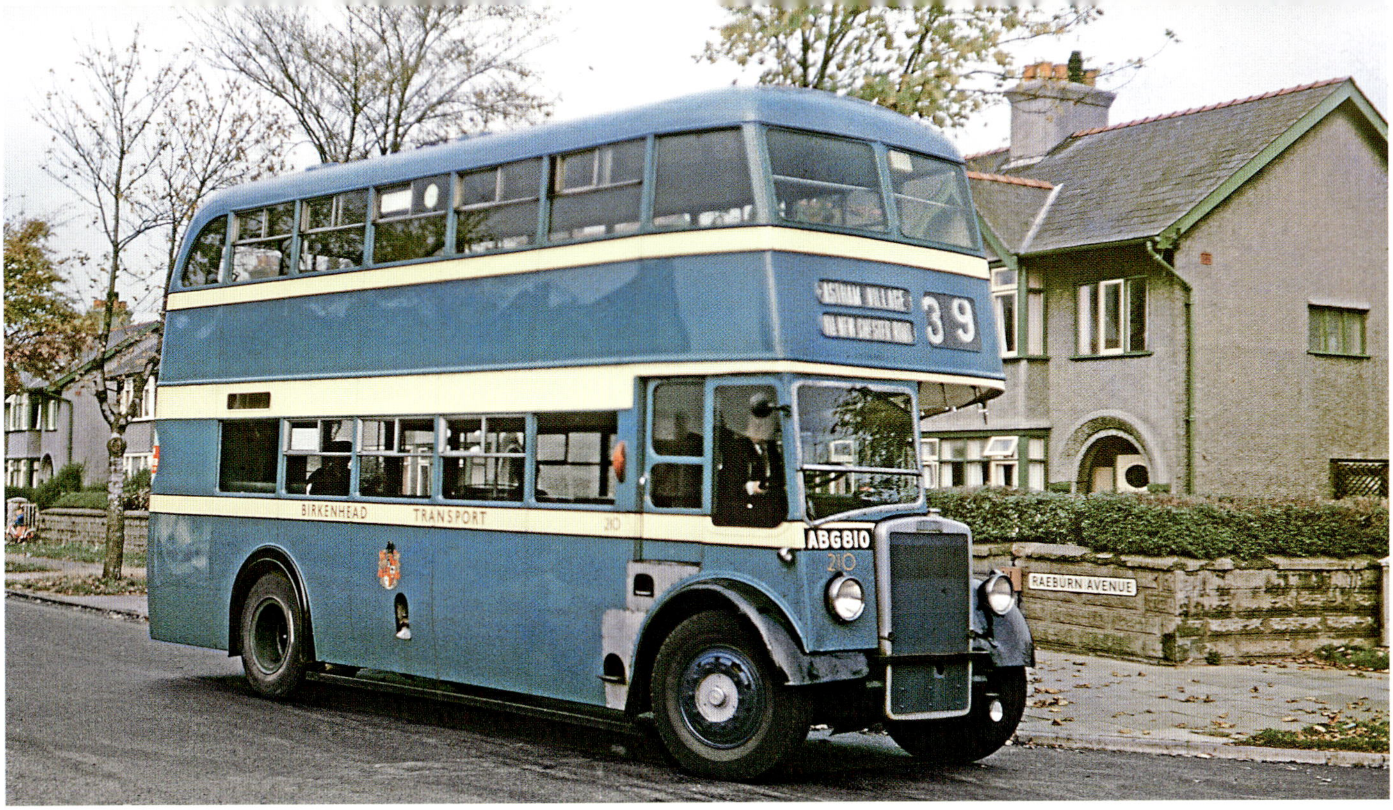

Birkenhead's first 8ft-wide vehicles were Leyland PD2/3s 206-225. Their Leyland bodies had an unusual seating arrangement of 31 upstairs with the normal 26 downstairs. They were the last to have offside indicator boxes (in which an intermediate point was displayed) use of which was soon abandoned, the apertures being panelled over at overhaul. Late in 1962, 210 was painted in the former 'three band' version of the livery. This was not approved by the transport committee and it was altered to standard livery after three months. On 24 October 1962 the newly-painted bus is turning from Raeburn Avenue into Heygarth Road towards the end of its journey to Eastham Village. *Reg Wilson/Online Transport Archive*

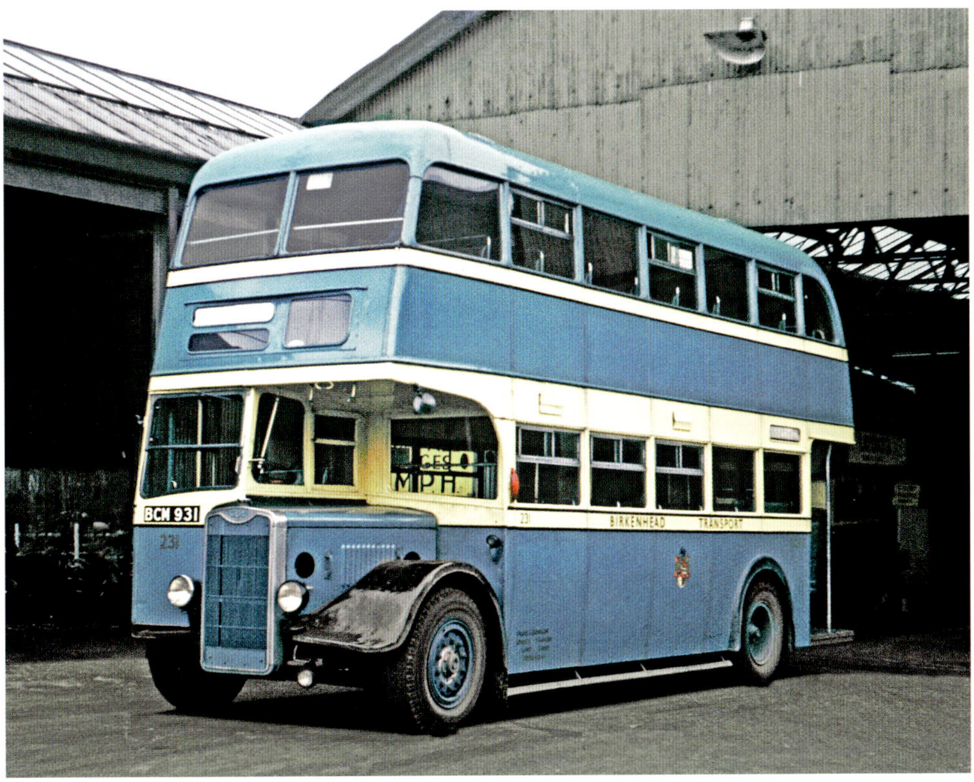

Birkenhead continued to buy Guys until 1956 and 15 6LW-engined Arab III (226-240) were delivered in 1952. They had bodies by East Lancashire Coachbuilders, a new supplier to Birkenhead but one with a fine reputation. 231 is in Laird Street depot, the original part of which was opened as a tram depot and works in 1903; the bus garage was added in the 1930s and its open parking area covered over in the 1960s. September 1967 *John Kaye*

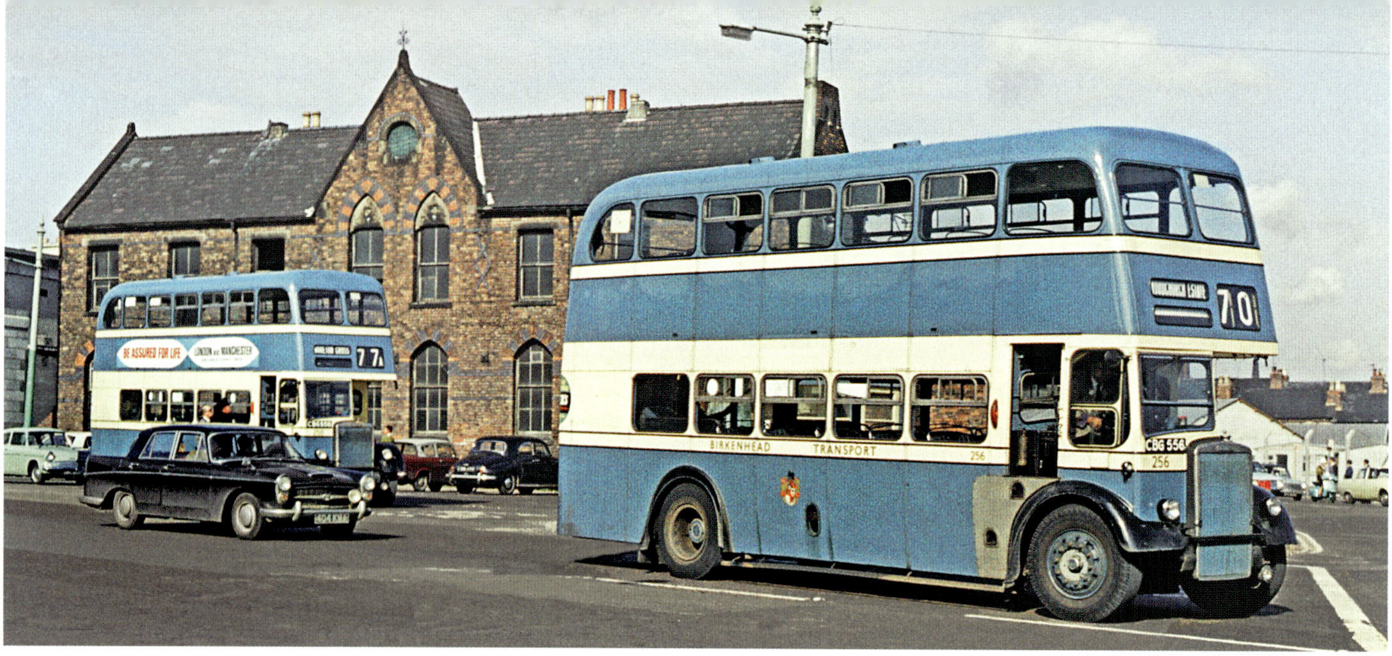

Weymann supplied bodies for Leyland PD2/12s in 1954 and 1955. In this picture 256 and 258 are approaching Birkenhead Central Station on services 70 and 77 which served the town's post-war housing estates in Woodchurch and Irby and carried heavy peak period traffic. *John Ryan*

The other five PD2s of 1954 (266-270) had bodies built by the Birkenhead firm of Ashcroft. In the 1950s Vernon's Pools of Liverpool was cash rich and owner Vernon Sangster began funding a variety of new small firms in a philanthropic effort to expand industry and employment on Merseyside. One such was Ashcroft Brothers Ltd. Formed in 1953 to build bus and other bodies, it had connections with staff at Birkenhead Corporation Transport's Laird Street Works. In addition to money, Sangster rented an existing building in Dock Road, Birkenhead, and Ashcroft bought a brand new Leyland PD2/12 chassis and a Metal Sections body frame, intending to build a prototype/demonstrator. To support this local initiative, Birkenhead Corporation ordered five bodies. Delivered in July and August 1954, they looked good, were well finished and proved durable – aspects of their design were clearly copied from Massey and East Lancs. The Dock Road premises were not high enough to build double-deckers and completed upper and lower decks of each body were taken to Birkenhead's Laird Street Works to be joined and the paint job finished. Sadly, trade union problems arose and Ashcroft gave up bus work, the chassis and frame for the demonstrator passing to Manchester-based coachbuilder Bond, which completed it and sold it to Bolton (66). The Ashcroft firm moved to other work and was not wound up until 1972. *Chris Bennett/Online Transport Archive*

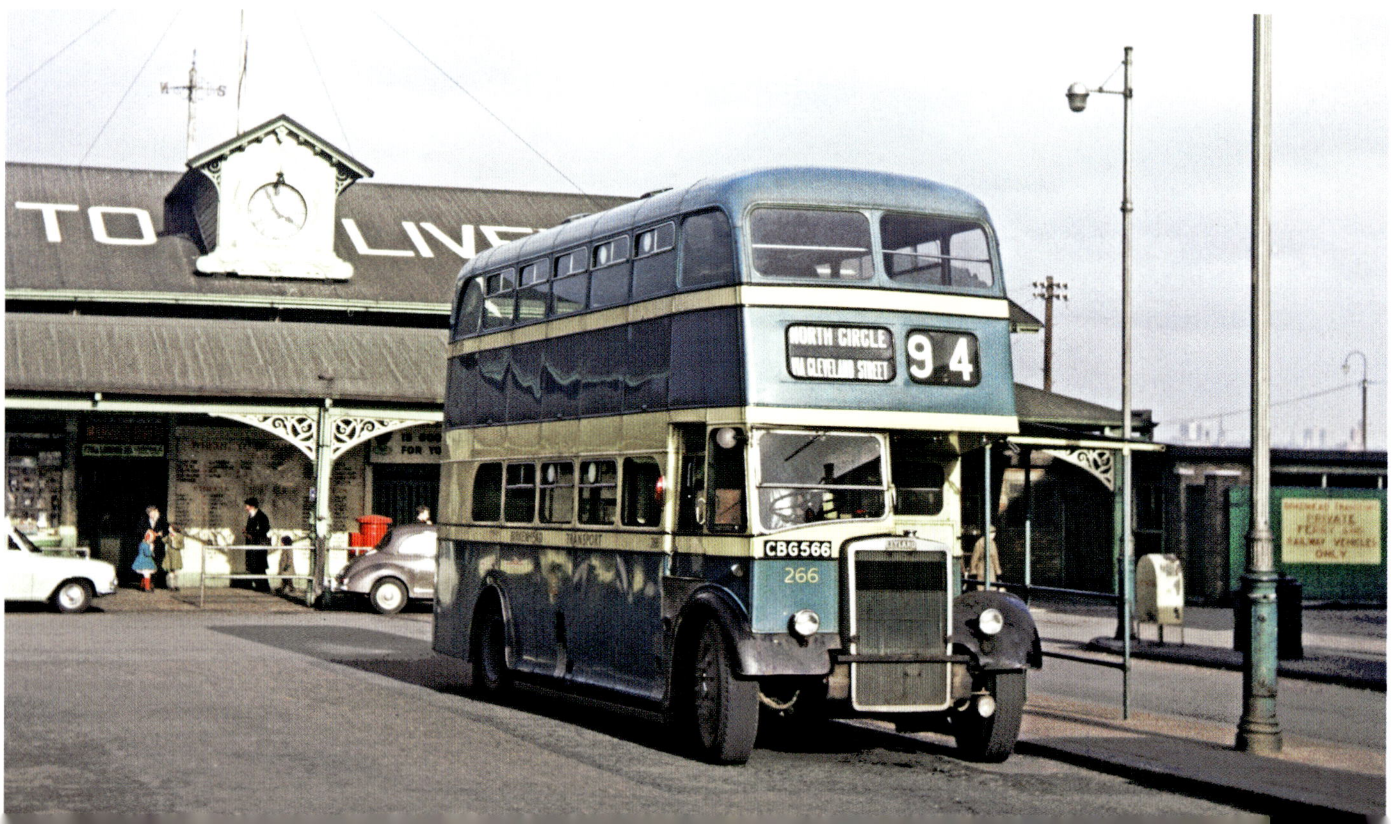

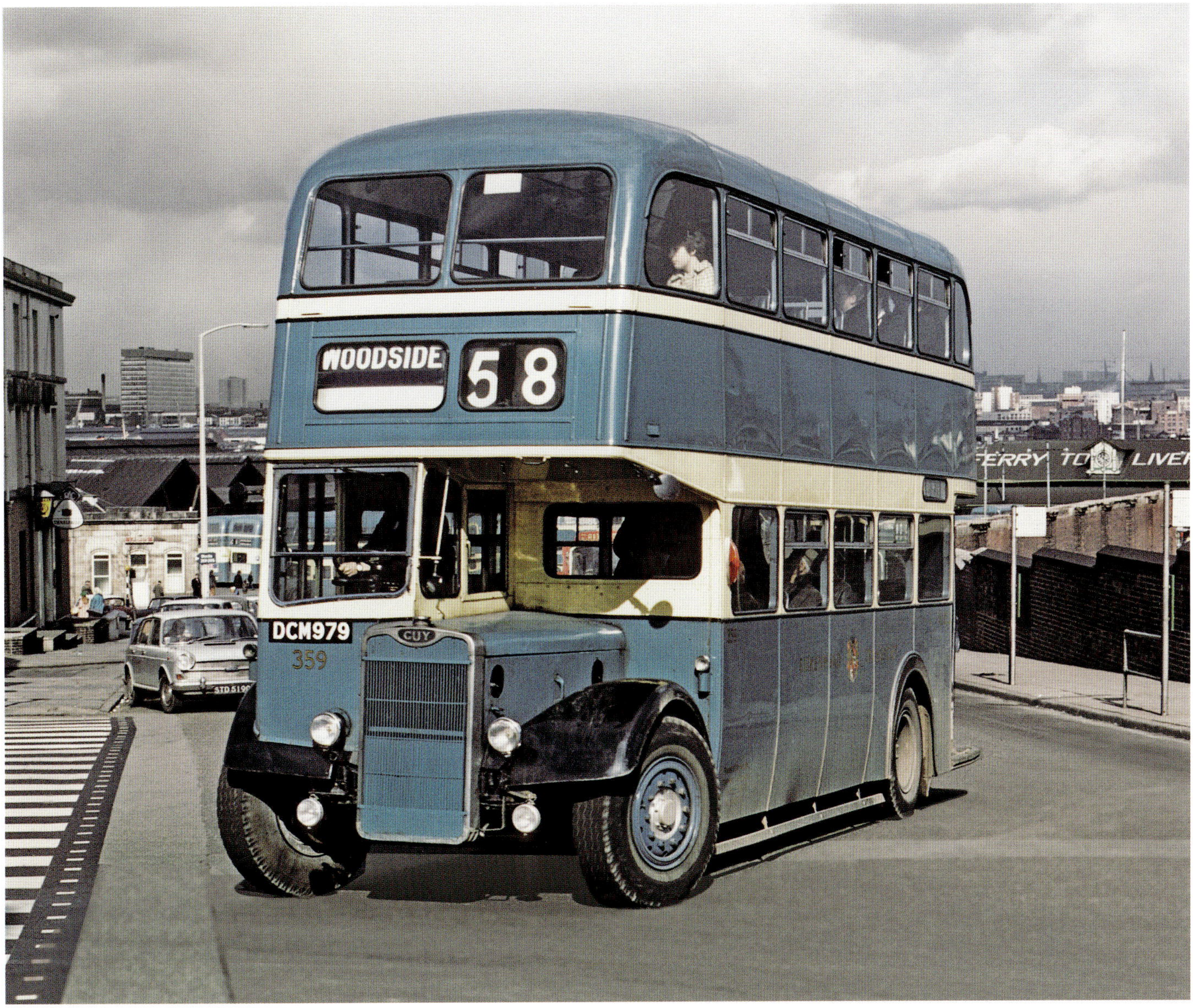

The 1955 batch of new buses consisted of seven Guy Arab IV and ten Leyland PD2/12. Numbers 355-361 were Arab IV with Gardner 6LW engines and 59-seat Massey bodywork. They were the first new buses in the revised livery which eliminated the band of cream below the lower deck windows and placed the fleetname on the lower side panels, either side of the coat of arms. In the background of this 1969 view Woodside Station has been demolished and its site has become a car park – the station closed in 1967. *Geoffrey Morant*

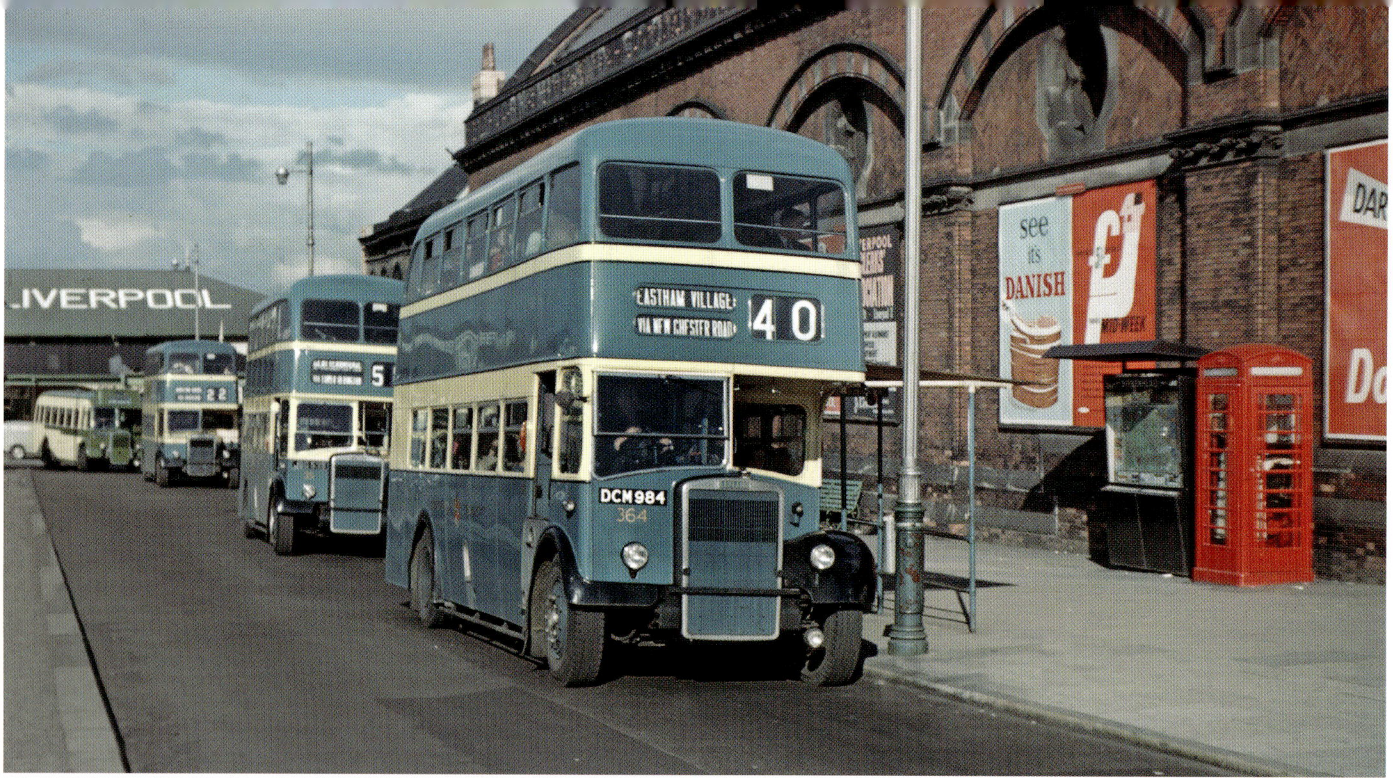

The body order for the ten Leylands was split – fleet numbers 362-366 had East Lancs bodies whilst 367-371 had Weymann's version of the Orion body. With a fairly heavy load, 364 prepares about to leave Woodside on route 40 to Eastham Village. In the far background is an ECW-bodied Crosville Bristol L6B in Tilling express-service livery. Alongside the telephone kiosk is a cabinet-mounted street map, which had buttons that one could press to illuminate and pinpoint particular places – high technology in 1960. *Geoffrey Morant*

To some the Orion's styling is basic and utilitarian, to others it is a classic. Whichever, it was durable and the looks of 367-371 were undoubtedly enhanced by Birkenhead's livery. This picture shows 370 at Woodside in April 1969. *Roy Marshall*

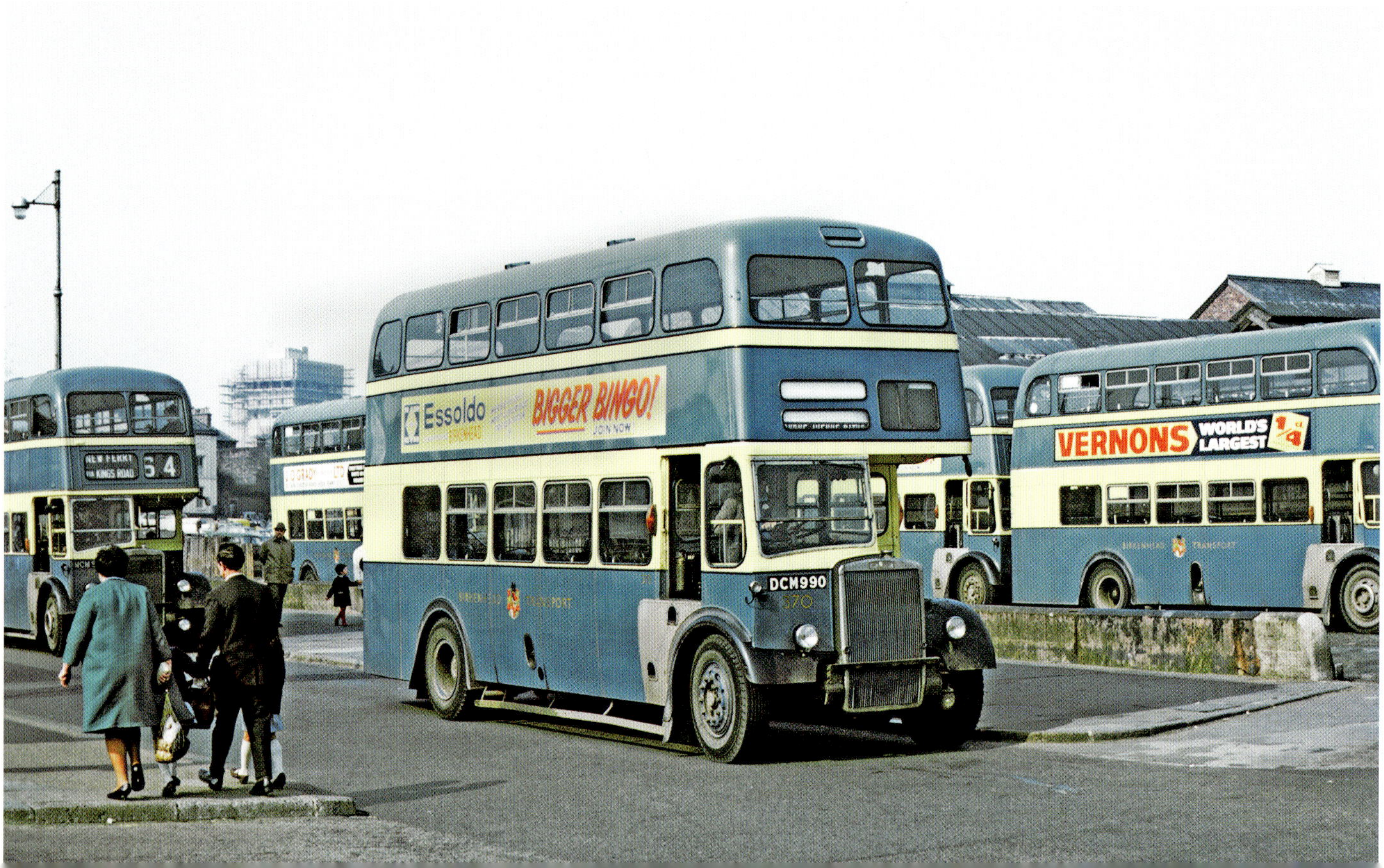

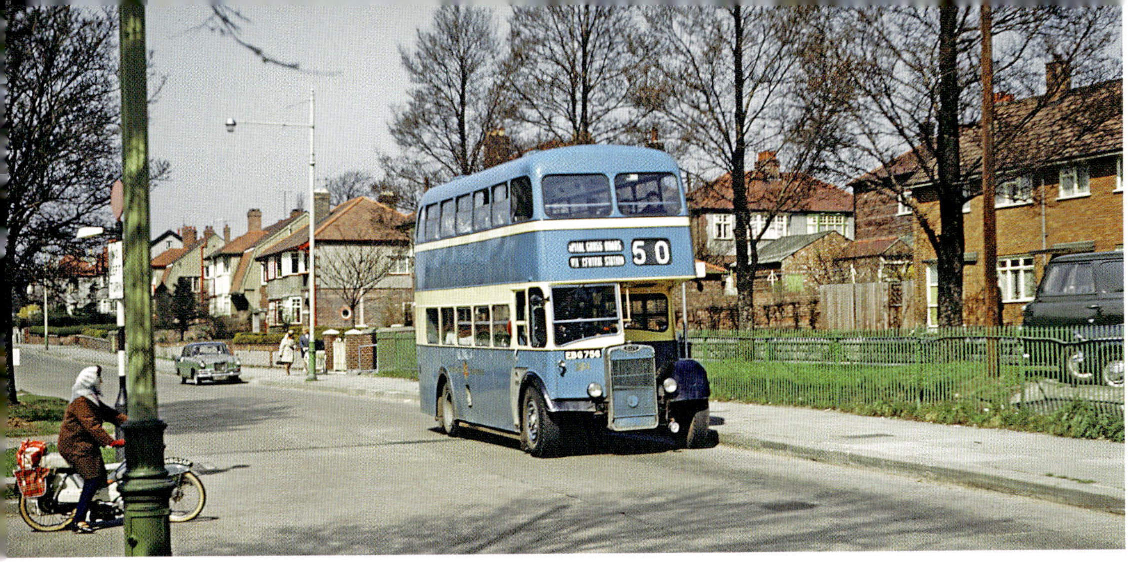

Birkenhead's last Guys arrived in 1956. The body order was ten Massey and five East Lancs. Fleet numbers 382-386 had the East Lancs bodies and here 384 is heading for Spital Cross Roads along a short dual-carriageway section of Old Chester Road, near the Oval athletics stadium. The lady on the moped motor-cycle waits in the gap in the central reservation for the bus to pass. 386 was the highest fleet number carried by a Birkenhead bus, fleet numbering then recommencing at 1. *Ted Jones*

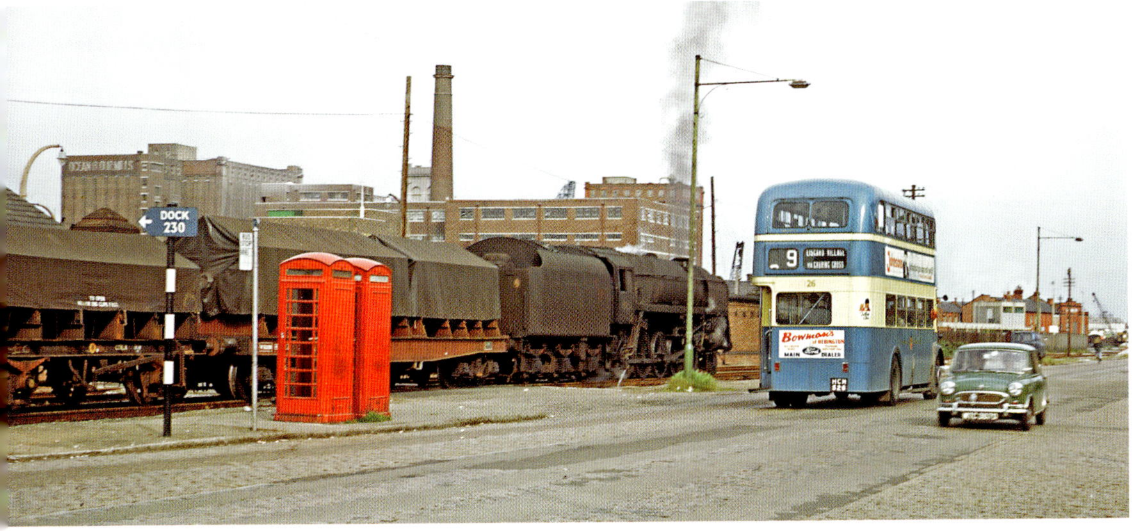

With one exception, for its future orders Birkenhead chose Leylands and 120 Massey-bodied PD2s (1-45, 61-90 and 110-154) entered service over the years 1957 to 1967. In this picture number 26, one of the 1959 delivery, overtakes a BR 2-10-0 9F locomotive at the head of a slow-moving goods train rumbling along Beaufort Road on the Birkenhead side of the dock system with the Joseph Rank Ltd's massive Ocean flour mill in the background – in the 1930s Birkenhead was the second largest flour milling centre in the world. In the heyday of the docks, goods trains like this caused long delays at several major road crossings. *A S Clayton/Online Transport Archive*

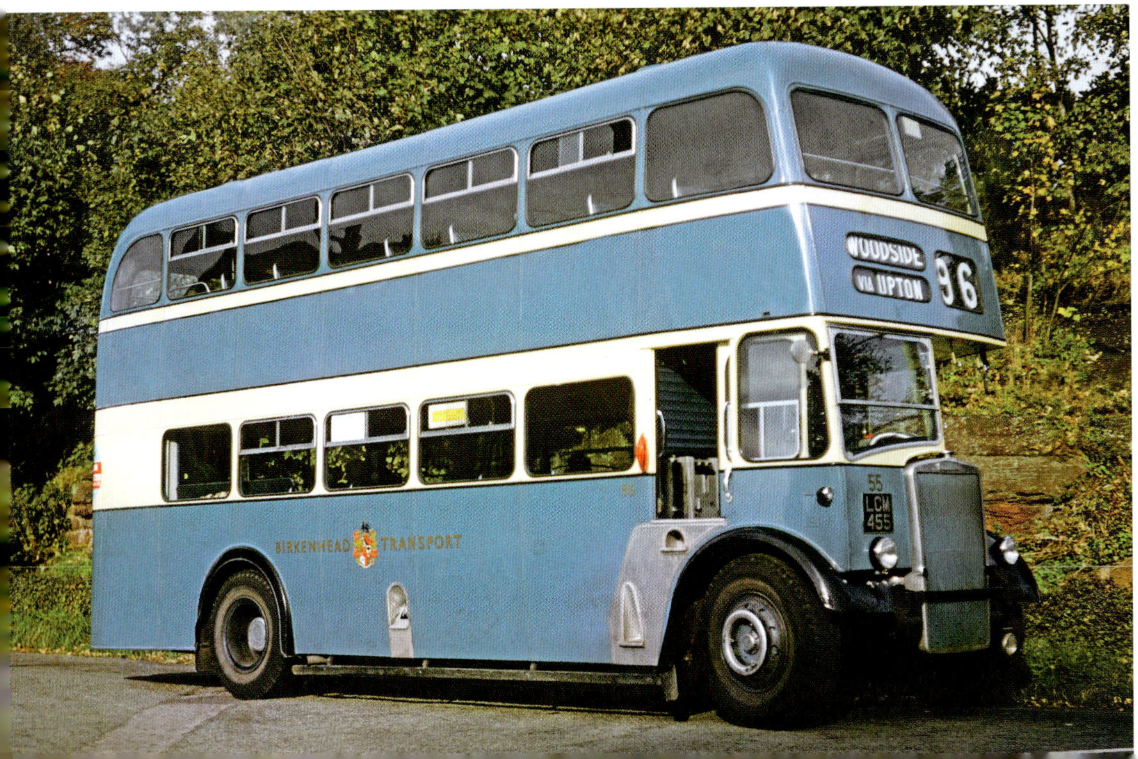

Fleet numbers 46-60 were handsome East Lancs-bodied Leyland PD2/40s readily identifiable by their square-shaped front number plates. This June 1968 picture shows an immaculate 55 at the Thurstaston terminus of service 96. Started in 1932 as service 85, it was one of those which took Birkenhead buses well beyond the town's boundary – in this case into the Wirral villages of Greasby, Frankby and Thurstaston. Renumbered after the war, the service was gradually curtailed and when this picture was taken there were just two journeys beyond Greasby, one in each peak. *Reg Wilson/Online Transport Archive*

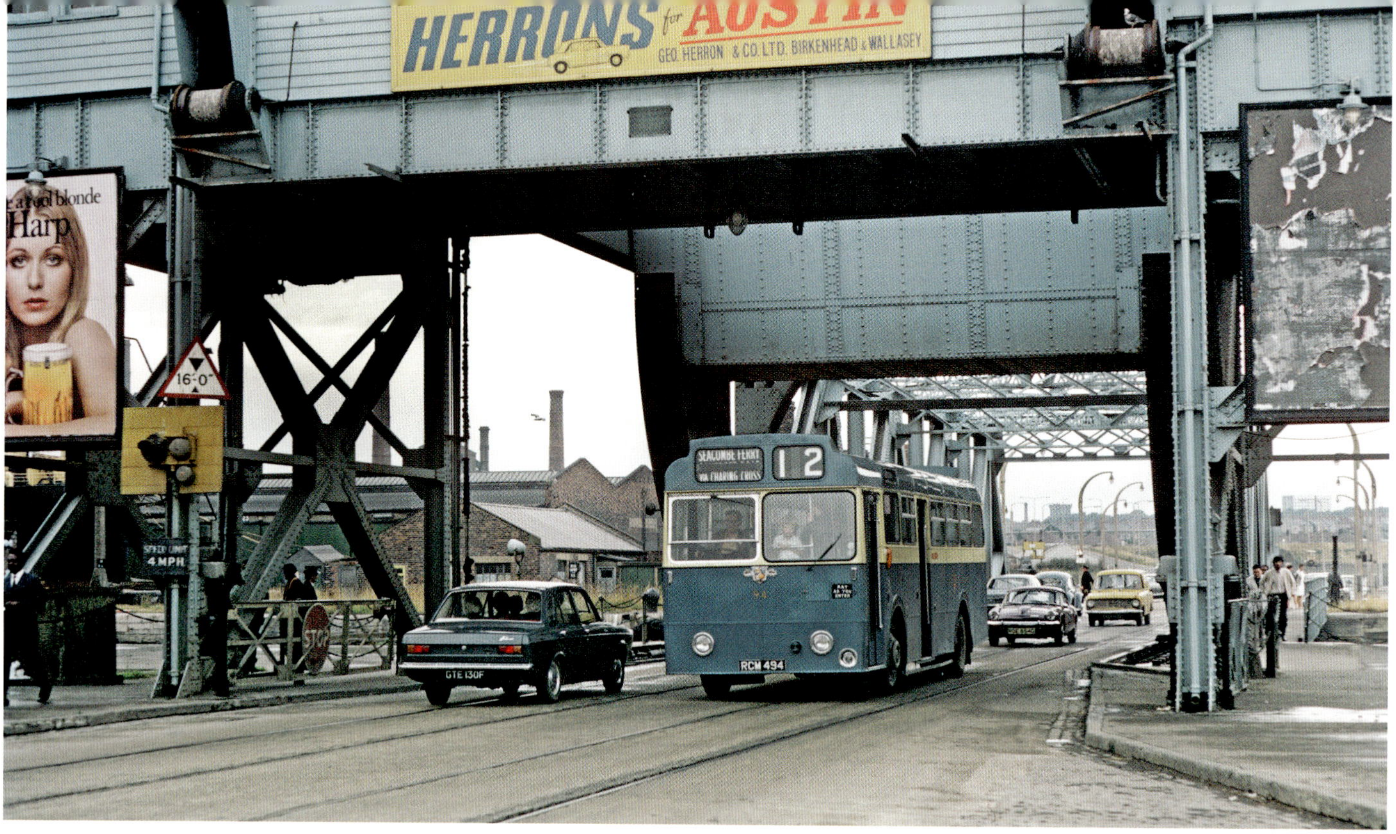

The 1948 Leyland PS1s were replaced in 1964 by four dual-entrance Massey-bodied Leyland Leopard L1s, numbered 91-94. When the 44 service was re-routed to avoid the low bridge, they became regular performers on routes 12 and 97. The former was the shortest of the cross-docks routes, shuttling between Seacombe Ferry and Charing Cross. The cross-docks services were worked jointly by Birkenhead and Wallasey, but when the 12 was converted to one-man operation in March 1967, the latter had no suitable vehicles and duties were adjusted so that the 12 was worked by Birkenhead. The one-man timetable was tight, with a 17-minute journey time and 3-minute turn around at each end, and this led to drivers setting the blind display permanently (if misleadingly) to Seacombe Ferry *via* Charing Cross, as in this July 1969 picture of 94 crossing Duke Street bridge bound for Birkenhead. *Roy Marshall*

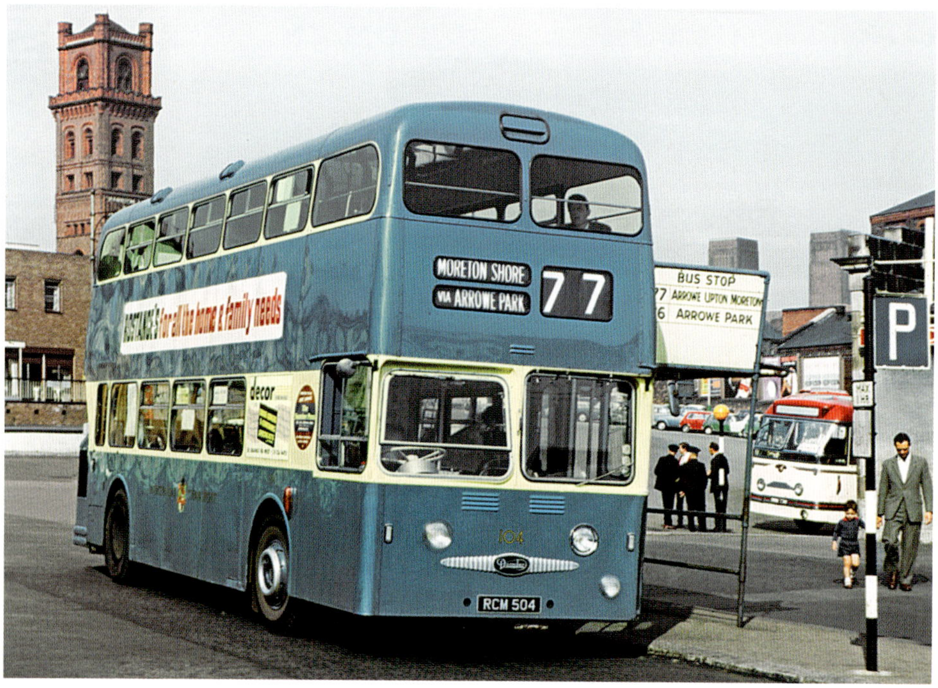

The exceptions to all those Leylands were the nine Weymann-bodied Daimler Fleetlines, 101-109, which entered service in July/August 1964, principally on the 77 from Woodside to Moreton Shore via Arrowe Park and Upton. Their initial livery had a simplified arrangement with minimal cream window surrounds and blue front and rear upper-deck domes. The arrangements for setting the front indicators were unusual with the winding handles on the outside of the body above the nearside windscreen. To allow the conductor to reach them there was a step which could be pulled out from beneath the body – its edge is visible beneath the numbers of the registration plate.

In this June 1965 picture 104 is at Woodside ready to make the 34-minute journey to the shore. Behind the bus is the tower which housed the machinery for the lifts at Hamilton Square station and on the right, above the stop sign and Ribble Leyland Royal Tiger coach 808, are the twin towers of the Queensway Mersey Tunnel ventilation shafts. *Geoffrey Morant*

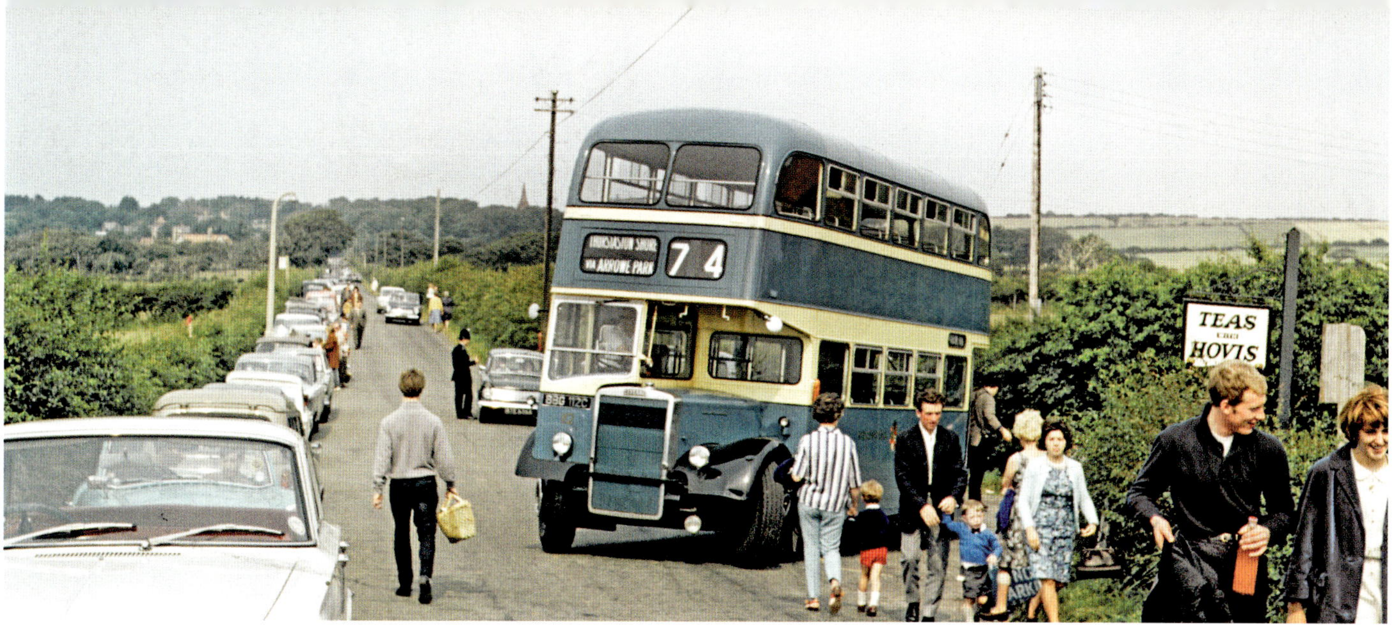

Leyland PD2/40s 110-124, new in mid-1965, were the last with the rounded style Massey bodywork – a neat-looking, well-finished and durable design that dated back to Birkenhead 201 of 1950. On 18 July 1965, the crew carefully reverse 112 into the former station approach road at the Thurstaston Shore terminus of route 74. By this time, the 74 operated only on summer Sundays and two journeys out of the timetable's three had the footnote 'These journeys will be withdrawn during inclement weather'. In this picture it is clear than the majority of people have come by private car. *John Ryan*

Situated on the River Dee estuary side of the Wirral peninsula, Heswall was firmly in Crosville's operating area dating from 1924 when John Pye sold Crosville his Heswall bus business, started during the first World War. The deal included land at Heswall on which Crosville then built a bus station (probably the first in the north of England) and a garage towards the back of the bus station behind the double-decker. When the garage was demolished a pub named the Johnny Pye was built on the site. Even though it was well outside the town boundaries, Birkenhead's 71 and 71A ran to Heswall as part of the heavy price the corporation extracted in 1930 in exchange for allowing Crosville into Woodside terminal but there were no jointly-operated company/corporation services. It was an exceptionally good deal for the corporation – and one for which Crosville never really forgave it. This 1969 picture shows Massey-bodied PD2/40 leaving for the 8-mile run to Woodside, with three Crosville Bristol Lodekkas and a Bristol RE single-decker in the background. *Online Transport Archive*

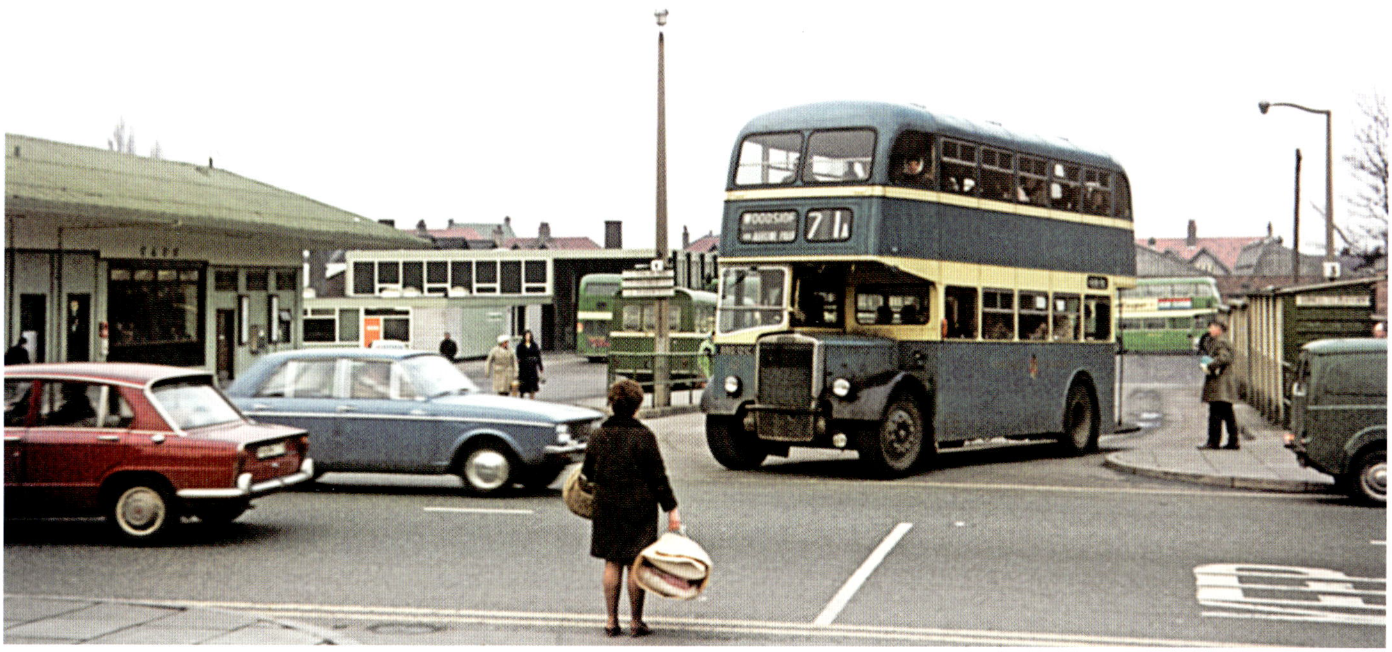

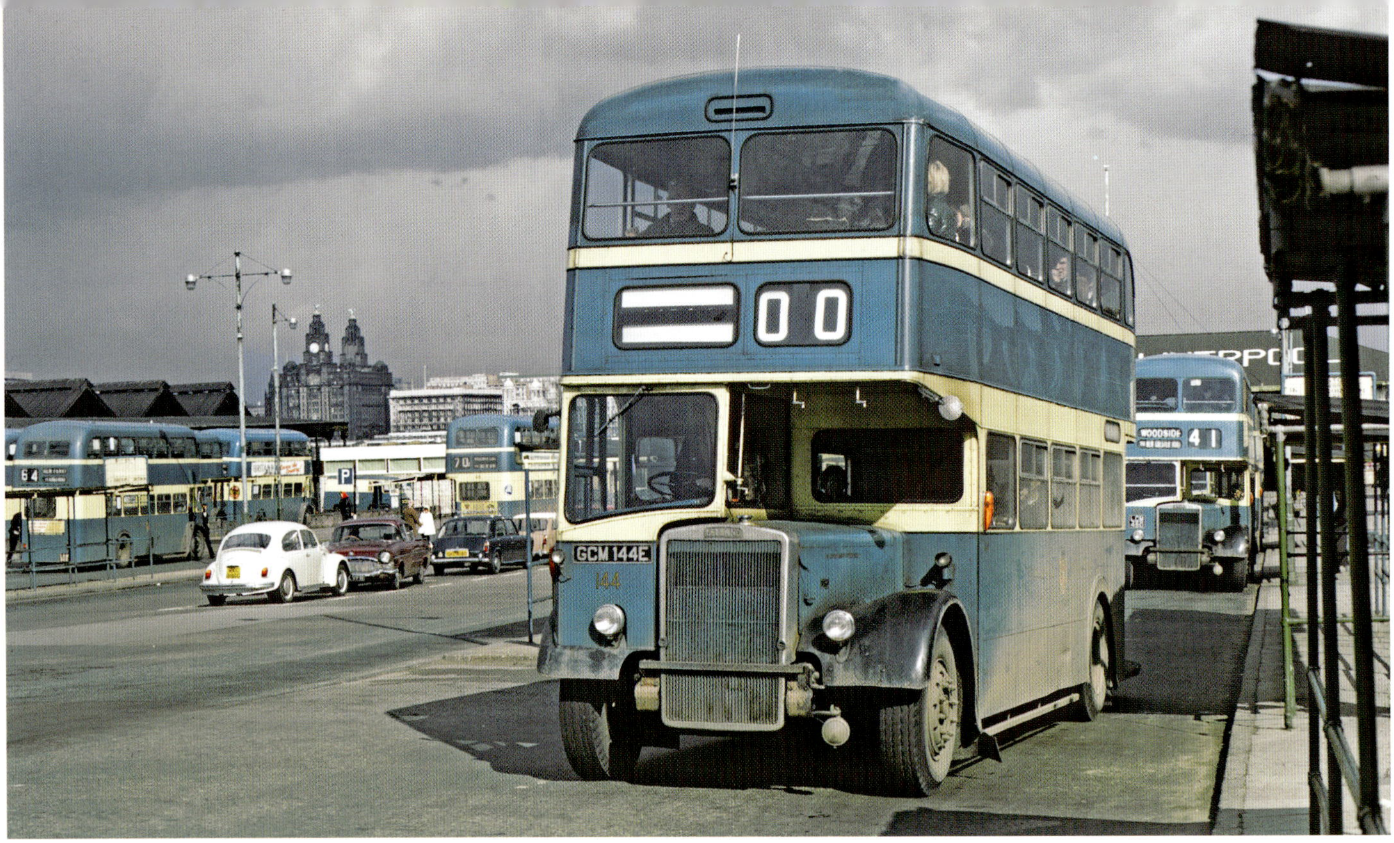

The final two batches of PD2s arrived in 1966/67 with bodywork to Massey's revised design. The upright squared-off front was in stark contrast to the previous styling and had much in common with the firm's box-like body for the Atlantean and Fleetline. Delivered in 1966, 125-139 were vacuum-braked PD2/40s whereas the 1967 batch, 140-154, were air-braked PD2/37s. In April 1970, working unusually-numbered route 00, 144 waits at Woodside, its lower panels covered in road dirt. The 00 was a network of services to and from the Unilever margarine plant in Bromborough (served by Birkenhead – another valuable result of the Crosville deal), the precise workings being something of a mystery to the general public as latterly they did not appear in the timetable. One of the contributors to this book recalls putting his hand out to a 'double-O' and being surprised when it stopped – he then had to buy a ticket without knowing which route the bus would take. *Geoffrey Morant*

With the 1965 authorisation of one-person operation of high capacity double-deckers, Birkenhead bought rear-engined double-deckers – in contrast to the operators across the Mersey which chose high capacity single-deckers. It was no surprise that they were Leyland Atlanteans rather than Daimler Fleetlines, for general manager Frank Brimelow, appointed in 1964, was a firm believer in Leylands. Northern Counties supplied the bodies having acquired Massey in 1967. 155-167 entered service in 1968 on the Oxton Circle routes 2 and 6 which were converted to double-deck one-person flat-fare operation, although in this April 1968 picture 165 is working service 70. *Roy Marshall*

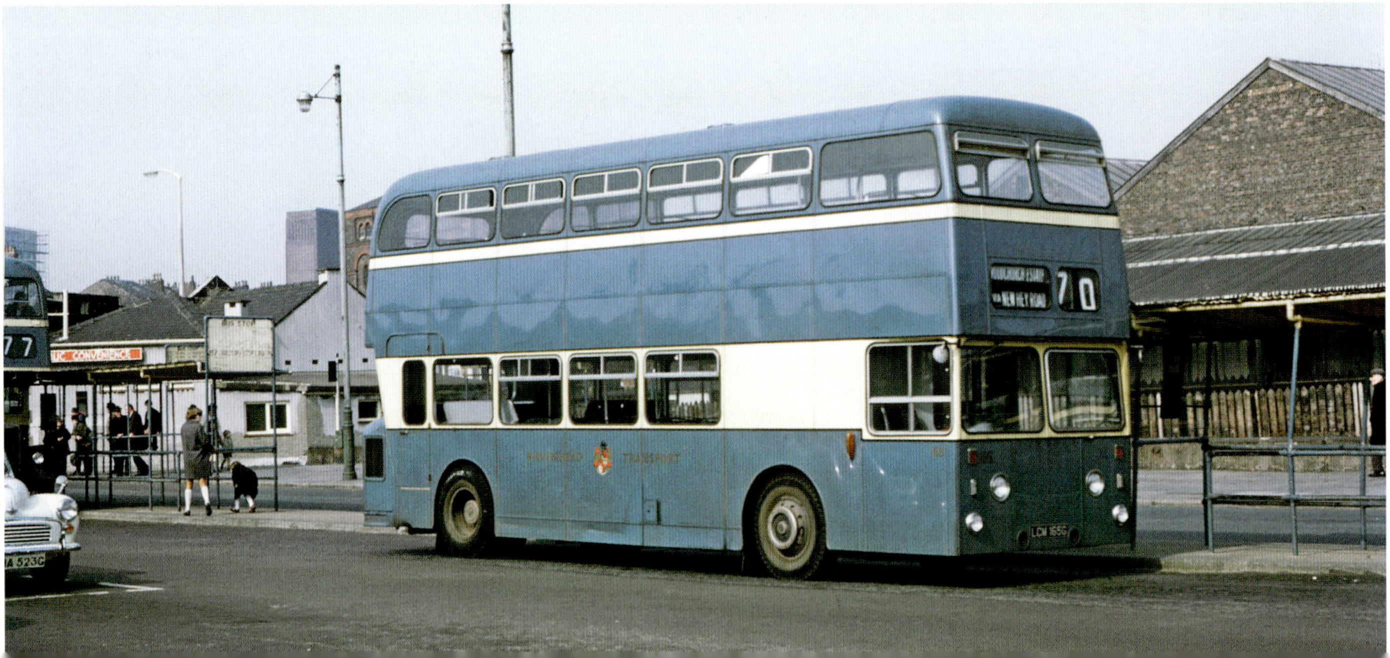

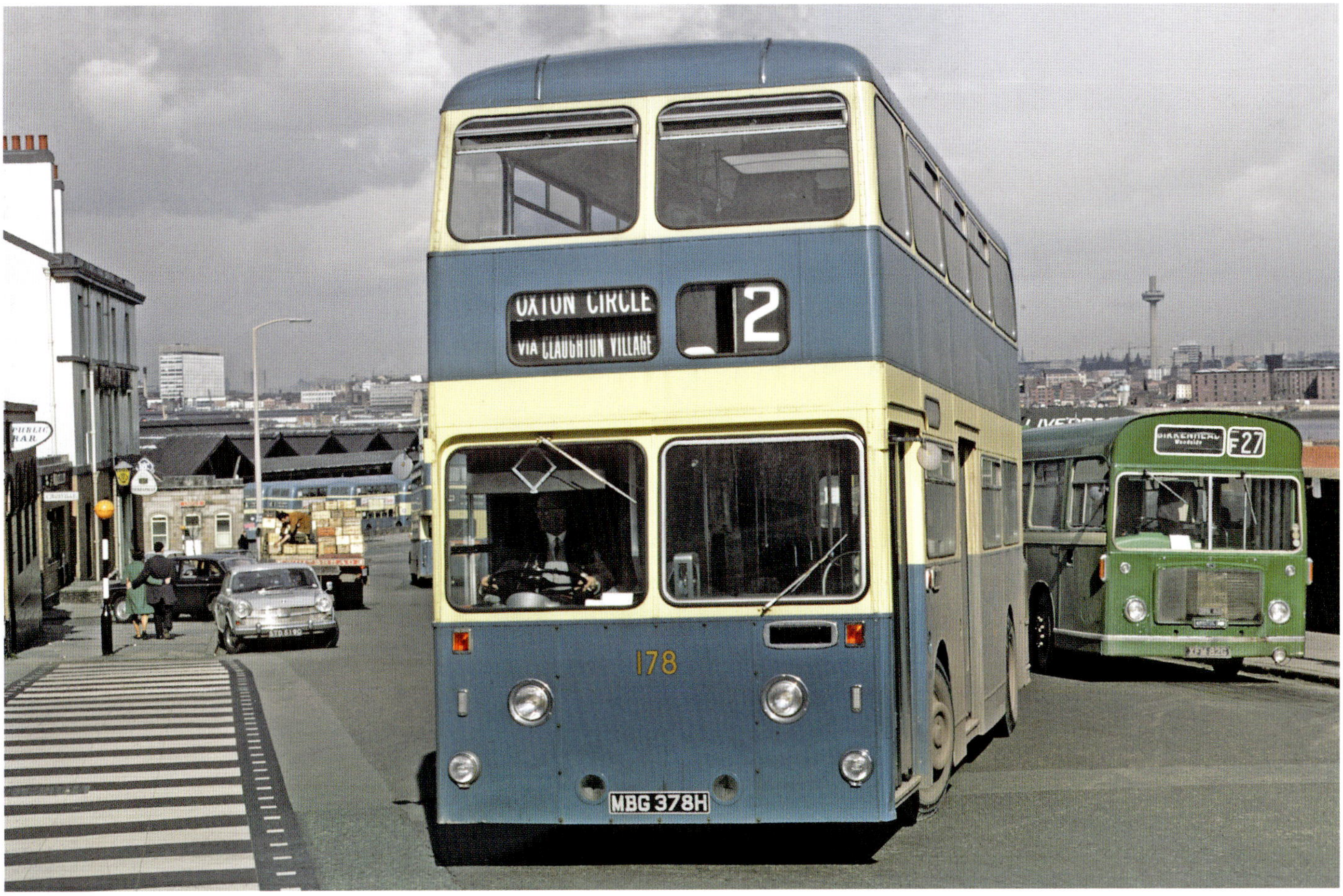

Birkenhead's final new buses, Northern Counties-bodied Leyland Atlanteans 168-182, went into service in November 1969 – the Passenger Transport Executive took over on December 1st. They had dual doors – a passing fashion of the time intended to speed up loading and unloading – and were also equipped with Loadmeters which counted passenger footsteps up and down the centrally-located staircase and, in theory, displayed the number of seats available on the upper deck. The latter device was not a success – schoolchildren quickly worked out that it could be confused by jumping up and down on the steps out of sequence. The livery was revised with increased amount of cream but they were the only vehicles to carry this livery. The first picture, taken in April 1970, by which time the bus was owned by the PTE, shows 178 leaving Woodside on the Oxton Circle service, the flat-fare farebox visible through the nearside windscreen. *Geoffrey Morant*

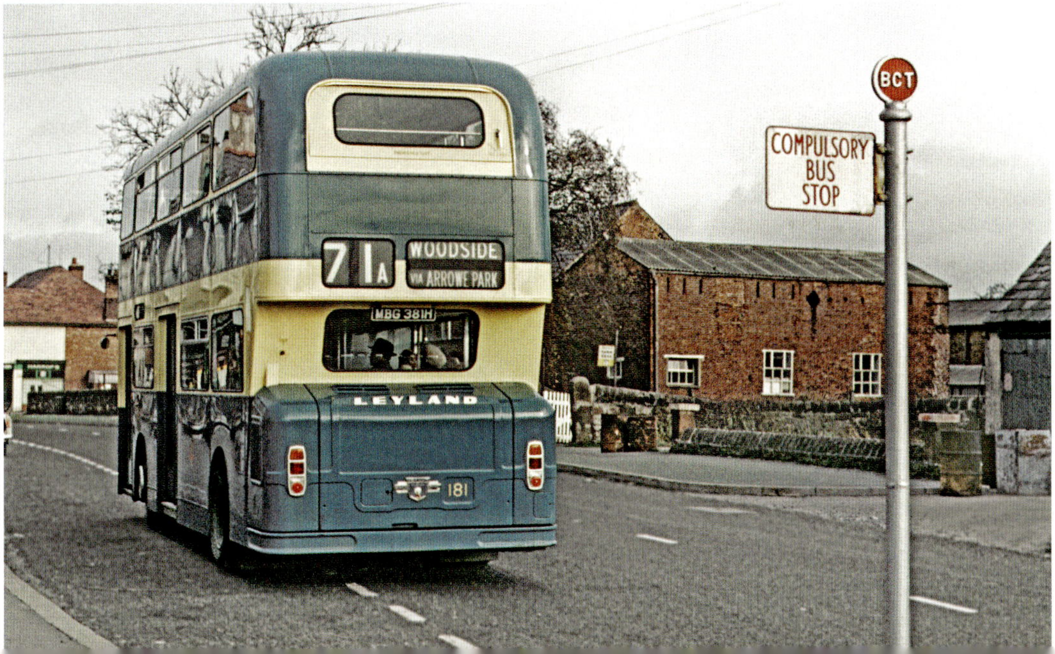

The second picture is of the rear of 181 in Irby on 2 November 1969 on what may have been its first day in service. Although one-person operated, all the Atlanteans had Birkenhead's full destination indicators at the rear but these quickly ceased to be used and were painted over or removed. The same indicator layout, front and rear, was also used by Wallasey. The red disc on a BCT stop signified fare stage; those on ordinary request stops were blue. *John Ryan*

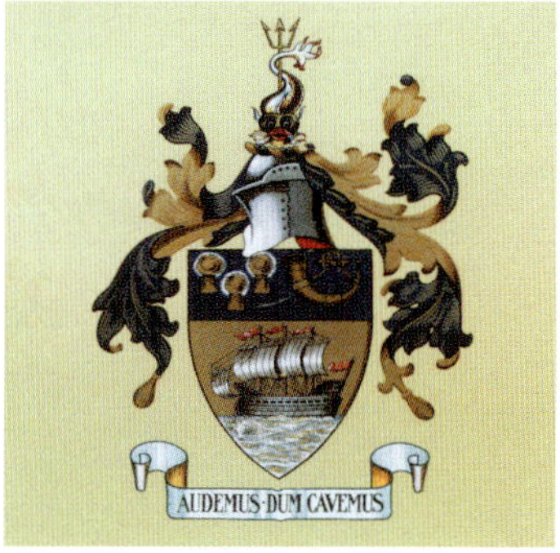

Wallasey

In contrast to Birkenhead, the borough of Wallasey was principally residential with only a limited industrial base close to the docks. For many years, over 40% of the adult population worked in Liverpool, the majority using the bus to reach the corporation's ferries at Seacombe. The seaside resort of New Brighton was part of the borough and at weekends and during the season thousands visited it for its sands, funfair, marine lake, promenade and the rest.

Its bus services were therefore mainly arranged to serve residential areas and connect them with the ferry. There were several cross-dock services operated jointly with Birkenhead but no joint services with Crosville, which was refused access to New Brighton and Seacombe. Peak traffic flows were high and the size of the fleet reflected this.

In the 1960s the industry-wide downturn caused by increased car ownership was made worse in Wallasey by a continual reduction in the number of people travelling to Birkenhead and Liverpool for work, a severe decline in the popularity of New Brighton, staff shortages and worsening labour relations. What had been a prosperous medium sized undertaking turned into a problem one. A new general manager, Geoffrey Harding, introduced several changes to counter the decline, not least being a survey of use and a consequent revision of almost all the services – it was the first of what became known as market analysis projects. Minibuses were another innovation.

Wallasey's bus fleet was straightforward. After a mixed fleet of AECs and Leylands, from 1937 the formula was Leyland chassis and off-the-shelf Metro Cammell bodies, bought in large batches. Most notable was an order for 20 and then 10 more Atlanteans more or less straight off the drawing board – quite remarkable for a fleet of just over 100 buses.

A pictorial review of Wallasey has to start at Seacombe ferry. Contrast these pictures with those of Birkenhead's Woodside – although busy at peak hours, with its central lawn Seacombe was the opposite in style and ambience. On arrival buses off-loaded outside the main ferry building with its impressive clock tower and then moved to the south side to load in 'herring-bone' bays, passengers waiting under a colonnade. Forward-engined buses reversed in, Atlanteans loaded front-in. June 1963 *Roy Marshall*

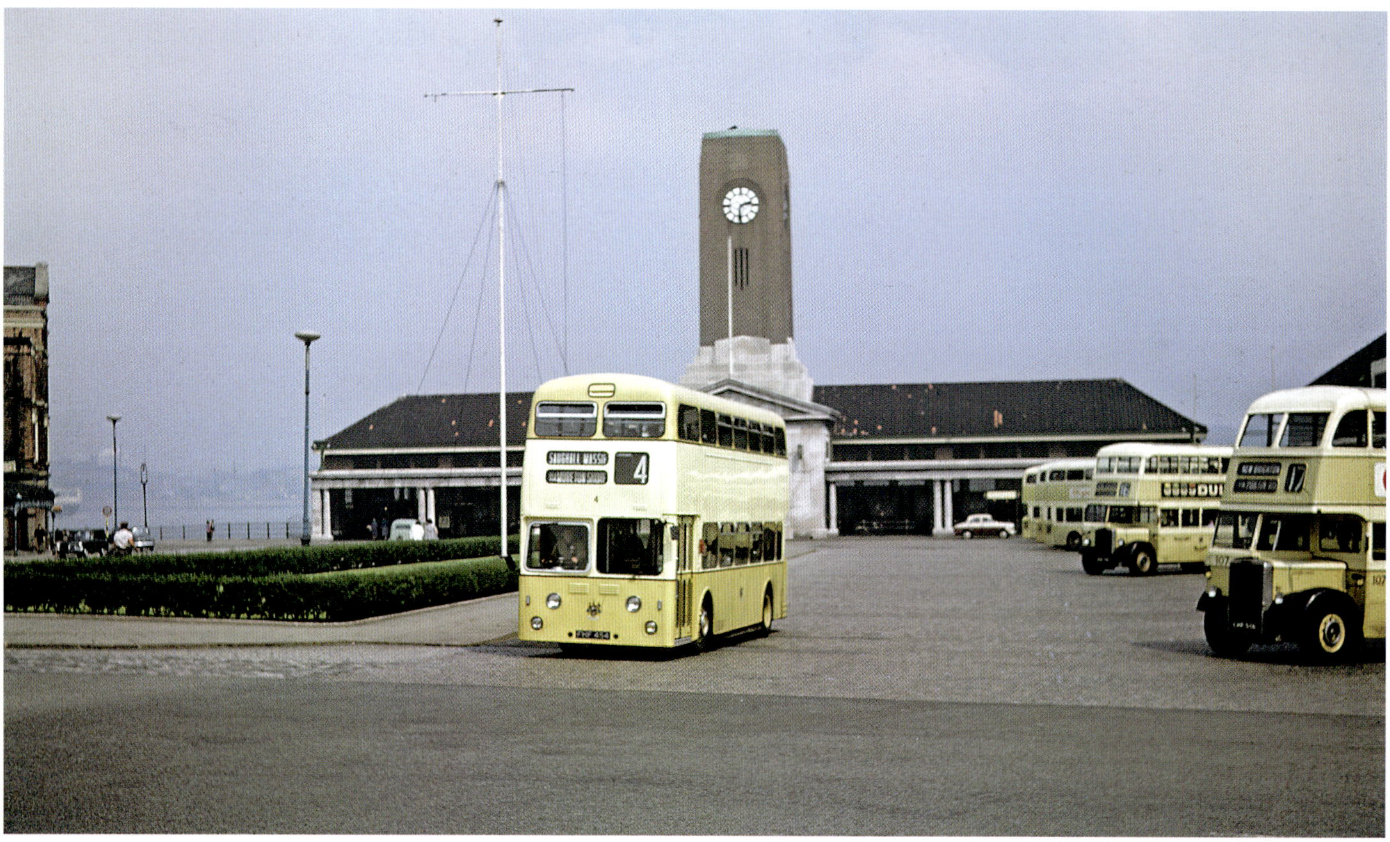

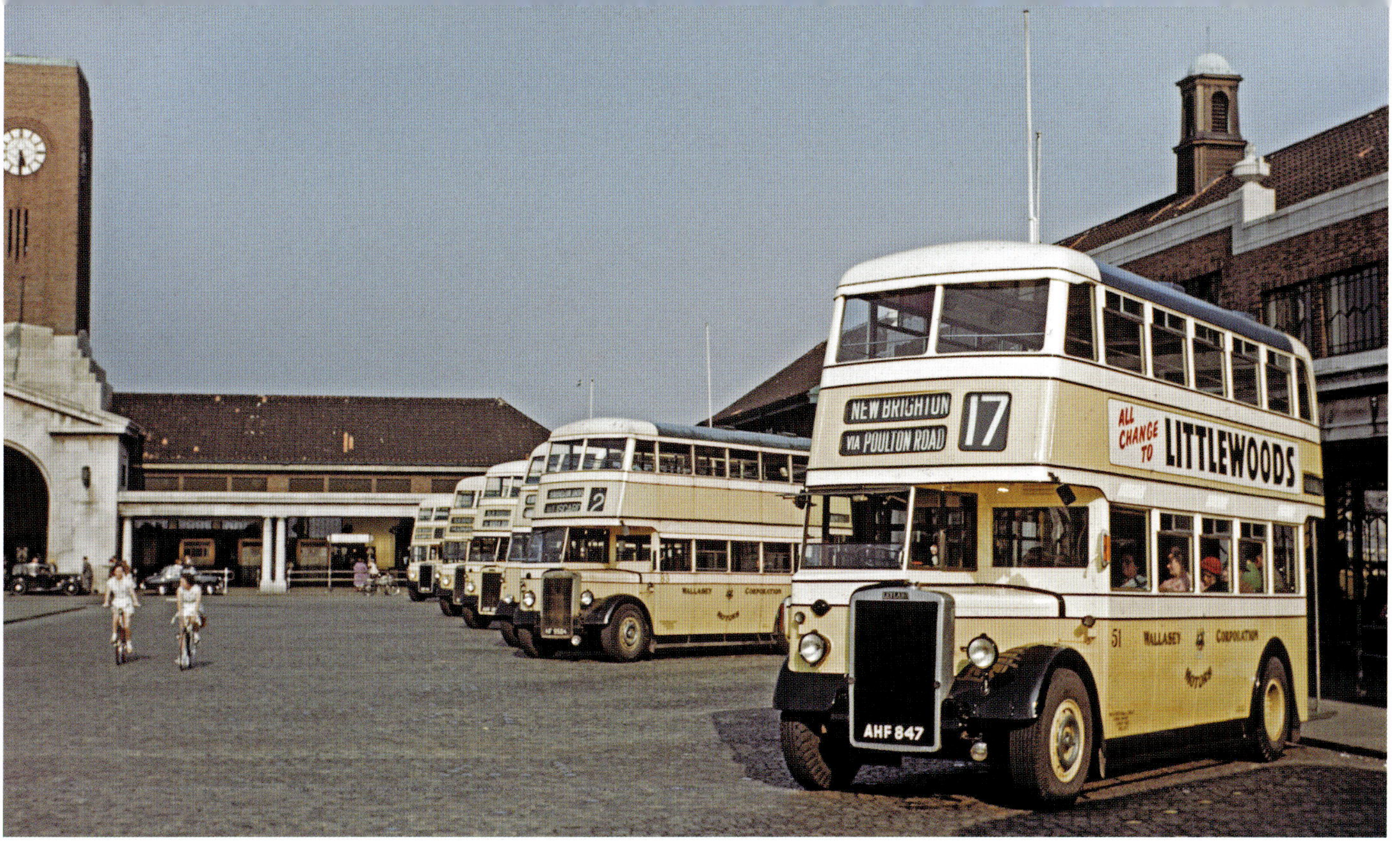

Until the early 1960s the Seacombe bus/ferry interchange handled hundreds of cross-river passengers especially at rush hours. Bus/ferry connections ran with clockwork precision and for many years buses carried a dummy clock on which would be set the time of the connecting ferry departure. Evening rush hour departures at Seacombe were worth watching. Every ten minutes when the duty inspector blew his whistle up to 15 buses including several short workings departed simultaneously. This view of the departure bays was taken in 1957; at the front is fleet number 51, one of the Metro Cammell bodied PD2/1s of 1951; beyond is PD1 number 83, new in 1946. *Phil Tatt/Online Transport Archive*

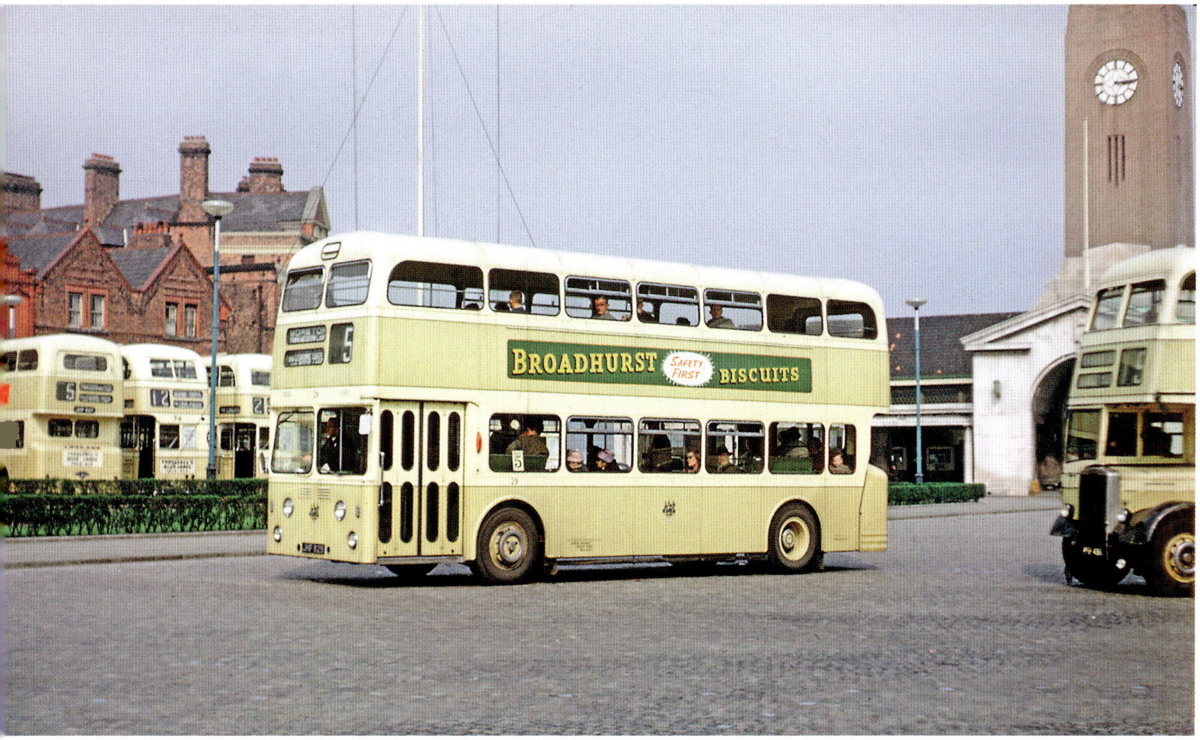

To the north side there was a spacious parking area for peak-hour duty vehicles, avoiding dead mileage to and from the depot at Seaview Road. Relations between the Corporation's separate Bus and Ferry Departments were sometime strained until they were amalgamated in 1963 under general manager Geoffrey Harding who, in addition to his bus background, was a member of the Royal Navy Volunteer Reserve. He held a current ship's master's 'ticket' and to get away from the continual stresses of combating declining traffic, outdated services patterns and trying to change working practices, would sometimes spend a day as captain of one of his ferries. August 1973 *Geoffrey Morant*

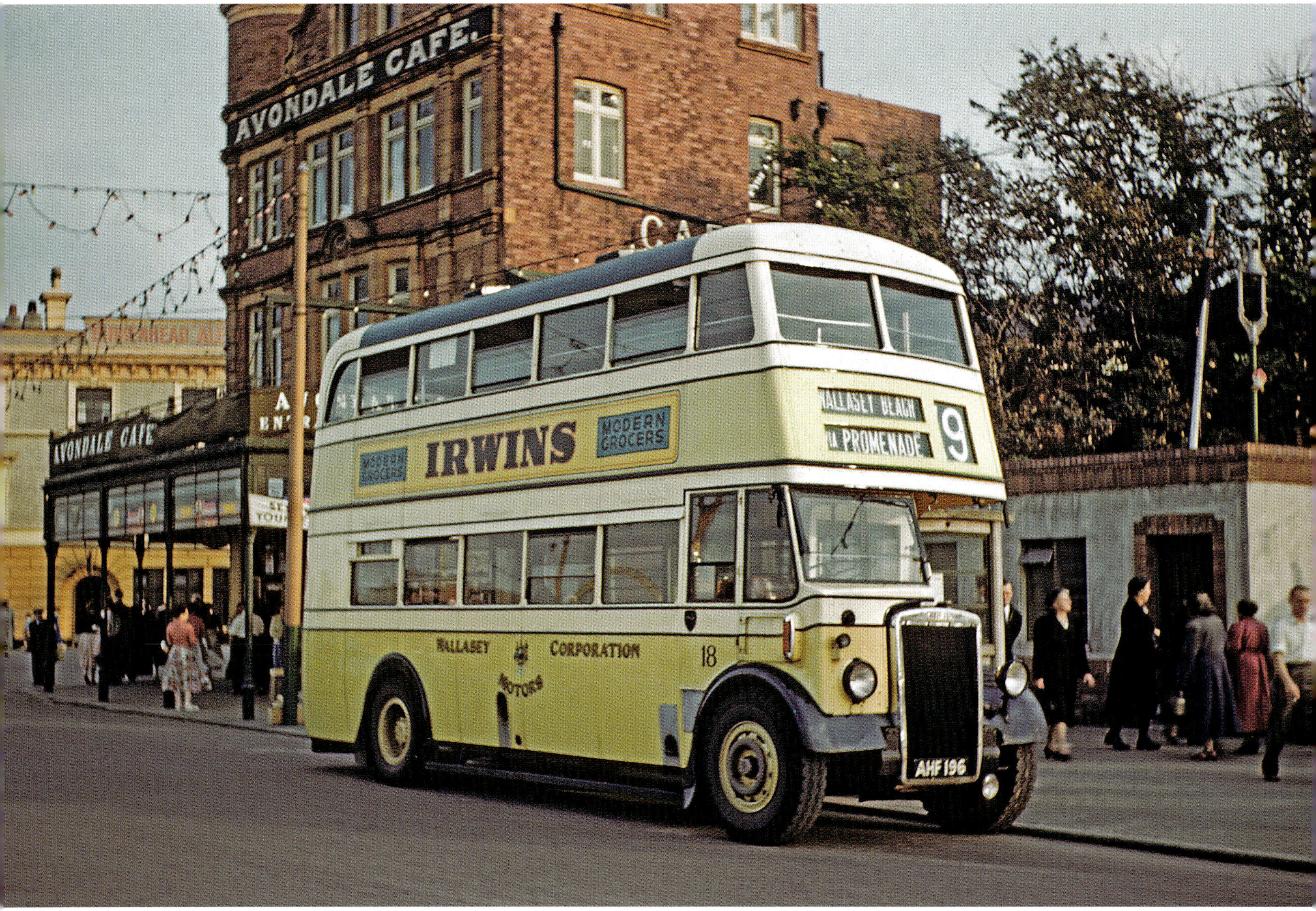

Wallasey's first three batches of postwar buses were Leyland PD1s with Metro Cammell's standard metal-framed body – a simple and functional yet elegant and fit-for-purpose design even though it dated from 1934. There were 48 of them – 78-101 new in 1946 and 11-34 new in 1948, replacing almost half the fleet; still in service were 46 pre-war Leylands with the same type of body. By some quirk for the HF- four digit series the Wallasey Motor Tax Office issued all the odd numbers first and then the even numbers, so that 78-101 were registered HF 9574 to 9620, even numbers only. This picture shows the somewhat dated livery with its title 'Wallasey Corporation Motors' around the coat of arms, large black signwritten fleet numbers, the offside intermediate route indicator in the rear lower deck window and the small advert or clock holder forward of the cab door. Pictured at Marine Promenade, near to New Brighton Pier, number 18 is working summer-only route 19, which ran along the Promenade to Wallasey Beach. *Phil Tatt/Online Transport Archive*

Opposite top Much of Wallasey's service network served residential areas and this picture captures the character of the quieter roads with their elegant villas. The 15 (formerly 5) service between New Brighton station and Seacombe exclusively served several residential areas of Wallasey. In this picture Leyland PD2 54 is in Penkett Road near Strathcona Road en-route to Seacombe ferry. *Online Transport Archive*

Opposite bottom The 48 PD1s were followed in 1951 by 24 Leyland PD2s, 35-58, with the same standard Metro Cammell body. Newly painted 58 in the modernised livery introduced in 1961, it has also had the rain shields removed from the side windows and some attention to its cab. *Reg Wilson/Online Transport Archive*

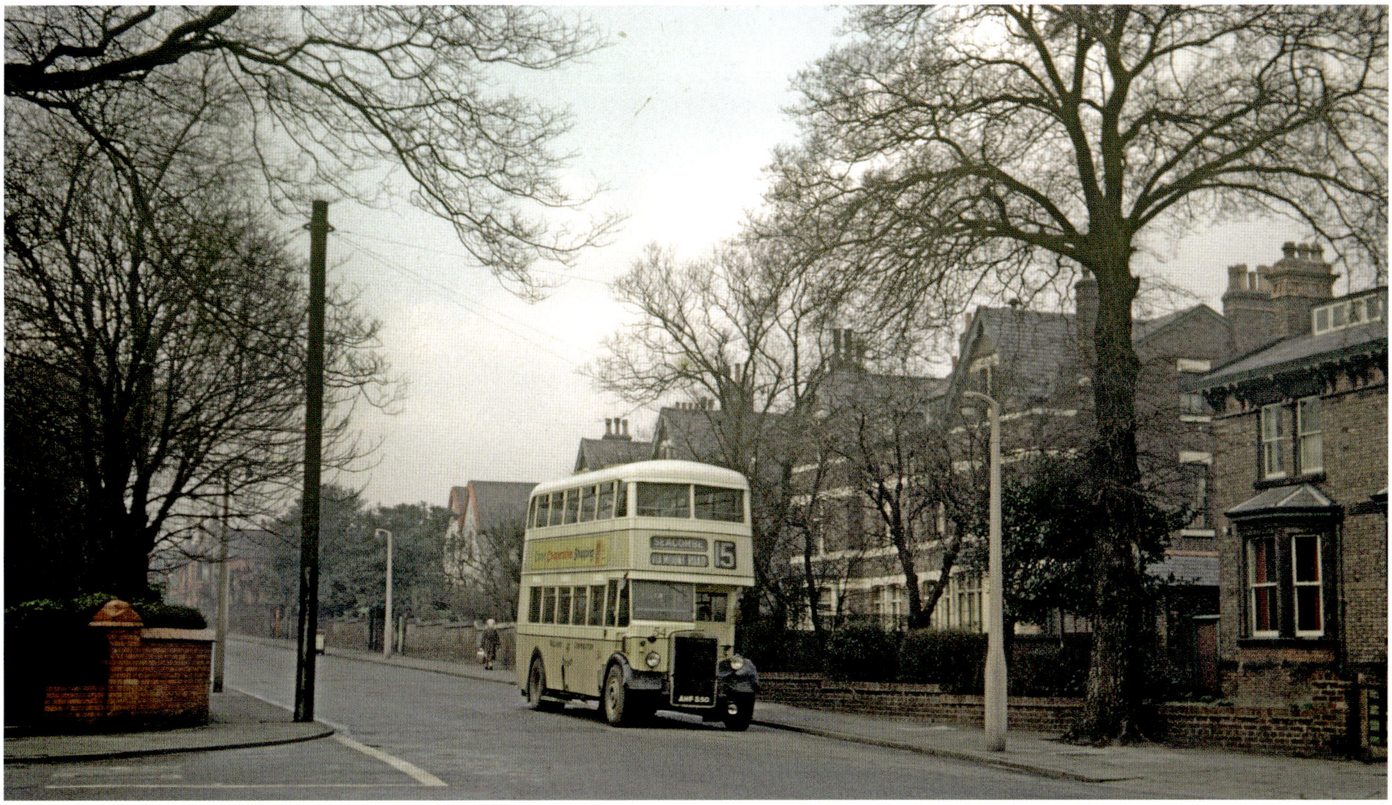
15
54

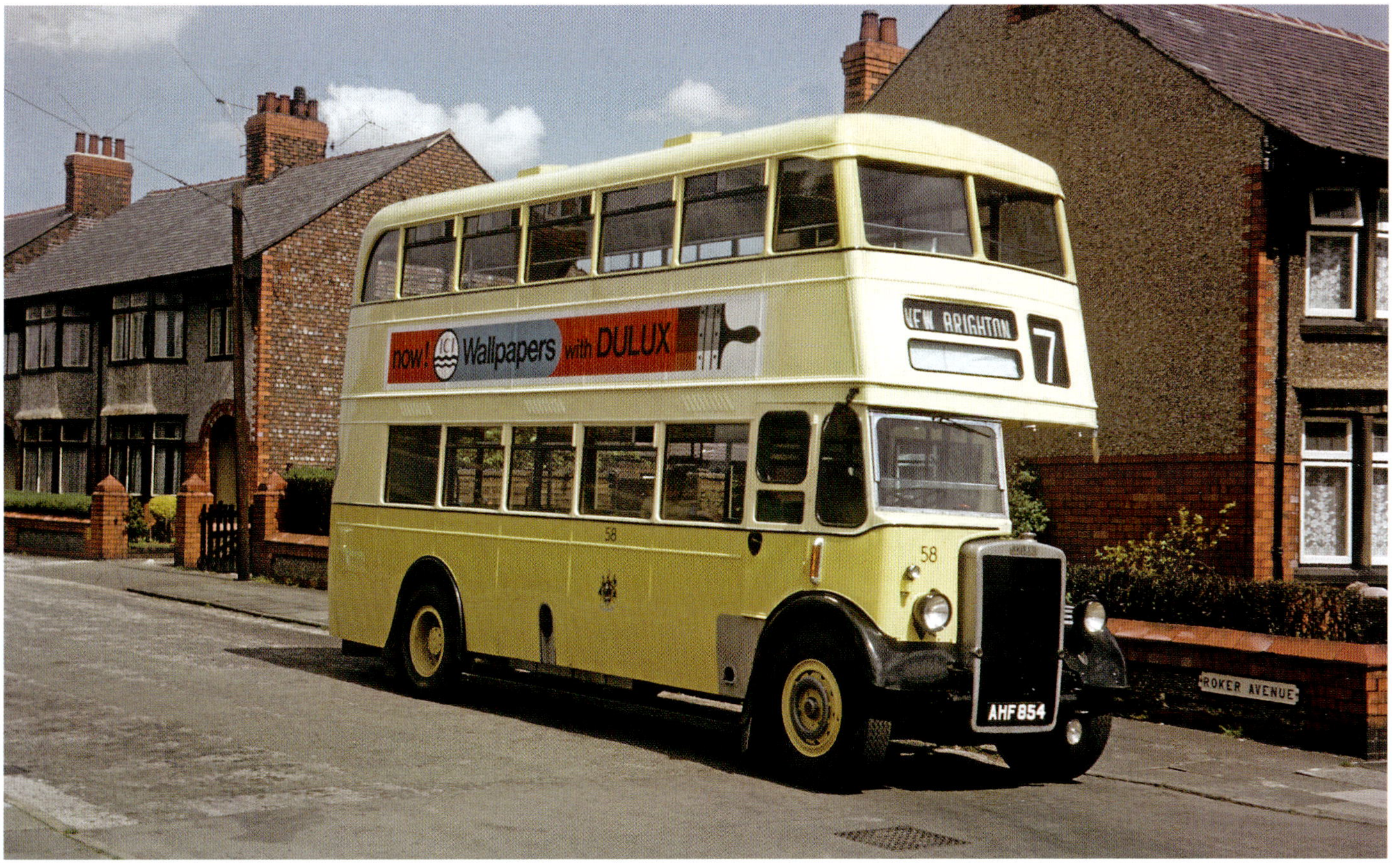
now! ICI Wallpapers with DULUX
NEW BRIGHTON
7
58
58
AHF 854
ROKER AVENUE

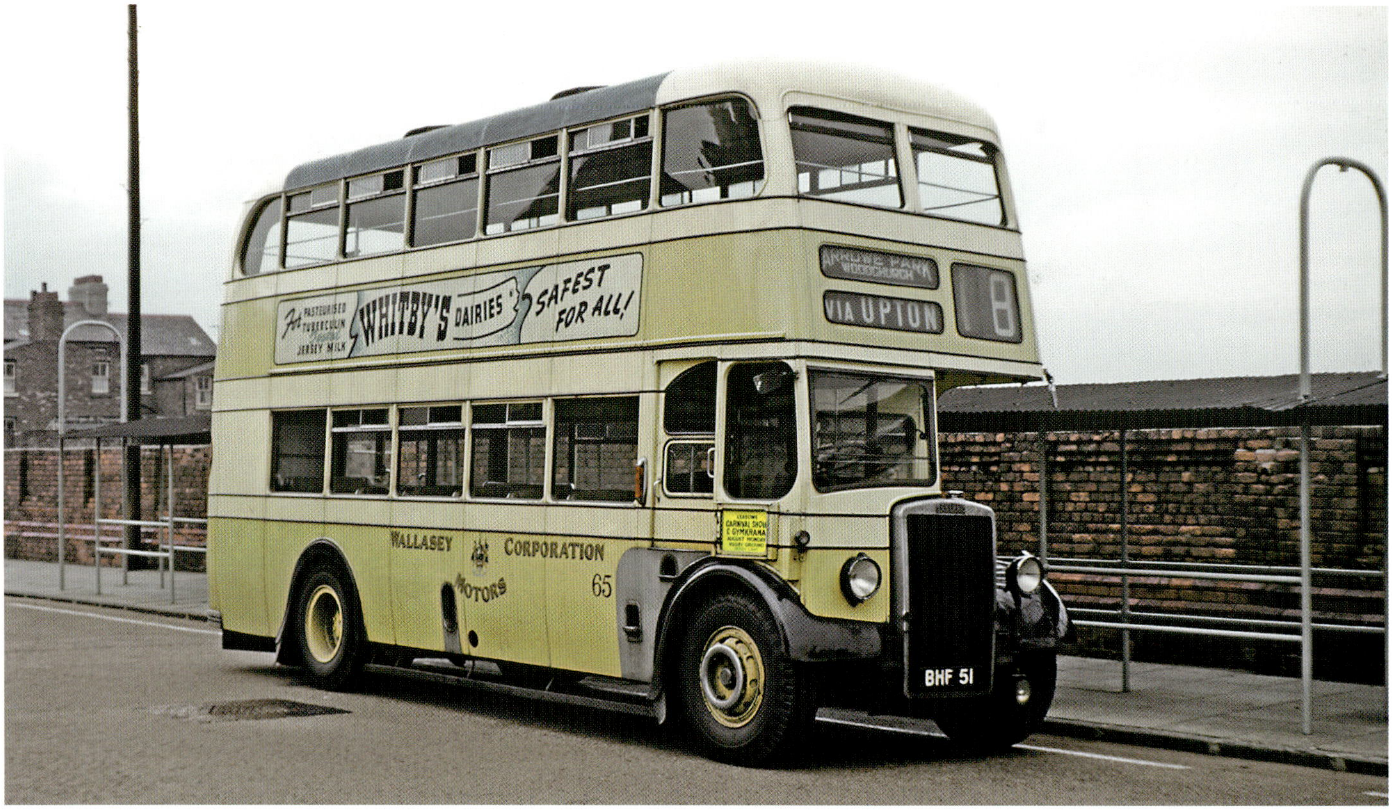

Wallasey's first 8ft wide buses were 22 Leyland Titan PD2/12s, 59-80. New in 1951/52 they replaced the last unrebodied pre-war double-deckers. With the familiar Metro Cammell design about to be replaced by the Orion, the body order went to Weymann. On a dull July day in 1959, number 65 waits to leave New Brighton on jointly operated service 18 to the Birkenhead suburb of Woodchurch. External advertisements were first carried in 1952 – their content was strictly controlled with a ban on any references to politics, money-lending or rival resorts. The small cabside frame carries a drop-in advertisement for the Leasowe Carnival and Gymkhana at Reeds Lane Rugby Ground on August Bank Holiday Monday 1962. *Ian Stewart*

In this picture Weymann-bodied PD2 72 has crossed the rolling bascule Duke Street Bridge in 1966 on the jointly operated service 10, one of the network of cross-docks routes operated jointly with Birkenhead across the then bustling Dock Estate. Delays could be considerable as bridges were opened to allow ships to pass through and slow-moving goods trains crossed the main road – one comment made was that 'we always allowed at least 90 minutes to make the relatively short journey from our house near New Brighton to catch a coach or train at Woodside, just in case the 10s were full or the bridges up – and all too often they were'. *A S Clayton/Online Transport Archive*

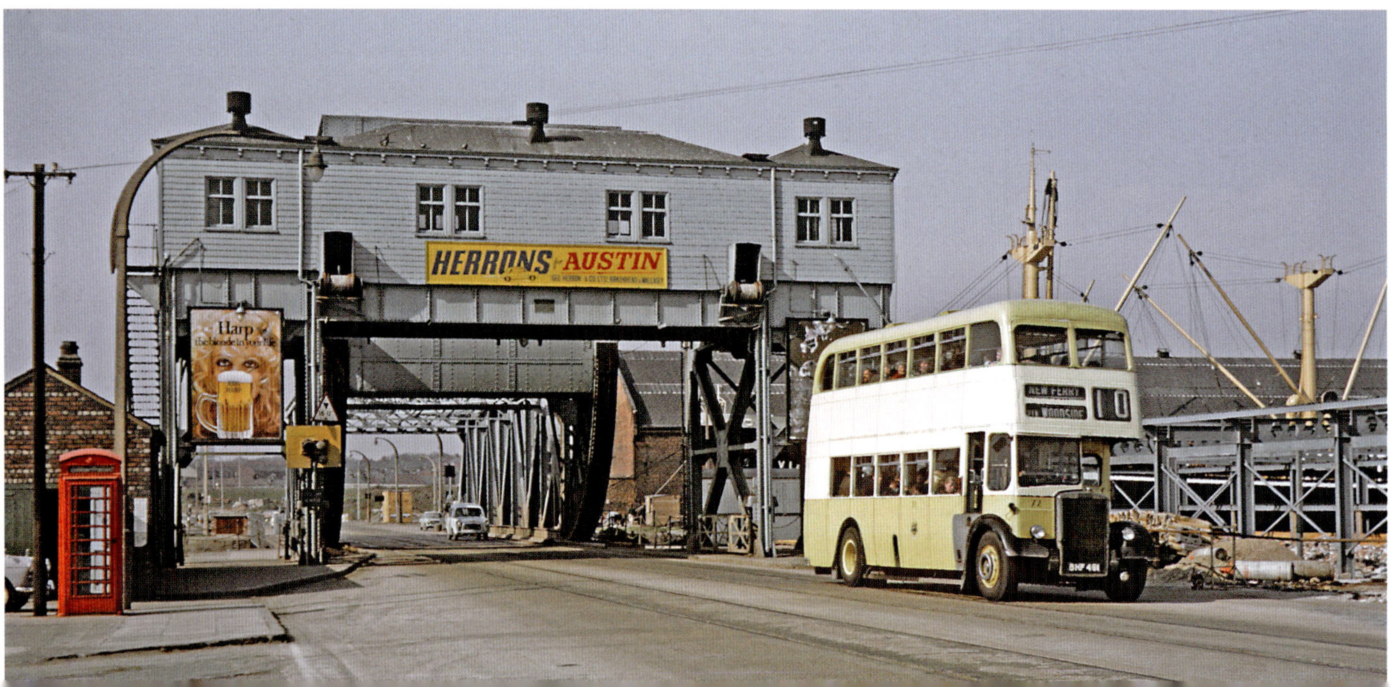

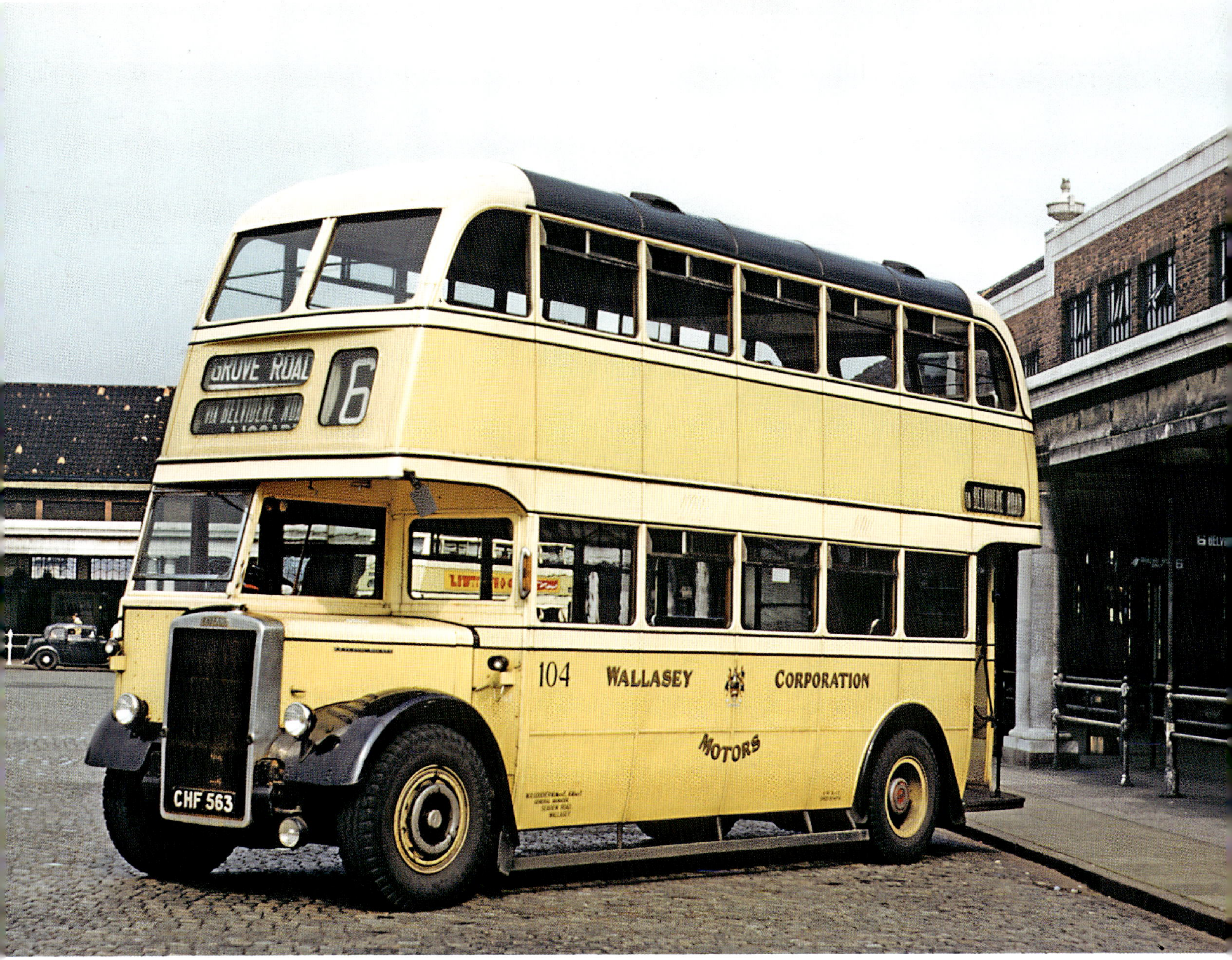

Six Leyland TD4c new in 1936 had been rebodied by Burlingham in 1948 – the firm was doing something similar on a large batch of Ribble vehicles – and renumbered 102-107. In 1955/56 the bodies (and their fleet numbers) were transferred to six new Leyland PD2/10 chassis. This is 104 at Seacombe in mid-1957. *Dennis Kerrison*

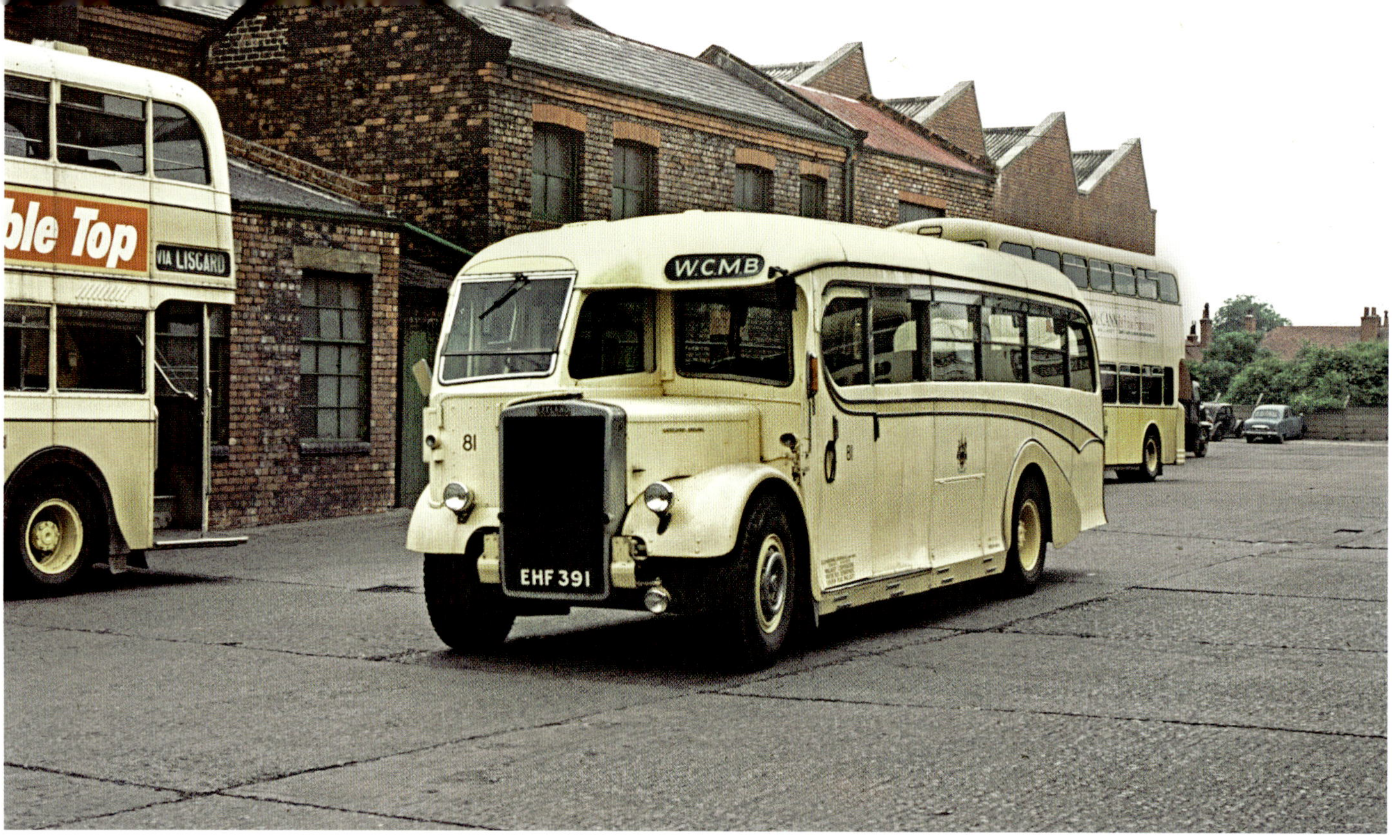

Wallasey had a small fleet of coaches and they had a complex life. Early in 1948 four Leyland TD4c double-deck chassis from the same batch as 102-107 had been rebodied by Burlingham with 29-seat coach bodies. Renumbered 7-10 they were used on seasonal routes 19 and 20, summer excursions and at peak times in summer were often hired to other coach firms. In 1957 the bodies from 7 and 8 were fitted to two new Leyland PD2/10 chassis; the other two TD4s continued in service. With the imminent arrival of Leyland Atlanteans 1-30 the four coaches were renumbered 81-84. TD4s 83/84 (formerly 9/10) were withdrawn in 1962, PD2/1-based 7 became 81 and is at Seaview Road depot in this June 1965 photograph. It had been used for driver training for some months. *Alan Mortimer*

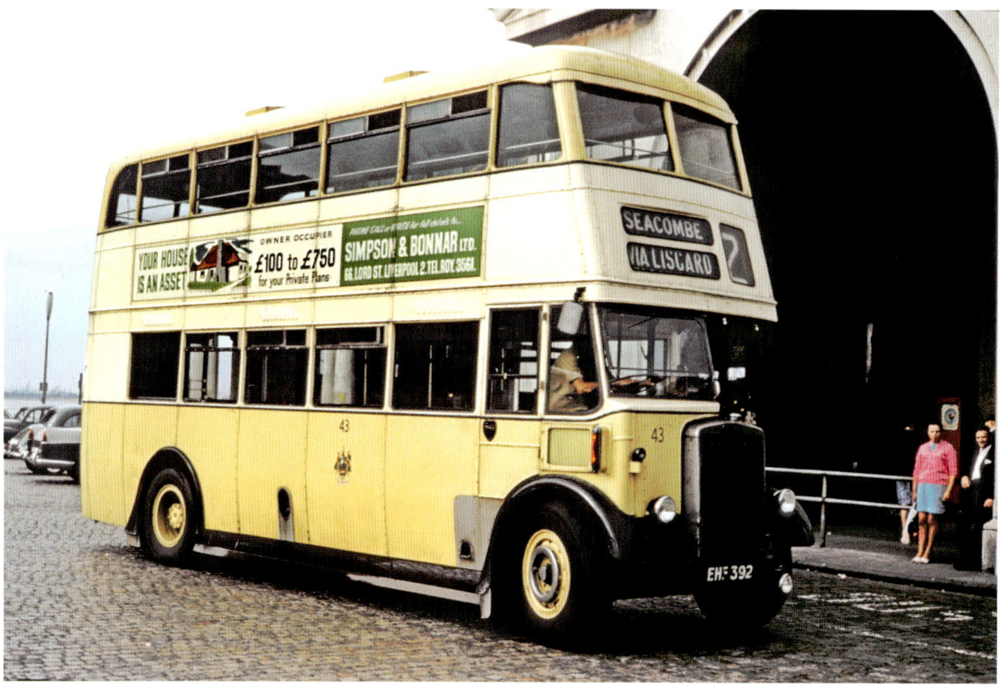

Coach-bodied PD2/10 number 8 (EHF 392) had a complicated life, involving PD2/1 43 and PD1 89. Following an accident in 1959, the badly damaged chassis of PD2/1 43 was not worth repairing; not so its Metro Cammell body which was rebuilt and fitted to the PD2/10 chassis from coach 8. The resulting Metro Cammell-bodied bodied PD2/10 was numbered 43 (EHF 392). The coach body was then fitted to the chassis of 1946 PD1 89 which had suffered severe body damage and the resulting PD1 coach (HF 9586) became 82 in the coach series. PD2/10 number 43 survived to be transferred to the PTE; it is seen here at Seacombe in 1963. *Roy Marshall*

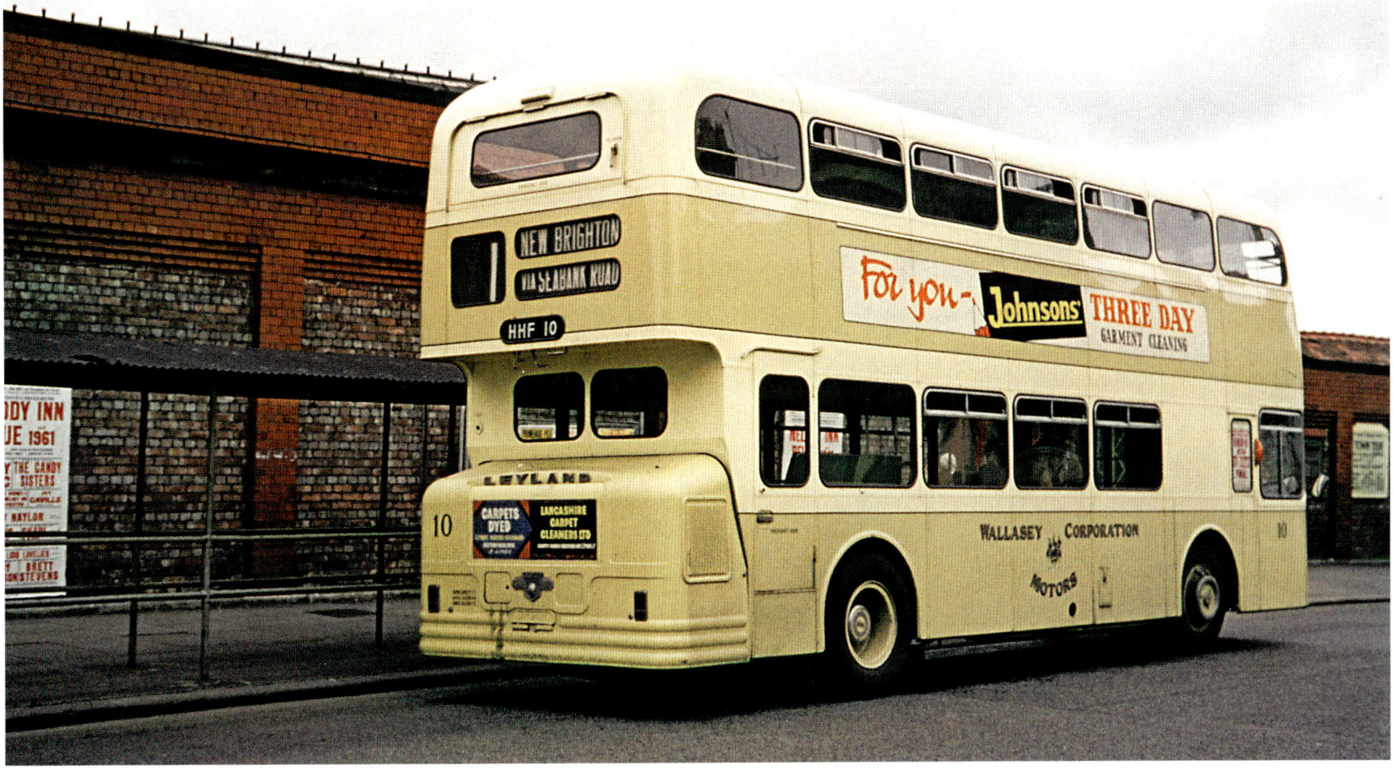

For a small municipality with a fleet of 100 to place an order for 20 and a further 10 of the ground-breaking but then untried and unproven Leyland Atlantean was a brave move – but general manager W R Goodier did it. Fleet number 1 was handed over by Leyland at a formal ceremony on 10 December 1958, numbers 2-6 followed in September 1959, 7-20 in 1960 and 21-30 in 1961 and with them the fleet needed no more new double-deckers until it was taken over by the PTE. Goodier retired in 1960 and new manager Geoffrey Harding inherited the mechanical problems of these early Atlanteans – 'they were a third of the fleet, so we simply got down to it and made them work'. On number 1's first day in service it had a crew of four – the driver getting used to two pedal control and having no engine noise to guide him; there were two conductors, one upstairs and one downstairs plus a busy inspector who alighted at every stop to guide passengers to the front entrance. Initially, rear-in herring-bone loading was retained at Seacombe with the bus reversing alongside a narrow wooden platform which provided access from the Colonnade to the front entrance – it was soon changed to front-in loading. 1-20 were finished in the 'traditional' livery as in this rear-end picture of number 10 at New Brighton when new. *Phil Tatt*

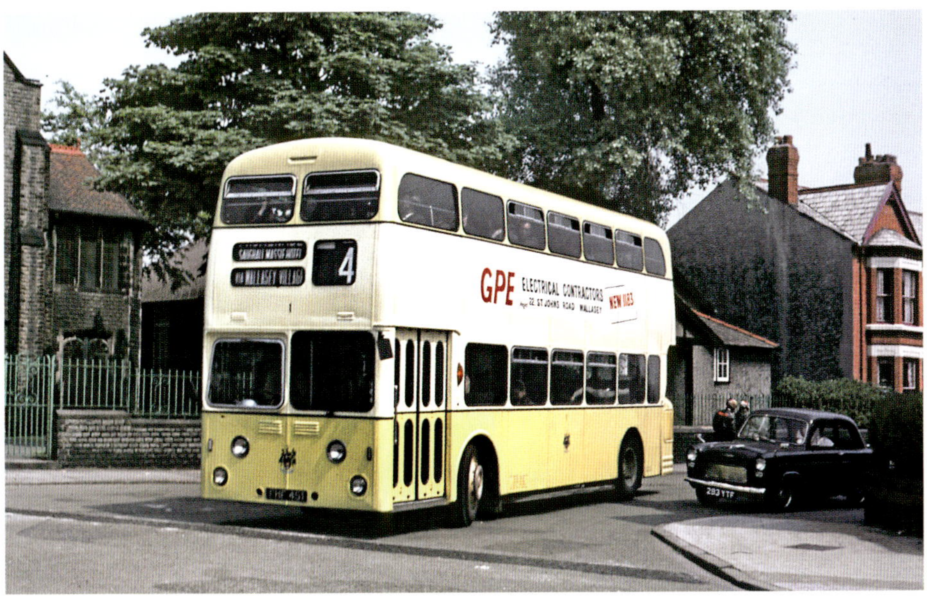

The livery was further simplified as in this late 1960s picture of that first Atlantean in Seacombe village at the junction of Brougham Road and Liscard Road on the half-hourly service from Seacombe Ferry to Saughall Massie. The Corporation had hoped that high-capacity buses would enable it to dispose of a larger number of older buses retained for peak hour short workings but traffic continued to decline and for much of the time these big 77-seaters ran with few passengers, as in this picture. Until one-person operation of full-size double-deckers was authorised in 1966 they were sometimes one-man operated with the upper deck closed off. *David Powell*

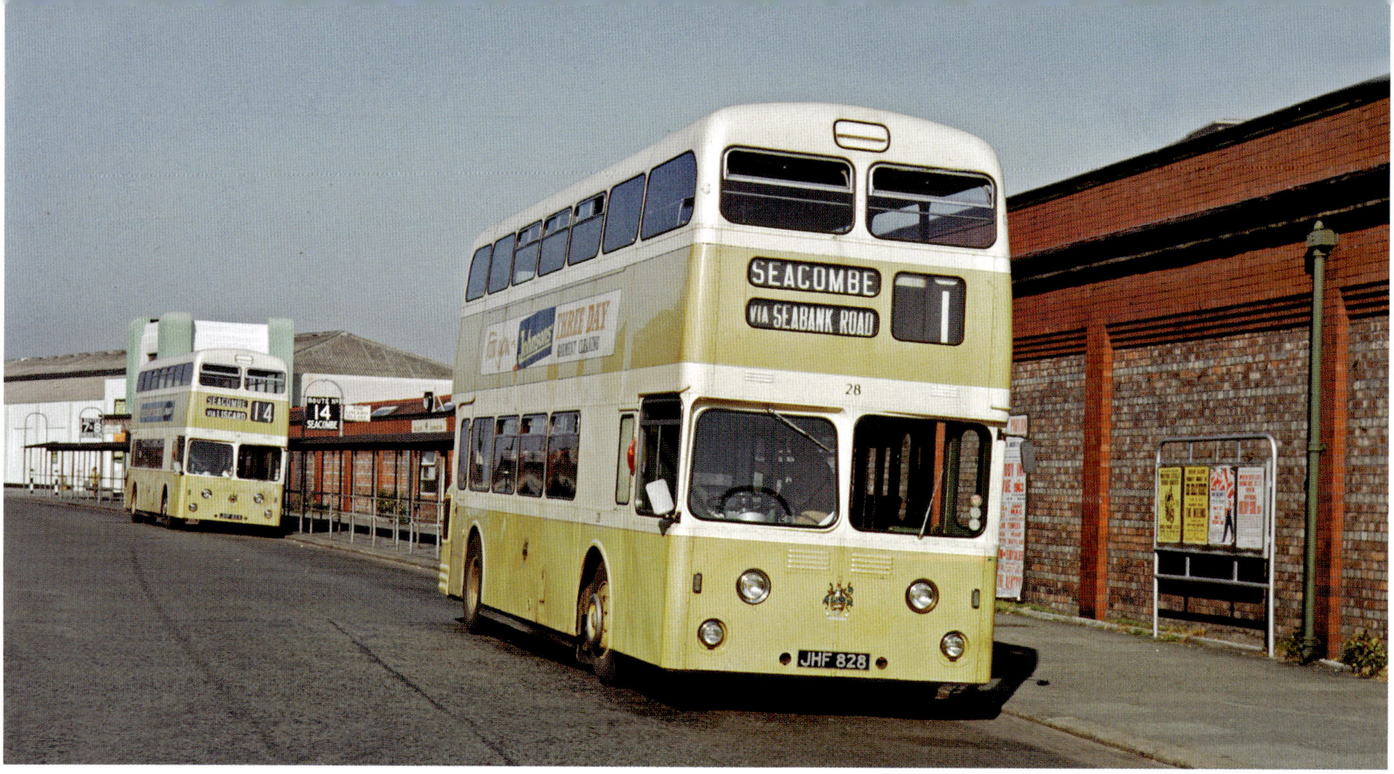

The last ten were delivered in a modernised livery shown in this picture of numbers 28 and 24 at New Brighton in 1962. The loading stands along the east side of Virginia Road were valuable when marshalling weekend seasonal crowds – queues of buses were often double-parked but by the time the Atlanteans arrived the crowds were already deserting New Brighton for the Costa del Sol. *Cedric Greenwood*

As part of the revision of routes to provide a more useful service and eliminate unremunerative running, a shoppers' service was introduced to link previously unserved areas to the main commercial centre at Liscard. It was operated by midi buses, something of a novelty at the time. New in 1962, Albion Nimbus numbers 31-34 had Strachans bodies with coach seats, enabling them also to replace the Burlingham coaches and to work off-peak duties on lightly-trafficked routes such as the 6 and 15. Seen shortly after delivery, 32 is in its original cream with primrose window surrounds – they were repainted with the colours reversed. *Reg Wilson*

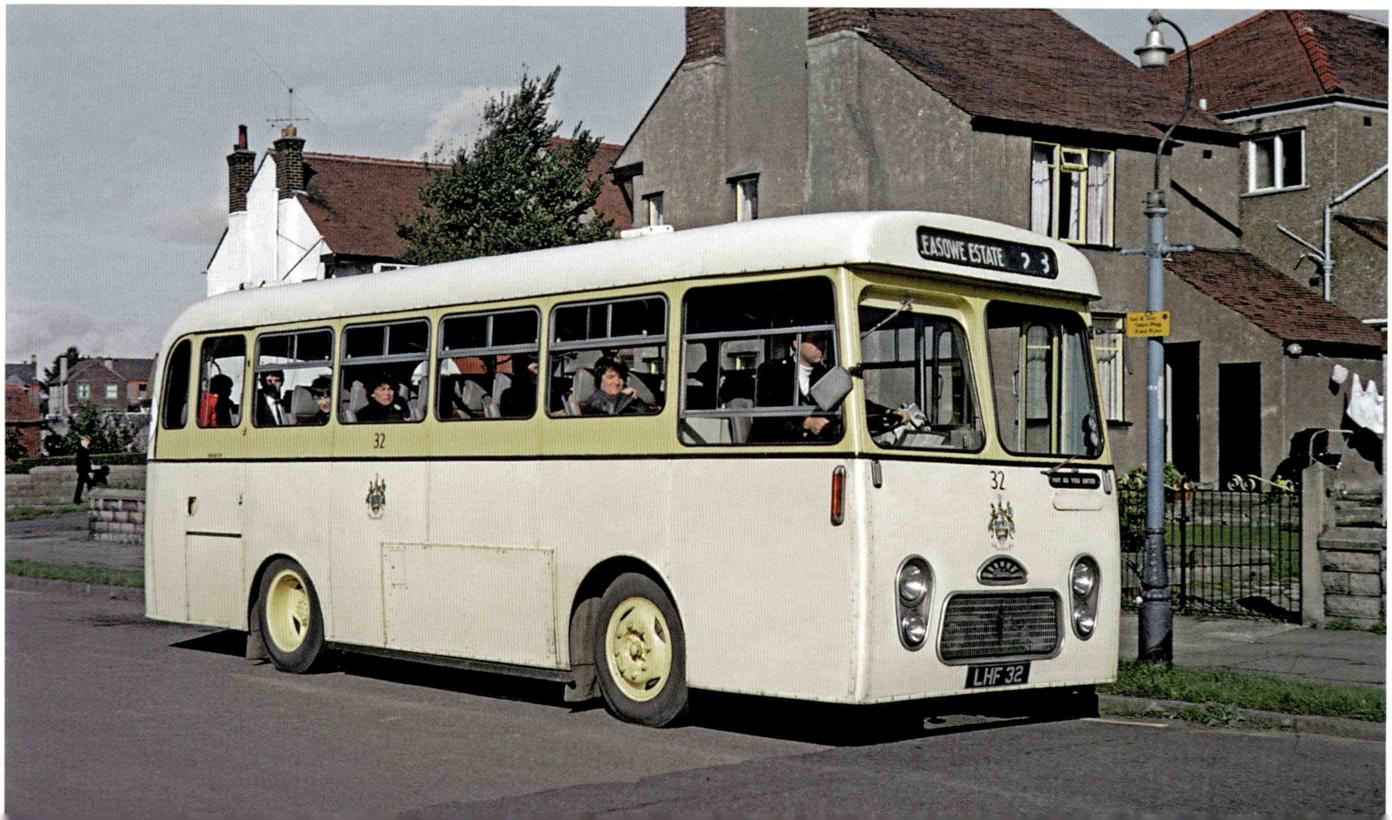

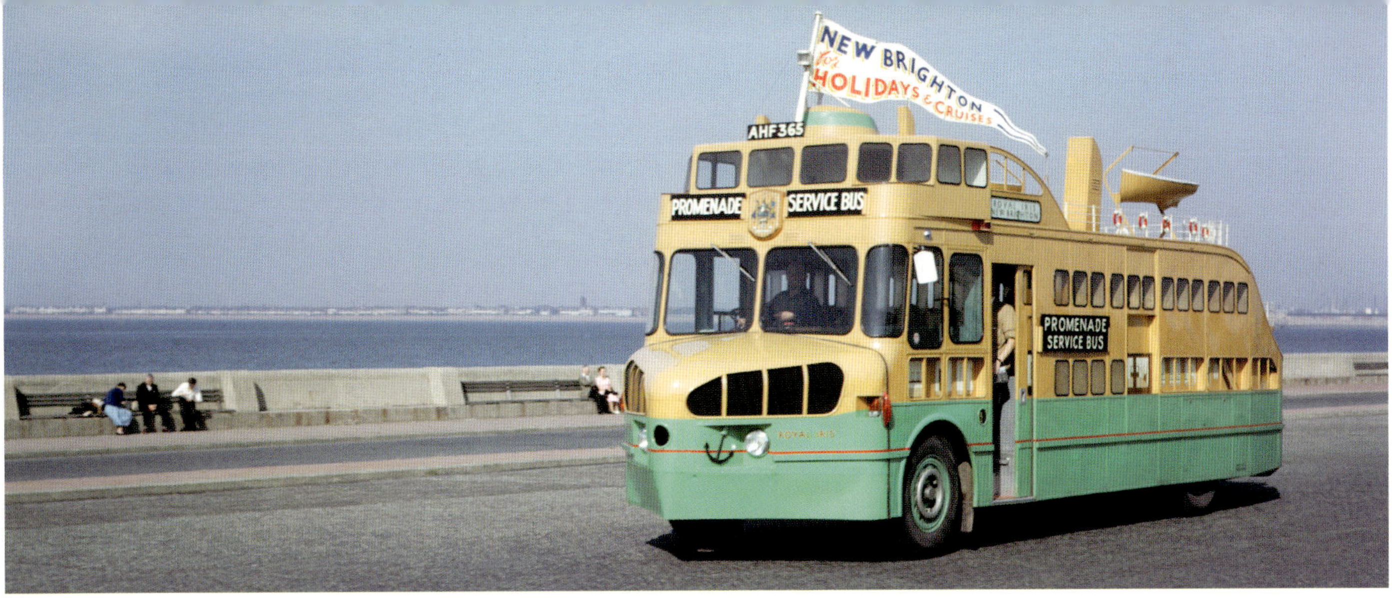

Although nothing like so busy as in the past, New Brighton still attracted holiday makers and day trippers. Prompted by Blackpool's decorated trams, during 1963 the Seaview Road workshops removed the body from Leyland PD1 127 (renumbered from 27 on the arrival of the Atlanteans) and replaced it with this representation of the department's popular cruise vessel *Royal Iris*. Numbered 84 in the 'coach series' (the fleet number was not displayed on the actual bus), it seated 22 and entered service in July 1964. Delicensed each winter, it did promotional work around the country from February to May and worked service 19 from June to September. Unlike most seaside resorts, Wallasey never had open top buses. *E J McWatt/Online Transport Archive*

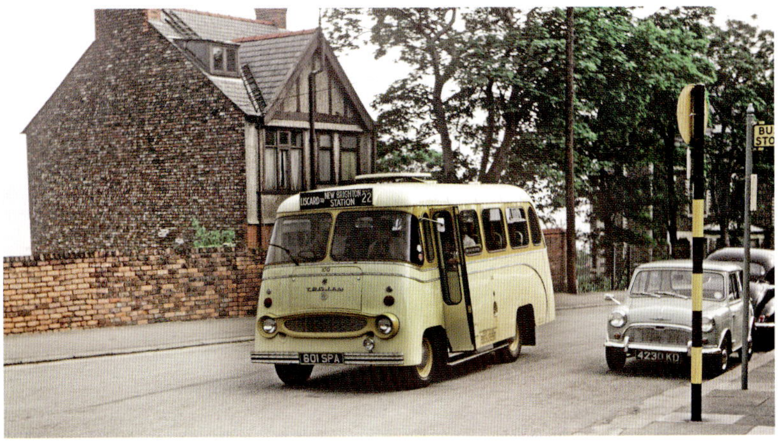

A further innovation as part of the restructuring of Wallasey's bus services was the minibus. Although they would become increasingly familiar in the late 1980s and onwards, in the early 1960s their introduction was a very advanced piece of thinking. New to Banstead Coaches of Surrey in 1960, 13-seater Trojan 601 SPA (fleet number 100) was acquired to operate new shoppers' service 22, introduced on 15 May 1963 and seen here the following month. *Roy Marshall*

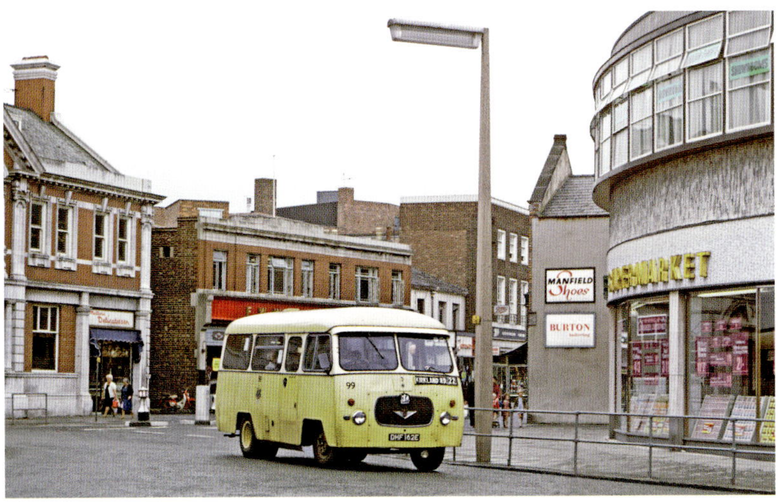

The Trojan was sold in 1966 and replaced the following year by a new petrol-engined Bedford J2 with a 19-seater Duple Midland body, fleet number 99. This picture shows it on 26 July 1969 in Liscard, at the time the commercial centre of the town. The little Bedford was the last bus bought by Wallasey Corporation. On December 1st 1969 the transport undertaking with its reduced bus fleet of Atlanteans 1-30, Albions 31-34, PD2s 40-80 (some withdrawn), Royal Iris 84 and Bedford 99 passed to Merseyside PTE. Not so the general manager. Having invented and successfully implemented what later became known as Market Analysis Projects, which in some ways revolutionised bus operation, and introduced the first municipal minibus service, in September 1969 Geoff Harding was appointed Director of Engineering and Operations at the SELNEC PTE. *Roy Marshall*

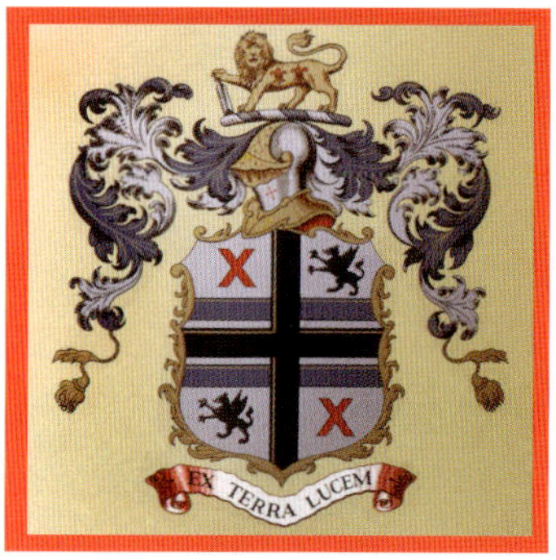

St Helens

St Helens' bus (and trolleybus) fleet was different. Compared with the neighbouring municipal fleets which stayed within their local boundaries, St Helens had operating agreements and joint bus services with Crosville, Lancashire United (LUT), Ribble and the corporations of Leigh, Liverpool, Salford, Warrington, Widnes and Wigan, and until 1955 a joint trolleybus service with LUT subsidiary South Lancashire Transport. St Helens buses worked into Liverpool, Southport, Warrington, Wigan and Atherton – and there were some notable ones, not least the fleet of 40 'London Transport' AEC RTs – bought new.

Being a busy and heavily industrialised town with glassworks, collieries, pharmaceuticals and chemicals, St Helens had a large working class population many of whom travelled considerable distances to work. Its buses worked hard and as a result were sometimes not in the pristine condition of, say, Southport's fleet. That said, the smart new layout of the livery, introduced in 1950 by new manager Edgley Cox, and similar to that of Southport, did much to brighten the town.

The undertaking attracted innovative general managers and over the period covered by this book there were four – George Robb, Edgley Cox, John Wake and Alex Barlow and vehicle policy varied as they changed. For most of the period, however, the fleet of around 130 was a mix of AECs and Leylands with bodies by Weymann and East Lancs but there were unusual ones too – Roe-bodied Bristol single-deckers with centre entrances; Leylands with bodies by D J Davies. When the Metropolitan County of Merseyside was formed in April 1974, St Helens was within its boundaries and the transport undertaking became part of the Merseyside PTE.

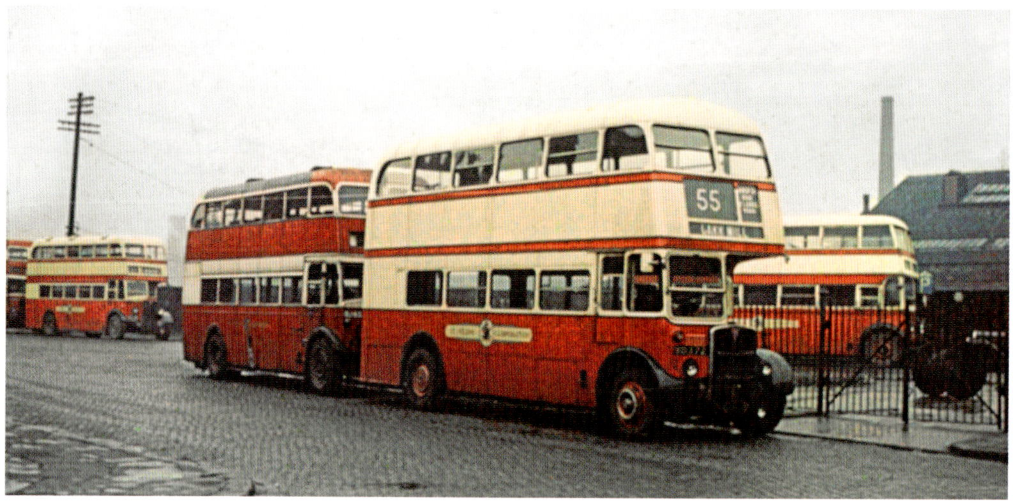

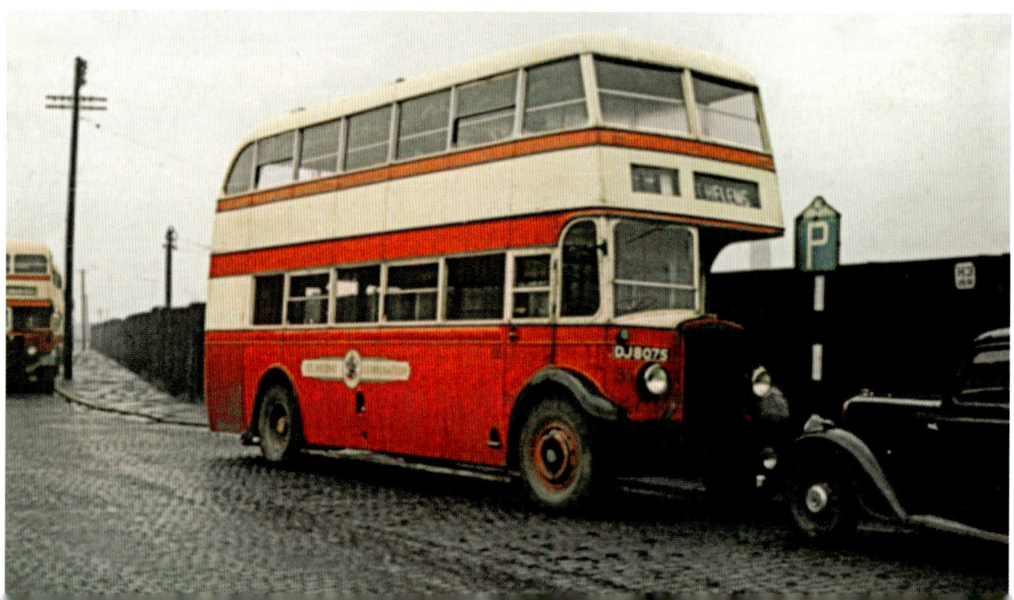

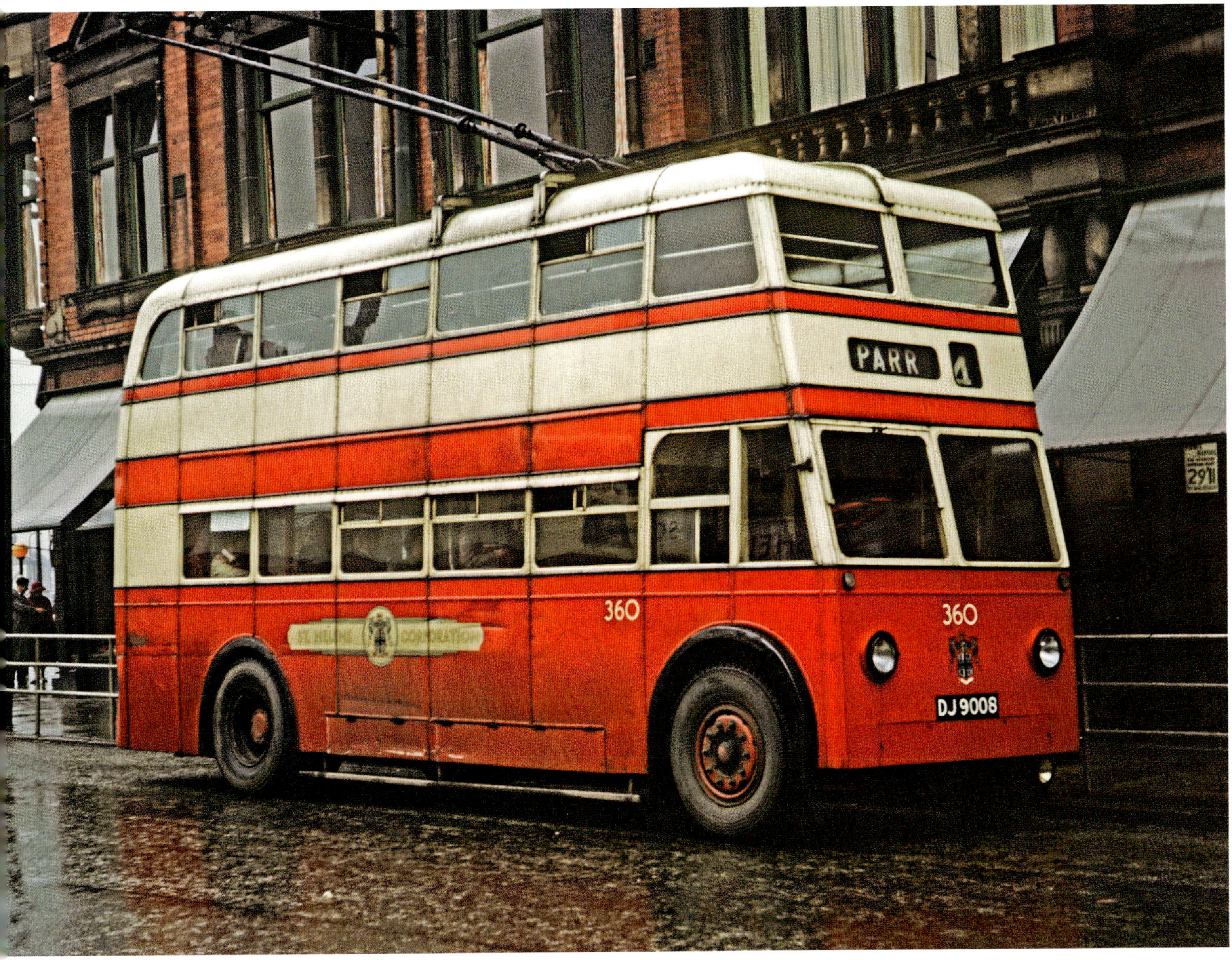

Originally numbered 157-166, Massey-bodied Sunbeam MF2 trolleybuses 357-366 were unusual. Built in 1941 they were intended for Johannesburg. The war prevented their shipment and the government allocated them to St Helens, giving special authorisation for their use as they were 8ft-wide, the then limit being 7ft 6in. A few months before it was withdrawn late in 1955, 360 is at the Parr service stand in Baldwin Street. The trolleybus fleet had been renumbered into the 300-series in June of that year. *Jim Copland/Online Transport Archive*

Opposite top This early colour picture, taken in 1953 at the junction of Hall Street and Shaw Street at the side of the garage, shows the old and new liveries. Park Royal-bodied AEC 'London Transport RT' number 72 is in the new livery, behind is one of three East Lancs-bodied Bristol K6As delivered in 1947. Across the road behind the Bristol is fleet number 39, a 1948 AEC Regent II also with an East Lancs body and across the yard to the front of the RT is a Leyland-bodied Leyland TD5, one of four new in 1939. *J H Price courtesy LRTA*

Opposite bottom The four Leyland-bodied TD5s were 85-88; three were withdrawn in 1954 and the fourth in 1955. This picture, taken in 1953, is of number 86. *J H Price courtesy LRTA*

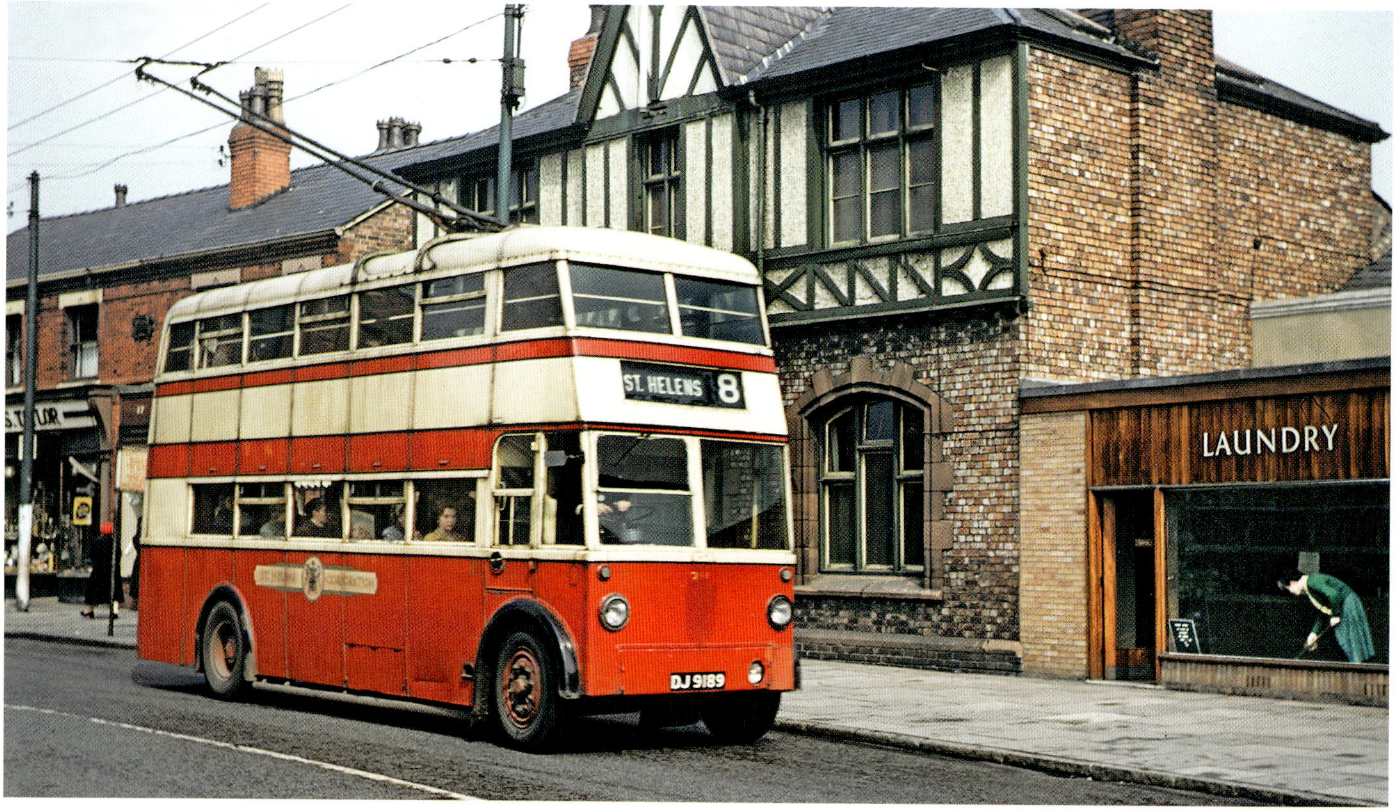
ST. HELENS 8
DJ 9189
LAUNDRY

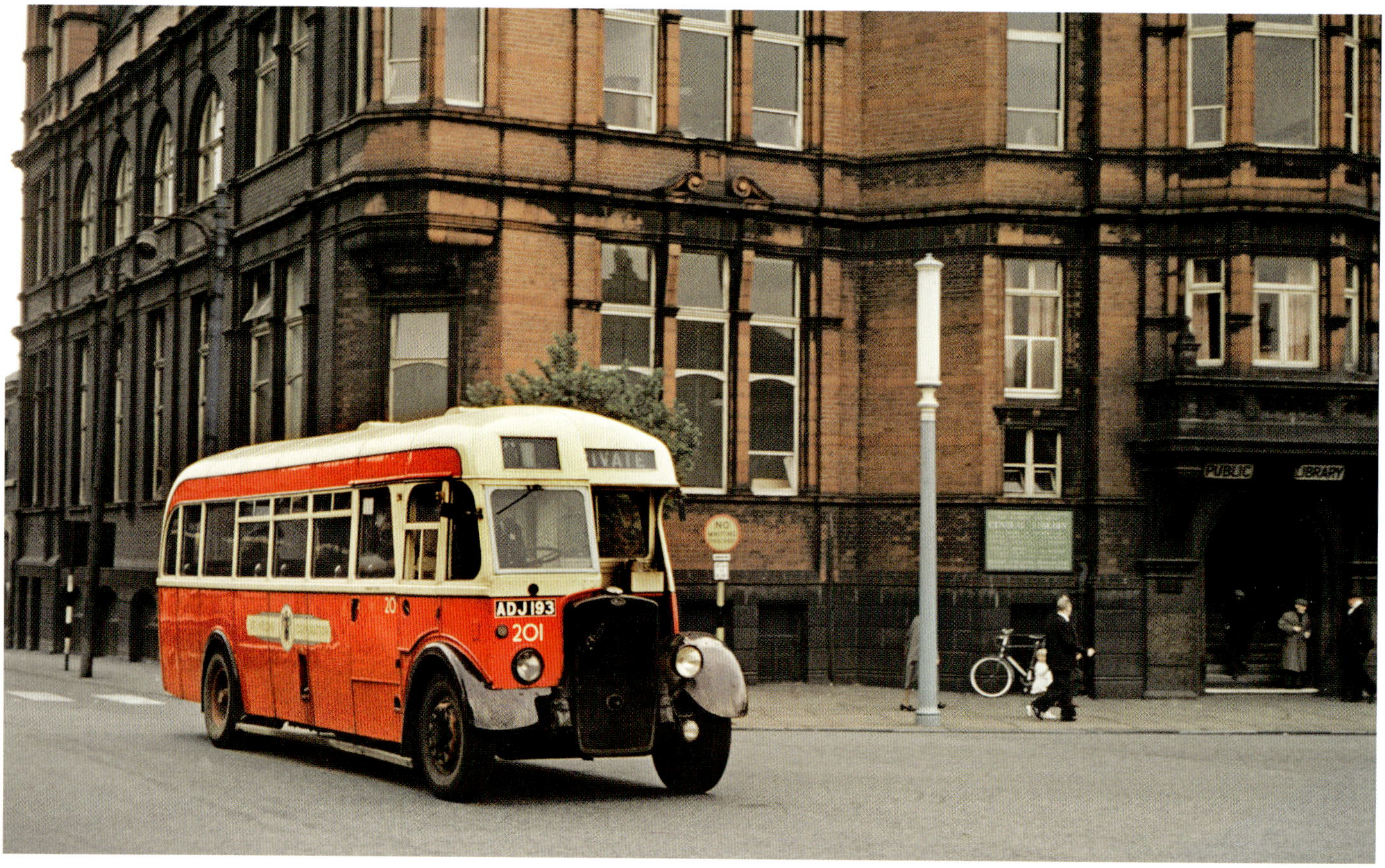
ADJ 193
201
PUBLIC
LIBRARY

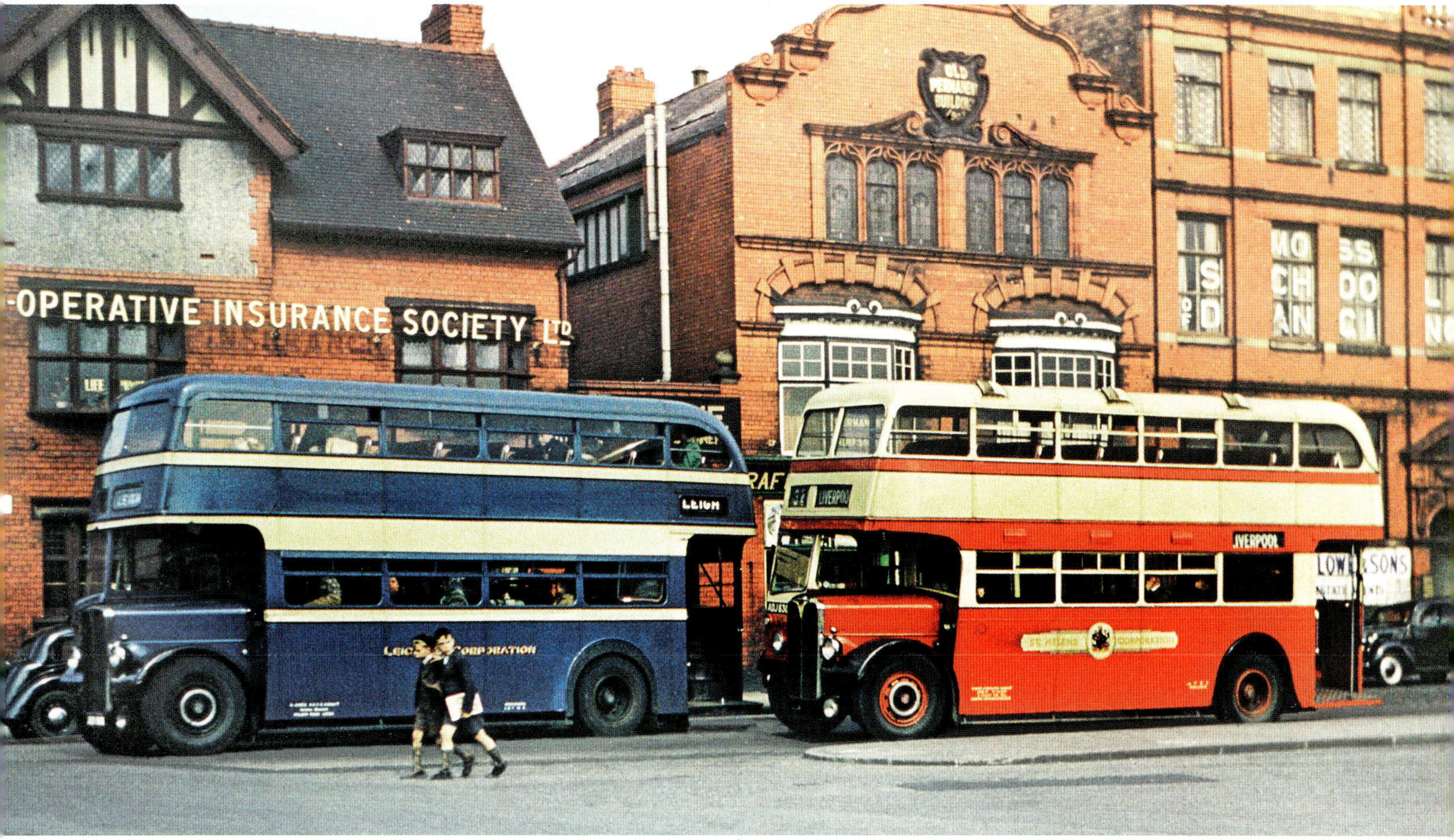

St Helens' buses could be seen in most of the surrounding towns. In May 1950 Leigh Corporation's Roberts-bodied AEC Regent III fleet number 25 is ready to leave Wigan Bus Station for its home town and the St Helens East Lancs-bodied AEC Regent III is going to Liverpool on the limited stop service jointly operated by Ribble, Lancashire United, St Helens and Wigan. New in 1949, fleet number 30 was one of eight. *C Carter*

Opposite top There were ten 'utility' Sunbeam W with Roe lowbridge bodies numbered 105-114 (later 305-314). Most were withdrawn in 1955 but 311 and 312 ran until 1957 and 1958. This picture of 311 inbound on the Prescot Circular was taken in 1957. *Jim Copland/Online Transport Archive*

Opposite bottom The low bridge at Rainford required use of single-deckers on the Warrington – St Helens – Southport service worked jointly with Ribble. Eight Roe-bodied Bristol L6A single-deckers were delivered in 1948 and numbered 201-208 in a new single-deck series, their half-canopy bodies of a style popular with Ribble before the war. Road and bridge were altered in 1952; St Helens then had no services requiring single-deckers and their usefulness declined. 201 is pictured passing the Central Library in Victoria Square on 7 July 1962; it was sold the following year. *John Ryan*

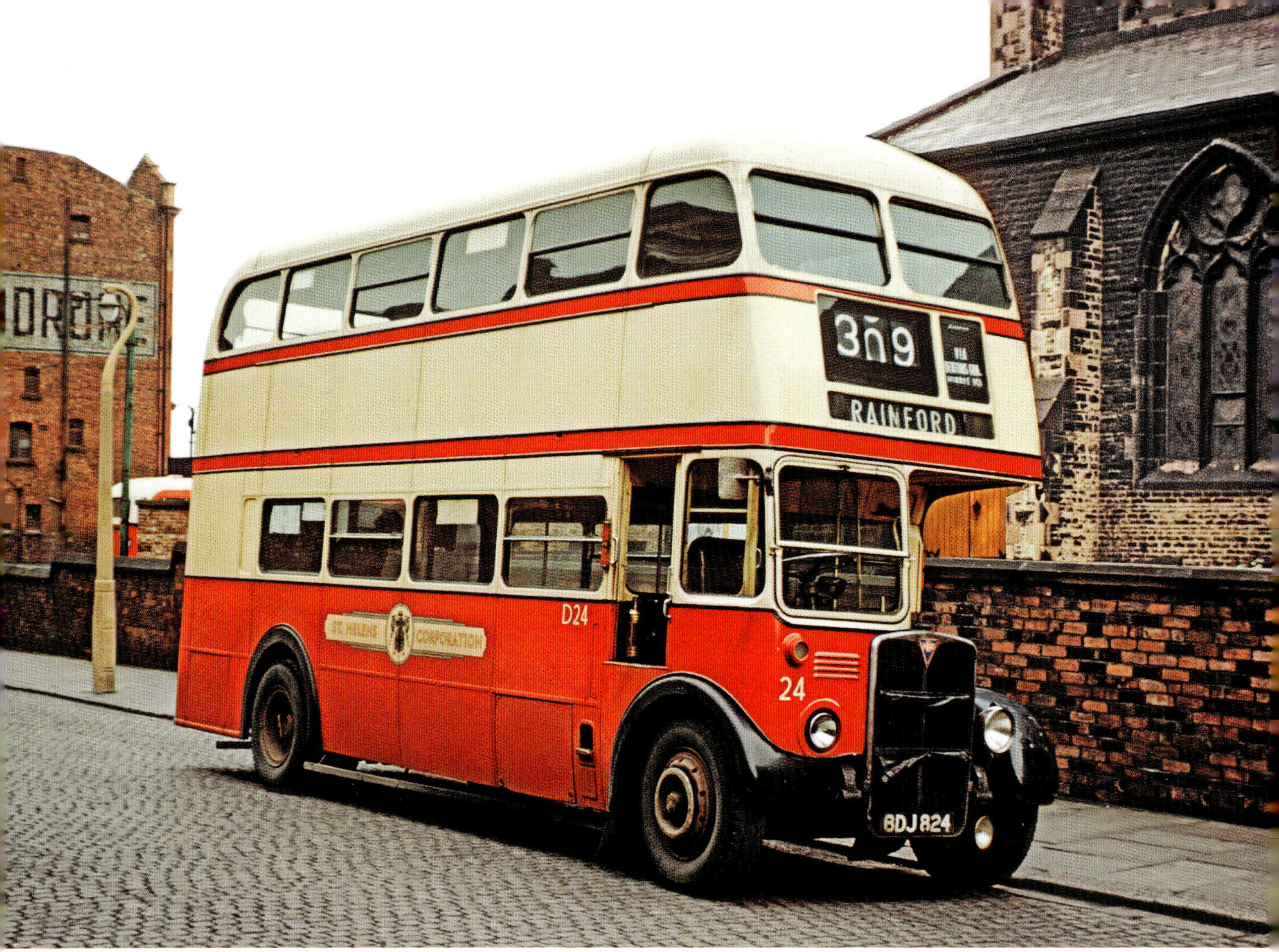

Appointed in 1949, general manager R Edgley Cox had been an engineer with London Transport. With something of a reputation for being a free thinker, he had an innovative solution to St Helens' low bridge problem. London Transport's famous RT-type had a slightly lower overall height than other highbridge buses. Careful measurement showed this was sufficient to clear the two major low bridges. Although they cost more than, say, a Leyland PD2, the transport committee agreed and late in 1949 orders were placed for 40 Park Royal-bodied AEC RTs, renewing one third of the bus fleet.

Identical in all but their exterior paintwork to the London fleet, the first fifteen (59-73) were quickly taken from the London production line and delivered in June 1950, the others (numbered 1-25) following in 1951/52. In an odd reversal of London practice, the largest of the three front indicators was used for the service number with intermediate points in the small nearside aperture. The changes appear to have been made after delivery and are perhaps further evidence of Edgley Cox's free thinking. The rear indicator was used for the service number.

Edgley Cox moved to Walsall in 1954 and his successor, accountancy-trained John Wake, introduced a system of prefix letters corresponding to each purchase of a group of new vehicles. The pictures above and opposite top show number D24 in 1961 and D64 in July 1962. In addition to the 40 RTs there was also a solitary Roe-bodied AEC Regal IV, 209. Intended for the Southport service, the rebuild of the bridge at Rainford made it unnecessary and the others that were planned were not ordered. Sold in 1962 there is no colour picture of it.

Designed for London Transport's unique in-house methods, the RTs proved expensive for St Helens to overhaul and their pre-selector transmission made them heavy on fuel. When they were due for major overhaul John Wake decided that it would be too costly and they were sold in 1960, 1961 and 1962. Maybe so but all saw further long service elsewhere – nineteen, including number 24, being sold to Hull Corporation. *John Ryan*

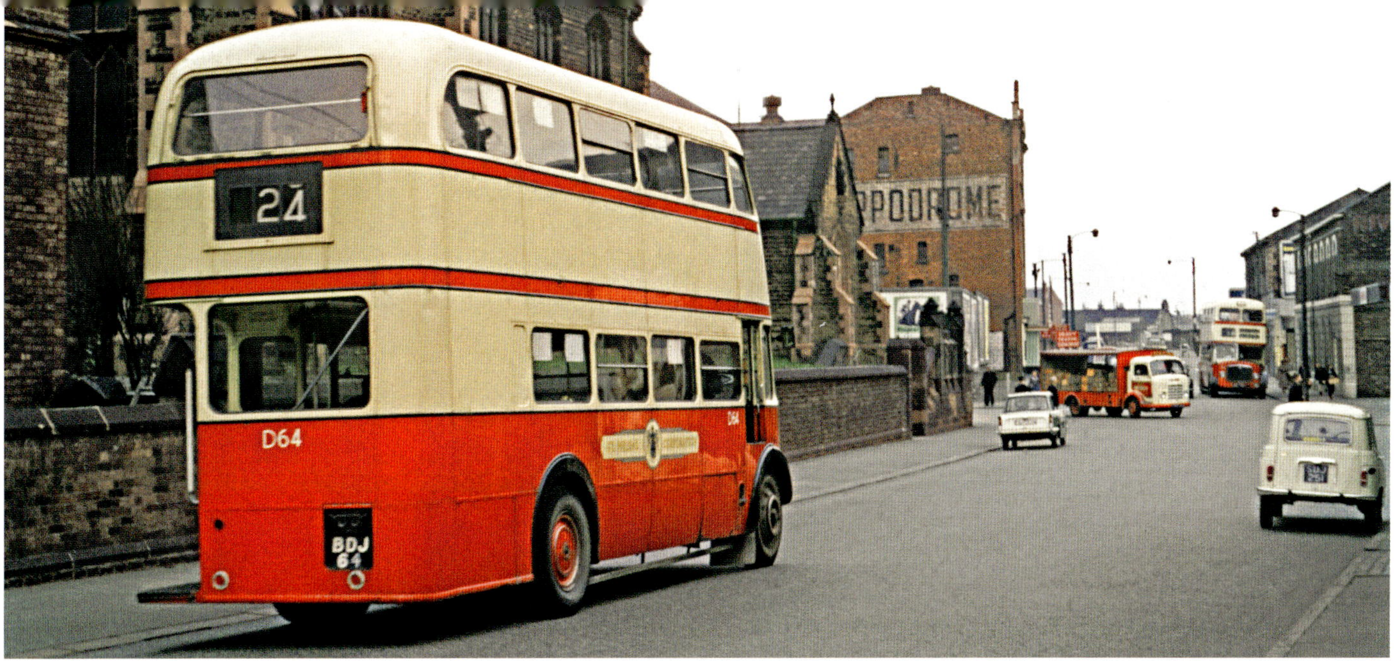

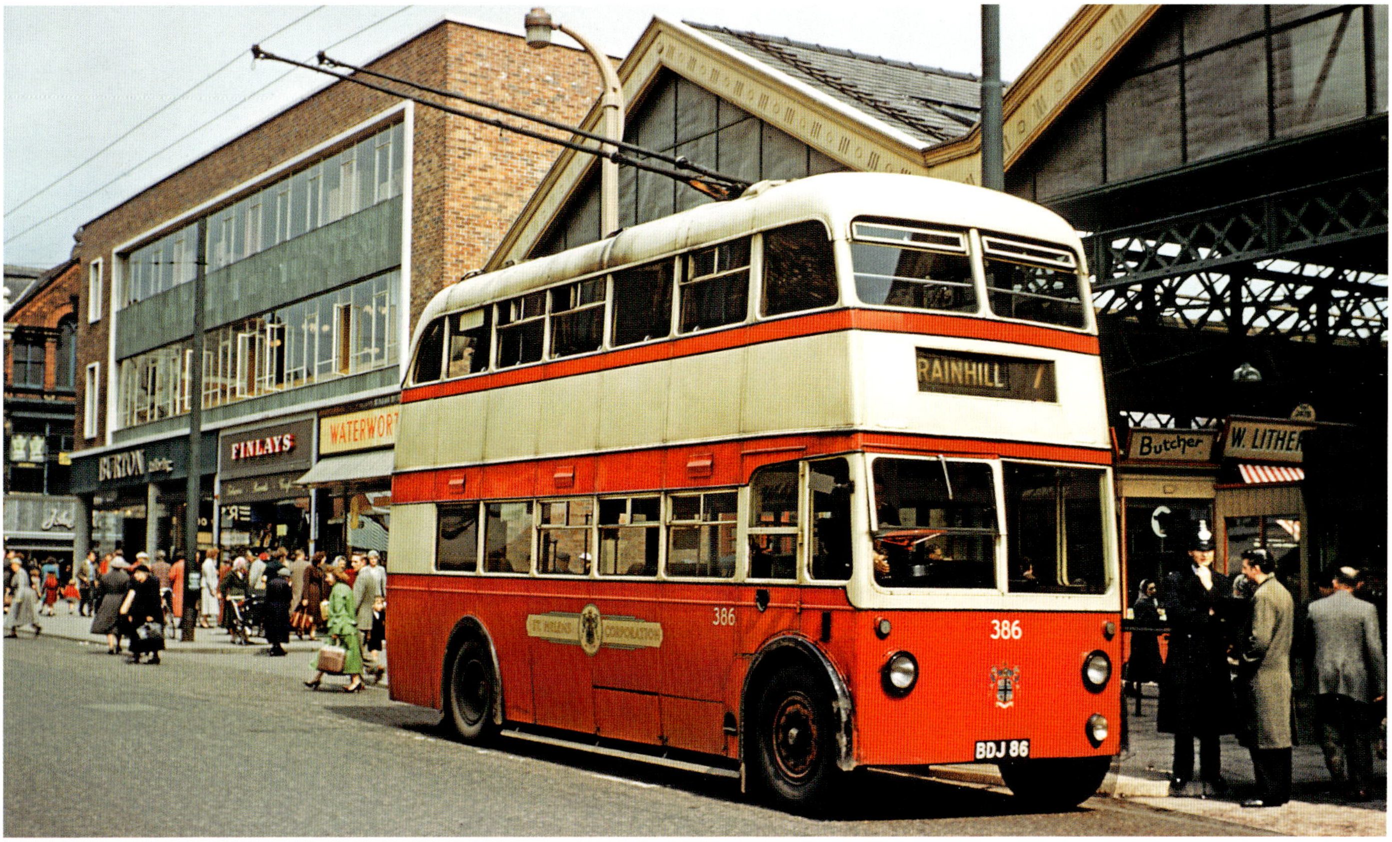

In addition to the RTs, there were 16 new trolleybuses for the busy Rainhill/Prescot circulars. The chassis order was split – 8 Sunbeam (174-181) and 8 BUT (182-189) all with East Lancs highbridge bodies. A detection system was installed on the overhead wiring at Peasley Cross to prevent them going under the low bridge there if accidentally allocated to the St Helens Junction route. The two types looked identical – by then renumbered, this is 386 loading for Prescot outside the Old Market Hall on Bridge Street in 1958. Although Edgley Cox was an advocate of trolleybuses and would extend the Walsall system, the infrastructure of the St Helens system was in a bad state and he had little choice but to recommend closing four of the routes in 1952. Successor J C Wake was not a trolleybus man and converted the rest of the system – in 1955 (Parr), 1956 (the Atherton route which was jointly operated with LUT's subsidiary SLT) and 1958 (Prescot and Rainhill). The Sunbeams were sold for further service to South Shields and the BUTs went to Bradford, where Wake would meet them again when he moved to be manager there in 1961 – and scrapped the trolleybuses. *Phil Tatt/Online Transport Archive*

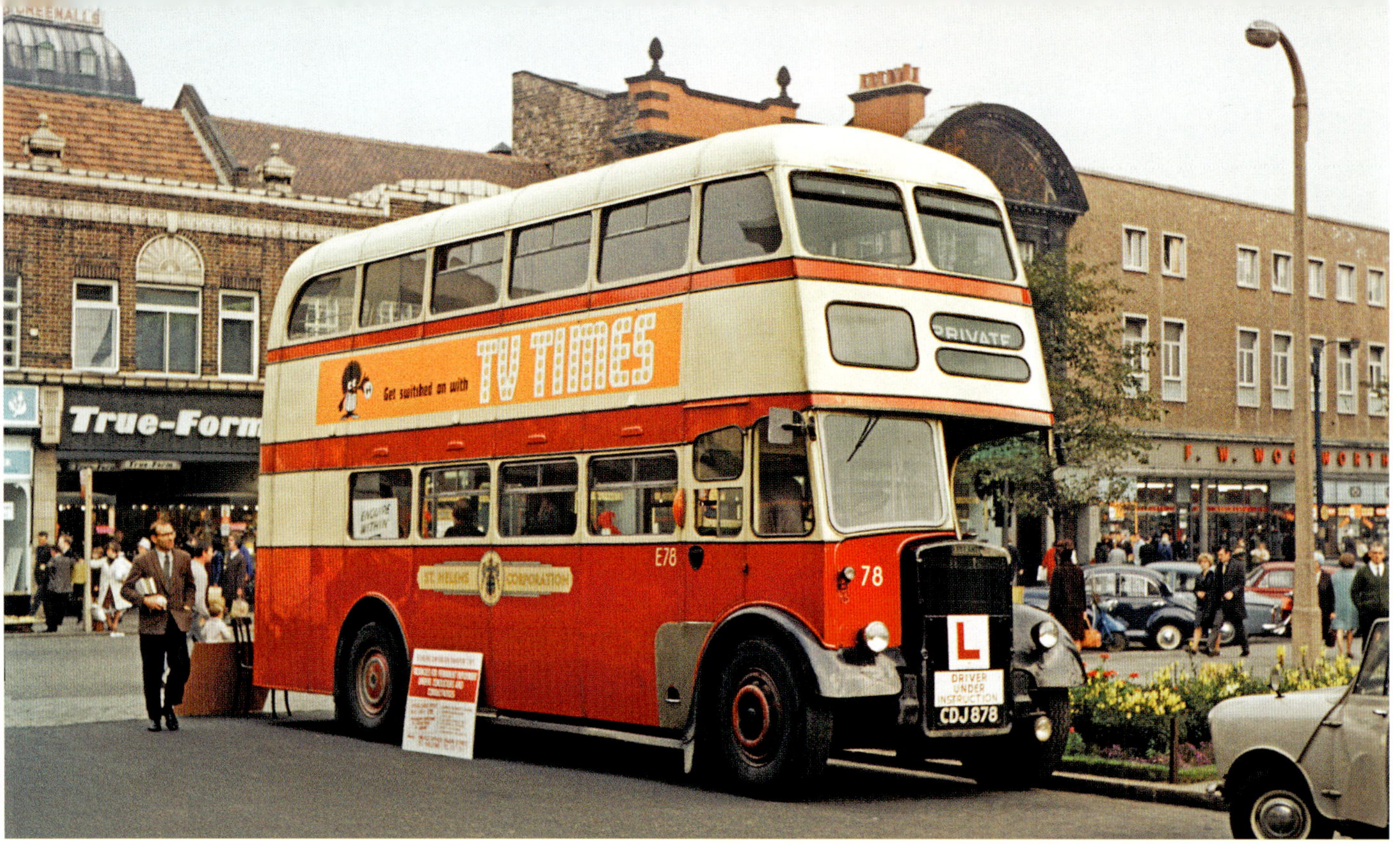

Although the RTs impressed, they were expensive and an alternative solution was devised by fairly simple modifications to Leyland's PD2 chassis. Special to St Helens, the PD2/9 had a slightly reduced overall chassis height which with a body using the RT frame produced a vehicle of the same height as an RT at less cost. Like the RTs they were also 7ft 6in wide – there was a licence width restriction in Woodlands Road on service 55 to Carr Mill. PD2/9s 74-82 were delivered in 1954; their bodies had Park Royal frames finished by D J Davies of Merthyr Tydfil – a small firm which Wake had used in his previous post at Burton upon Trent. This picture shows number 78 on a staff recruiting campaign in St Helens town centre in September 1966. *John Ryan*

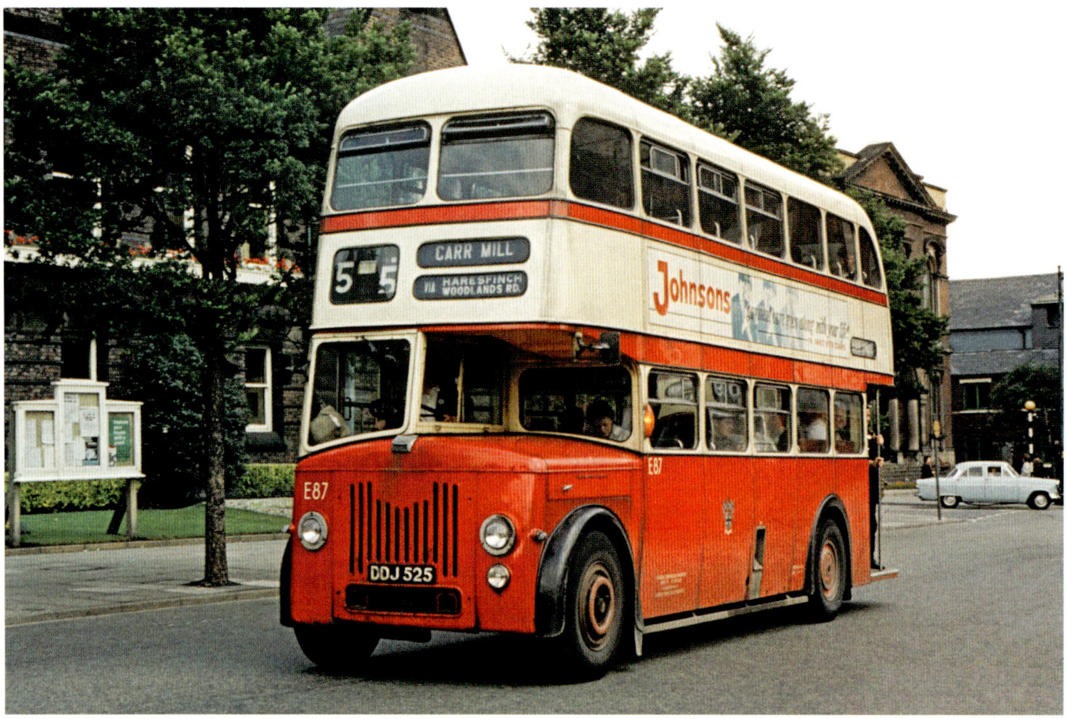

East Lancs and Weymann then offered to build a highbridge body with the necessary reduced overall height of 14ft 3½in on standard chassis and 7ft 6in-wide East Lancs-bodied Leyland PD2/22 E83-E91 were delivered in 1954. E87 is seen working the 55 service on 15 July 1967, a year before it was withdrawn by which time the livery had been simplified by removing the large fleetname with its cream ground. *John Ryan*

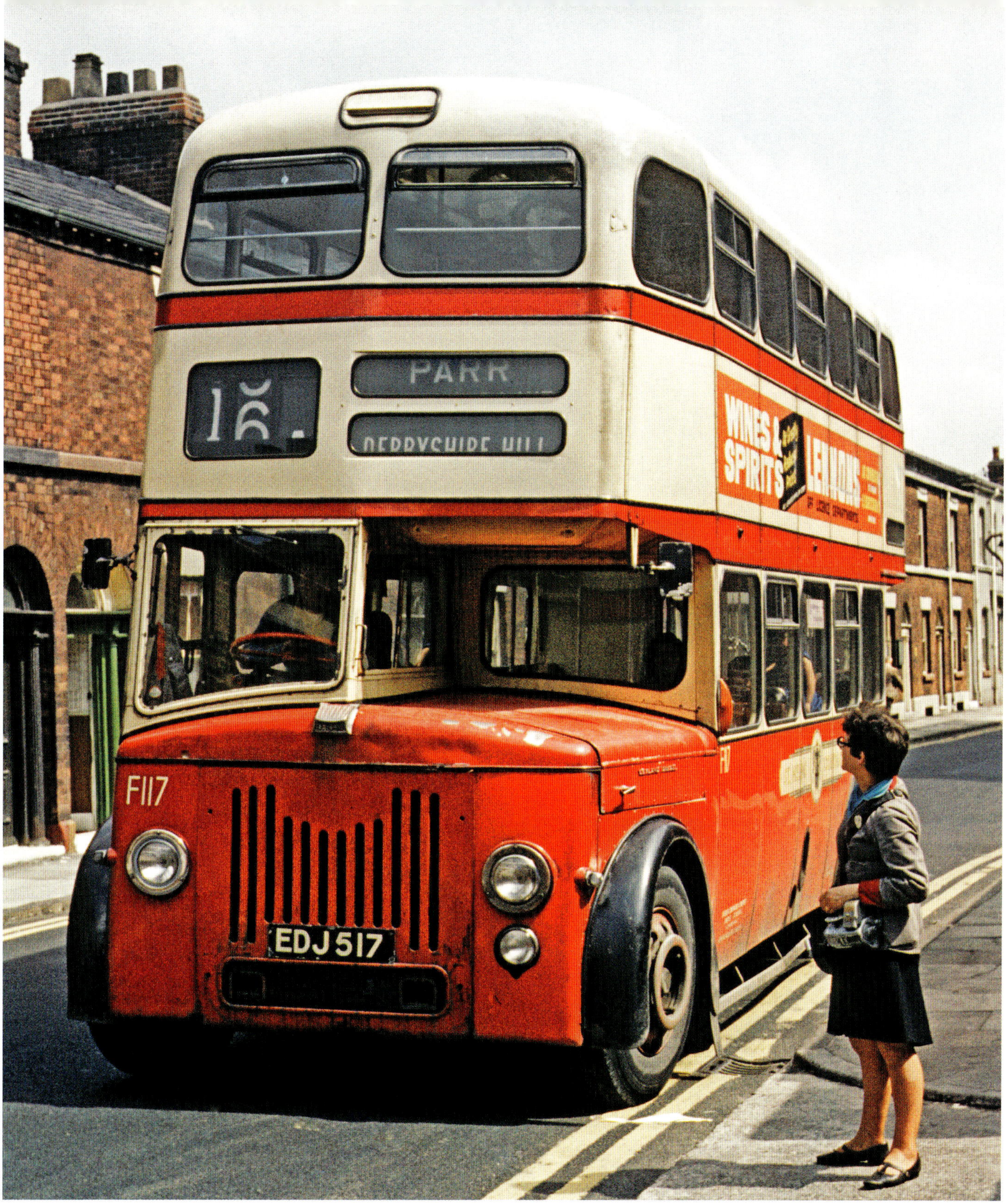

On a sunny day in July 1967 the smart young conductress checks the destination display before departure. The somewhat worn condition of Weymann-bodied Leyland PD2/20 117 was a not uncommon condition in the St Helens bus fleet. *John Ryan*

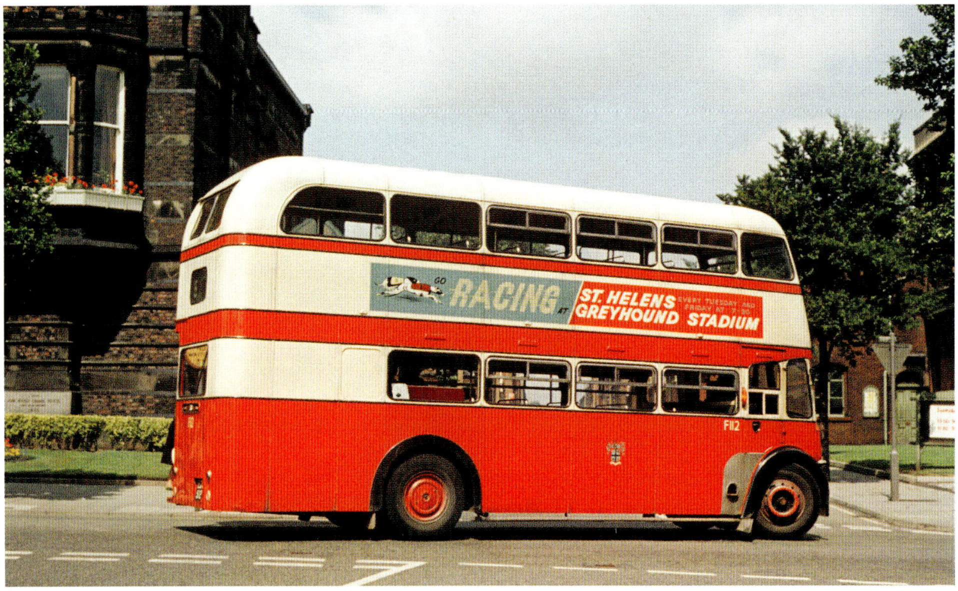

There were thirty three 8ft-wide Leyland PD2/20s – F101-109 (1955) and G121-127 (1956/57) had East Lancs bodies and G128-133 (1956) were Weymann. F110-120 were to have had Davies bodies on Park Royal frames but only 112 was part completed when D J Davies died intestate – his firm was not a limited company. 112 and the chassis of 110/11/13-17 were at his works and were impounded by the administrators. It was a year before matters were resolved and they could be extracted, whereupon the chassis of 110/11/13-17 were speedily sent to Weymann for bodying. The chassis for G118-120 had not yet been delivered and were added to the East Lancs batch. Taken from an unusual angle, this July 1967 picture of a smartly turned out F112 nicely shows the Park Royal lines of the Davies body. *John Ryan*

The next 38 vehicles were AEC Regent V. Numbers H134-139, J140-155 (1957/58) and K164-171 (1959) had Weymann bodies and J156-163 (1958) East Lancs. Waiting at the Old Market Hall terminus on what used to be the trolleybus service 8 to Rainhill, 159 was still carrying its letter prefix in June 1968, although the system had been stopped in January. The square-shaped logo on the front upper-deck side panel marked the celebration of St Helens' centenary as a municipal borough. *Roy Marshall*

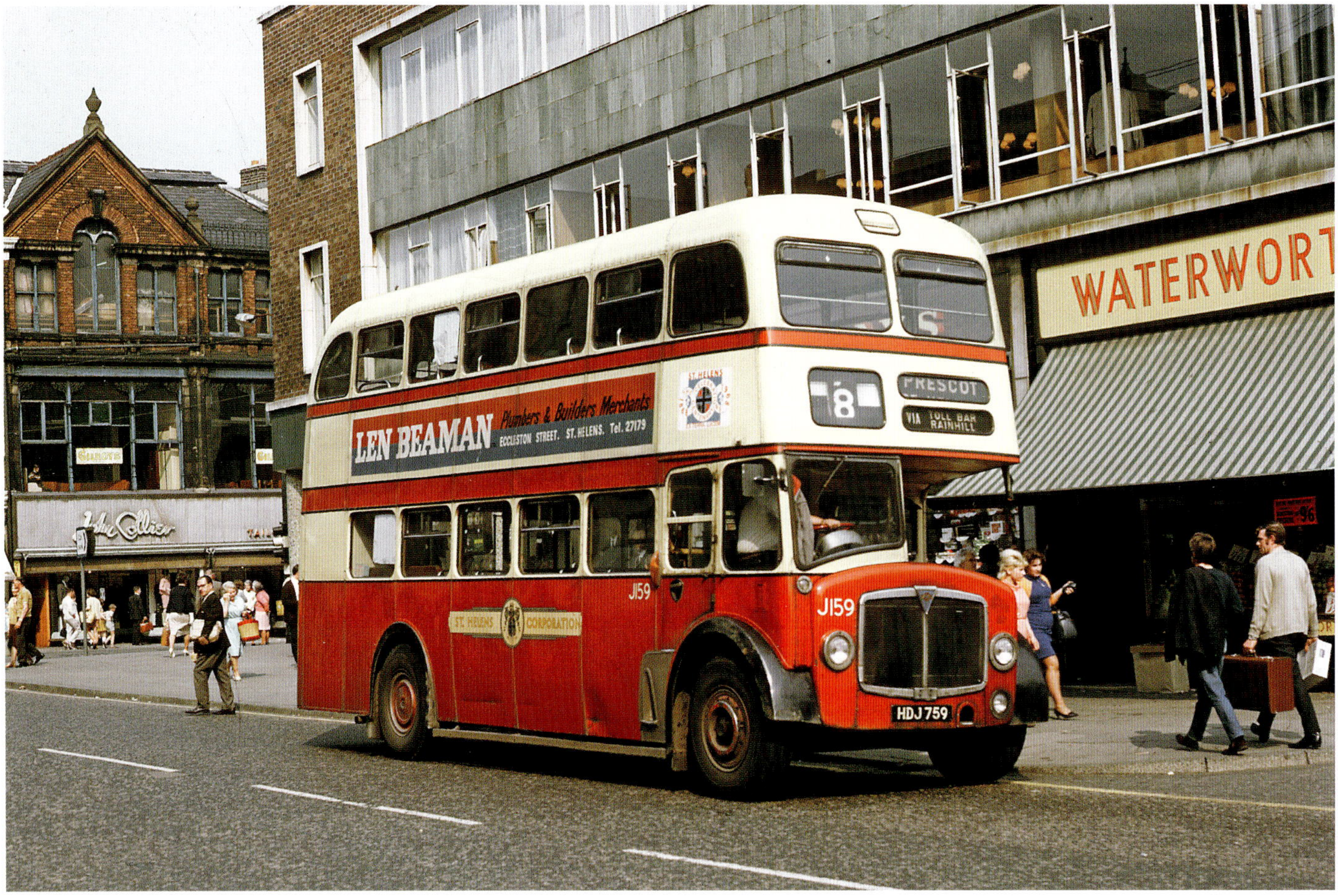

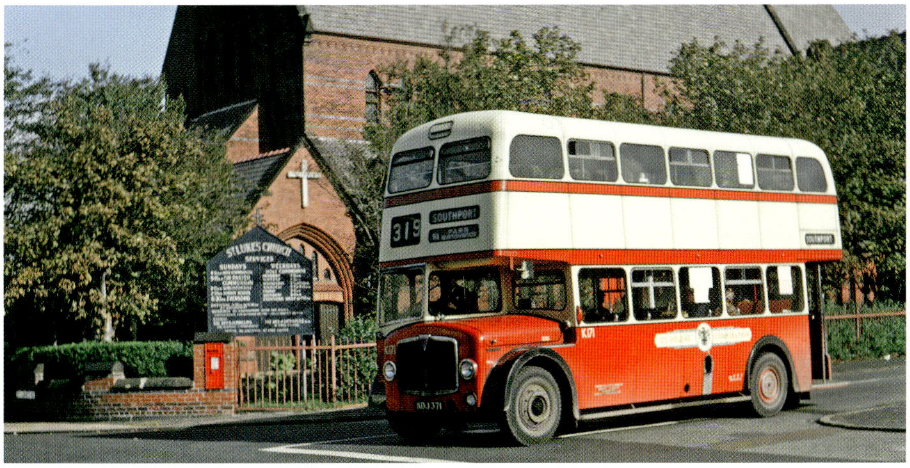

A long way from home and a quarter of a mile from the end of its 32-mile journey on the 319 from Warrington via St Helens, Rainford and Ormskirk, Weymann-bodied AEC Regent V K171 passes St Luke's Church, at the corner of Hawkshead Street and St Luke's Road, Southport in October 1962. St Helens was not the only municipality which worked into Southport. Bolton Corporation had a share in the similarly long 122 Bolton – Chorley – Southport service which it worked jointly with Ribble. *Roy Marshall*

St Helens had only one 30ft-long double-decker. Delivered in 1959, K199 was an AEC Regent V with a forward-entrance East Lancs body. It was planned also to buy a 'highbridge' Leyland Atlantean but this was 2.5 inches in excess of the maximum safe height of 14ft 3.5in at Rainford bridge and a lowbridge Atlantean with its awkward half highbridge, half lowbridge upper-deck seating was rejected. Unsurprisingly, K199 provoked union opposition and was at first confined to routes 7/8 and 15/16. Thereafter it was used on the Southport 309/319 service on which it would sometimes run out of fuel on its last journey back to St Helens due to its small fuel tank. Alex Barlow was appointed general manager in 1961 and favoured single-deckers, considering it unwise to reduce service frequencies by operating higher capacity vehicles at less frequent intervals. August 1967 *Roy Marshall*

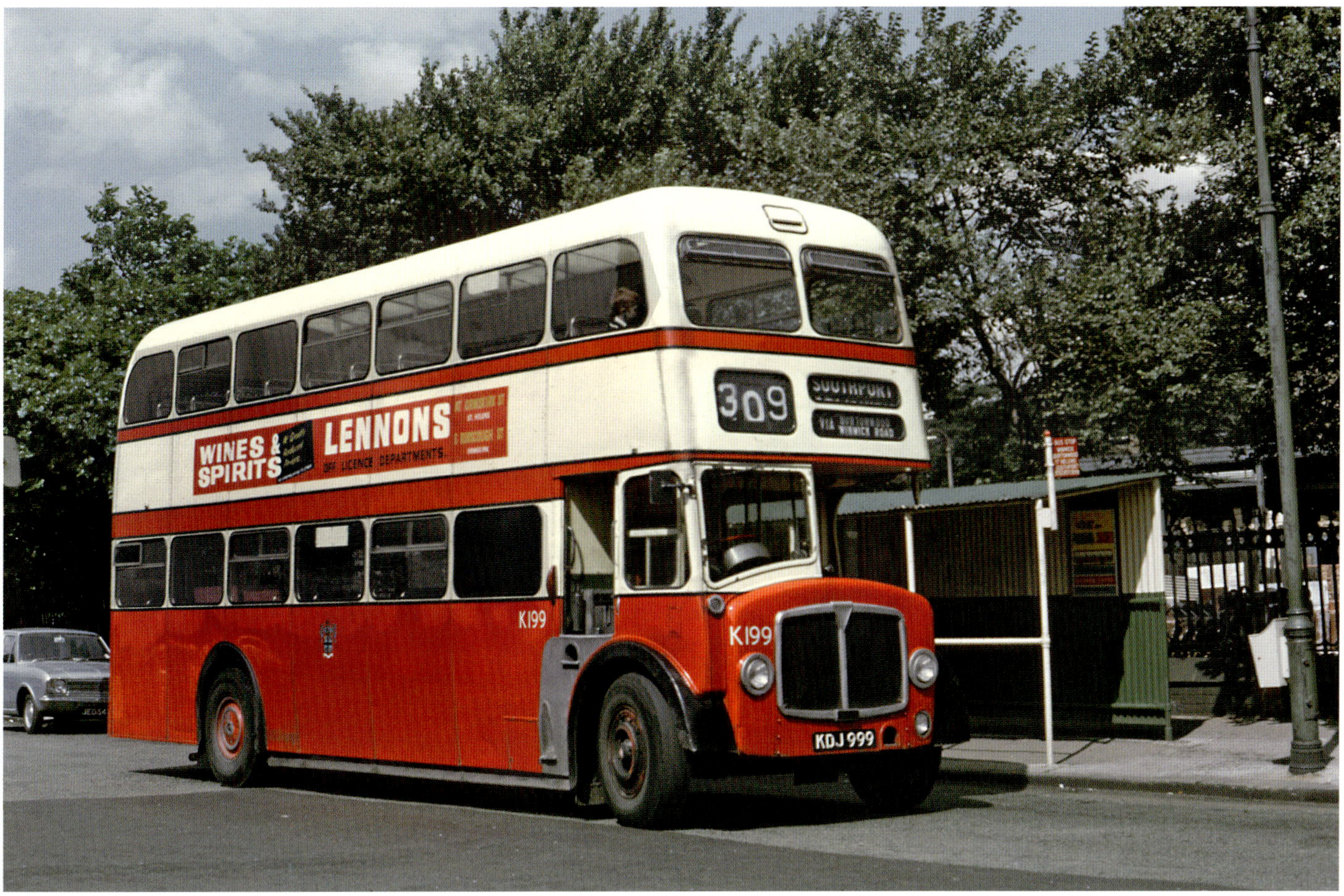

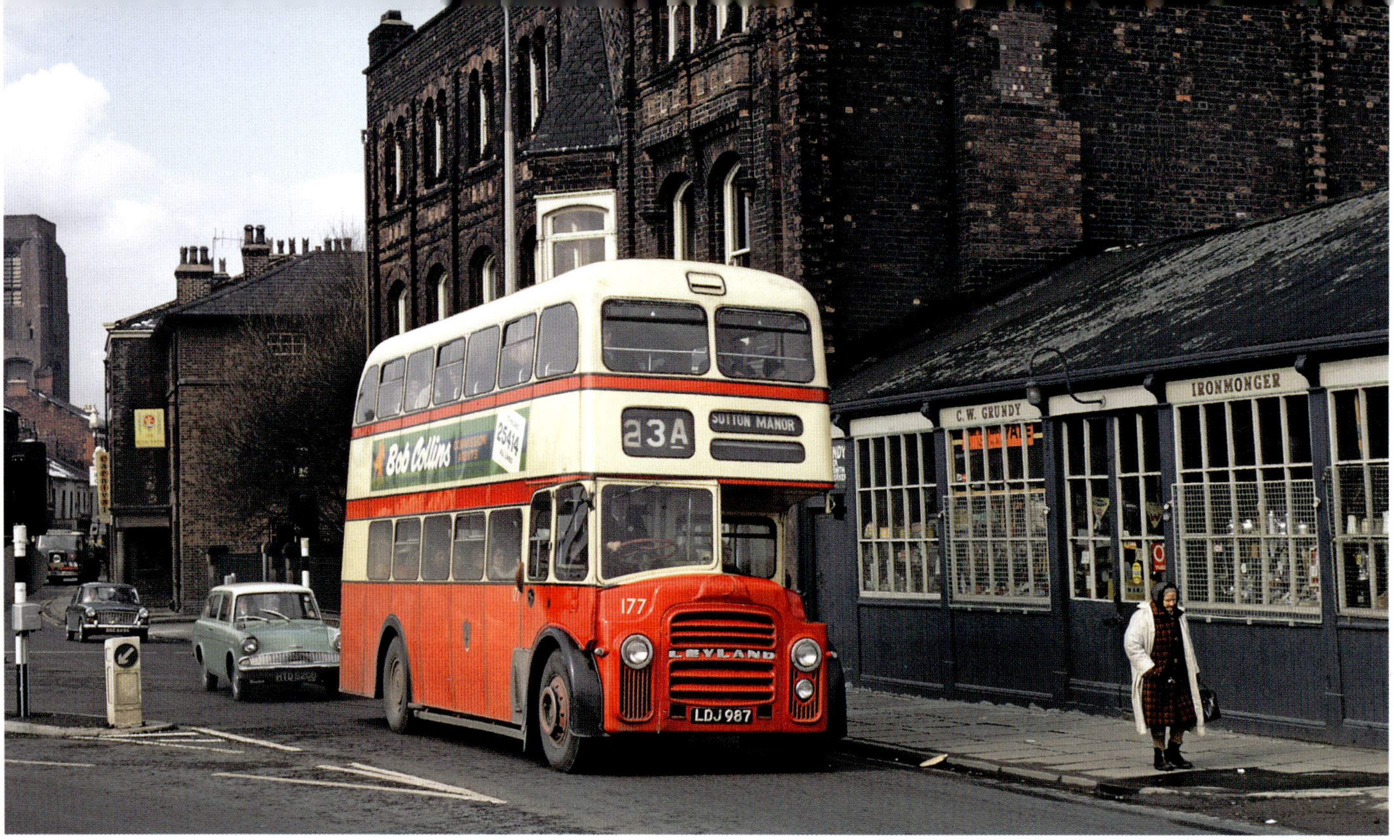

There had been many grumbles about Leyland's bulky bonnet and radiator cowl assembly, not least from John Wake who decided to make Leyland produce something cheaper, smaller, easier to repair and which gave the driver a better view of the nearside kerb. Made from moulded glass-reinforced plastics, the result was known as the 'St Helens front'. Leyland added an A to the model number and PD2A/30 K172-179, new in 1960, were the first, 172-175 with Weymann bodies and 176-179 with East Lancs. Outbound for Sutton Manor, 177 passes Grundy's fine ironmonger's shop in Church Street in April 1970. *Geoffrey Morant*

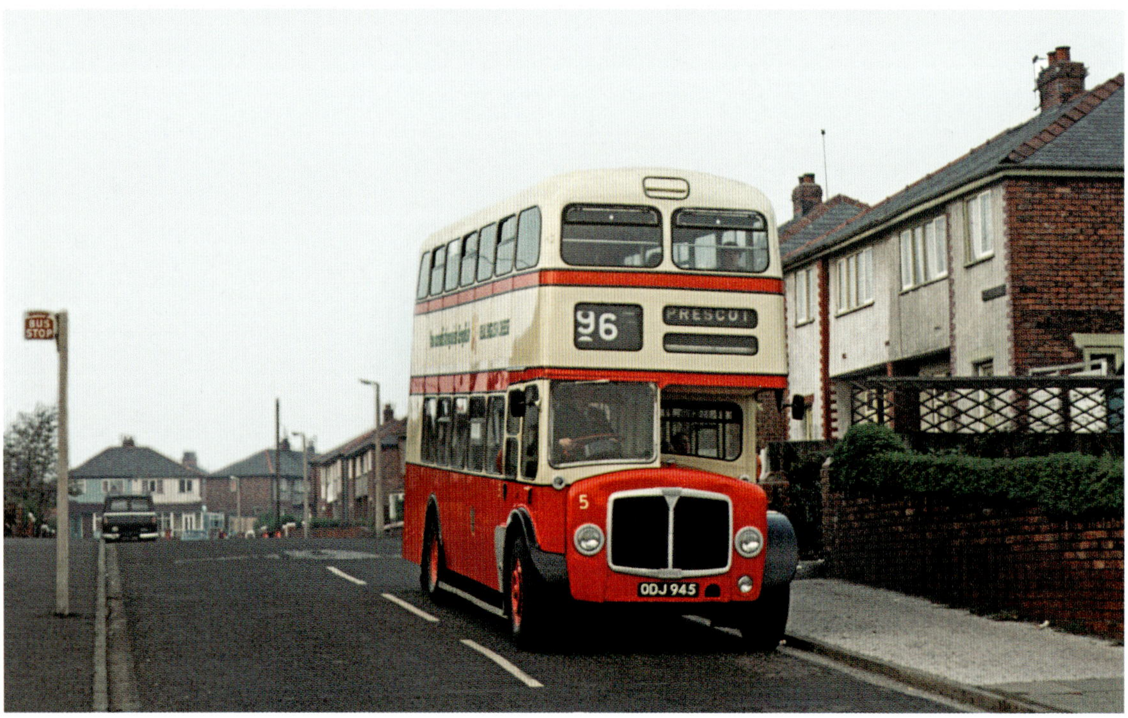

Fleet numbering reverted to 1 in 1961 and until 1967 double-deck orders were split between Leyland and AEC, the AECs and some of the Leylands having Metro Cammell bodies, the rest of the Leylands were East Lancs. Photographed in Beechwood Close, Prescot on route 96, newly delivered number 5 was one of 15 Regent V (L1-7, L33-40) which entered service in 1961/62. *Peter Jackson*

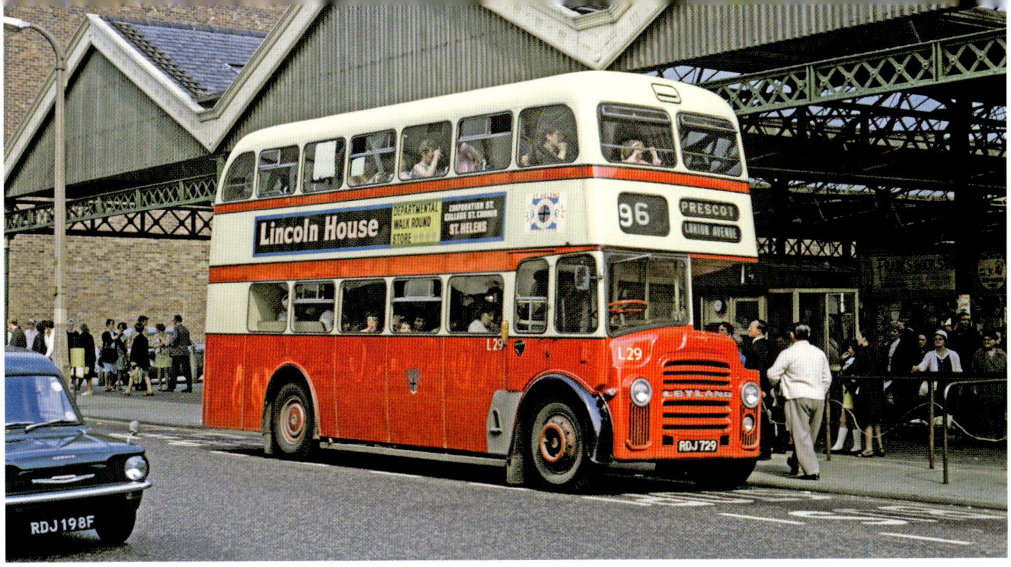

Numbers L8-12 and L26-32 were East Lancs-bodied Leyland PD2A/30. Although it is not yet departure time from the stand outside the market, East Lancs-bodied 29 already has a full load on the 96. The flush-mounted windows which St Helens specified for its East Lancs bodies on and after 176 and 199 gave them something of an Orion-style look. The first version of the new front had old fashioned 'bullet' sidelights set outboard, which required an odd looking cut off to the bodywork. June 1968 *Roy Marshall*

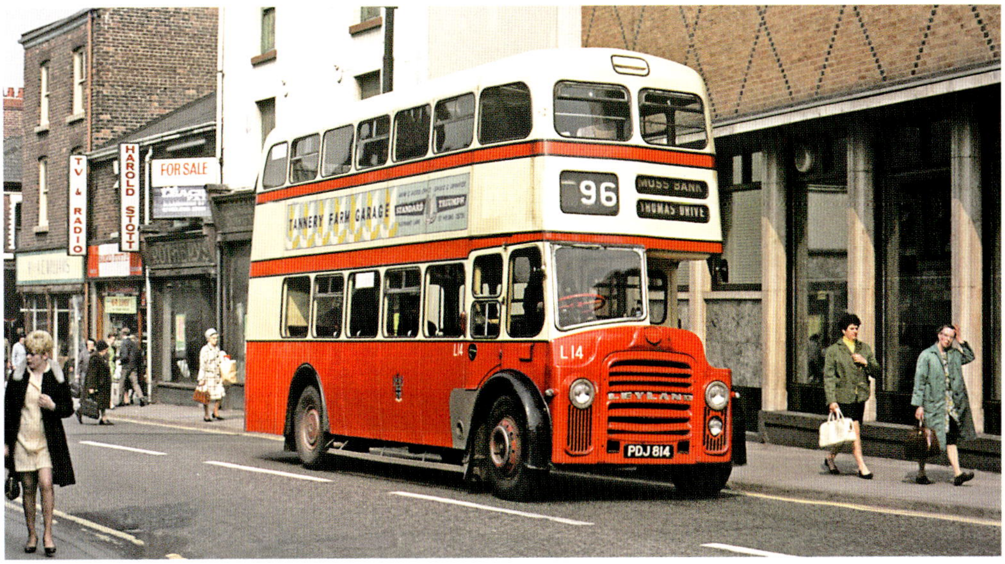

Metro Cammell's solution to the sidelight problem was to fit the 8ft body with the 7ft 6in-wide front end – a mix that had regularly been used on Orions that had the previous Leyland cowl. The result looked tall and gaunt. L13-L25 had this body. *David Powell*

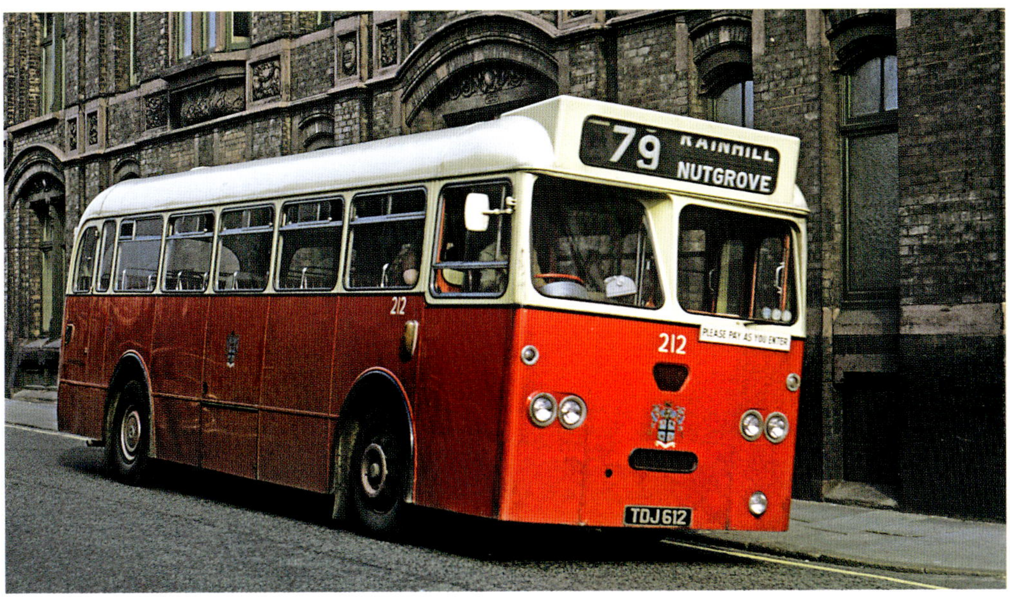

Three AEC Reliances with bodies by Marshall of Cambridge were delivered in 1963. Their fleet numbers, 210-212, followed on from the previous single-deckers. At first often used on private hire work, in 1967 they were converted for one-person operation. This picture, taken on 1 June 1968, shows 212 on service 79 to Rainhill Stoops which was jointly operated with Crosville. *Roy Marshall*

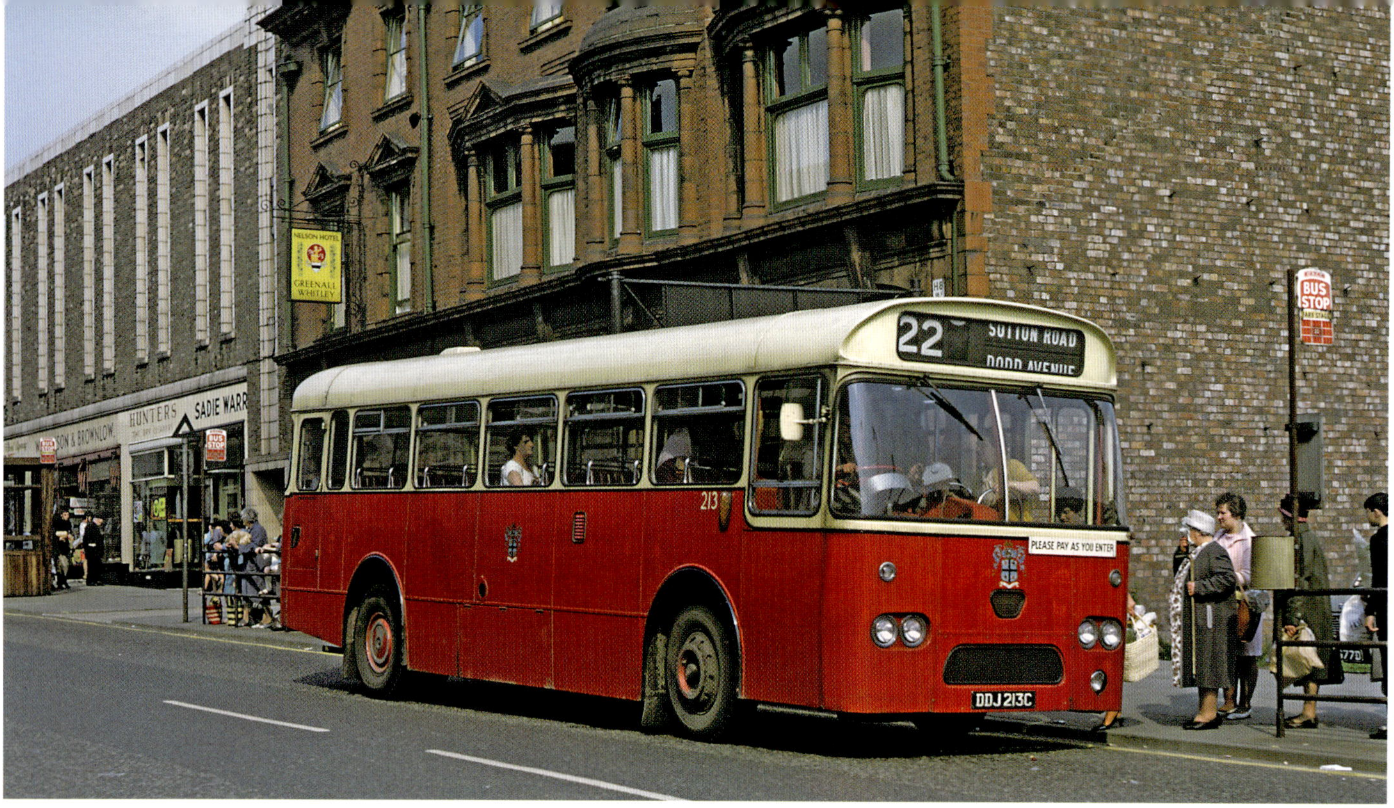

Two more Marshall-bodied AEC Reliances (213-214) came in 1965, this time with more modern looking BET-style bodies. New with front entrances, late in 1966 they were converted for one-person operation, a central exit door being added to speed loading and unloading. This is 213 outside the Nelson Hotel in Bridge Street. June 1968 *Roy Marshall*

The Reliances were followed by eighteen more Leyland PD2s (41-58), nine in 1965 and a similar number in 1967. As previously, eleven had East Lancs bodies and the others MCW (successor to Weymann) – both types looked much the same as the previous ones. The St Helens front was updated to have the sidelights inset into the cowl. *Geoffrey Morant*

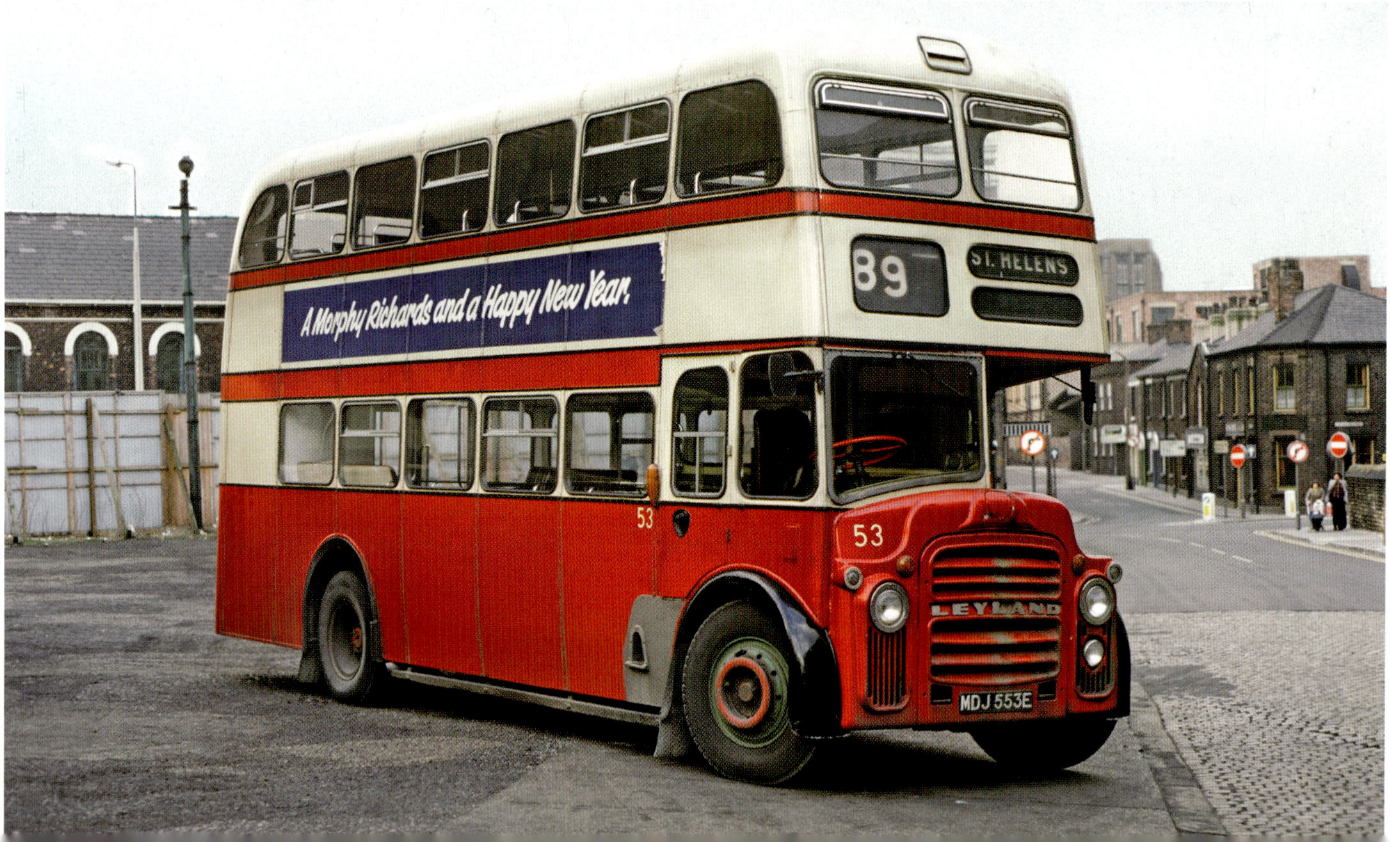

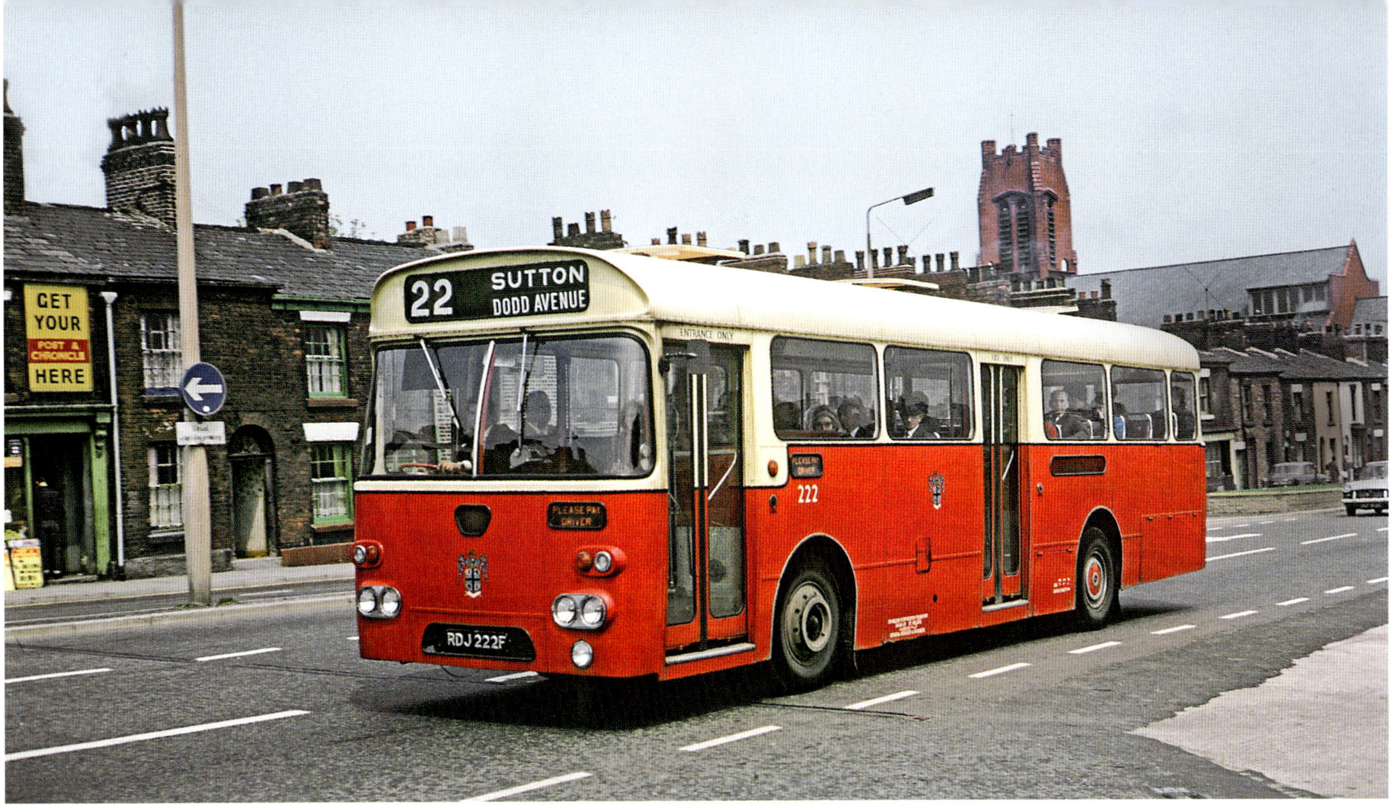

Large capacity one-person-operated single-deckers were widely adopted in south west Lancashire – at Liverpool, Southport, Warrington and Widnes. St Helens bought the type exclusively from 1968 and when it was merged into the PTE in 1974, St Helens had a fleet of 63 with more on order. Numbered 215-277 they all were AEC Swifts with Marshall dual-entrance bodies seating 44 with 20 standees. *Reg Wilson/Online Transport Archive*

Lancashire United also bought a substantial number of high capacity single-deckers over the same period but with a variety of makes of body and chassis. Amongst them were three Alexander-bodied AEC Swifts, new in 1968. Odd men out in the LUT fleet, in a mutually useful deal, they were sold to St Helens in 1973, retaining their LUT fleet numbers 291-293 – the gap from 277 would have been filled by more Marshall-bodied Swifts, some of which were on order but delivered to the PTE. In this picture, taken in February 1974, 291 with a good load on board negotiates the roundabout at the bottom of Bridge Street with four Marshall-bodied Swifts in the background. *Roy Marshall*

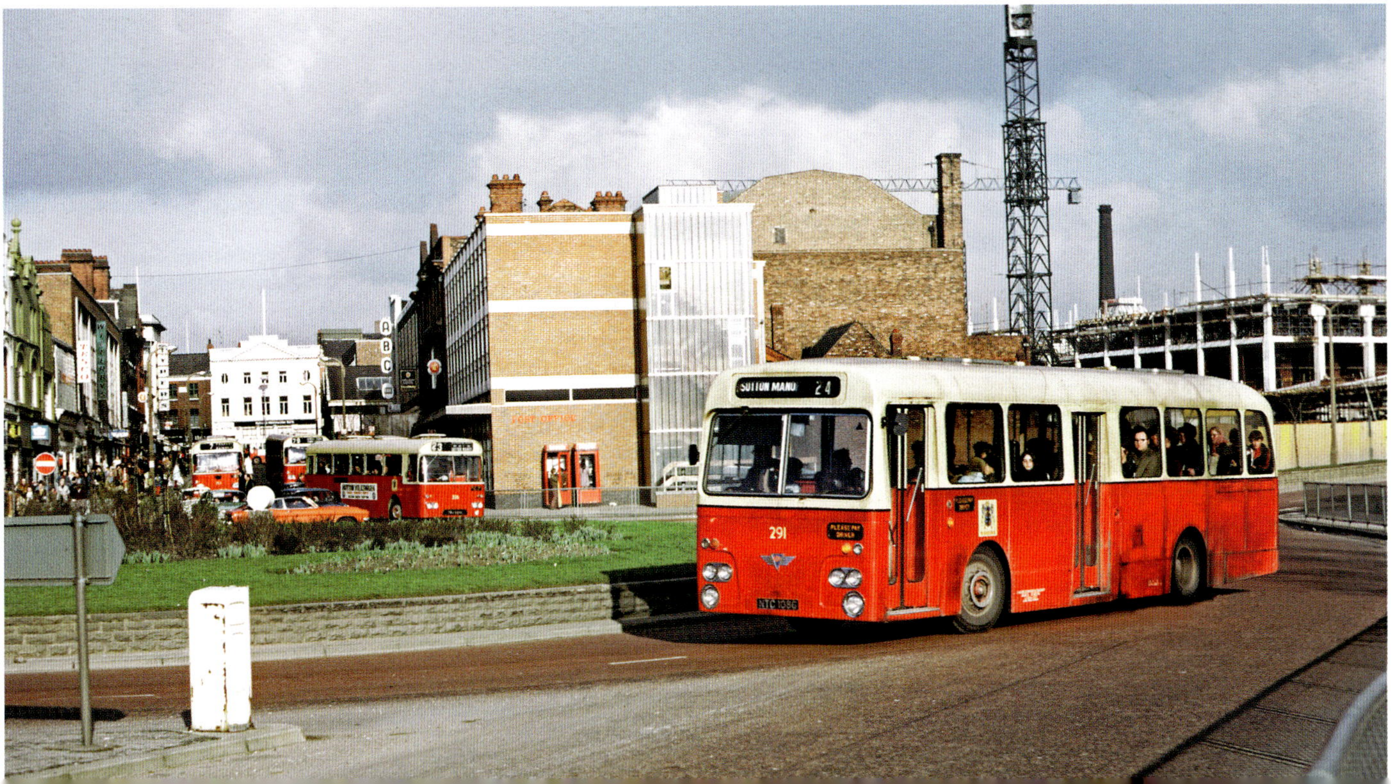

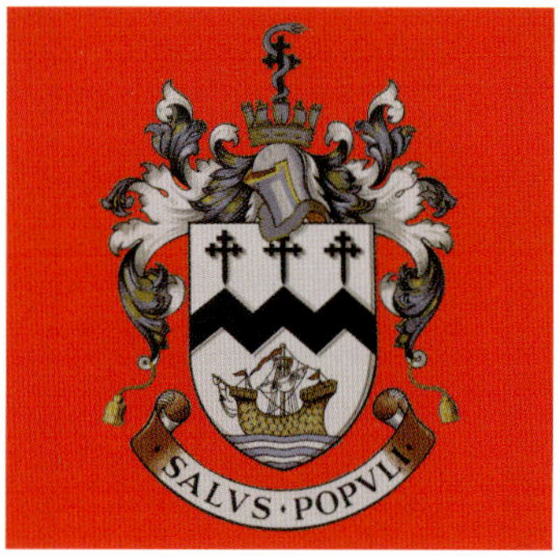

Southport

With its miles of sandy beaches, pier, large marine lake, prestigious golf links and botanic gardens Southport was and is still a popular seaside venue but its dignified affluence began with the railways when it became a popular place to live for mill owners, ship owners and the like from Liverpool, to which there was a frequent electric train service, and Manchester, which was connected by fast trains. Whereas Blackpool had its illuminations; Southport had the International Flower Show and took its turn in hosting world famous international golf tournaments.

Such was the civic pride that only the corporation's immaculate buses (there was never any question of them carrying external advertisements) were allowed on Lord Street, the town's principal road. Lord Street was an elegant tree-lined boulevard with flower gardens, monuments, civic buildings, high quality shops with glass and cast iron verandas, restaurants and cafés. Ribble's buses and the many coaches that brought visitors to the town had to use the sea front, one block away, and other less visible streets.

The transport undertaking's early buses were built locally by the Vulcan Motor and Engineering Company based in the town but from 1932 the fleet was principally Leyland. However, it did have some of the most unusual buses in the country – a fleet of ex-military Bedford QL trucks with open top bodies used on a unique off-road 'Shore Service' along Southport's miles of golden sands.

Southport's bus operations were focused on providing excellent services within the borough boundary; there was no need for any joint operation. For some 25 years the undertaking was managed by Jackson Hoggard who was the youngest general manager in England when he was appointed in 1947. The comprehensive maintenance and engineering facilities at the Canning Road depot, Blowick, kept the fleet of some 70 buses in exceptional condition.

Southport's buses had style and it seemed a shame that due to the creation of the County of Merseyside in April 1974, it had to be taken over by the PTE which was, in truth, focused miles away.

At the centre of Lord Street is The Monument war memorial and garden, in front of which, in this picture, is open-top Leyland PD2 number 88. In the background is a small section of Lord Street's shops with their glass and cast iron colonnades. Shortly after this picture was taken, the bus was shipped to a museum in the United States. April 1964 *Roy Marshall*

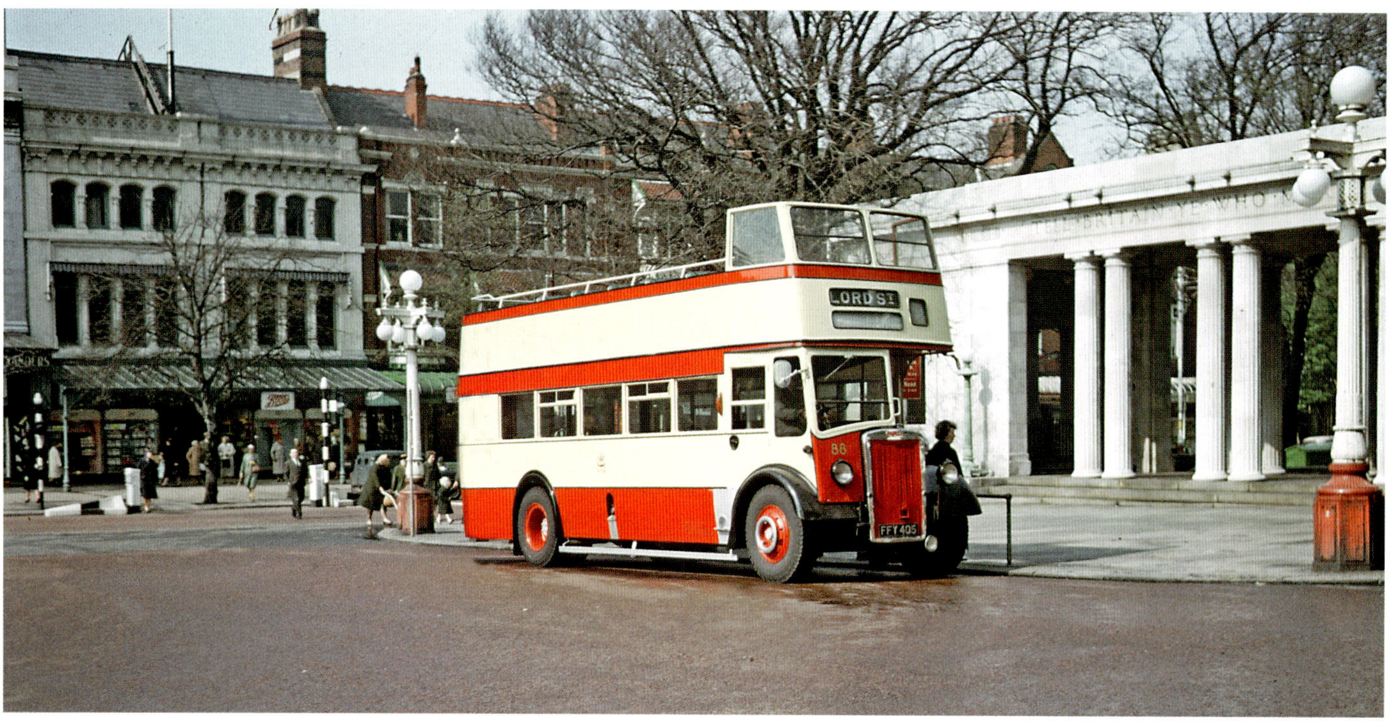

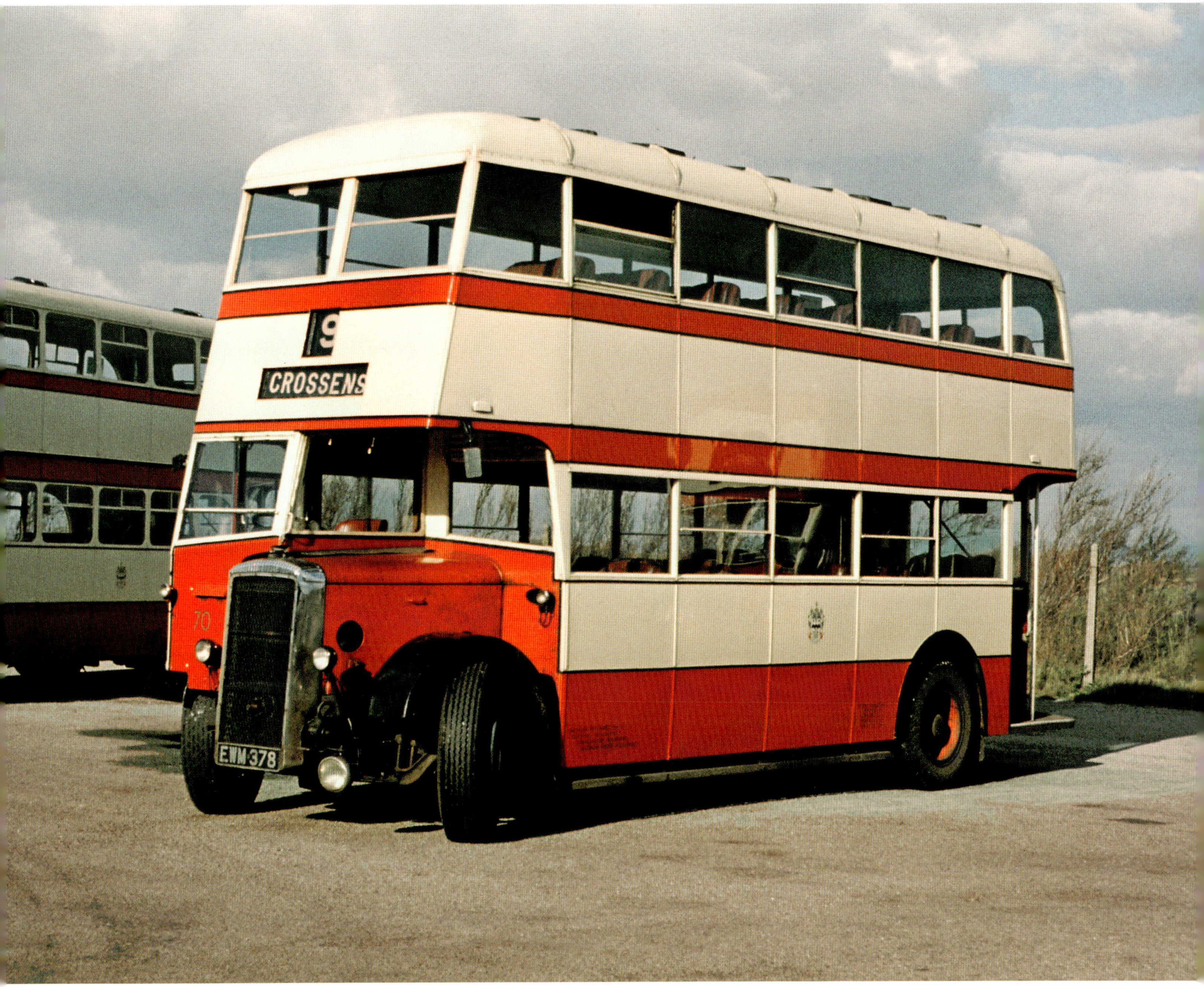

It was once said that there were more Daimler car owners in Southport than in any other town in the country; that Southport's wartime vehicle allocation was Daimlers rather than Guys was therefore somehow appropriate. Delivered in 1944/45/46 and numbered 56-83, there were 25 CWA6s, (56-65, 69-83) the first four with Northern Counties bodies, the remainder Duple and three CWD6s (66-68) also bodied by Duple. This picture is of Duple-bodied CWA6 70 on the Hesketh Park Aerodrome depot forecourt in September 1957. This second depot, used from 1947 until 1963, was in the hangars which also housed aircraft used on short pleasure flights from the beach. *Dennis Kerrison*

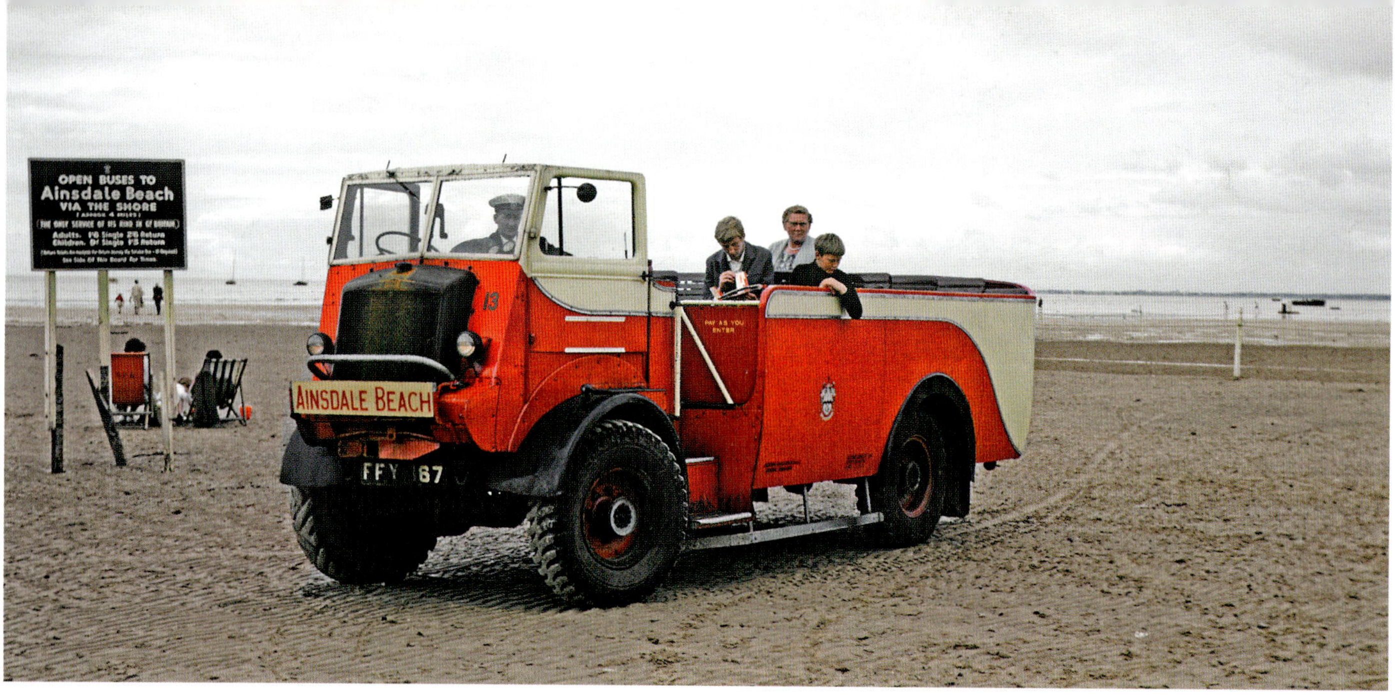

Southport's huge beach is long, wide and flat with a very long tidal reach. For many years private cars were allowed on the sands and many a youngster had his or her first drive there, for it was not a public highway. Years back, a sea-front service along the promenade was the corporation's first service and a bus service running along the beach had been planned in 1939 before war intervened. The war over, to operate these services general manager F E Cook bought twelve war surplus petrol-engined Bedford QL 4x4 military truck chassis/cabs in 1946 which he had fitted with 23-seater open bodies, the first built by the transport department and the others by local firm Rimmer, Harrison and Sutherland. Some worked the Shore (beach) Service which between 1947 and 1953 was the operational responsibility of the town's Publicity and Attractions Committee. Not carrying passengers on public roads, they did not need PSV licences; those working the promenade service and town tours (the responsibility of the transport department) did. The QLs were numbered 1-4, new in 1946, and 11-18 new in 1947. In 1964, number 13 waits to leave Ainsdale for its four-mile trip across the sands to The Pier and Marine Drive. The board which marked the terminus noted that it was 'The only service of its kind in Great Britain' and also warned there were liable to be cancellations and delays due to the tides. With a maximum permitted speed of 10mph and a journey time of 20 minutes, the trip was well worth the single fare of 1s 6d (2s 6d return) and it could exciting when the four-wheel drive QLs ploughed through sea water up to 18 inches deep. Numbers 13, 14, 17 and 18 were the last to be withdrawn, in 1966. *Harry Luff/Online Transport Archive*

The 'Circular Tour' was advertised to run every few minutes, the board listed the route: Lord Street – Hesketh Park – Promenade – Monument. This is number 17, turned out specially out of season in September 1957 for an Omnibus Society visit. *Dennis Kerrison*

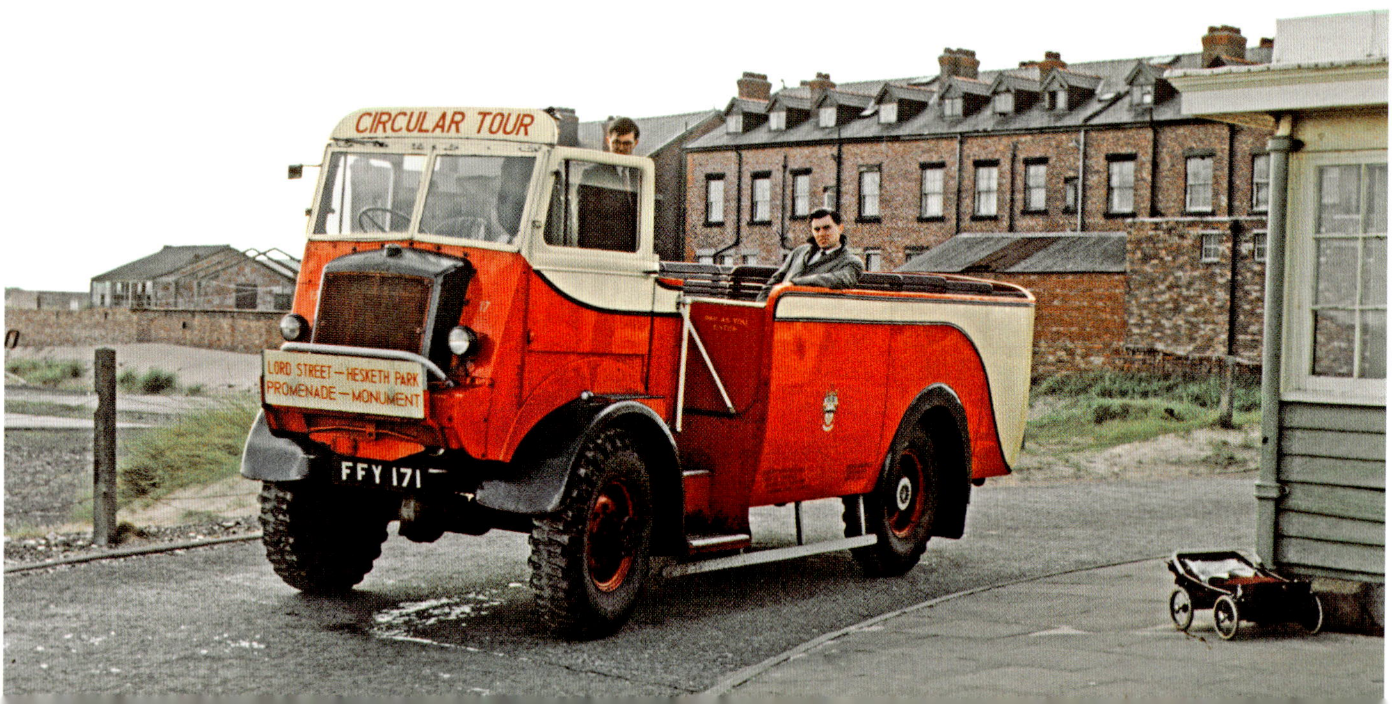

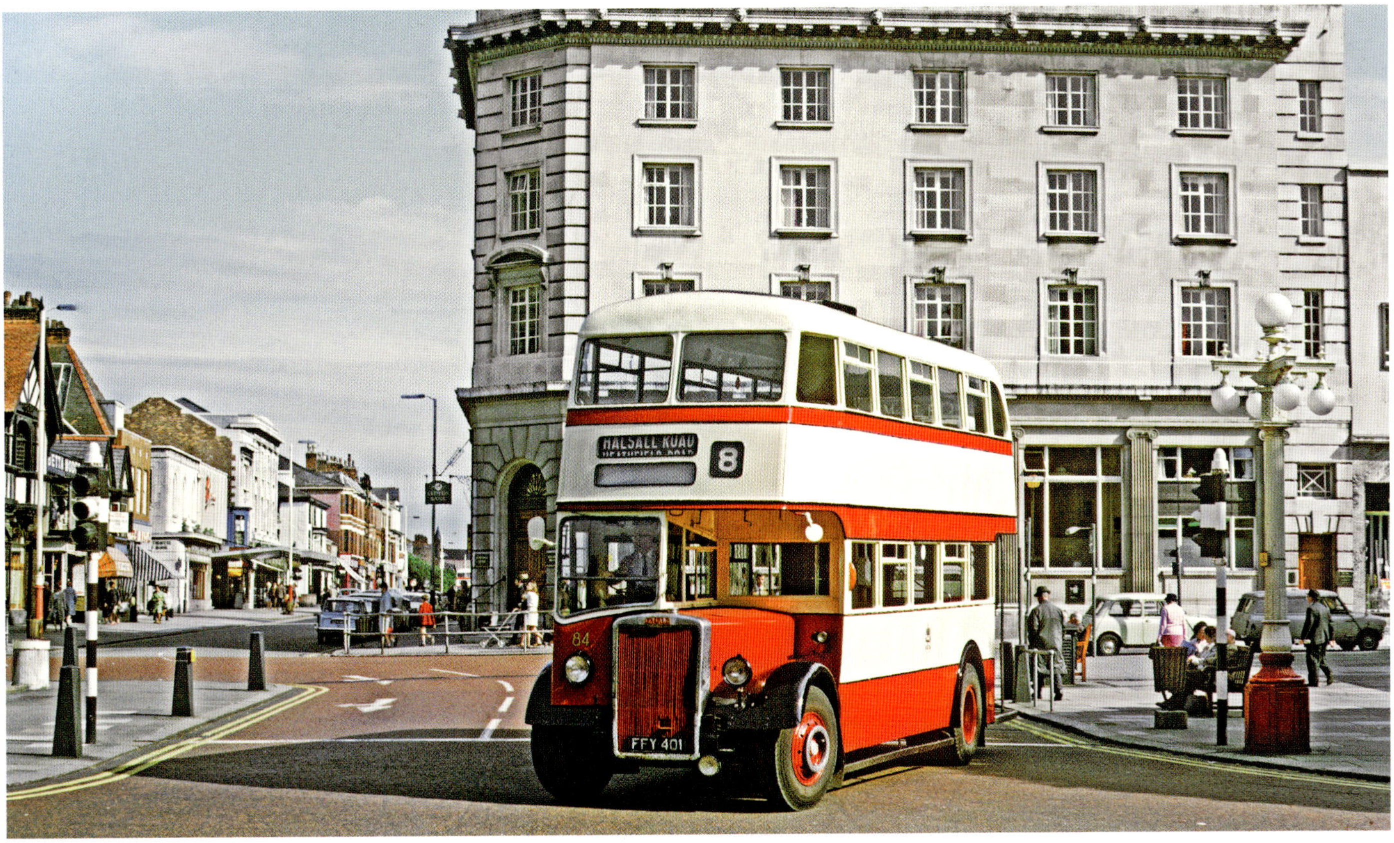

Although its operating territory had virtually no hills, Southport bought no Leyland PD1s but went straight to the larger-engined Leyland PD2. Twelve PD2/3 (synchromesh gearboxes) with Leyland bodies (84-95) entered service in 1947 and were the first PD2/3s in the country – PD2/1s for Todmorden, Potteries, Halifax and two demonstrators preceded them. On a sunny day in June 1968 number 84 is turning into Lord Street. 84-89 had been altered in 1962/63 to have a removable upper-deck roof and side windows. The job was very neatly done and the only evidence in this picture of 84 with its roof on is the slightly thicker beading of the joint below the second to sixth upper-deck windows. *Roy Marshall*

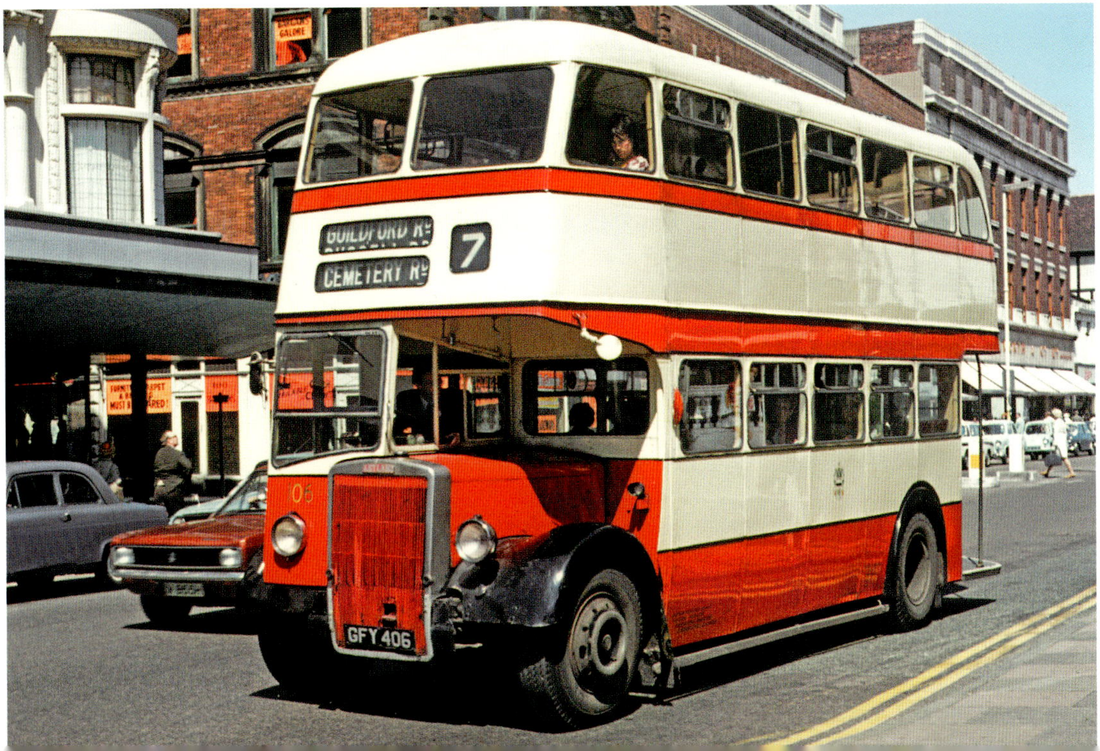

Just how well Southport's buses were cared for is nicely shown in this picture of 106. The bus was 21 years old but its paintwork was as glossy as the day it was new. Photographed in Chapel Street in May 1971, it was one of 15 Leyland PD2/3s delivered in 1950 (96-110) with Leyland's 'Farington' style bodywork, which had flush-mounted windows. Southport's cross town services such as this one displayed a different number in each direction – 7 when going south-west to Guildford Road and 8 on the return journey. 106 would serve for another year. *Alan Murray-Rust*

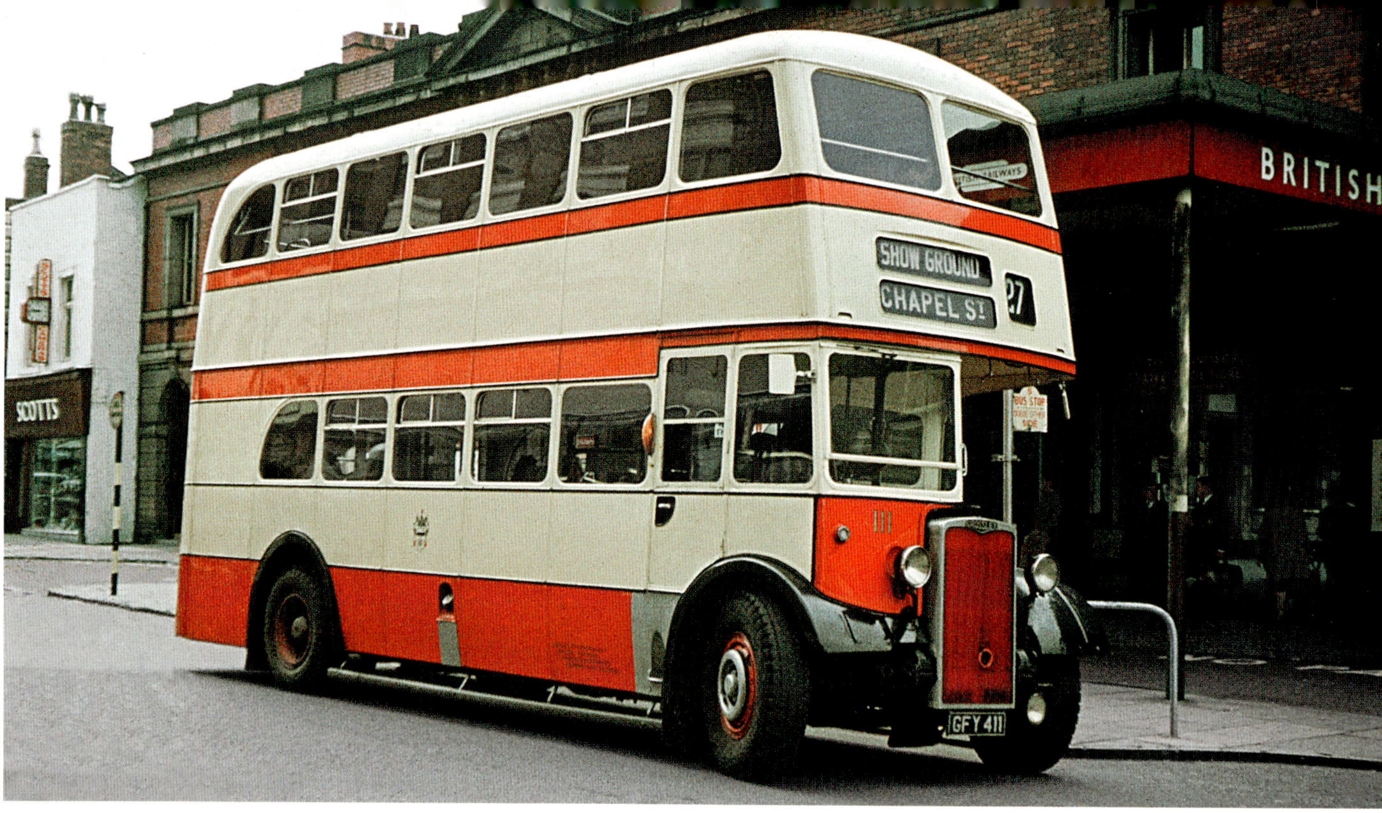

Three things combined to produce a temporary variation from Southport's buying Leylands. First was Leyland's long delivery times which could then be as long as five years. Second was that general manager Jackson Hoggard's brother Len, who was Crossley's municipal sales manager, was under severe pressure from AEC which had bought Crossley in 1947. Third was 'support local industry' agitation from local firm Brockhouse Engineering that the department buy the latest version of its Brockhouse-Salerni Turbo-transmitter – a form of automatic transmission using a torque converter which had so far not proved over successful. The result was an order for two Crossley DD42 double-deckers, one with the Brockhouse turbo-transmitter, thee AEC Regent III double-deckers and two Crossley SD42 single-deckers, all with Crossley bodywork.

New in February 1950 and numbered 111-112, the Crossley double-deckers had the improved, more powerful (and more reliable) 'downdraught' version of the HOE7 engine. 111 was a DD42/8T with turbo-transmitter transmission – it was removed at first overhaul in 1957 and replaced with the same type of Crossley synchromesh gearbox that was fitted to DD42/8S 112 from new. This 1959 picture shows 111 at Chapel Street (later Southport) Station, working Flower Show service 27. In the mornings, most services that travelled south along Lord Street made a short diversion to call at the station allowing business people to transfer easily to the frequent trains to Liverpool and Manchester. *Ian Stewart*

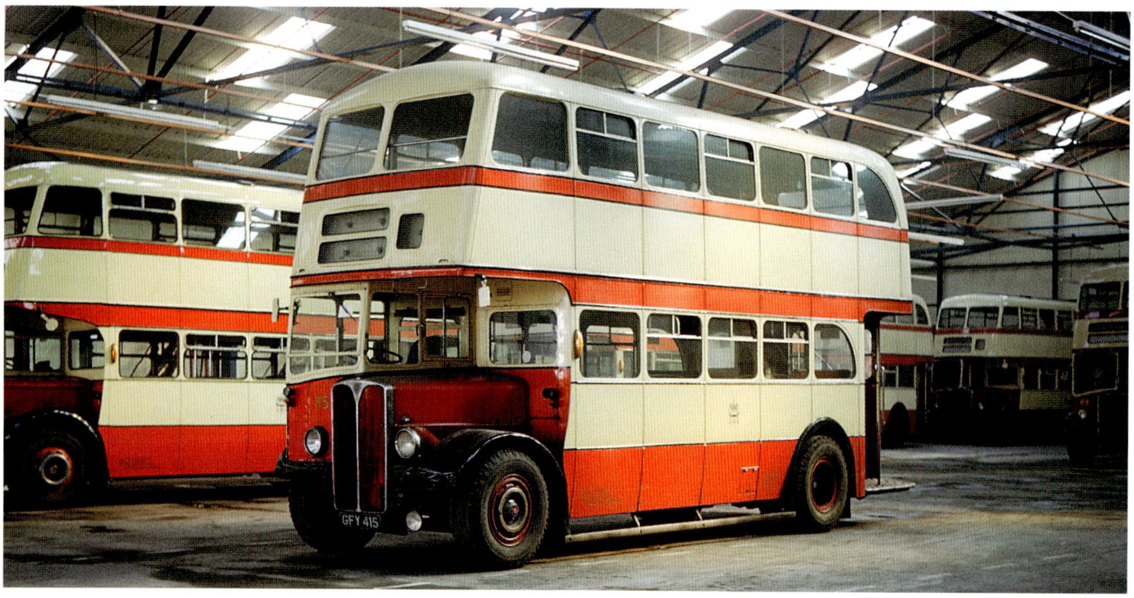

The three AEC Regents arrived in December 1949, a couple of months before the Crossley DD42s. Numbered 113-115 they had pre-selector gearboxes. They were withdrawn in 1962, a year before the Crossleys and still in fine condition, they and the two DD42s passed to the Northumberland firm of Bedlington and District which ran them for three years. On 12 March 1963, 115 was awaiting collection inside the garage at Canning Road, Blowick. *Roy Marshall*

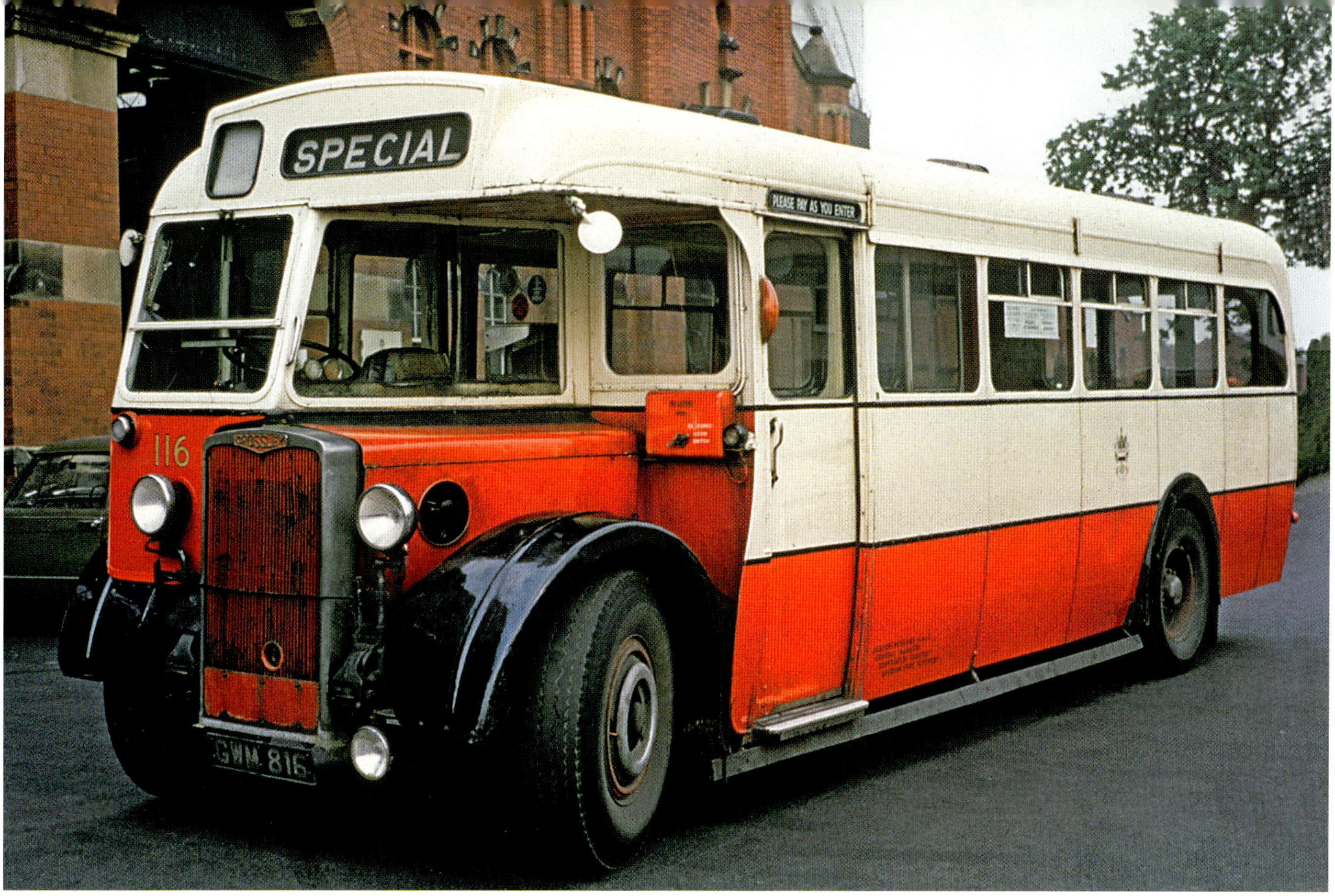

The Crossley SD42/7 single-deckers arrived in January 1951. Numbered 116-117 they were used on lightly-trafficked routes – Southport had no services which passed beneath low bridges. Both were later fitted for one-person operation when, in addition to the usual modification to the nearside cab window to allow the driver to turn and collect fares, the sliding passenger door was fitted for vacuum operation. The vacuum tank for this was mounted on the bulkhead – similar looking to a header tank for a turbo-transmitter it confused some enthusiasts into believing the single-deckers had had turbo-transmitters. Photographed outside Canning Road depot in 1964, 117 was withdrawn after being badly damaged in an accident in 1965. It was then sold to Oldham Corporation, which repaired the body and used it to replace the damaged Roe body on one of its own SD42s. *Arnold Richardson*

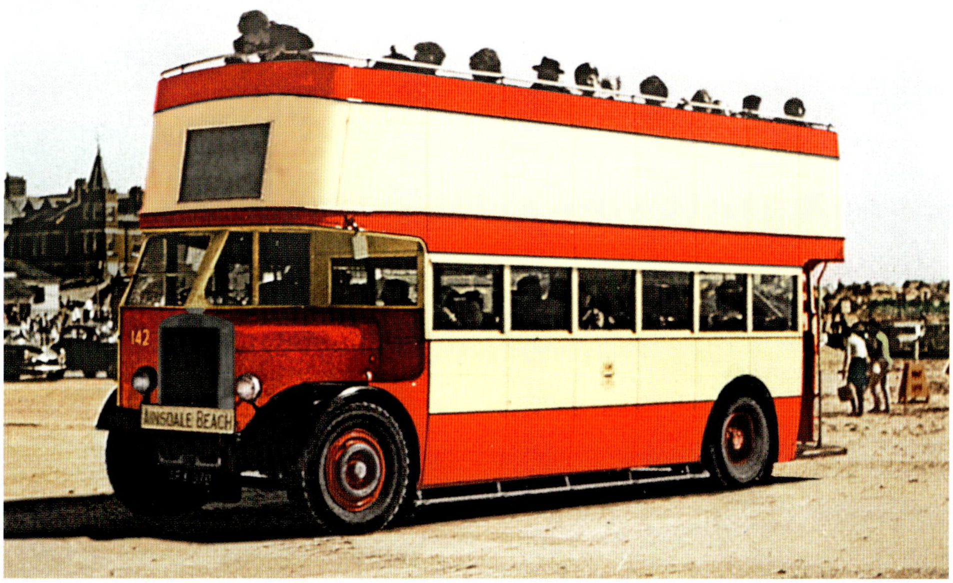

The open top PD2s were successors to four English Electric-bodied Leyland TD3s new in 1934 which had been converted to open top in 1951/52, the wooden seats on their upper decks coming from wartime Daimlers. Renumbered 142-145 the quartet worked the sea front service and the 'circular tour' service. They ran until 1963, 142 and 145 sometimes being used on the shore service as in this picture, taken near the pier in 1957, of 142 and private cars on the sands. It says much for the care Southport gave its fleet that 142 and 145 withstood the salt water and sand grit. *Roy Marshall*

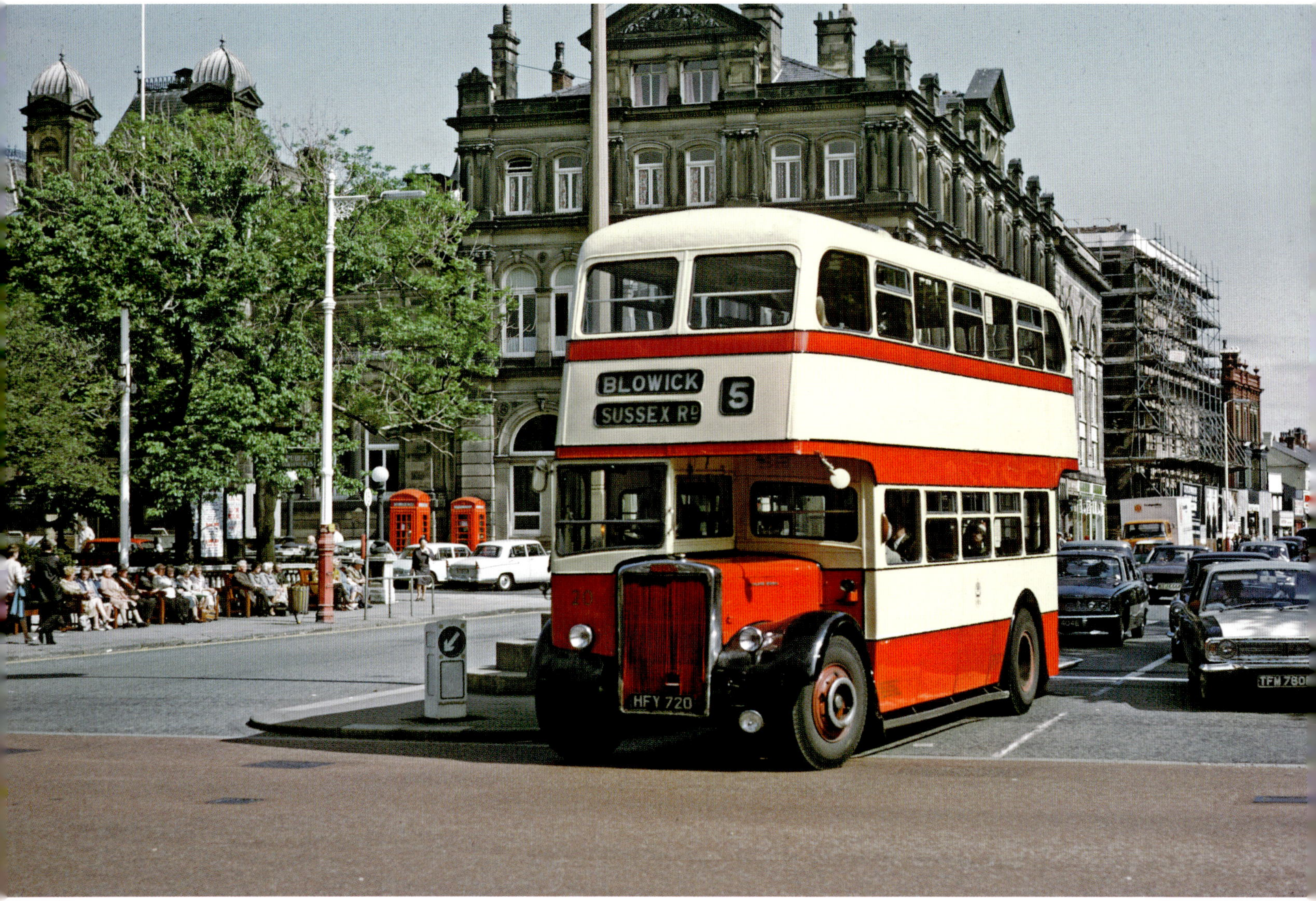

This picture shows one of the six Weymann-bodied Leyland PD2/12s delivered in 1952, numbered 20-26. In June 1968, visitors sit and enjoy the sunshine in Eastbank Square as the first of the batch turns into Lord Street from Eastbank Street. *Roy Marshall*

Opposite top Three batches of Leyland PD2/20s followed, all with Weymann bodies – four (27-30) in 1954, six (31-36) in 1956 and a final six (37-42) in 1957. The first picture shows 33 at Aughton Road level crossing over the Southport – Liverpool third-rail electric line. Converted in 1904 it was the first suburban electric line in the country. *Dennis Kerrison*

Opposite bottom The second picture is of number 41, plus some of the rear of 28 and, in the distance one of the 1947 PD2s. Fully loaded 41 is pulling away from the stops on tree-lined Lord Street near the Monument. *Alan Montgomery*

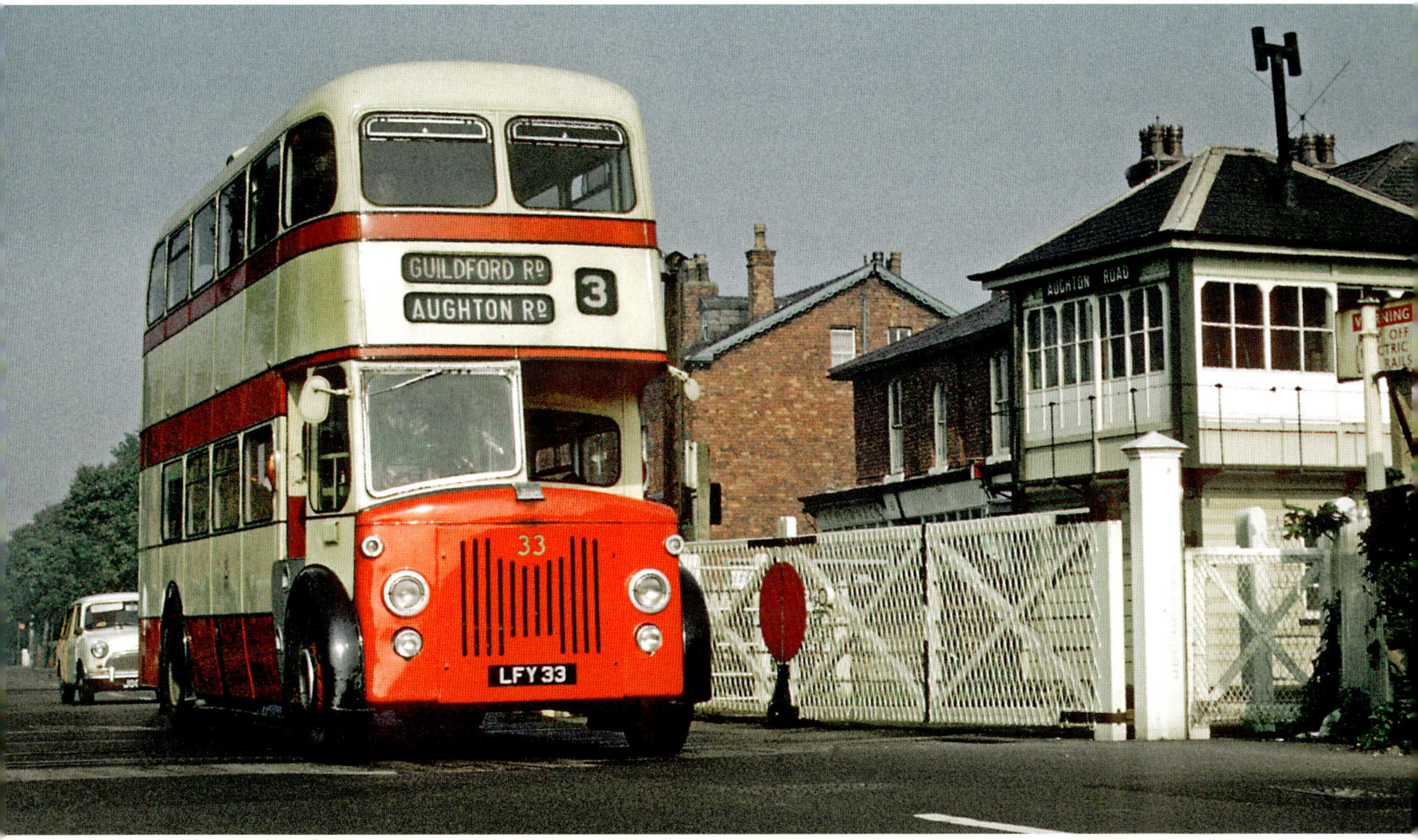
GUILDFORD Rd
AUGHTON Rd
3
33
LFY 33
AUGHTON ROAD

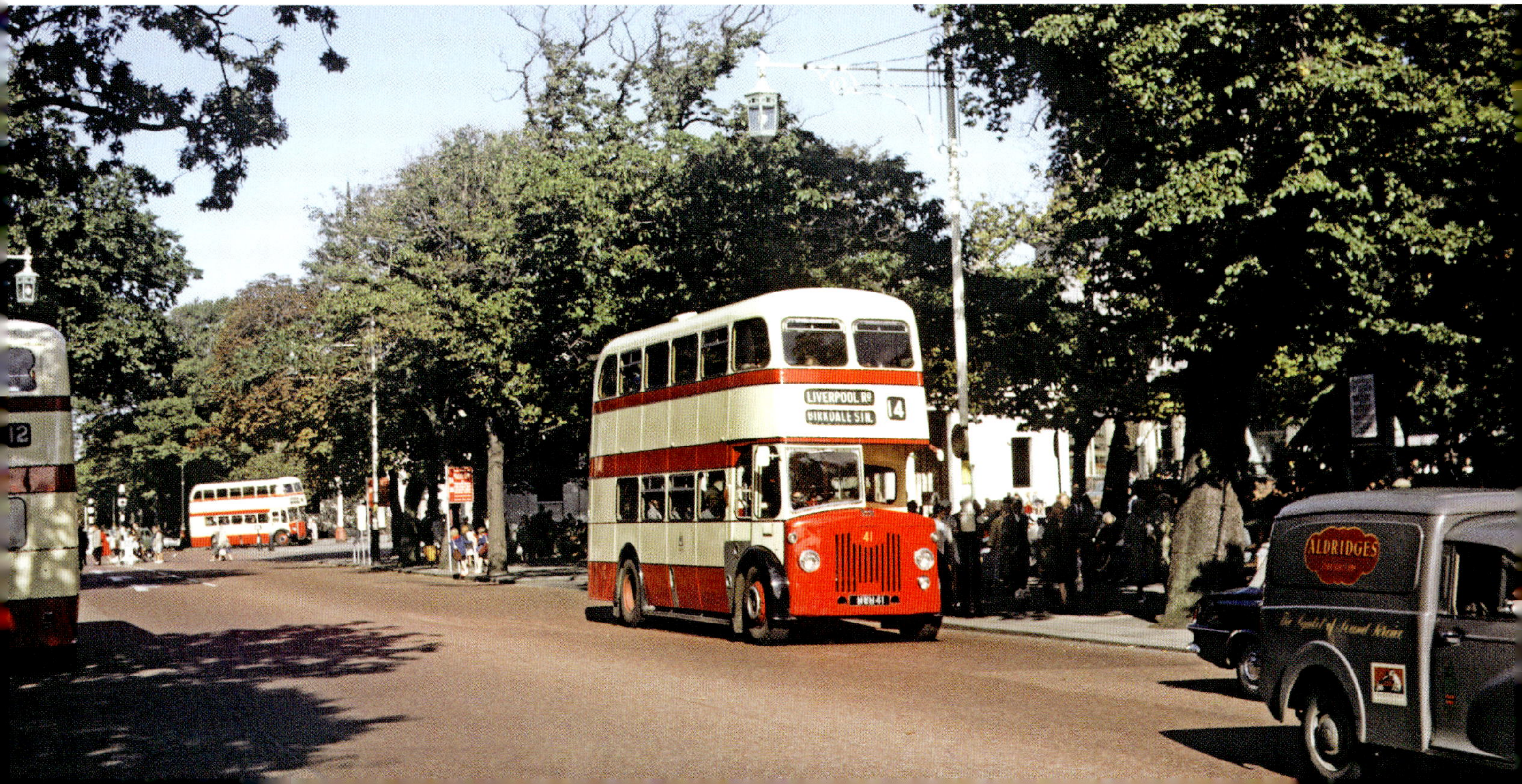
LIVERPOOL Rd
BIRKDALE STN
14
ALDRIDGES

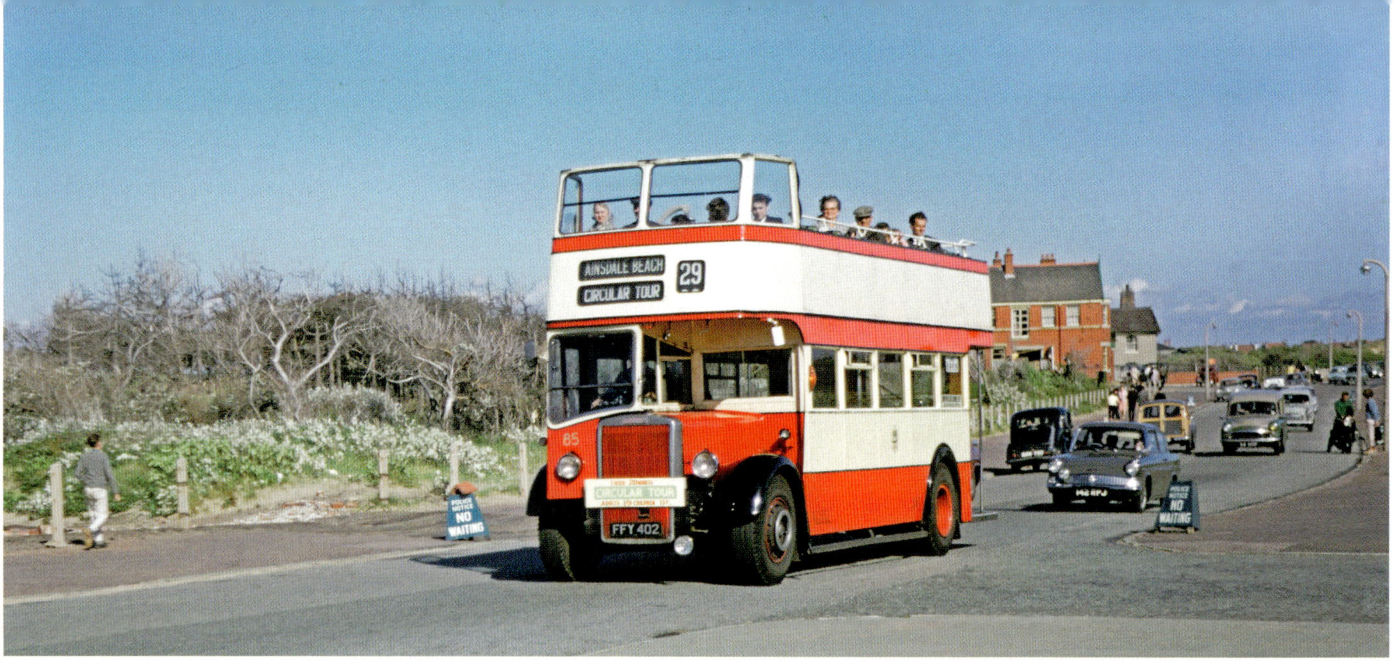

In 1962/63 PD2/1s 84-89 were altered to have removable roofs, replacing TD3s 142-145. On 5 August 1962 newly-converted 85 approaches Ainsdale Beach on the circular tour service. The journey time was 80 minutes and the fare 1 shilling and 9 pence for adults (1 shilling for children). From 1884 to 1952, the former Cheshire Lines railway branch into Lord Street Station crossed the road between the two buildings in the background. *Roy Marshall*

Three 1950 Burlingham-bodied Leyland Tiger PS2s were acquired from Ribble in 1963 for conversion to open top – the work was done in the Canning Road workshops. They were numbered 10-12 and Roy Marshall took this picture of newly converted 10 'straight out of the works' in July 1963. He was Traffic Manager at Southport from 1957 to 1966 and in one of several moves to reduce costs and improve traffic had replaced the open top cross-town 'promenade' open top service, which ran in summer, rain or shine, with a circular tour which only ran when the weather was good. *Roy Marshall*

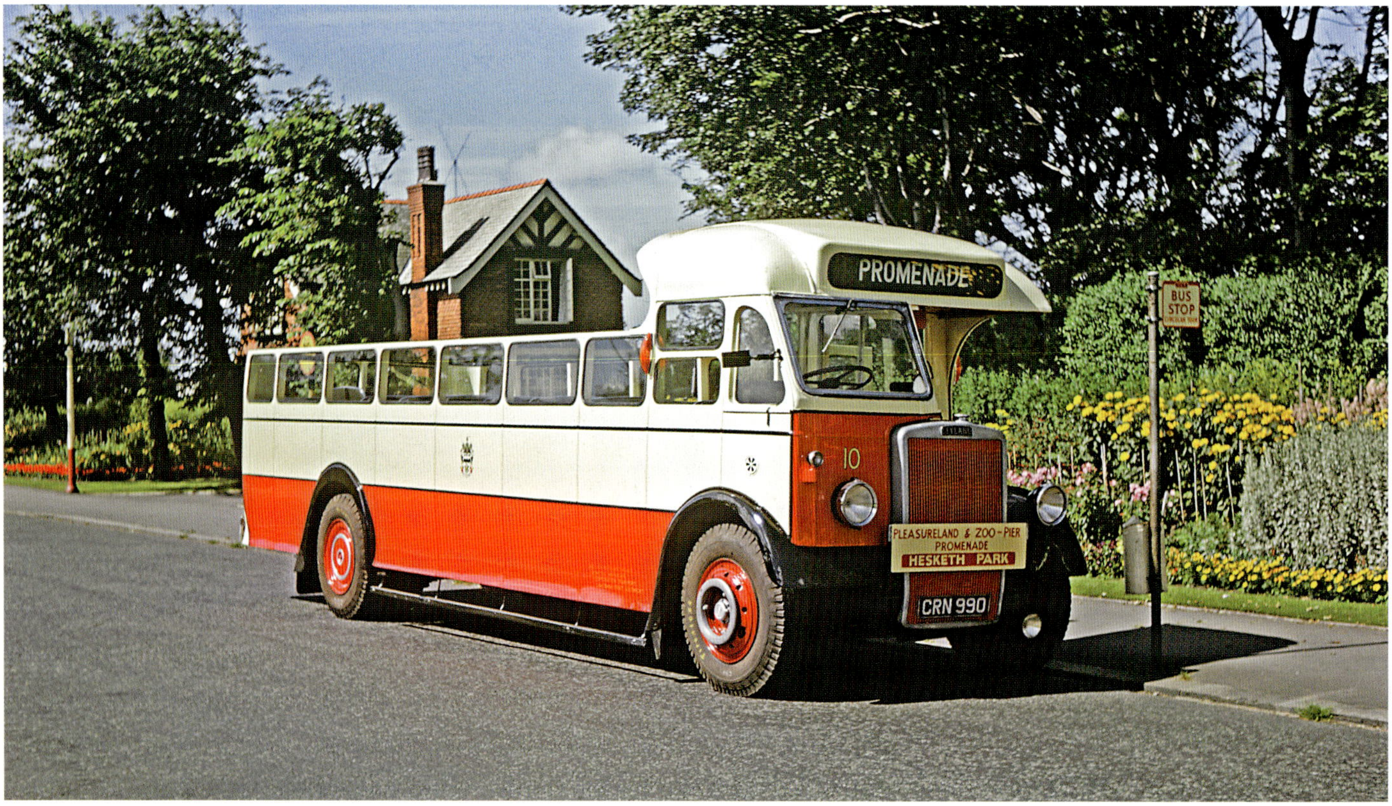

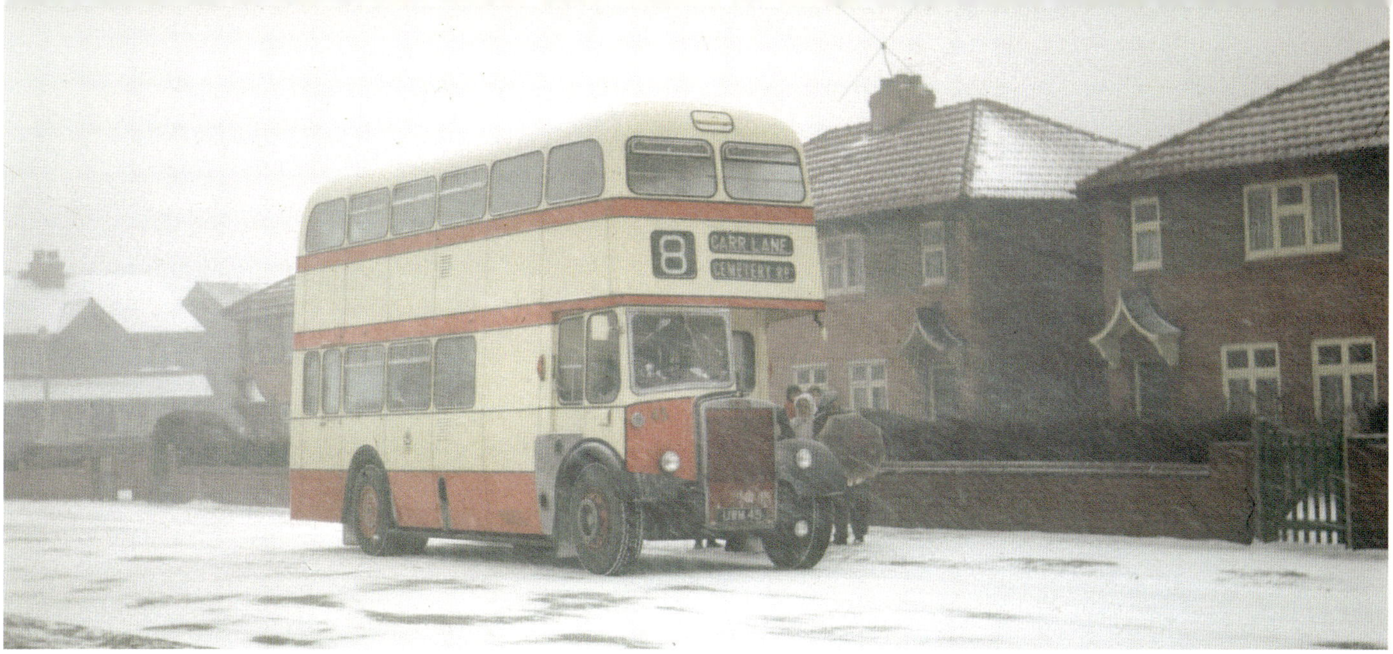

Although from the pictures so far it might seem as if it did, the sun sometimes didn't shine in Southport and the passengers would have been glad to get out of the snow and into 45's heated interior in this snowstorm in February 1973. Southport was early into forward-entrance PD2s with four in each of 1961 and 1962 all with Weymann 'Orion' bodies and numbered 43-50. The indicator layout was changed to place the service number indicator, which was made much larger, on the offside front. The bus is in Canning Road. *Roy Marshall*

This fine view of part of the Canning Road garage and workshops at Blowick, taken in July 1973, shows front-entrance Leyland PD2/40 57 – one of four (55-58) new in 1967; four similar ones, 51-54, had arrived in 1965. They had Weymann bodies whereas 55-58's were MCW, Metro Cammell and Weymann having been merged in 1965. All the front-entrance PD2s were converted for one-person operation in 1968-1970. Behind 57 is PD2/20 36, some ten years older, and across the road is open topper 187, renumbered from 87 in 1973. Facing into the garage is the department's AEC Matador recovery vehicle – one of its tasks was rescuing stranded QLs from the sands. *Roy Marshall*

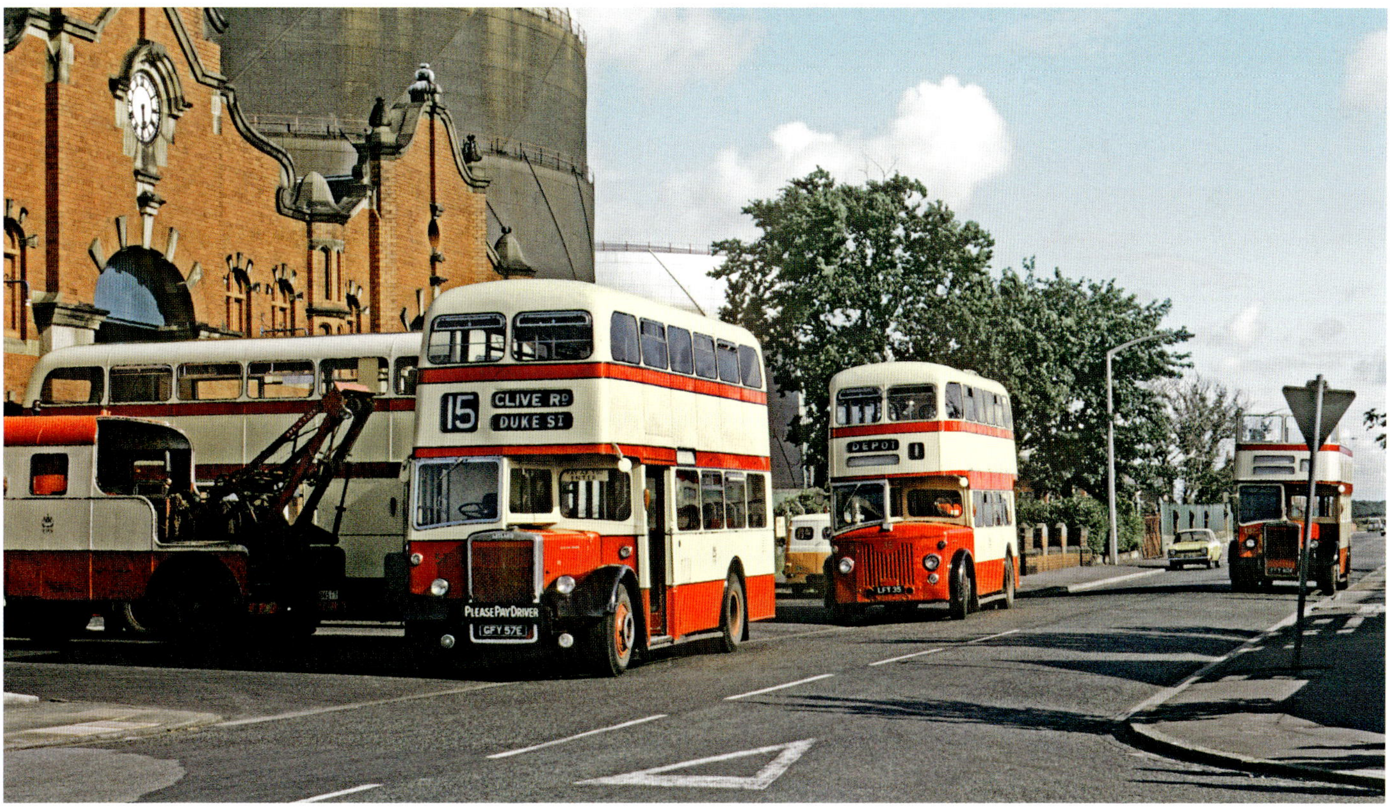

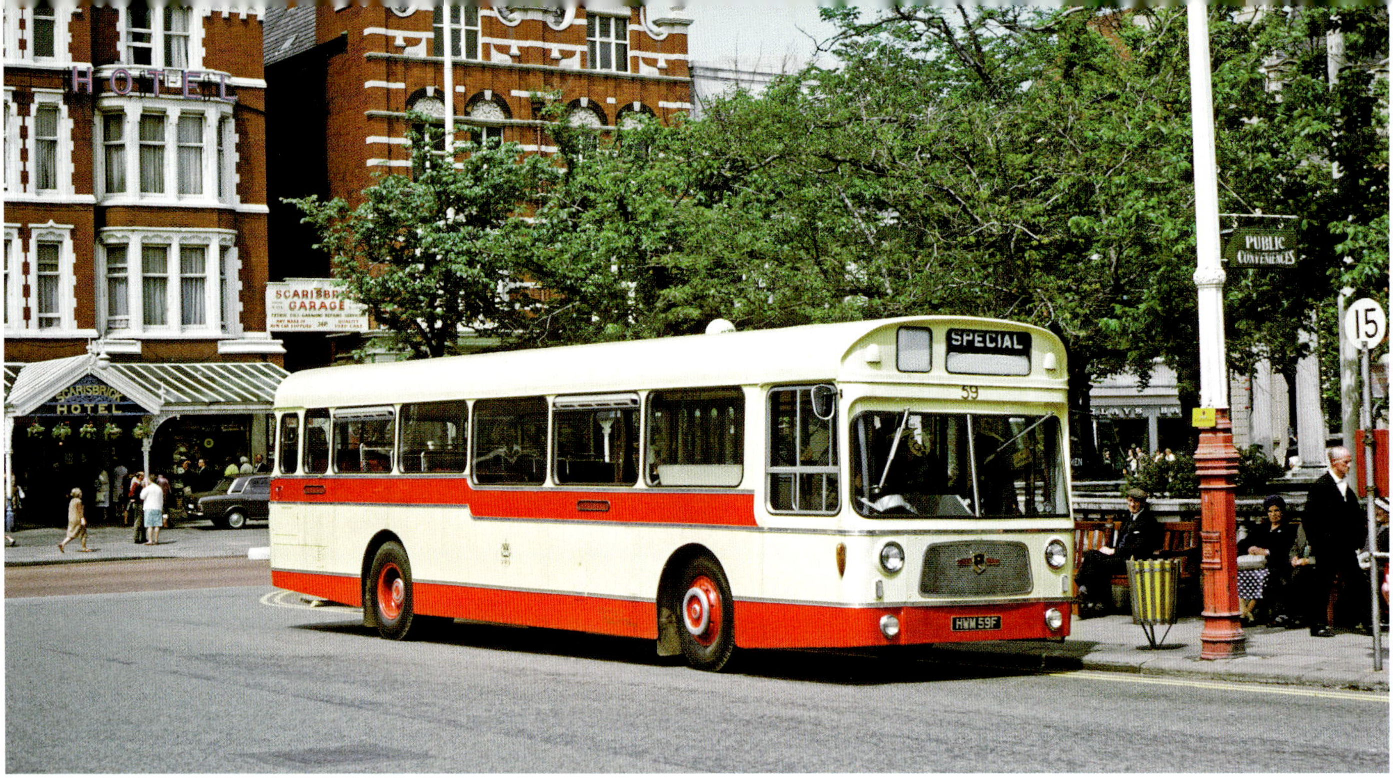

Like Liverpool, Southport chose to move to high capacity one-person single-deckers although the change was not at all popular with passengers. Two batches of six Leyland Panthers with MCW bodies with 45 seats and room for 17 standees (59-70) were delivered in 1968. This picture is of brand new 59 in Eastbank Square in June 1968. *Roy Marshall*

There were no more new buses until 1971 when two batches of five Marshall-bodied Panthers (71-80) entered service. Number 76 is passing the new Safeway supermarket on Lord Street. At the time Safeway was American-owned and, as befitted Lord Street, considered 'up-market'. The cinema building behind the bus was originally the Garrick Theatre, famous for its splendid art deco interior; sold to the Essoldo group in 1957 it became a cinema and then in the 1970s a bingo hall. *Roy Marshall*

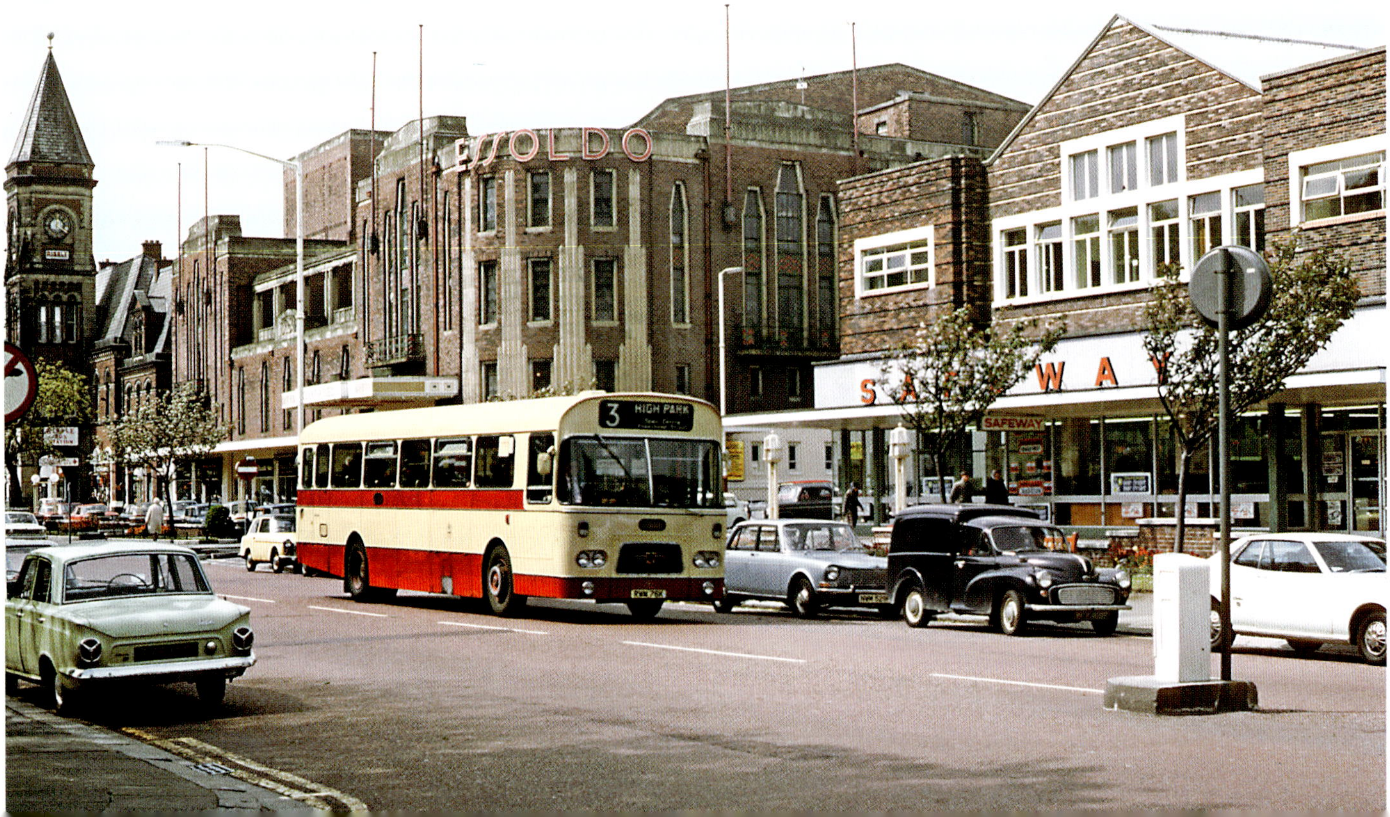

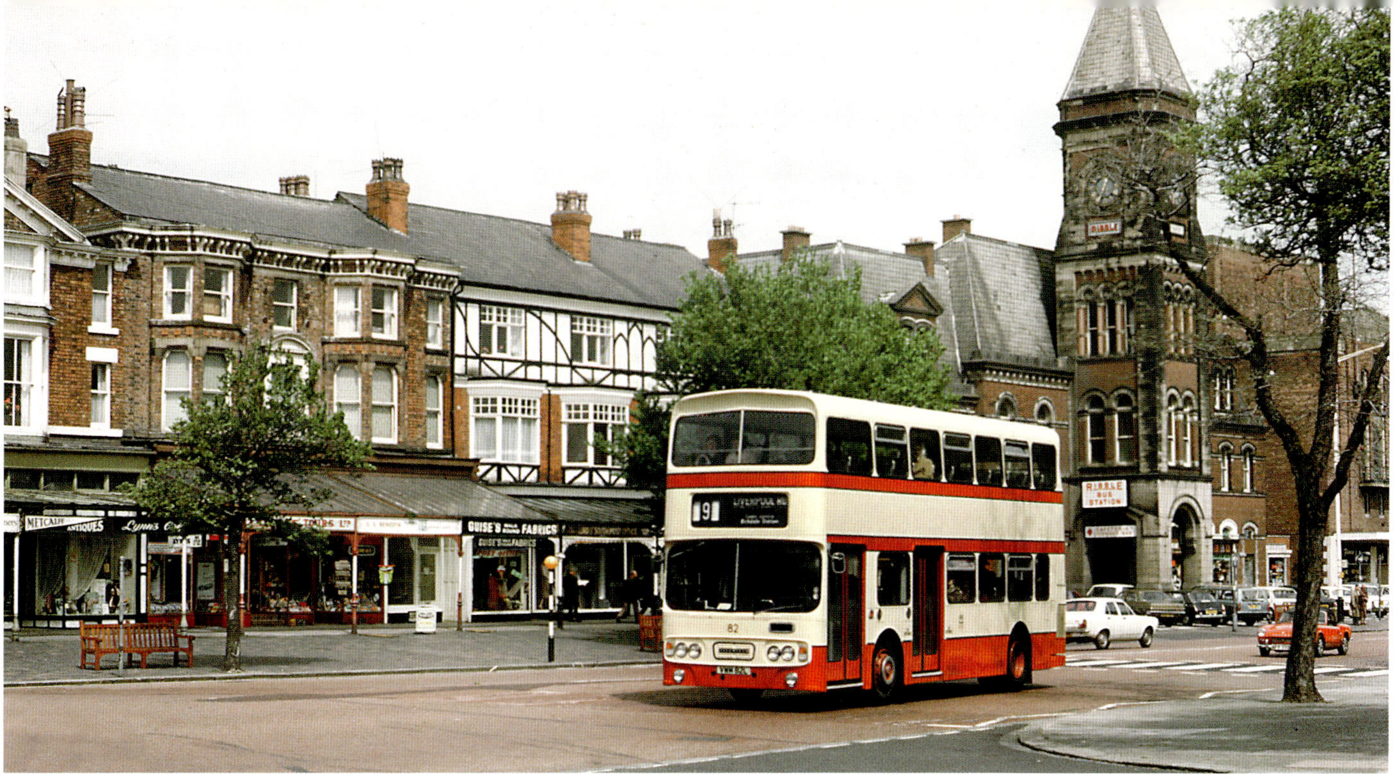

There is much of interest in this picture of number 82, one of ten Leyland Atlanteans with dual-doorway Alexander bodies new in 1973. The shops with their glass and iron verandas, the red-coloured road surface of Lord Street and the hardwood seats placed along the tree-lined pavement. However the most interesting thing in the picture is the Ribble Bus Station just to the rear of 82. Originally the Lord Street terminus of the Cheshire Lines railway, when it closed in 1952 it was taken over by Ribble and converted into a splendid bus station, retaining all of its architectural features – there is an interior picture in the Ribble section of this book. Ribble and others' buses were still not allowed on Lord Street and, like the trains, entered and exited from the Promenade side but Ribble now had a strong presence on the street. May 1973 *Roy Marshall*

It is perhaps unkind to the Leyland National's designers to comment that Southport could even make one look smart and shiny but numbers 1-8 of 1974 certainly did, with their white bumpers and Southport's red and cream livery which, unlike that of many other operators, remained unchanged from when Jackson Hoggard introduced it in 1947. March 1974 *Roy Marshall*

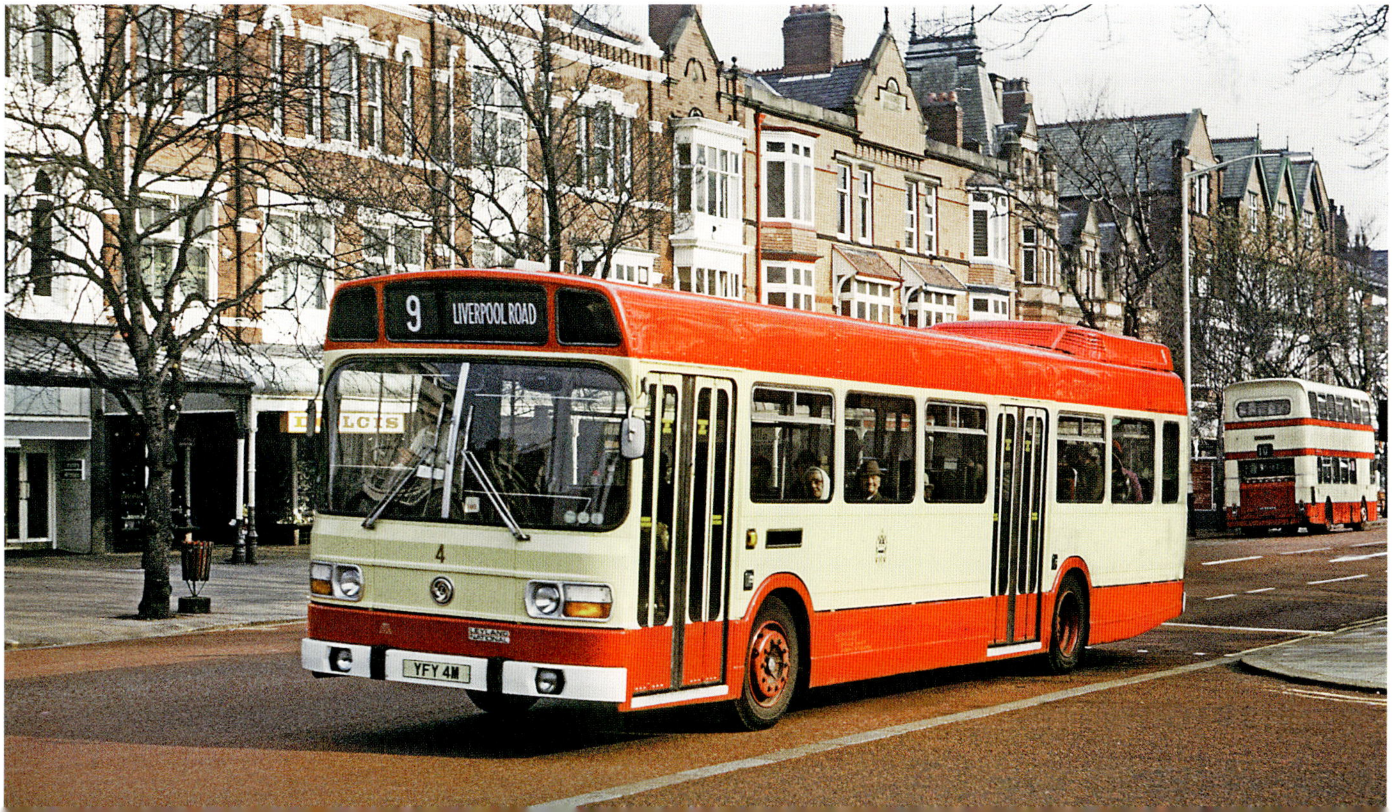

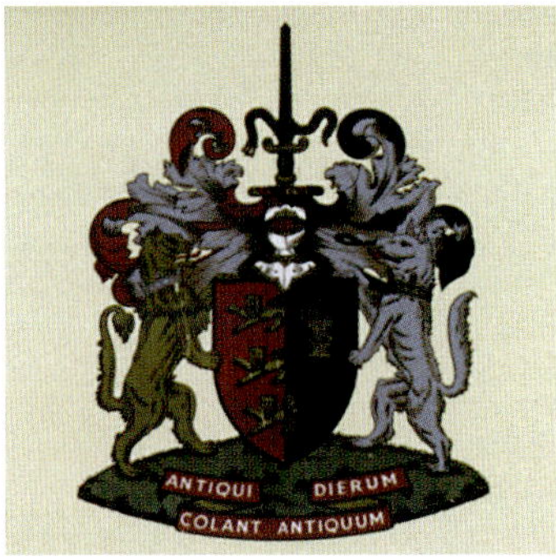

Chester

Named Deva by the Romans and the county town of Cheshire, the cathedral city of Chester is one of the best preserved walled towns in England, rich in architectural and archaeological treasures including the famous Rows – two-tiered rows of shops with the balustrade walkways of the upper levels accessed by steps from the street. Its bus fleet fitted well with all of this – strongly built Guy chassis, reliable and durable Gardner engines, stylish, well-finished Massey bodies and a dignified livery, the colours of which harmonised with those of the city's ancient buildings and sandstone walls.

The transport department had no buses until 1930 when a fleet of AEC Regents and Regals replaced the trams, more AECs and some Leylands followed. Wartime saw the usual mix of Daimlers and Guys; after came eight Daimlers, two AEC Regals and ten Fodens. A new general manager changed the policy and from then on its fleet of around 50 was Guy/Gardner/Massey with Daimler Fleetlines when Guy ceased building buses.

Development of Chester's municipal bus operations was severely hampered by Crosville, which had its headquarters in the town and tried to buy the undertaking in 1927. An operating agreement between the two was made in 1932 which limited Chester's operations but, like Birkenhead and Wallasey, there were no joint services. Relations with Crosville were never good, with, for example, continual argument about the restricted loading places in Town Hall Square. There is no better example of the friction than the livery. Originally Chester's buses were green and Crosville's maroon. When Crosville was moved into the Tilling group it was a group requirement that it choose either the Tilling standard red or green and, most of its area being rural, it chose green. Greatly affronted by this usurping of its livery, Chester's council complained bitterly. It was to no avail against 1000-vehicle Crosville and in 1946 the displeased council decided it had to change the livery of its own buses. It was somehow no surprise that it chose a brownish maroon which its smart looking buses carried for the rest of the undertaking's existence.

The local government reorganisation of April 1974 merged the city of Chester with the Chester and Tarvin Rural Districts to form the non-metropolitan district of Chester. The transport undertaking passed to the new larger body, using the fleetname 'Chester City'.

This picture of part of Bridge Street nicely captures the style of Chester during the period of this book. In 1972 Massey-bodied Guy Arab fleet number 11, new in 1955, takes on passengers for Eccleston. Just ahead of it other passengers, their bags loaded with shopping, wait at the Crosville stop for buses to Wrexham. Perhaps more striking than the bus is this section of The Rows, with their walkways; some buildings are black and white half timbered, some mellow brick and the modern structures continued the arrangement. *Geoff Hyde*

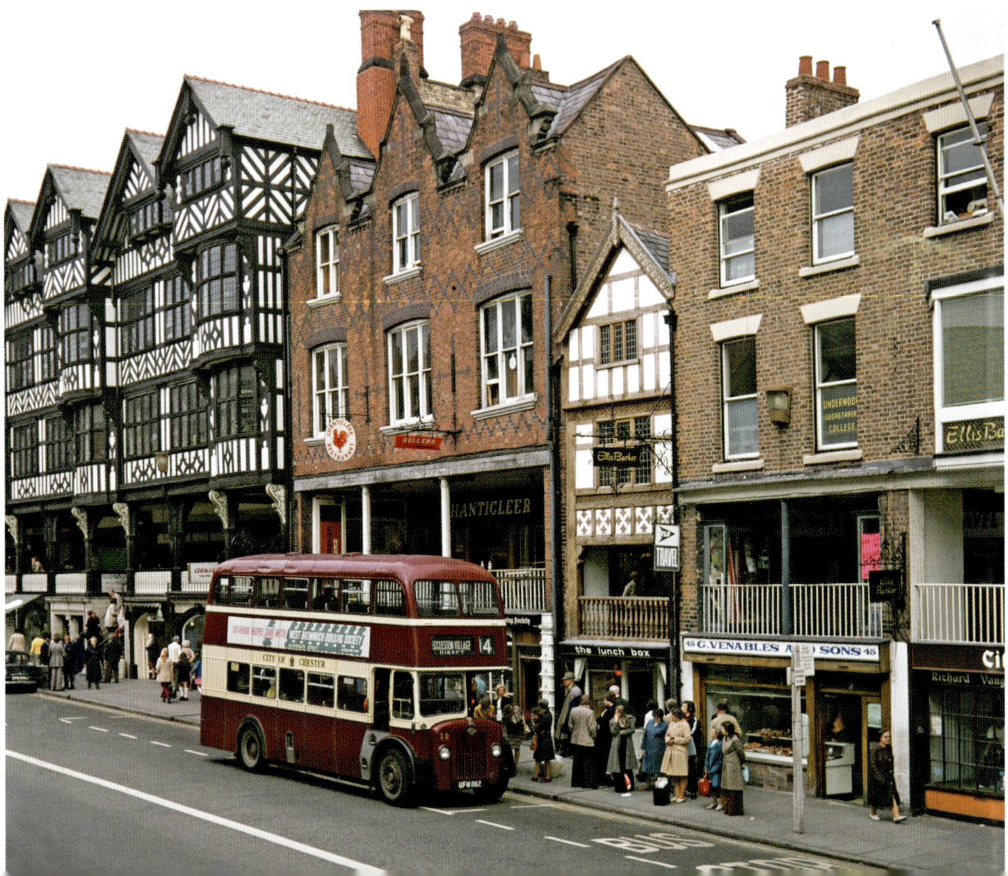

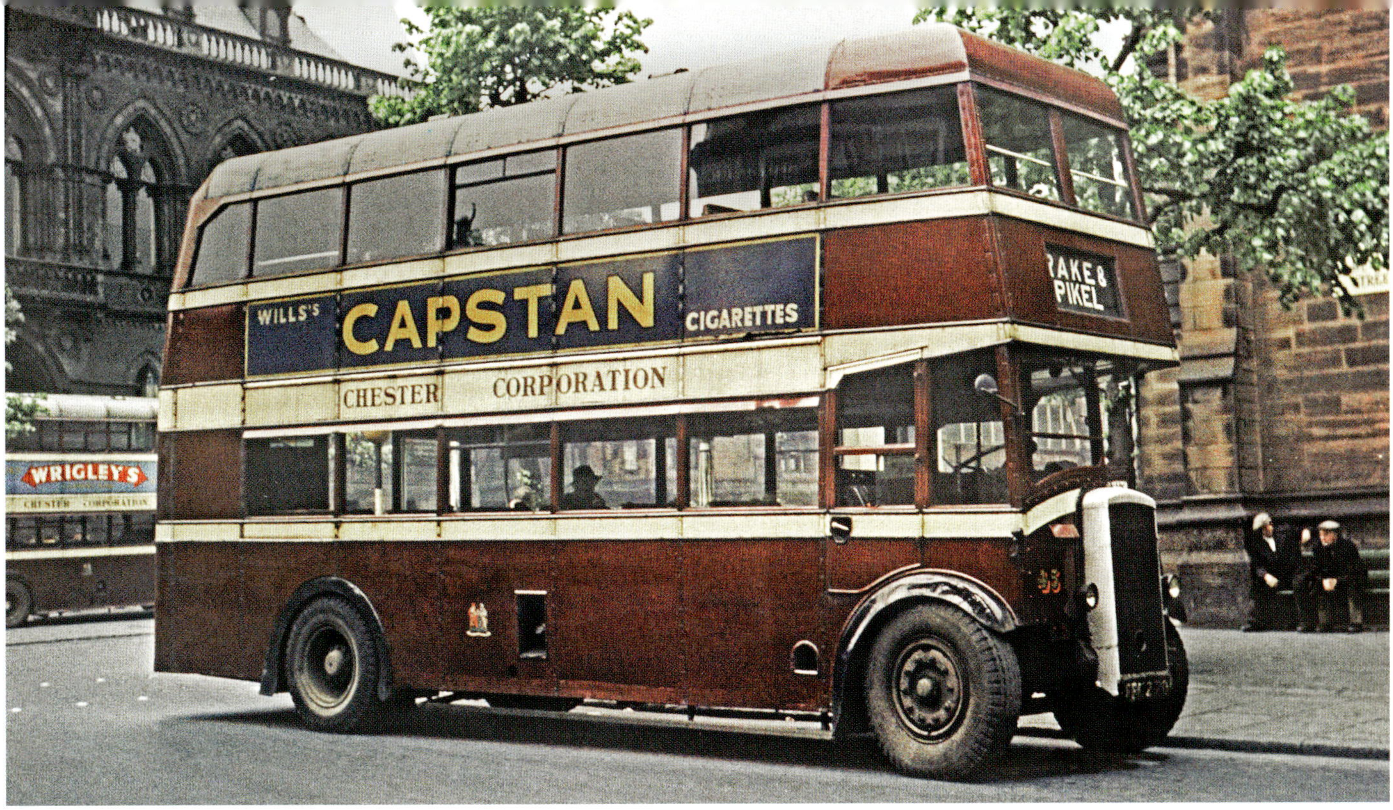

Many military bases and factories were built in the area during the war and the fleet was increased with seventeen 'utility' Daimlers and Guys to handle the resulting traffic. Dating from 1943, 45 was a Daimler CWG5 with a Massey body shown here in May 1950 waiting at the Huntington service stop outside the Cathedral. The indicator blind, showing simply 'Rake and Pikel' (a Huntington pub), was a 'left over' from the war when government security required operators in military or sensitive areas to remove district names from blinds and use something that (hopefully) only locals would know – pub names were the obvious choice. *C Carter*

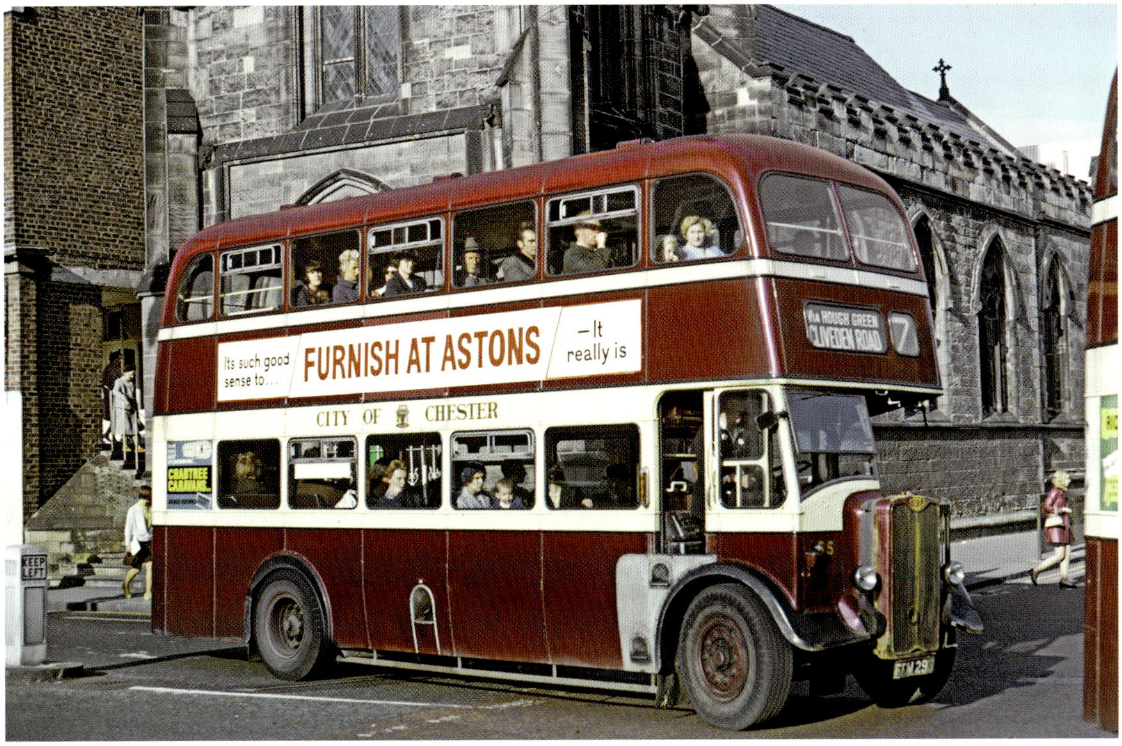

Four of the eight wartime Guy Arabs were rebodied in 1952, two by D J Davies – a small coachbuilder in Merthyr Tydfil – and two by Massey. The Davies ones were poor and were scrapped after only nine years – two more on Foden chassis only lasted seven. The metal-framed Masseys, on the other hand, were in service until 1968/69. This is number 55 passing St Michael's Church at the junction of Bridge, Grosvenor and Pepper Streets on 12 September 1968. *Roy Marshall*

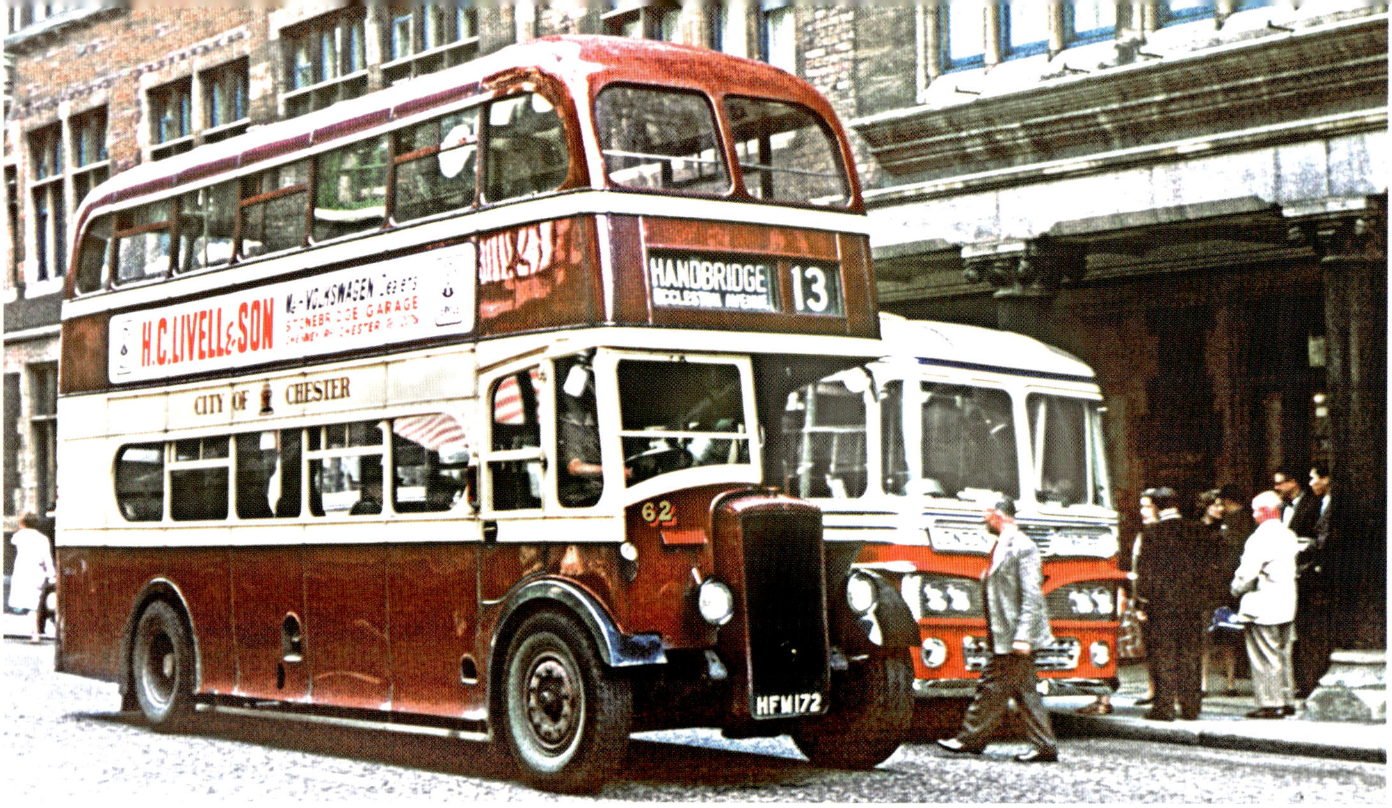

Metro Cammell was to have supplied bodies for eight Daimlers but could not offer delivery until the end of 1948. Massey was able to do the job more quickly and bodied CVA6 60/61, 67, 70 and CVD6 62/63, 66, 71 which entered service in 1947 and early 1948. Fleet number 62 passes an AEC Reliance coach parked outside the Grosvenor Hotel in Eastgate Street. *Dennis Kerrison*

The Metro Cammell bodies were built to Chester's specification late in 1948. Surplus to Chester's needs they were bought by Salford, then very short of buses, in which fleet the resulting vehicles were numbered 343-350, the most obvious Chester feature being their indicator boxes. August 1950 *C Carter*

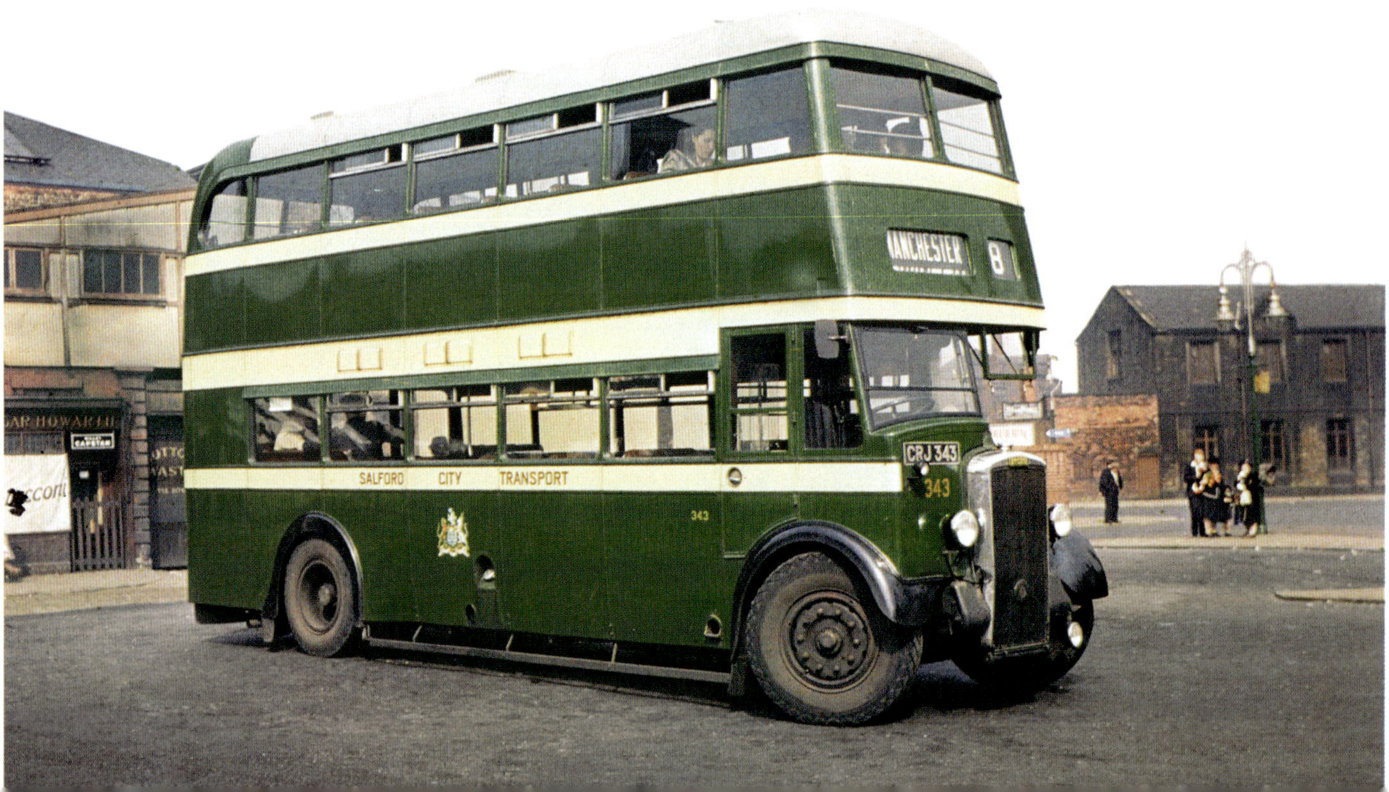

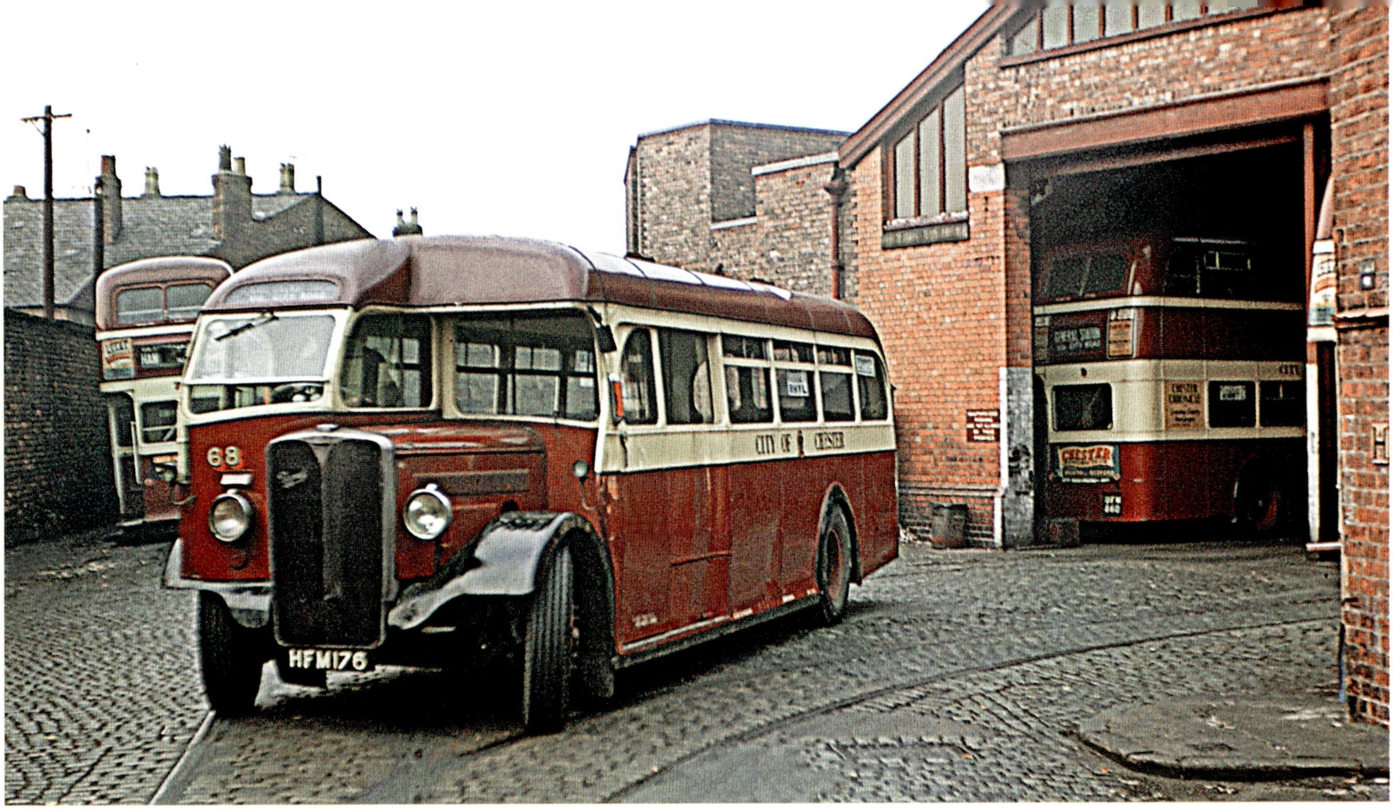

The gaps in the fleet numbers – 64/65, 68/69 – were filled by four AEC Regal single-deckers. Massey built the bodies which, with half canopy cabs and small single indicator box looked similar to Crosville's prewar specification. 64/65 came in 1946 and 68/69 late in 1947, their principal use being the services which passed under the low bridge in Blacon Hall Road. The picture, taken in 1963, shows 68 leaving the garage. Built as the tram depot, its entrances off Station Road were appropriately named Tramway Street and Car Street. Two of the four Regals lasted until 1967 by which time they were by several years the oldest of the type in municipal service, the design of the body making them look more like a bus from the late 1930s. *Peter Roberts*

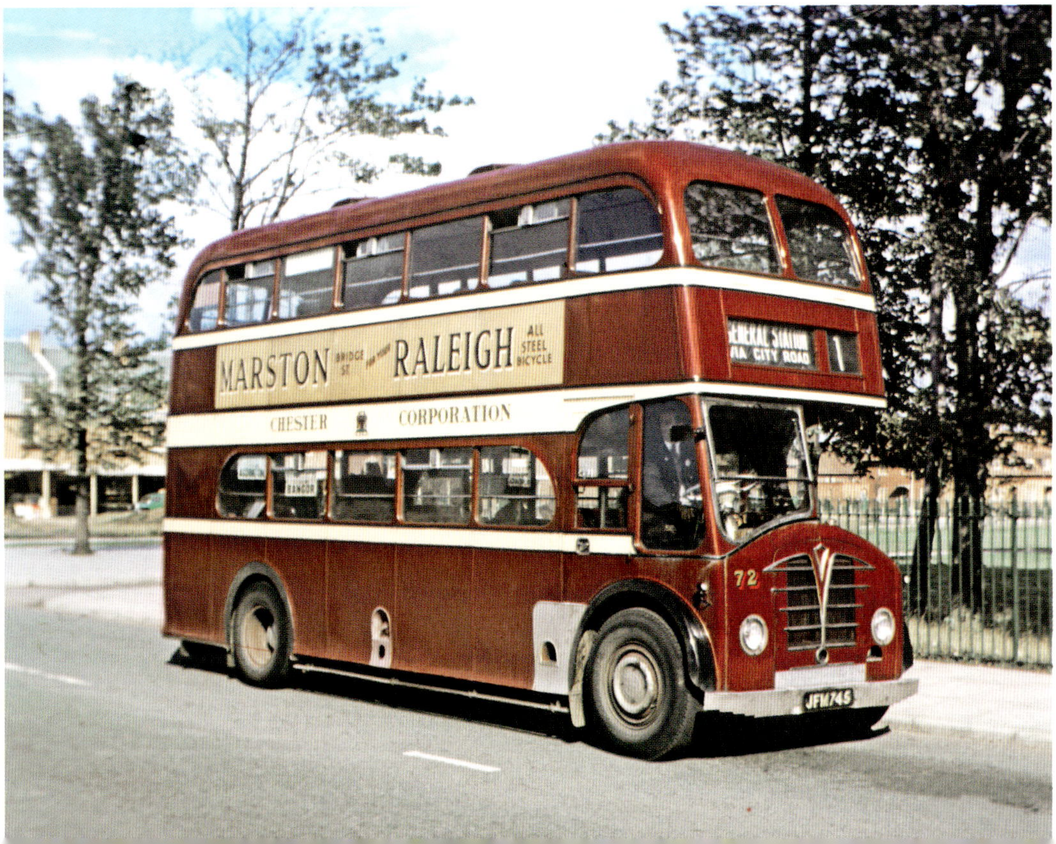

In 1946 Foden had ambitious plans for its new double-decker chassis. Based some 20 miles away in Sandbach it was an obvious move to show the first one to the transport committee of the county town. In 1946 the committee inspected a demonstrator – of which there is more to tell in the Warrington part of this book – and an order was placed for five Gardner-engined PVD6G with Massey bodies. There was then a delay whilst Foden carried out more development work. The prototype chassis, updated, eventually passed to Warrington and the first Chester Foden was shown on the firm's stand at the 1948 Commercial Motor Show. The five buses were numbered 72-76, the show model being the first. This is it, pictured at Blacon in 1955. *Bruce Jenkins*

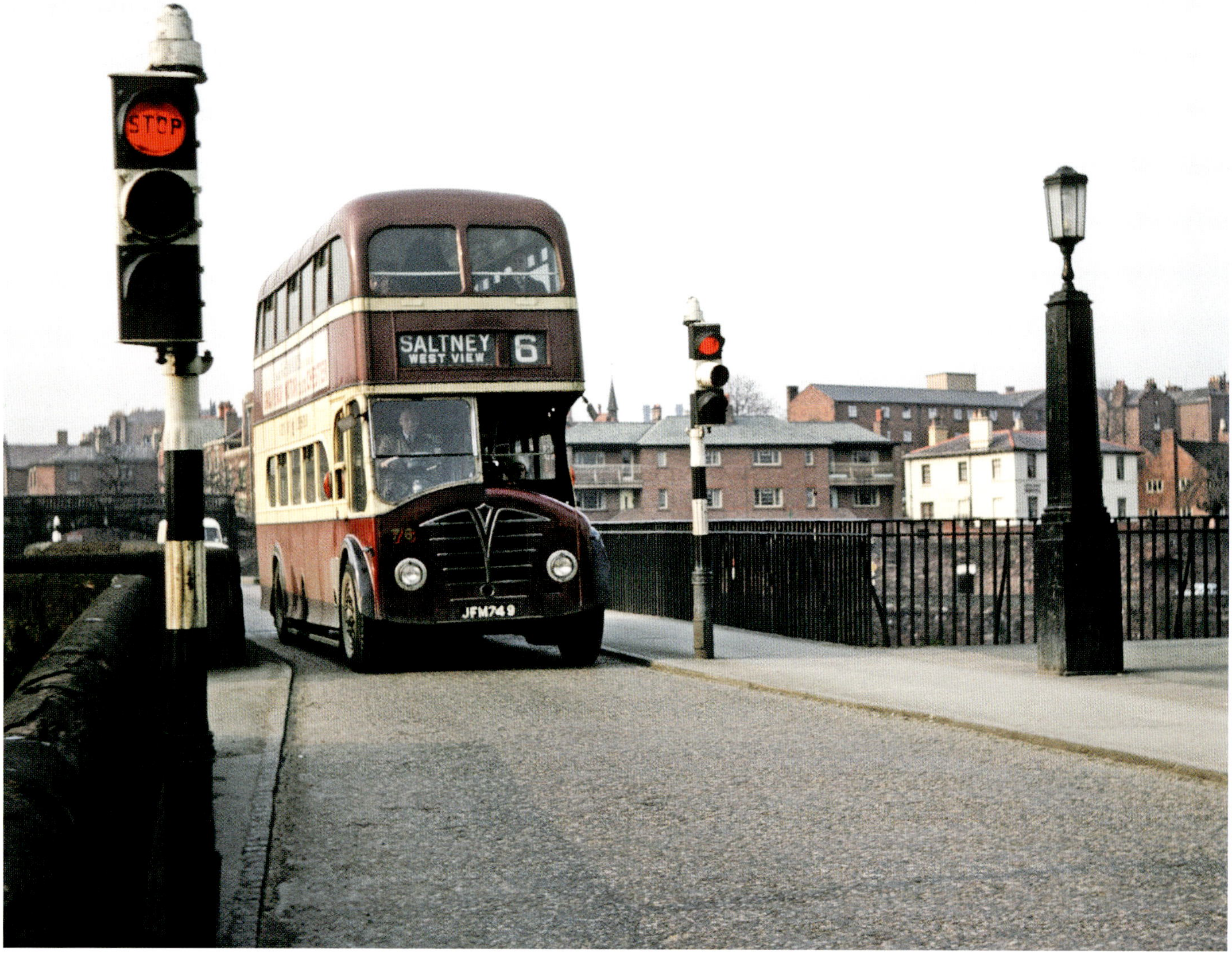

Five more Fodens followed – 77/78 in 1950, 79-81 in 1951. Numbers 77/78/81 had the usual Massey bodies and looked much the same as 72-76 and they ran until the late 1960s, the last, number 78 being withdrawn 1970. Not so the Davies bodied ones – their timber frames deteriorated and they were sold in 1959. In this nicely composed picture, fleet number 76, new in 1949, crosses the River Dee on the Grade 1-listed Old Bridge en-route to Saltney in April 1963; it would run for another two years. *Roy Marshall*

Opposite top There were no more Fodens and from 1953 until production ended in 1969 Chester bought Gardner-engined Guy Arab double-deckers – 47 of them. Fleet numbering restarted at 1 with an order for six – numbers 1-3 having Massey bodies. Just beyond the Old Bridge shown in the previous picture, number 2 passes the row of mock-Tudor buildings on Handbridge on 12 September 1968. *Roy Marshall*

Opposite bottom The bodies on numbers 4-6 were built by Guy Motors and entered service in 1954. Guy had an arrangement with Park Royal to use that firm's frames for the small number of double-deck bodies that it built and the result looked much the same as Park Royal's own product. With a wonderful backdrop of half timbered buildings, number 4 waits for its crew the one of the bus bays in the town hall square on Northgate Street. To the left of the bus is the well-known Clemence's Restaurant, where the Dennis Williams Quintet performed every Thursday and Saturday in the small dance-hall at the rear of the restaurant. There was jazz too and it was the first venue for the Wall City Jazz Men – 'Dance to Dixieland Music at The Wall City Jazz Club', admission 3 shillings (two shillings and sixpence if you were a member). The band played at the opening night of Liverpool's Cavern Club on 16 January 1957. *Ian Stewart*

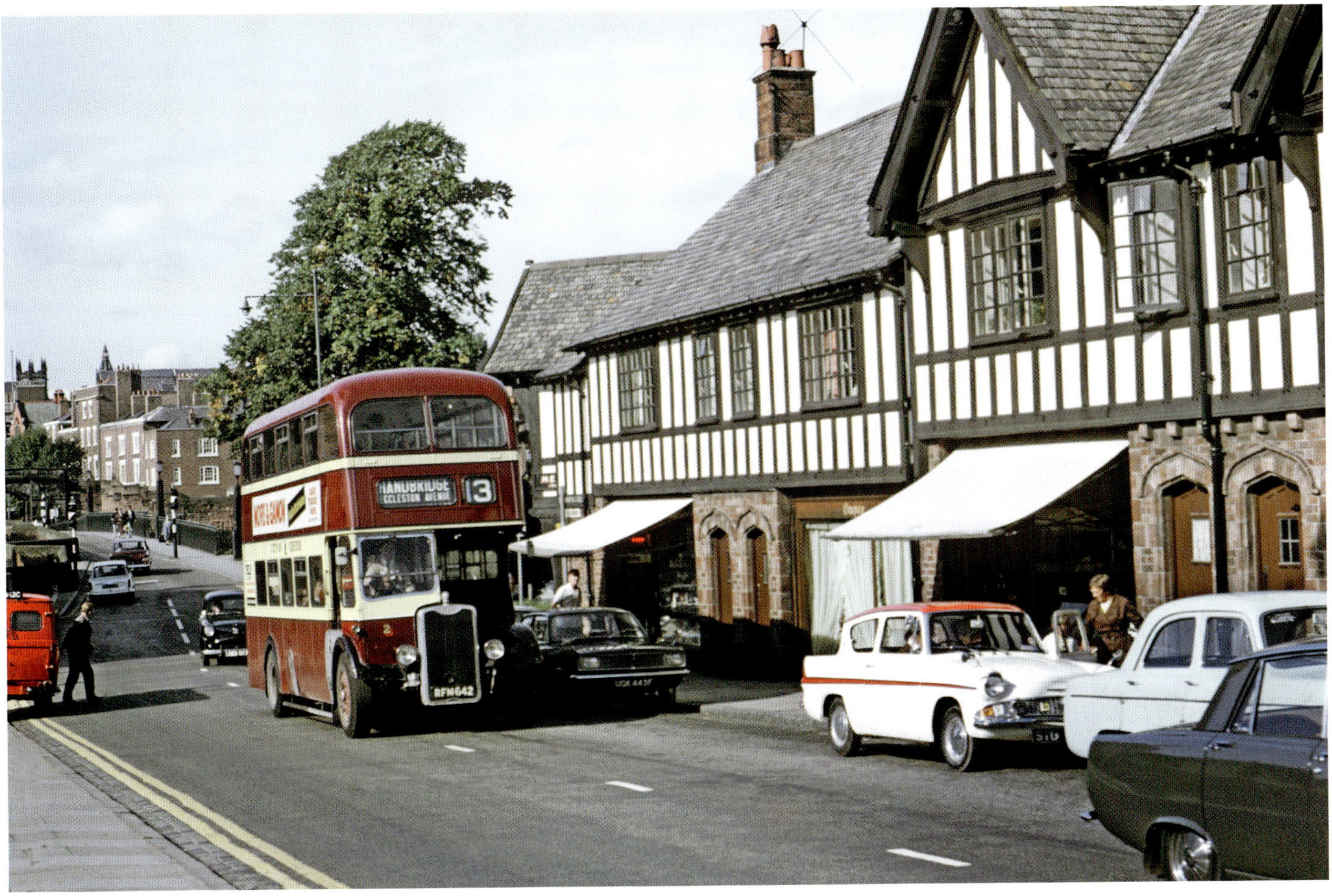
HANDBRIDGE
ECCLESTON AVENUE
13
RFM642

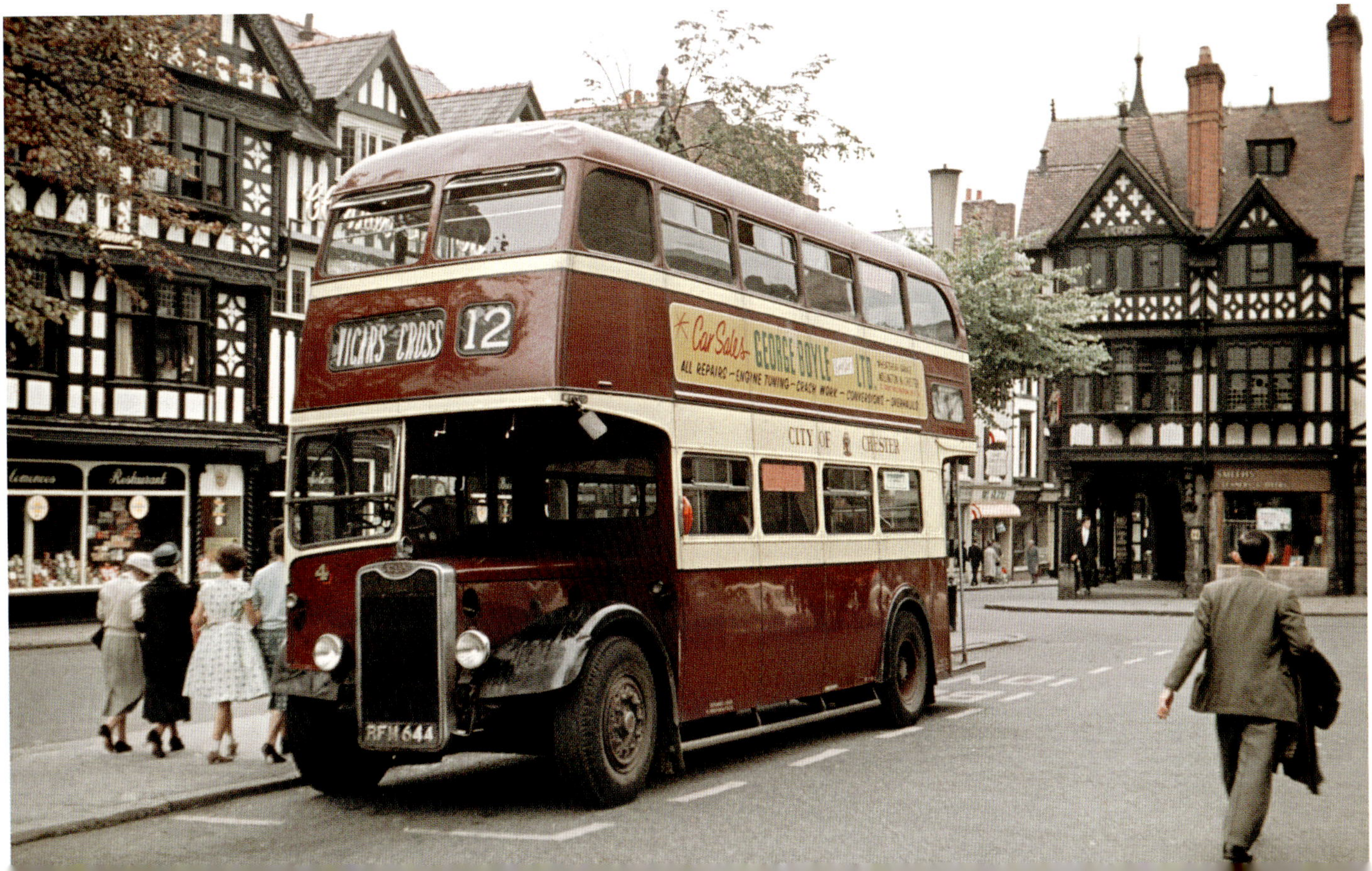
VICARS CROSS
12
Car Sales GEORGE BOYLE LTD.
ALL REPAIRS—ENGINE TUNING—COACH WORK—CONVERSIONS
CITY OF CHESTER
Restaurant

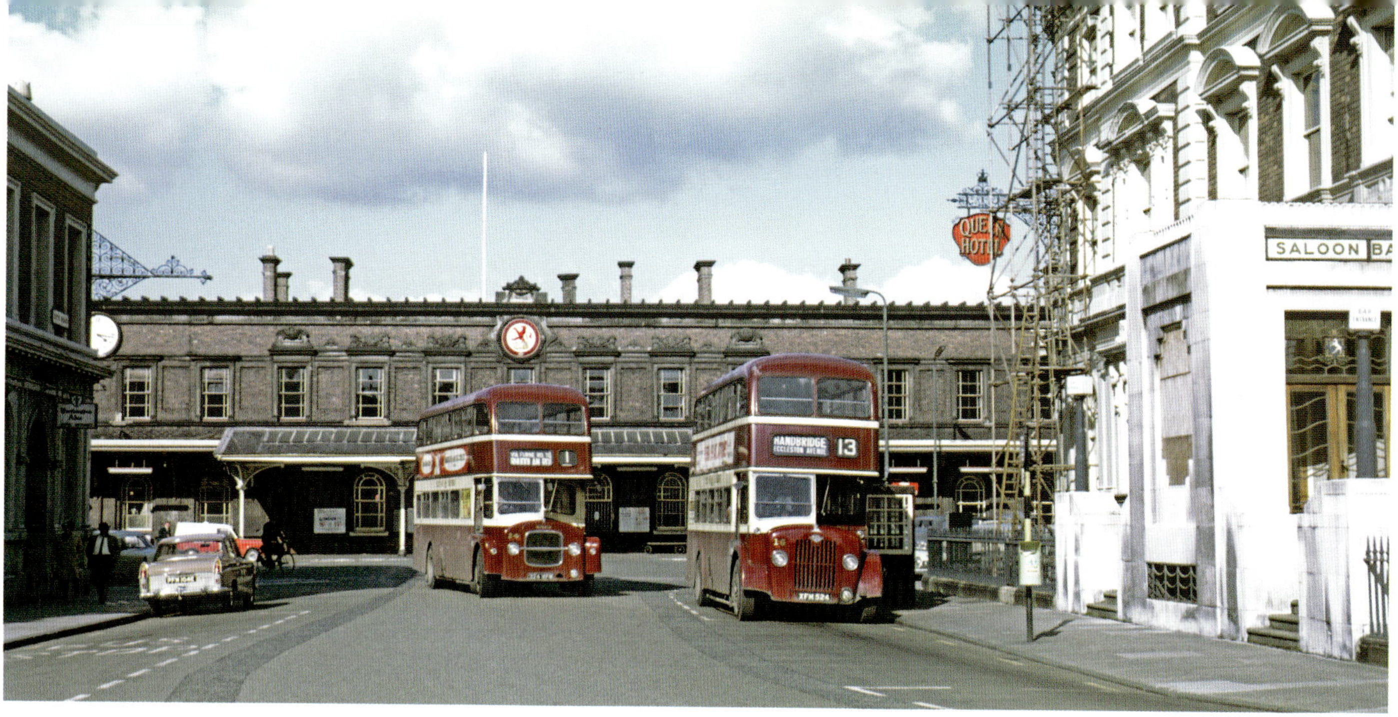

Two more batches of six Guy Arab/Masseys followed, numbered 7-18. Numbers 13-18 followed the current industry move to reduce vehicle weight and had five-cylinder Gardner 5LW engines, rather than the usual 6LW. At Chester General railway station number 16 is working the 13 service to Handbridge; alongside, on service 1 to Rhuddlan Road, is 24 which has the so-called 'Johannesburg' version of the bonnet/engine cowl. Built in 1848 and later shared by the GWR and LMS, the station was at the important and busy railway junction of lines from London (via Crewe), Holyhead, Liverpool, Manchester and Shrewsbury and the development of the railways contributed much to the city's growth. *Alan Mortimer*

With their Davies bodies too far gone to repair, the simplest thing was to replace numbers 79 and 80. Southampton Corporation was selling some of its fleet of Park Royal-bodied Guy Arabs; they were in very good condition and in February 1959 Chester bought two of the 1946 ones, fitted them with Chester-style indicators and numbered them 56/57 which were vacant numbers in the current list. They were a bargain and ran until 1968/69. This picture shows number 57 in Bridge Street in November 1967. It was sold to a Barnsley scrap dealer in 1968, its valuable Gardner 6LW engine almost certainly being shipped to Hong Kong and fitted to a boat. *Geoffrey Morant*

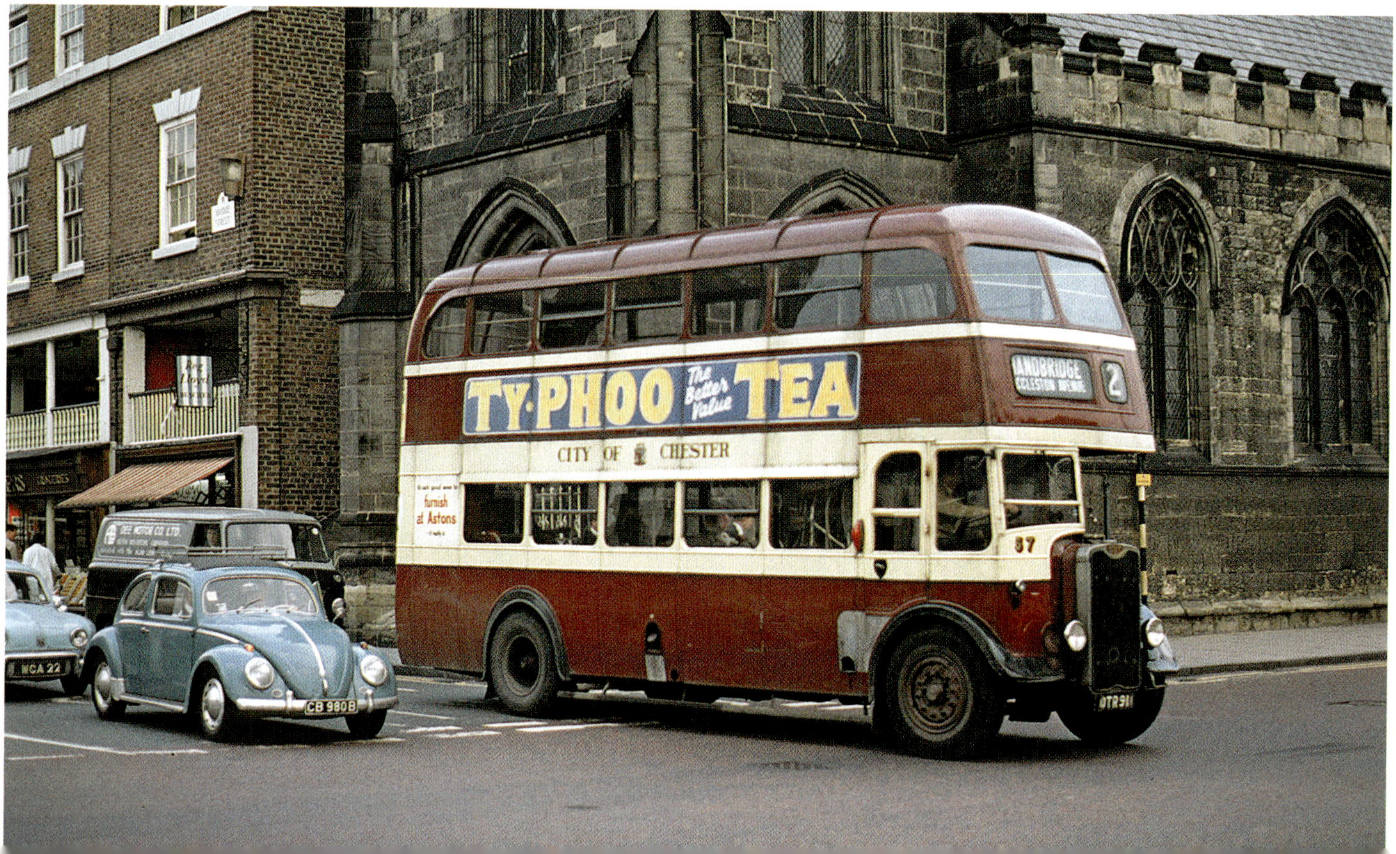

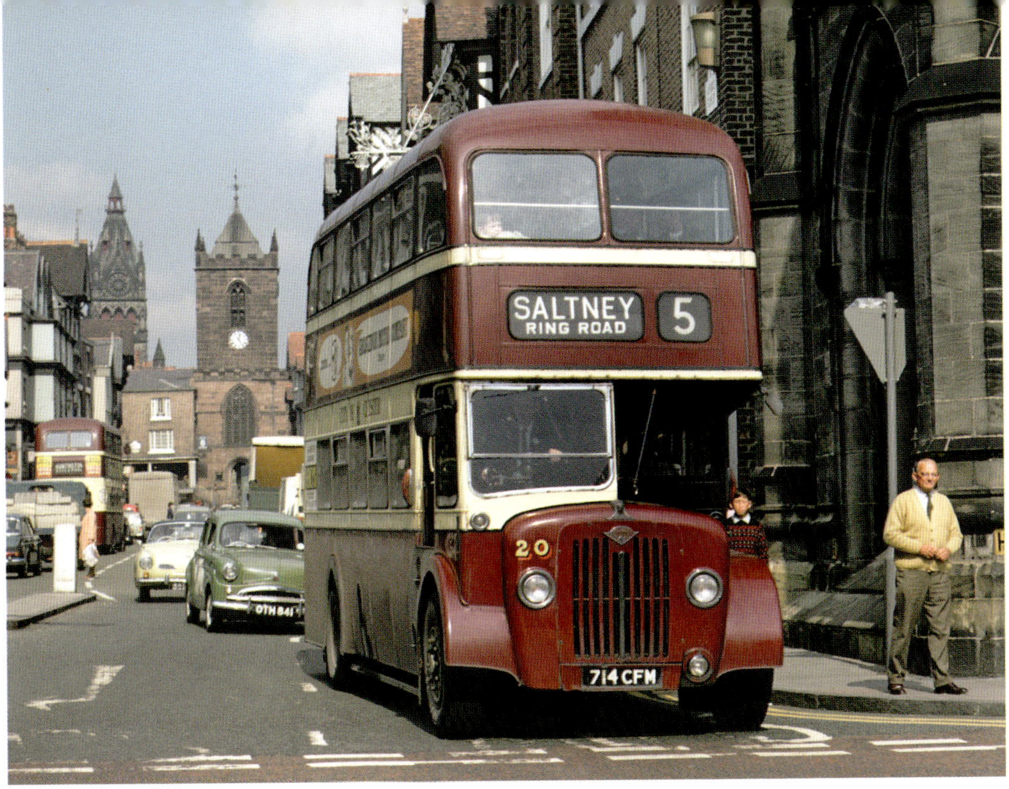

This splendid picture of Massey/Arab 20 at the junction of Bridge Street and Eastgate Street in September 1967 perfectly captures the city's streets – and their names which are taken from the gates in the city walls. Number 20 has come from Northgate and the similar Arab/Massey going in the other direction will turn right at the far end of Bridge Street at St Peter's Church into Watergate Street and then almost immediately left into Northgate, stopping by the Town Hall whose tower can be seen in the background. *Geoffrey Morant*

The seven Massey-bodied 6LW-engined Guy Arab IVs (24-30) delivered during 1961/62 were something of a change, not least because they were the corporation's first 8ft-wide buses – most other operators, including Crosville, had changed to 8-footers years before. They were up to date, however, in being 30ft-long with forward entrances. A feature which made them look different was the revised bonnet and radiator cowling. Guy had designed this for a South African order and supplied it to the home market for a short period, where it became known as the 'Johannesburg' front. Photographed shortly after delivery in 1962, fleet number 28 is turning from Northgate Street into the bus loading bays in Town Hall Square. The use of these and congestion therein was the subject of friction between the department and Crosville, two of whose ECW-bodied Bristol L single deckers are already there. *Phil Tatt/Online Transport Archive*

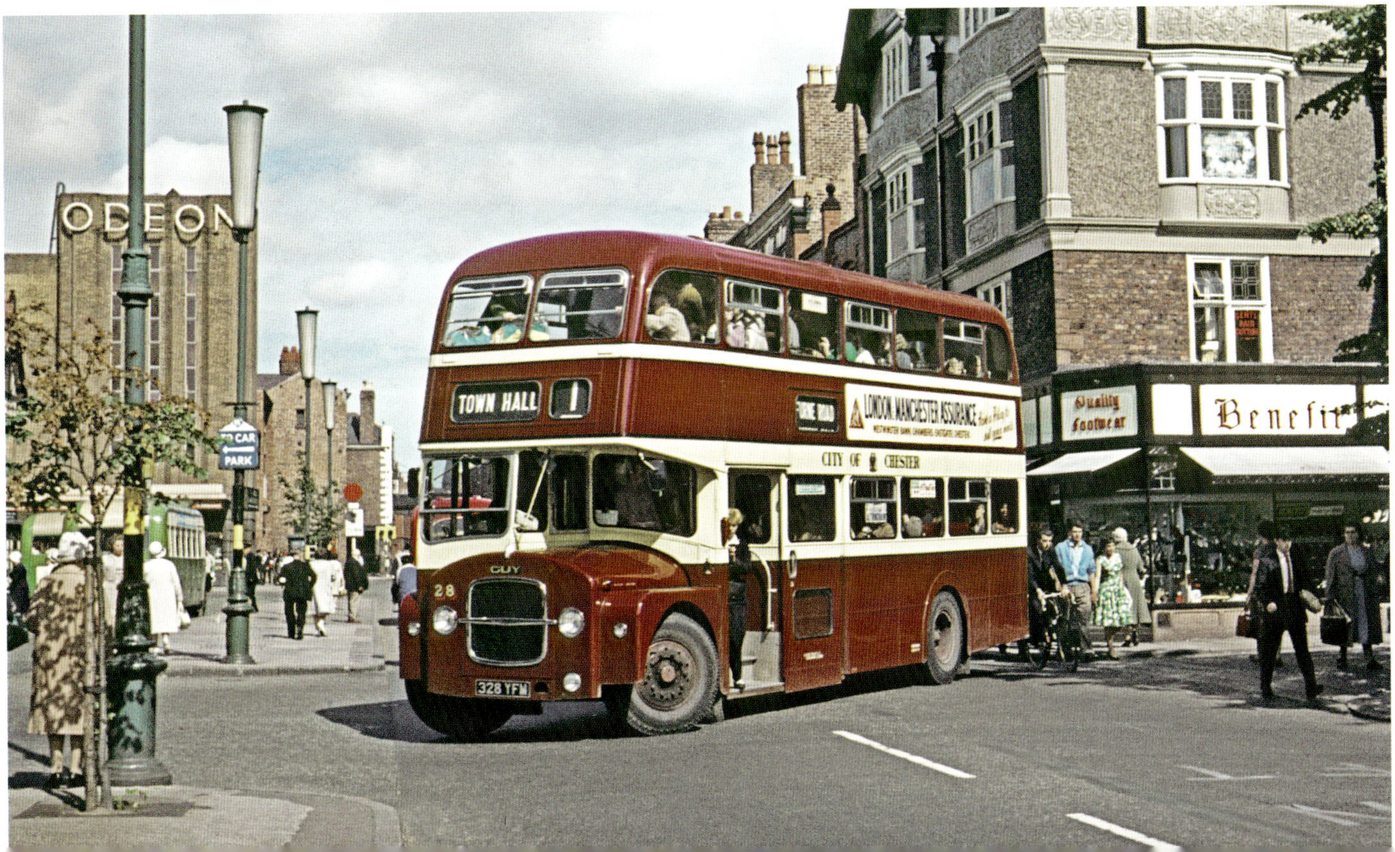

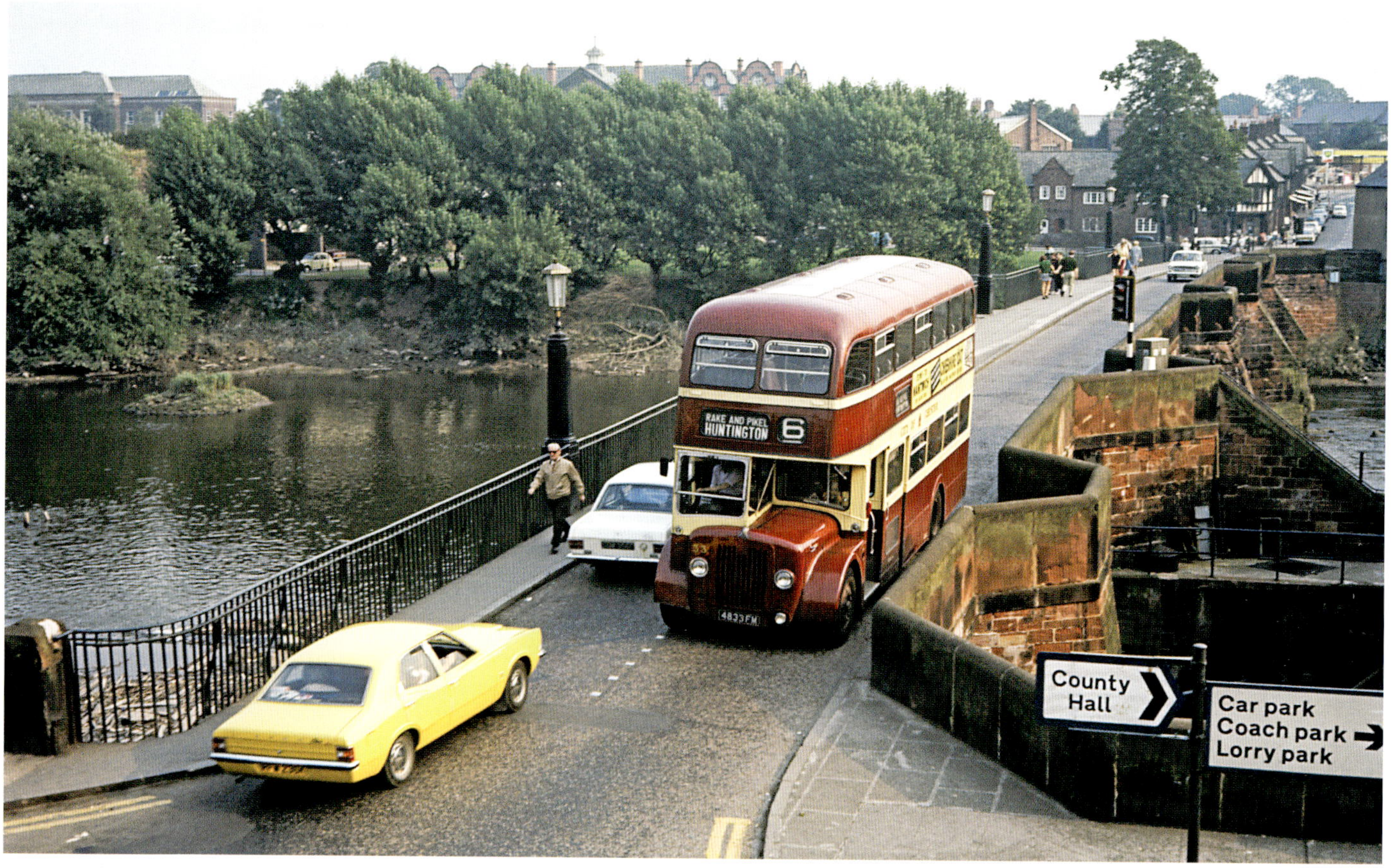
RAKE AND PIKEL
HUNTINGTON
6
4833 FM
County Hall
Car park
Coach park
Lorry park

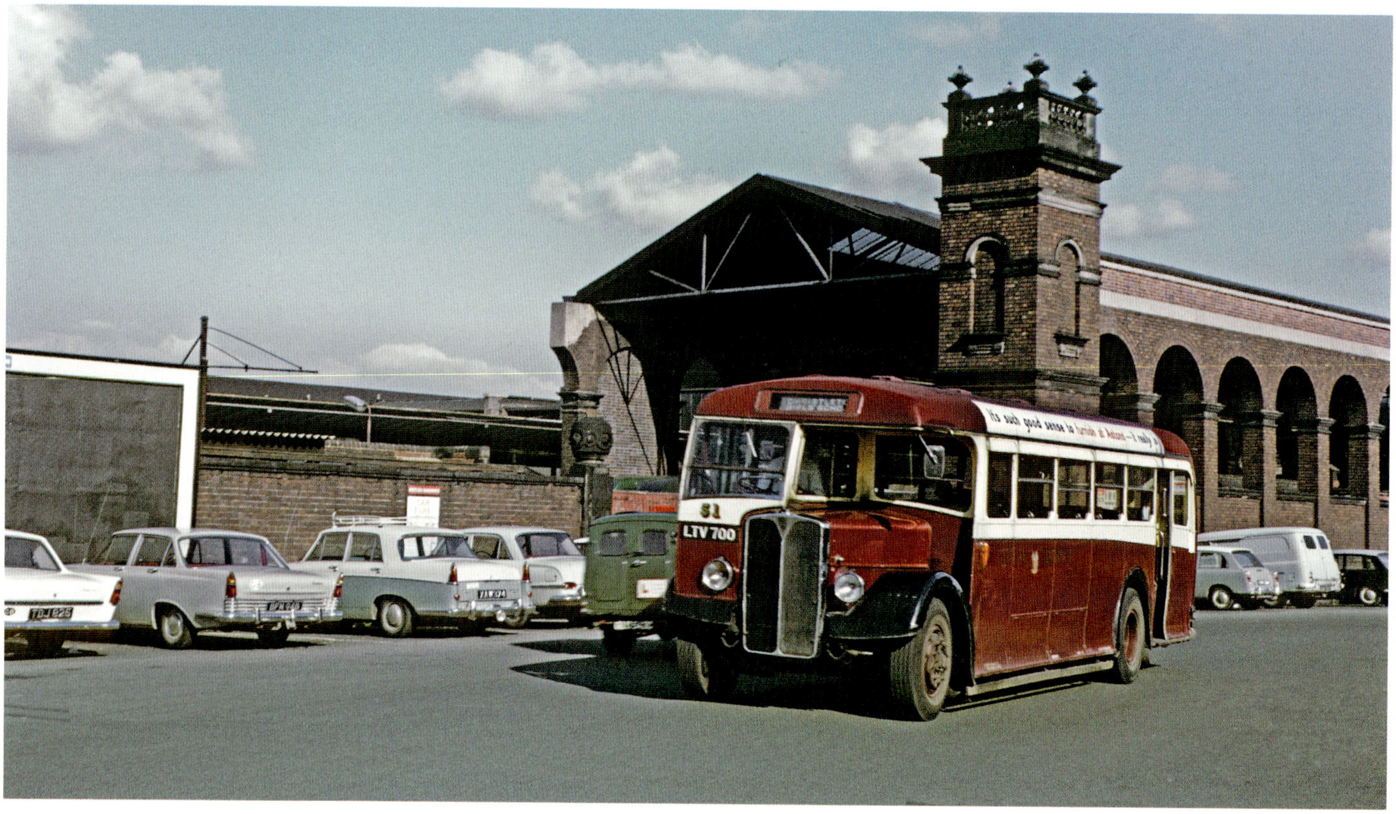
LTV 700

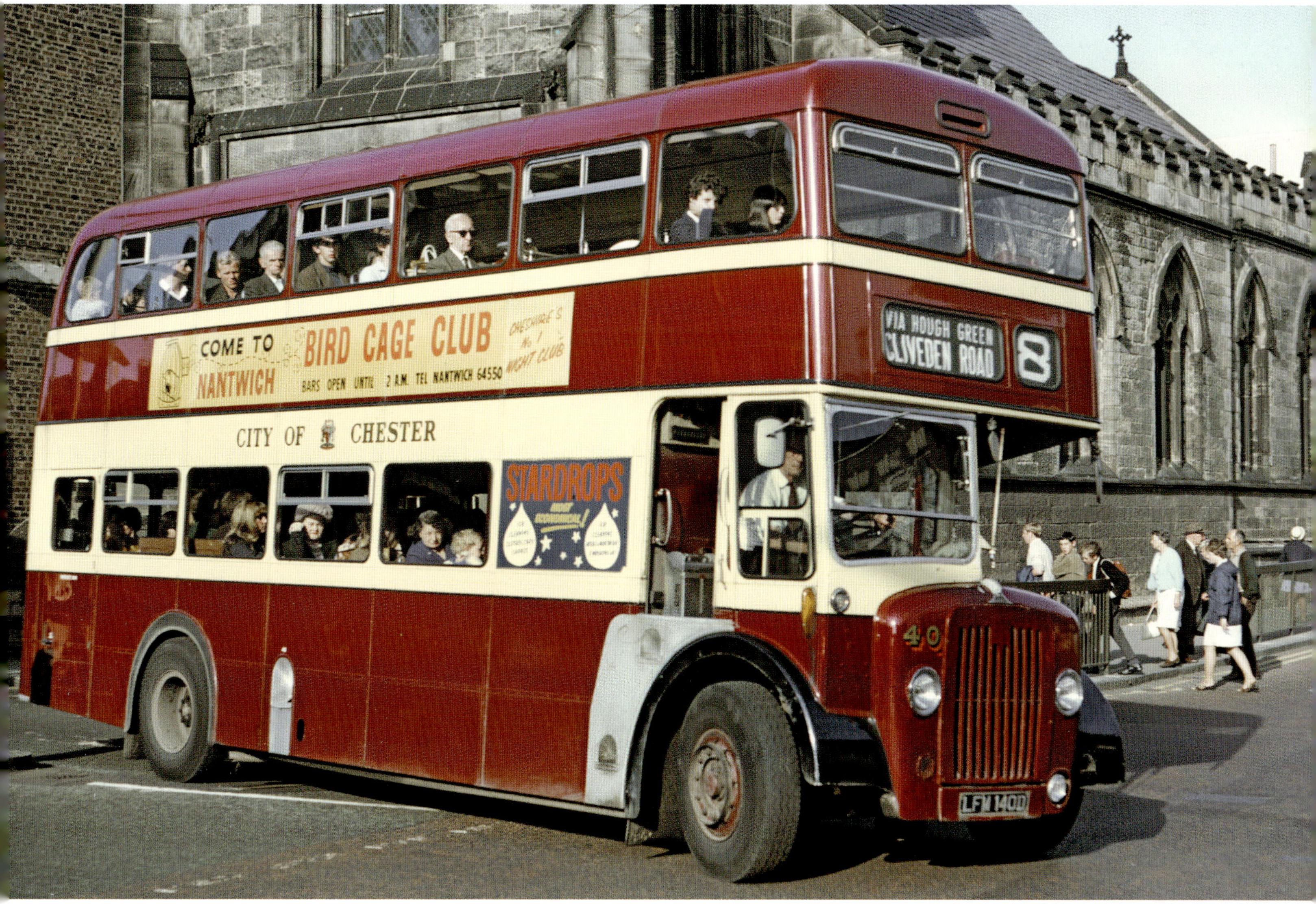

Massey updated its elegant rounded design in part to make it similar to its body for rear-engined double-deckers. With its severe squared off upright front the result was not entirely harmonious. Arab Vs 35-38 of 1965 and 39-41 of 1966 had this style of body. September 1968 *Roy Marshall*

Opposite top Chester normally bought its new vehicles in batches of four. Numbers 27-30 of 1962 and 31-34 of 1963 were the usual Guy/Massey combination, again 30ft-long. The second four had the Arab Mark V chassis which had a revised frame allowing a lower loading step for the front entrance. The city walls were a good place from which to photograph buses from different angles, as in this picture of 33 crossing the Old Bridge on 2 September 1972. *G D Parry*

Opposite bottom Two of the 1946/47 AEC Regals were withdrawn in 1962/63 and replaced by another second hand purchase. Bought from Nottingham Corporation in 1963, it was a 1951 AEC Regal III with a 35-seater rear-entrance East Lancs body. Numbered 51 in a new 'single decker' series, in this picture it is seen passing the General Station in 1965. It ran for five years. *Marcus Eavis/Online Transport Archive*

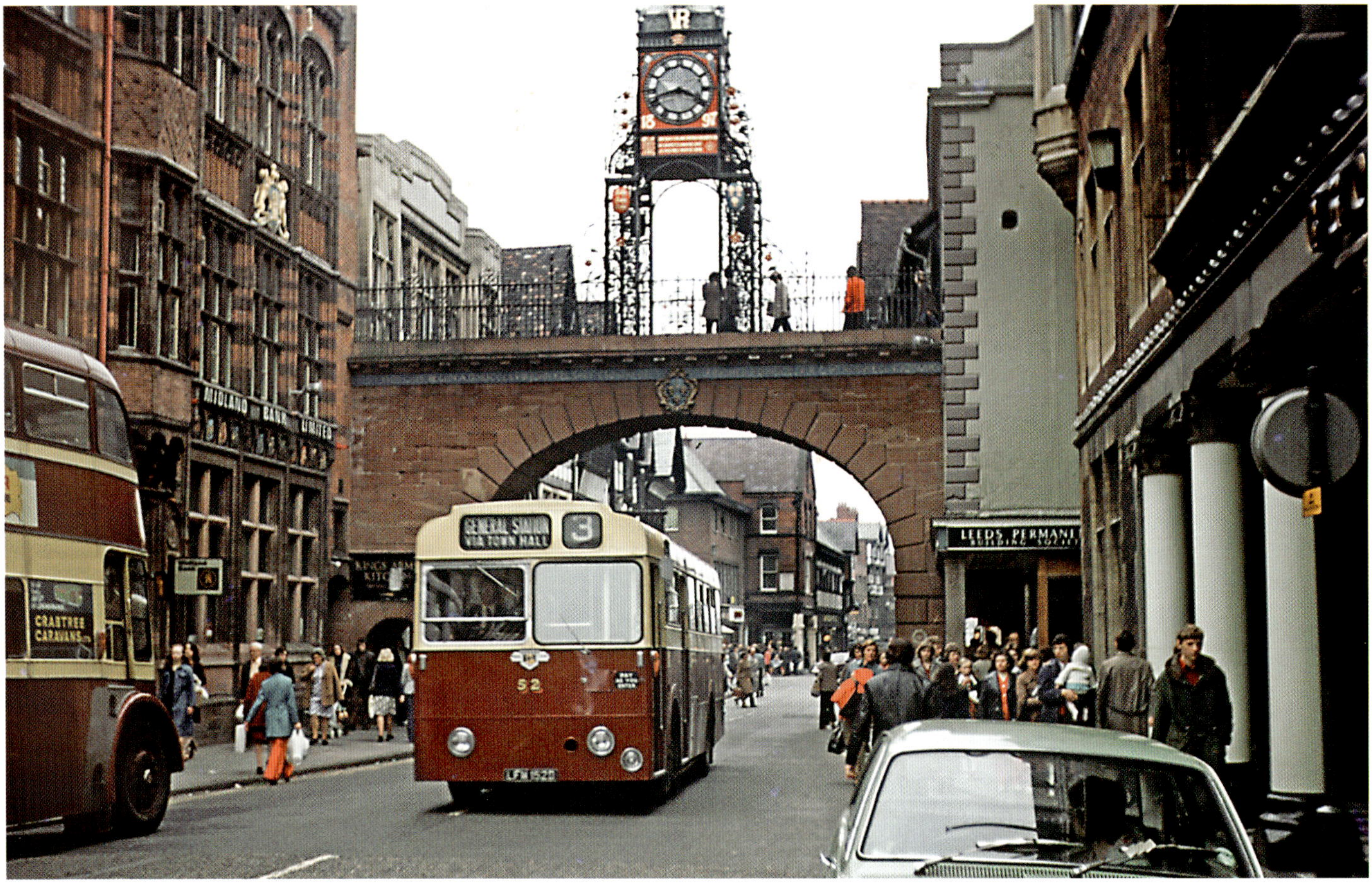

With nothing on offer from Guy, fleet numbers 52-54 were Leyland Tiger Cub single-deckers with dual-door Massey bodies equipped for one-person operation. One was delivered in each of 1966, 1967 and 1968. This picture shows number 52 when new, on a crowded Eastgate. The bus is passing beneath the sandstone East Gate with its famous four-sided clock which marked Queen Victoria's Golden Jubilee. *Peter Roberts*

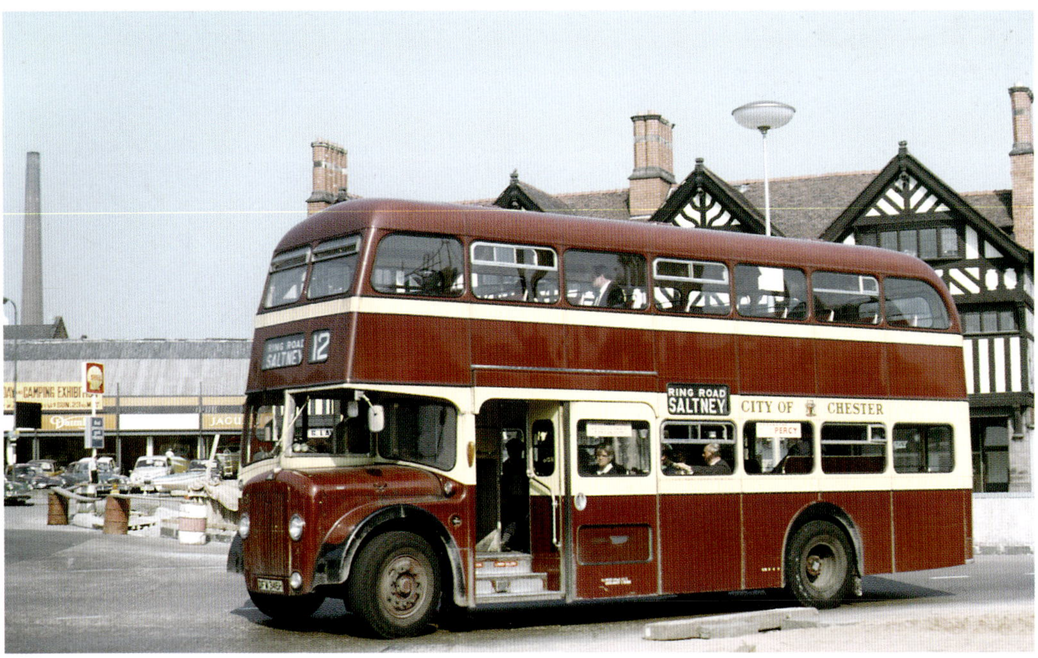

The six Guy Arab Vs (42-47) delivered during 1969 highlighted the changes in the UK bus building and operating industries. The directors of Massey Bros Ltd decided the time had come to sell the business and the firm was taken over by and absorbed into the other Wigan-based coachbuilder Northern Counties, which took over the contract and supplied the bodies for 42-47. The Guy Arab chassis for numbers 45-47 were the last bus chassis built for the home market by Guy Motors which had been taken over by Jaguar in 1961 and merged into British Leyland in 1966. Number 45 was one of those three final Guy Arabs and in this May 1971 picture is leaving the city on a 12 to Saltney. *Roy Marshall*

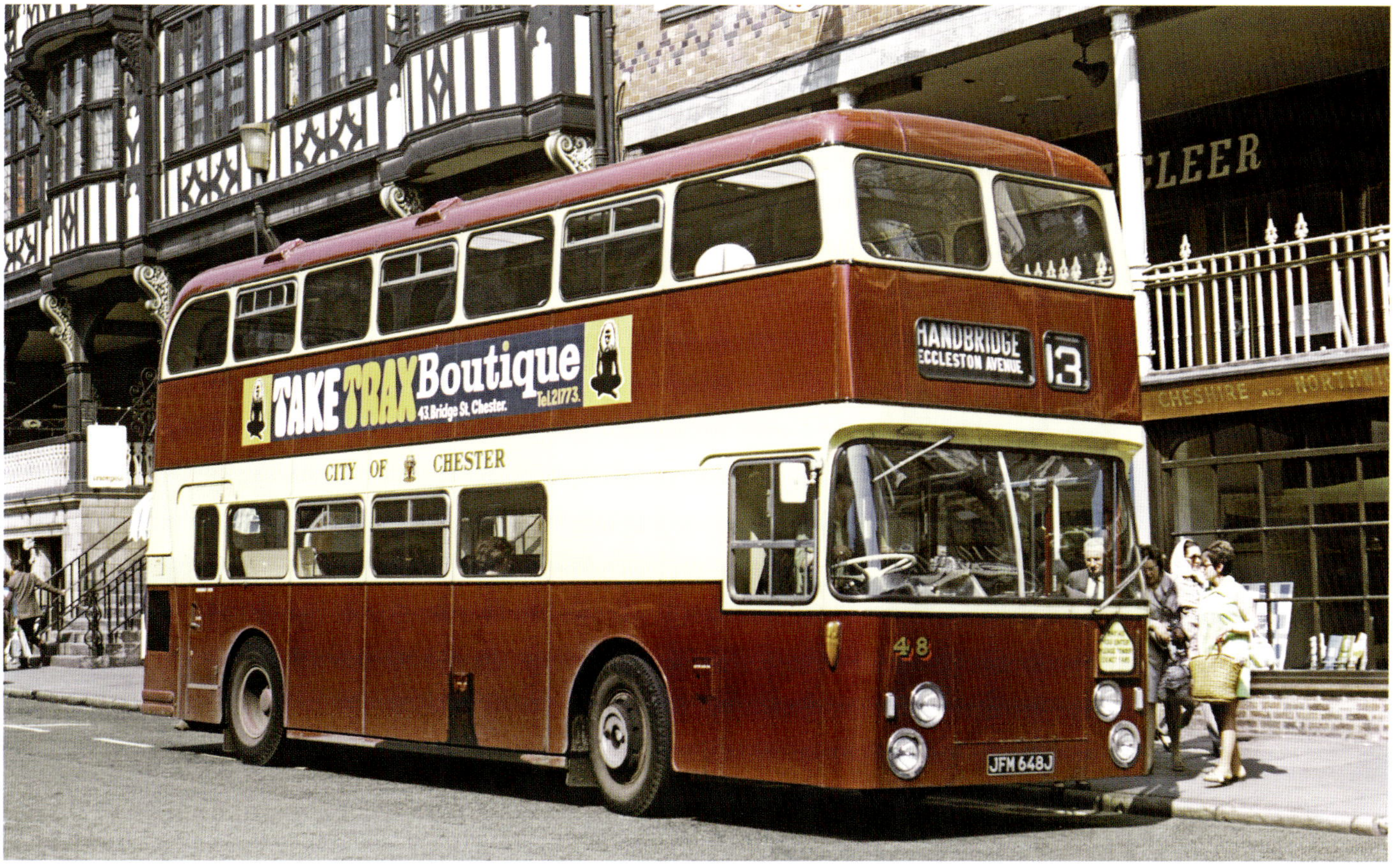

Chester could get no more Guy Arabs but it could still get Gardner engines and Daimler's Fleetline was generally acknowledged as the best of the rear-engined double-deck chassis. So Chester bought Northern Counties-bodied Fleetlines – three in 1970, two batches of three in 1972, and three in 1974, all equipped for one-person operation. They were numbered 48-50 and 55-63, the idea of segregating the single deckers (then numbered 51-54) having been given up. The bodies on all twelve were to the standard design from Northern Counties since the mid 1960s. *Roy Marshall*

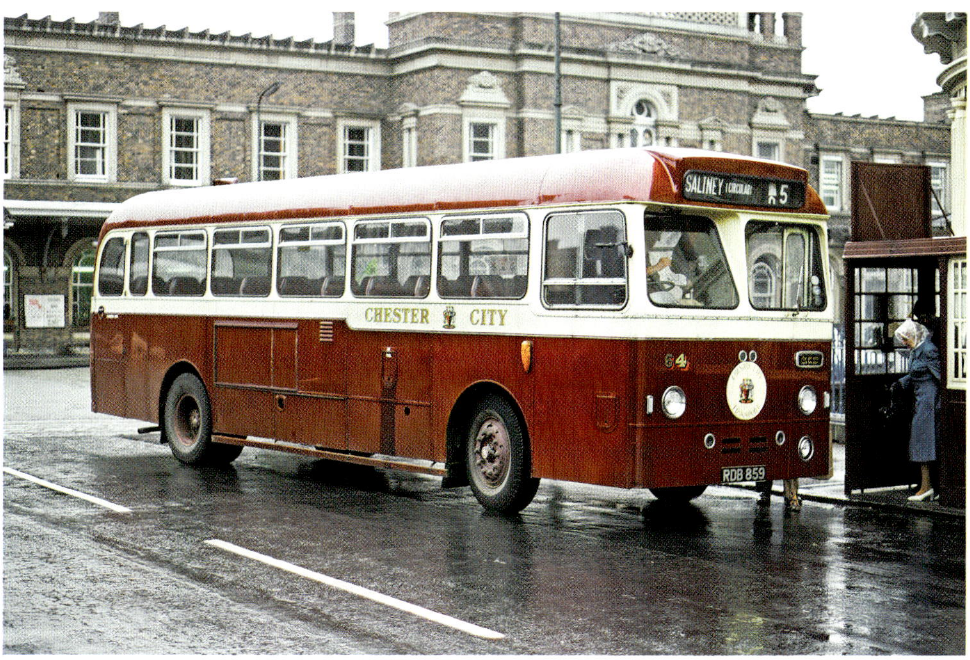

An experimental summer-time shoppers' town centre service required extra single-deckers. In 1973 the SELNEC Passenger Transport Executive had some surplus Willowbrook-bodied AEC Reliances which it had acquired when it took over the main part of the North Western Road Car Co in 1972. Chester bought two and, numbered 64/65, they entered service in early 1974 (64) and late 1973 (65). This picture shows 64 in July 1974 – the yellow roundel on the front and 'Chester City' fleetname were part of a revision of livery and branding introduced by the new local authority which took over on 1st April 1974. The new authority was not itself a city but Chester still was and proud of it. *Roy Marshall*

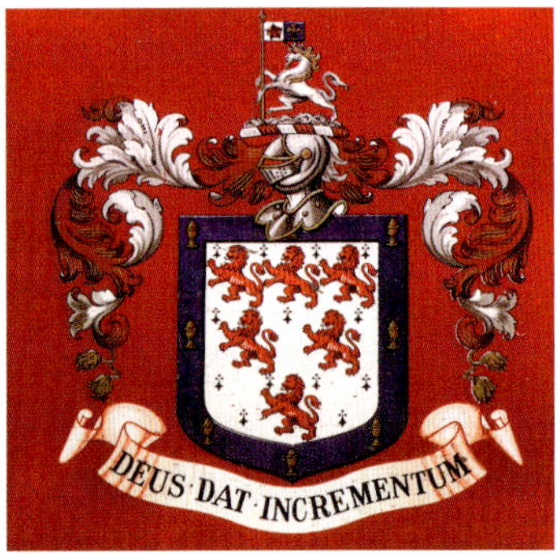

Warrington

There was great variety in Warrington's fleet of around 90 buses. Principally a Leyland user before and after the war, its postwar fleet also included Guy Arab double-deckers, three of the less common single-deck Arab, the largest fleet of Foden double-deckers anywhere – some of which had bodies removed from pre-war Crossleys, twenty nine Bristol Ks with Gardner 6LW engines, Daimler Fleetlines, an Albion Nimbus and specially-built narrow-width Leyland PD2/40s. There was rather less variation in bodywork, which was mainly by East Lancs. Fleet numbering was equally interesting, sometimes filling gaps and at others separating vehicles into makes and types, with several renumberings of the fleet as general managers changed – it had six managers in the years 1945 to 1974.

There was wider interest, too, for if you stood near Bridge Foot or the adjacent bus station in Arpley Station Approach you would likely see as many Crosville, North Western and Lancashire United buses as corporation ones plus an occasional one from St Helens and Salford Corporations and also independent Naylor's blue Guy Arab.

It was not an easy town in which to operate buses. Although strongly industrial, the town centre retained much of its central area medieval street pattern with narrow streets. Services to the south of the town were often interrupted for long periods by the three swing bridges across the Manchester Ship Canal, eventually replaced by over bridges, and, until 1957, the notorious Wilderspool railway level crossing.

The Corporation's tramways opened in 1902, the first buses arrived in 1913 although the bus network was not extended until 1928. The trams were replaced between 1931 and 1935 and bus services expanded with joint agreements with Lancashire United, North Western – the latter keeping its local allocation in the Corporation's bus garage – and Crosville, which had a garage in the town.

Warrington was outside the areas of the Merseyside and SELNEC PTEs and when they were formed, the town's buses remained under municipal control. The 1974 local government reorganisation created the much enlarged Borough of Warrington, which, having always been in Lancashire, suddenly became part of the county of Cheshire. The transport undertaking passed to the new borough, its title changed to Warrington Borough Transport, at which point its remit widened and this book's coverage ends.

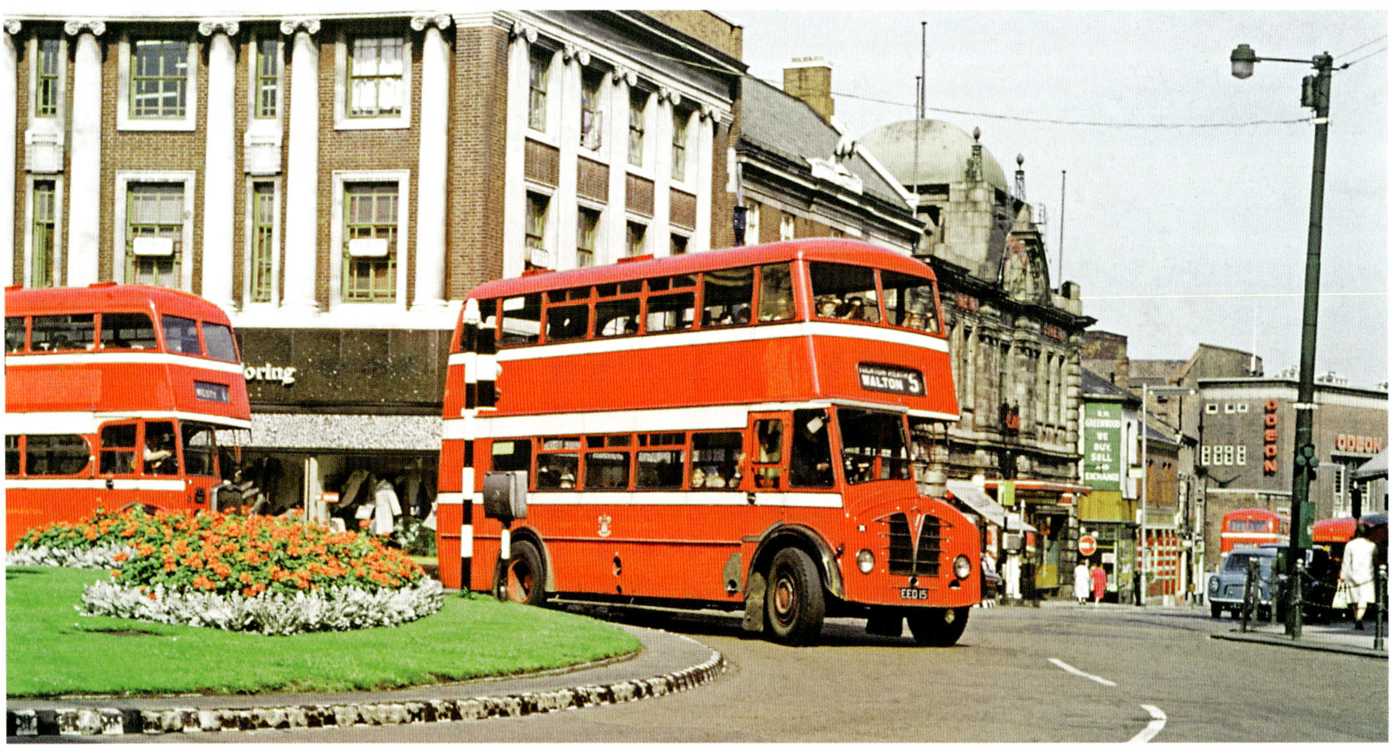

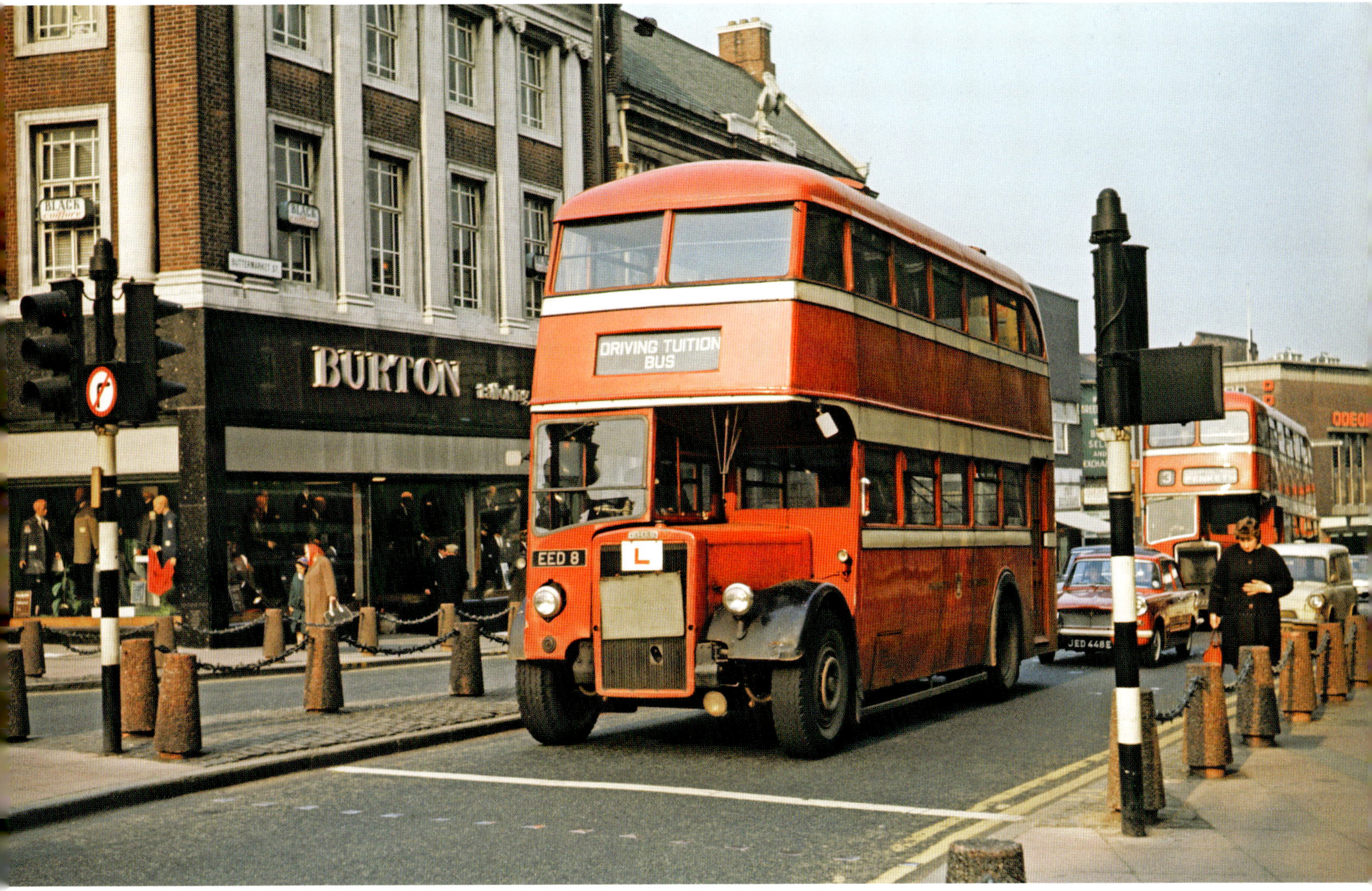

Warrington took delivery of fifteen Leyland PD1s in 1946/7. Thirteen had highbridge bodies built to Leyland design by Alexander under sub-contract to Leyland, the latter's body shops being fully loaded; the other two had lowbridge bodies by Bruce of Cardiff. When new they carried a short-lived maroon and cream livery, which was changed in 1947 to bright red and off-white. The Alexanders were numbered 16-20, 24, 25, 27, 29, 35 and 38, rationalised to 14-24 in the 1948 renumbering scheme. Seen here in Buttermarket Street on 27 March 1969, EED 8 was on driver training duty, its role from 1961 to 1974 for which it was fitted with a platform door and renumbered 4, having previously been 38 and 24. As in so many towns, men's tailors Burton's occupied a prime corner site at the town centre's principal cross roads at Market Gate. *Alan Murray-Rust*

Opposite Warrington eventually owned fifteen Foden PVD6 double-deckers, delivered between 1948 and 1956 all with Gardner 6LW engines. Seven entered service during 1948/49, the most unusual being number 36. Its chassis was the prototype PVD6. First registered as HMB 395 in 1945, Gardner-engined and Willowbrook-bodied chassis 23000 was Foden's demonstrator. Foden then built a new, updated chassis with a Foden two-stroke engine, fitted it with the Willowbrook body off HMB 395 and registered it KMA 370; registration number HMB 395 was cancelled. Chassis 23000 was then updated to the new specification and sold, unregistered, to Warrington along with six new chassis. New bus bodies from dependable builders were in short supply. With new Leyland and Foden chassis in store at its garage with no early prospect of bodies, the corporation decided to remove the Metro Cammell metal-framed bodies from six Crossley Mancunian chassis new in 1935 and one Metro Cammell –Crossley body from a 1936 Mancunian and have James Hilton & Company of Leigh (a firm which was doing a considerable amount of body refurbishment for municipal operators) fit them to five new Leyland PD1 chassis and two Foden chassis, one of which was 23000. The bodies fitted well on to the Leyland but on the Fodens (36, 37) the cab had to be extended to meet the Foden front, resulting in a short section of the cab protruding from the rest of the body. This is chassis 23000, fleet number 36, registered EED 15 and with the Metro Cammell body off Crossley Mancunian ED 8700. A bit of a mix it may have been but it ran until 1962. In this August 1961 picture it is negotiating the Market Gate roundabout at the top end of Buttermarket Street, followed by one of the FED-registered Bristol K6Gs. *John Ryan*

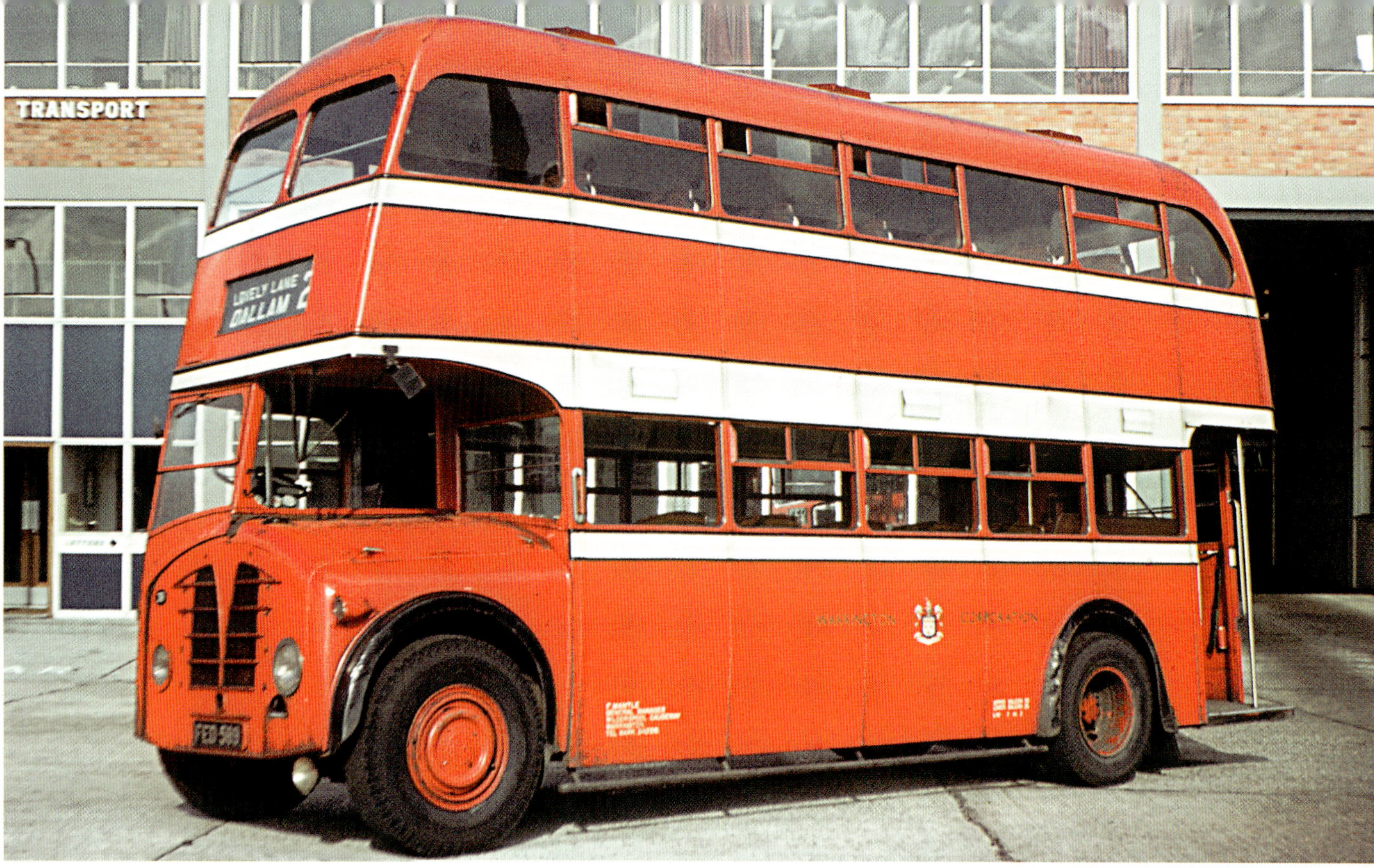

The other five Fodens (38-42) were to have had Saunders Roe bodies but a request for a large price increase caused the contract to be cancelled and re-let to East Lancs. This is number 39, taken in 1963 outside the Transport Department's fine new offices and workshops, which were built in front of the existing garage on Wilderspool Causeway and opened the previous year. Warrington's livery was unusual in that it used an off-white (formally 'ivory') rather than cream for the relief colour. *Peter Roberts*

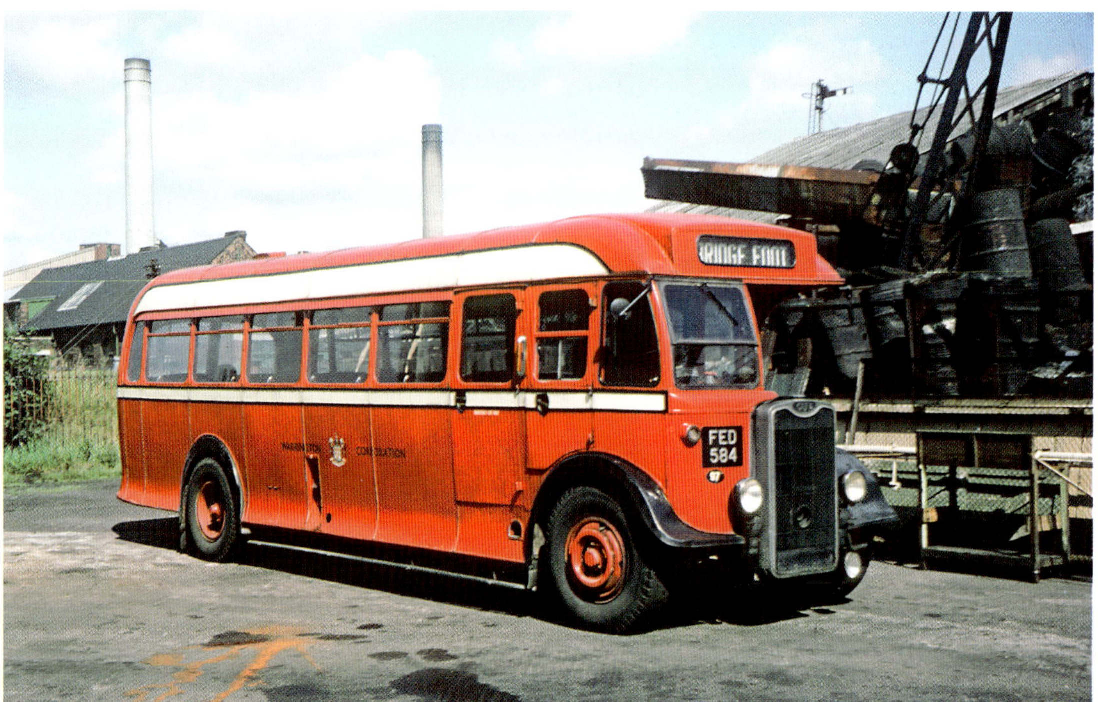

Three Gardner 6LW-engined Guy Arab single-deckers (95-97) with 33-seat forward-entrance Guy bodies joined the fleet in 1949. Number 97 was photographed at the back of the depot in August 1964. In 1965 it was adapted for one-man operation but union difficulties delayed its use for several months. When it was withdrawn in 1968, a plan to convert it to a mobile workshop fell through and it went for scrap. *Reg Wilson/Online Transport Archive*

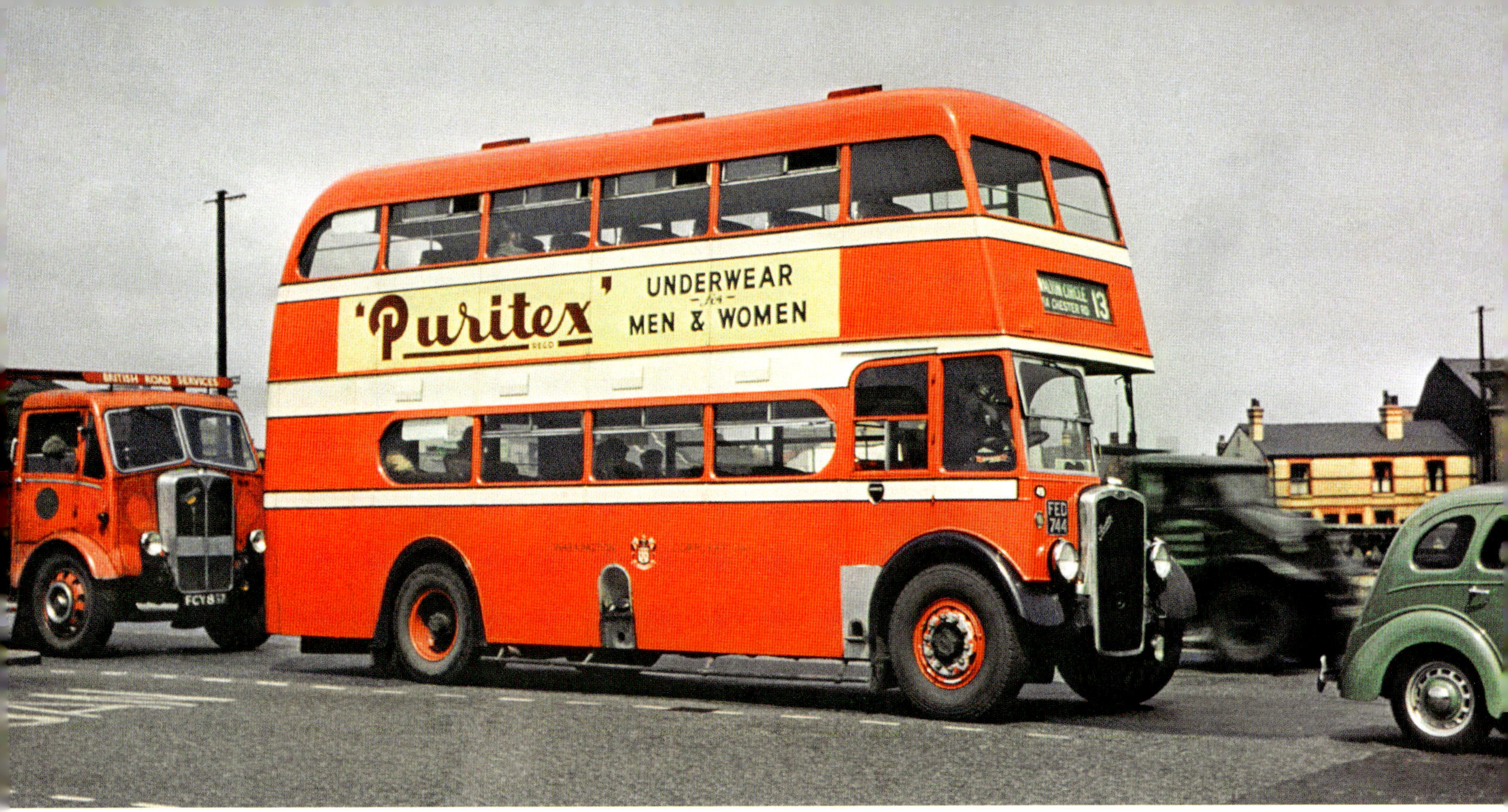

Early in 1947 twenty Leyland-bodied Leyland PD2s were ordered by new general manager Roddie MacKenzie, who was appointed in 1946 but left in 1949 to join the Road Haulage Executive (British Road Services) before returning to the bus industry in which he had a distinguished career. Leyland's earliest delivery forecast was 1950 but he was still able to obtain the Bristol chassis on order, as newly nationalised Bristol was allowed to fulfil existing orders, before being restricted to supplying only government-owned fleets, principally the former Tilling group. Gleaming in the sunshine on Warrington Bridge on 18 May 1950, and (somewhat appropriately) followed by a British Road Services AEC lorry, fleet number 49 was one of 29 Bristol K6Gs. The first two (numbered 14, 15 and then 43, 44) were delivered in 1947 and had East Lancs bodies whilst 45-71, delivered in 1949 and 1950, had similar-looking bodies by Bruce Coachworks of Cardiff. Bruce was a relative newcomer and had an arrangement with East Lancs to use the latter's frames. *C Carter*

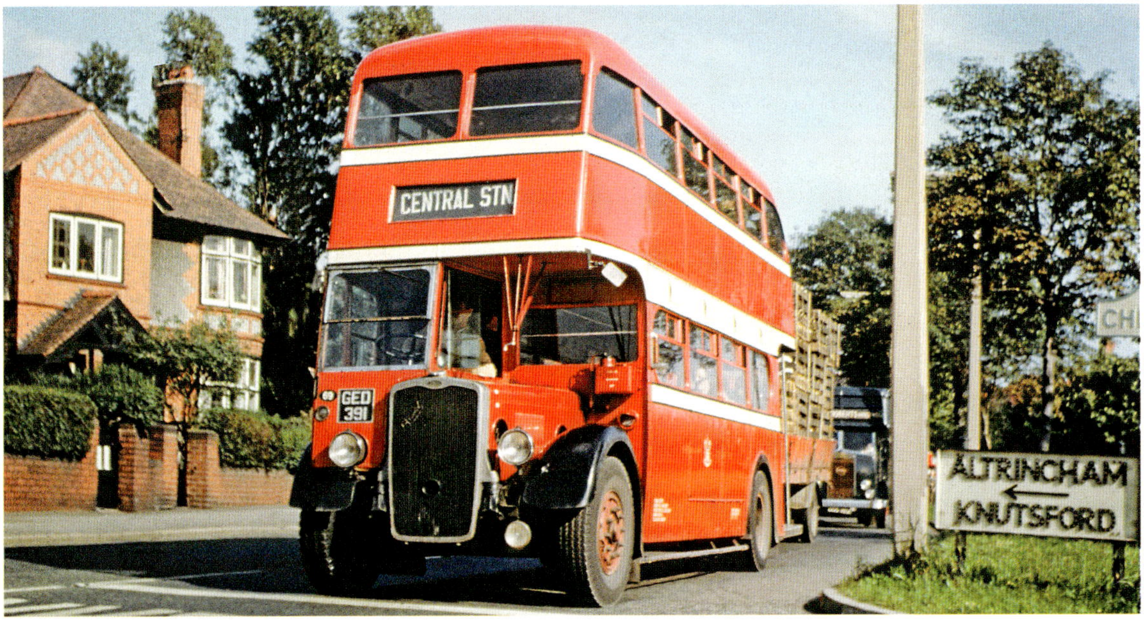

From the second batch of Bristol K6Gs, Bruce-bodied 69 is inbound for Warrington on Knutsford Road, Grappenhall, Cheshire, its inward journey likely to be prolonged if the swing bridge is closed. To the offside of the front number plate is the small oval white on black fleet number plate – in use from just after the war until the early 1960s, they were a feature of the Warrington fleet. *Arnold Richardson*

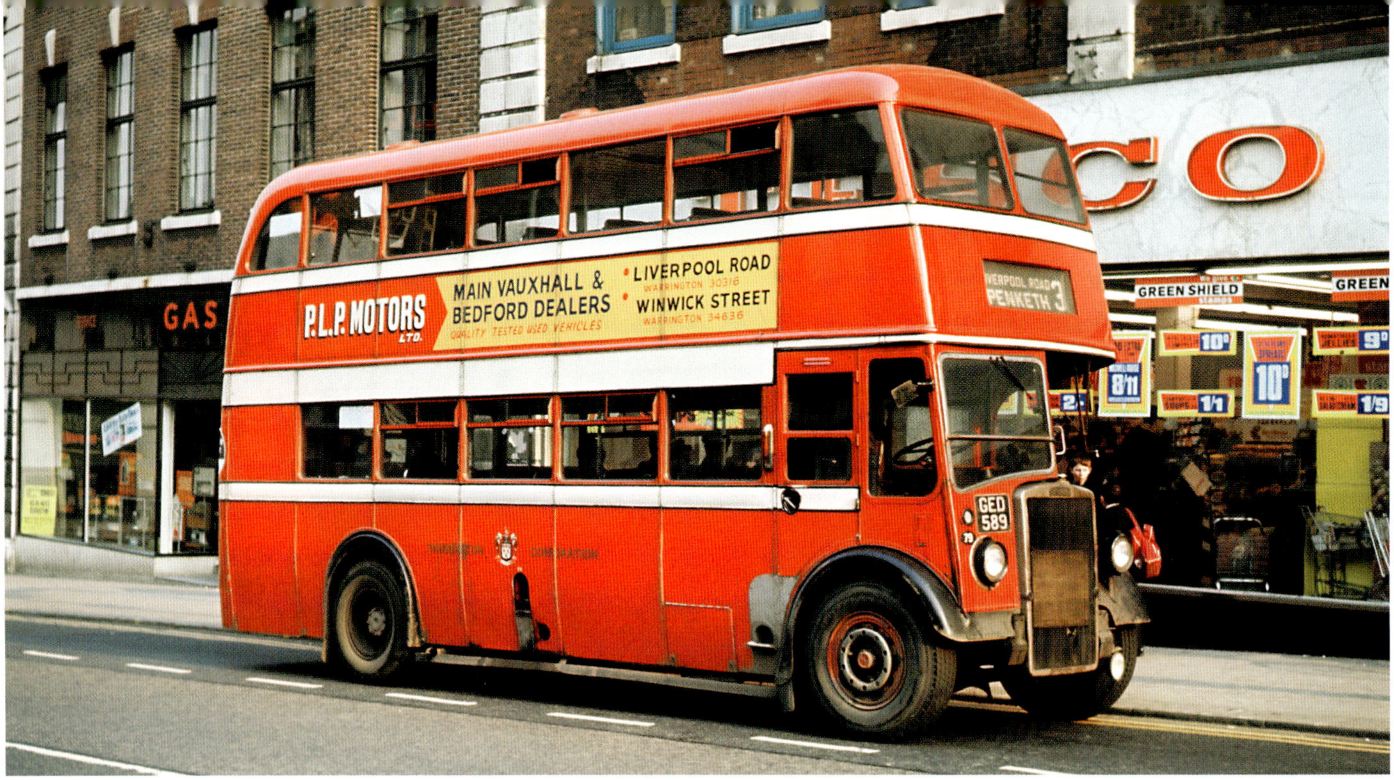

The first ten PD2/1s (1-10) were delivered in 1949 and the others (72-81), were delivered during 1950. In March 1969, 79 is loading on Buttermarket Street outside Tesco with its enticement to save Green Shield Stamps – 'collect the stamps, fill up the stamp books and exchange them for free gifts' was something that attracted many people in the 1960s and 1970s. A great advocate of the stamps, the 'pile it high, sell it cheap' Tesco of the 1960s and 1970s was a very different operation from that of the 21st century. *Alan Murray-Rust*

There was a gap of some five years before the next new buses entered service. Crossley-bodied Foden PVD6s 102-104 arrived late in 1954. The bus in this picture, 102, entered service after the others, having been Foden's exhibit at the at the 1954 Commercial Motor Show. Near the end of its working life, it was on a schools duty when photographed in March 1969 at Warrington Bridge. Crossley did a particularly neat job of matching the body to Foden's engine cowl. *Alan Murray-Rust*

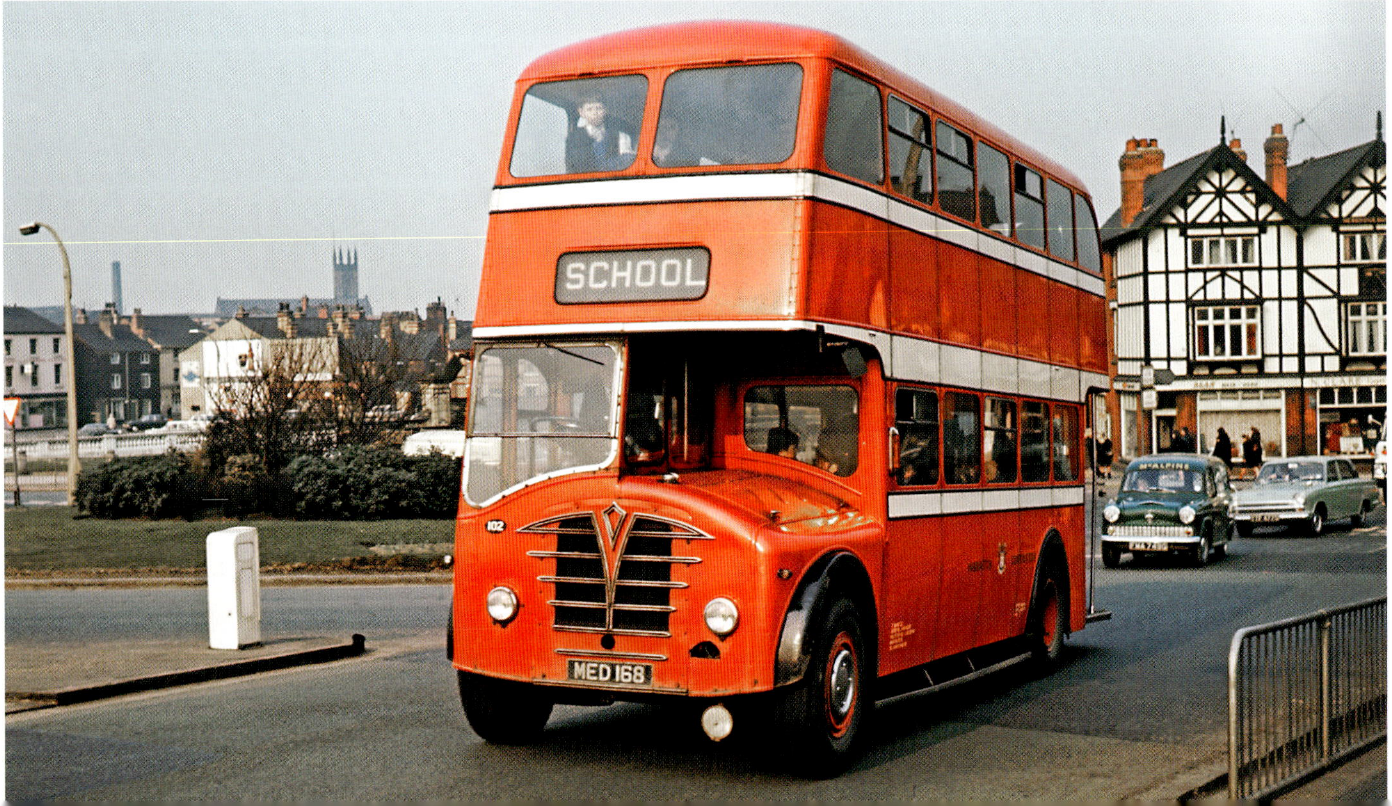

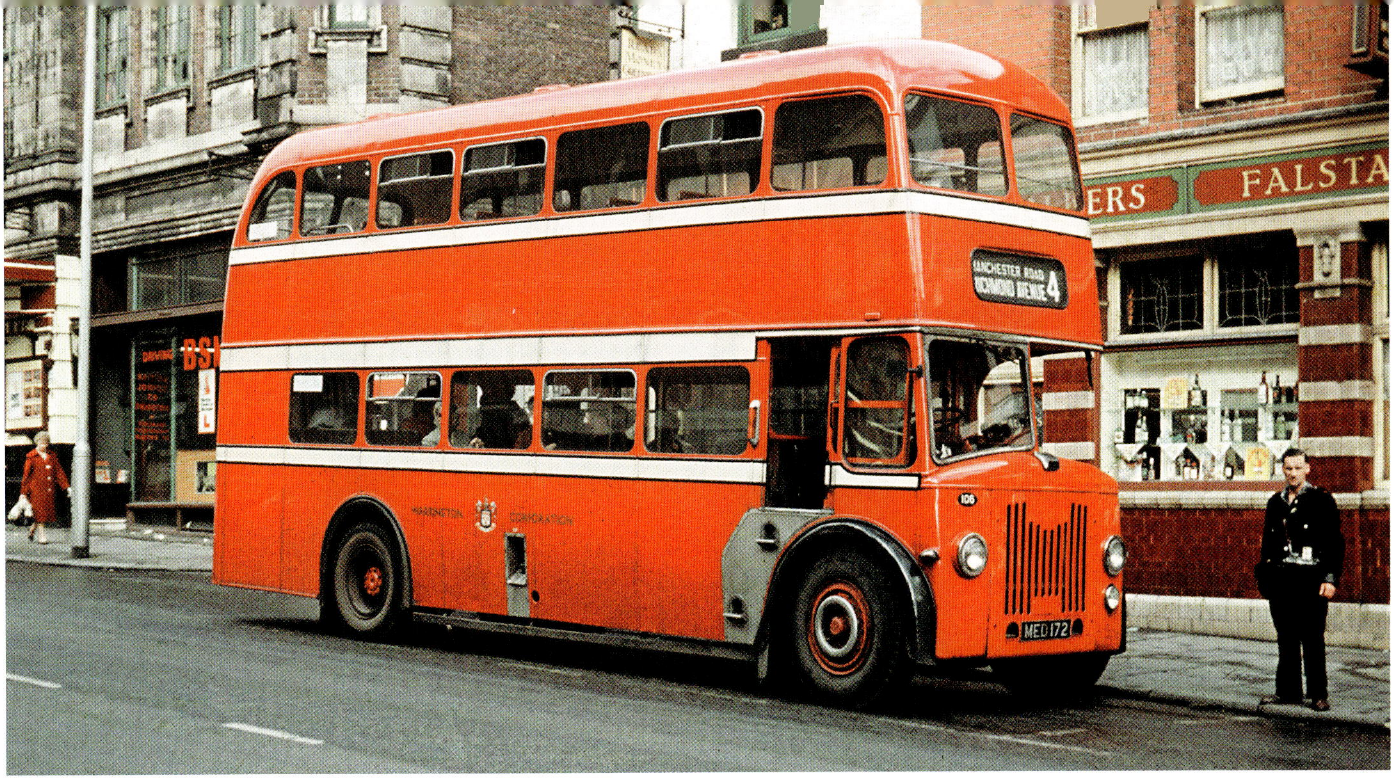

There was a licence restriction on the services using the narrow yet two-way Sankey Street in the town centre. A maximum vehicle width of 7ft 6in was stipulated and all the fleet so far was of this width although 8ft had long been general elsewhere. Arriving at the same time as the Fodens, East Lancs-bodied 105-107 were Leyland PD2/22 – the 7ft 6in version of the more common PD2/20 chassis. In Buttermarket Street in 1959 and outside the Lower Angel pub – Falstaff Ales were a product of the local Walker's Brewery – newly repainted 106 looks very smart. All three were withdrawn in 1970. *Ian Stewart*

Fodens 108-112 were the last PVD6s to be built. They had East Lancs bodies, the standard frame of which did not marry up with the Foden front, resulting in a slightly clumsy-looking join between the cab front and cowl. Photographed in 1970, a year before it was withdrawn, this is 108 passing Bridge Foot on the 78 service from the United States Air Force Base at Burtonwood into Warrington and thence Padgate and Fearnhead. It was one of the group of local services, numbered 76 to 81, which were worked jointly with Lancashire United (LUT) and had LUT numbers. *David Powell*

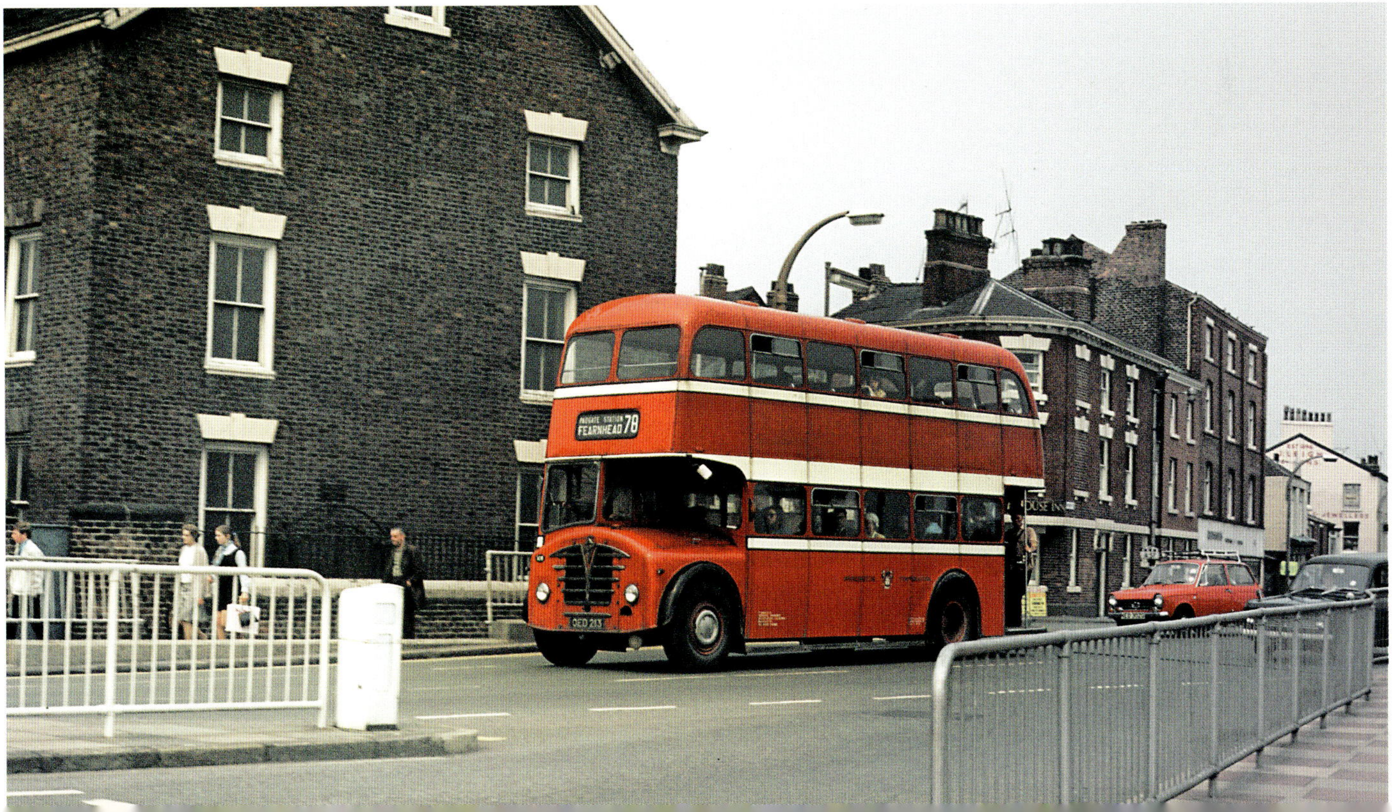

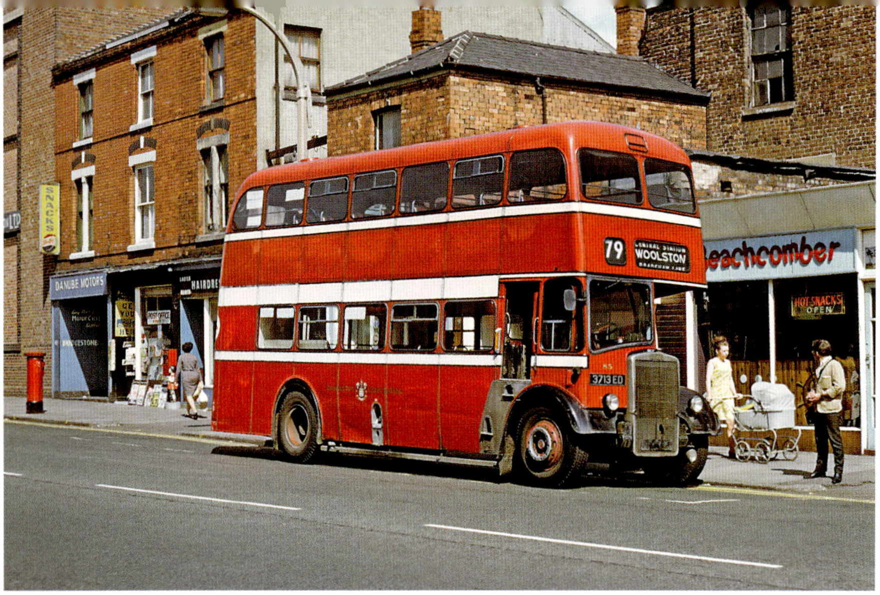

The first new buses for six years and the undertaking's first 8ft wide buses (in anticipation of a promised widening of Sankey Street) were eight East Lancs-bodied Leyland PD2/40s 82-89 delivered in 1962. Fleet number plates were replaced by small fleet number transfers, unusually not using a sans serif style font. This is 85 at the Central Station town stand of the cross-town joint LUT service from Longford to Woolston. August 1968 *Roy Marshall*

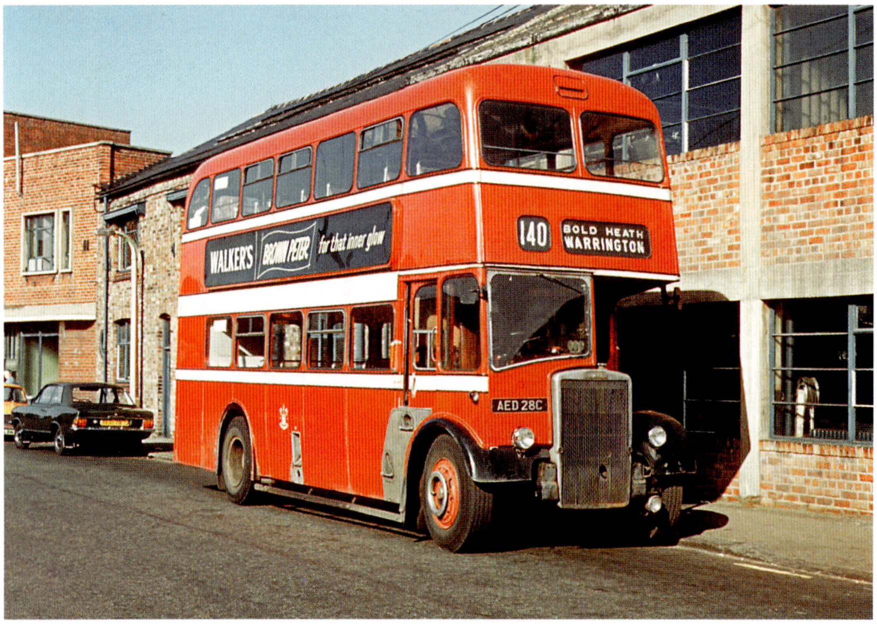

Seven similar vehicles, 11-17, came in 1964/65, their registrations (AED 26/27B, 28C, 29B, 30C, 31/32B) spanning the 'letter change' date, which was January 1st at the time. This is number 13 in August 1970 on the 140 to St Helens. Jointly operated by Warrington and St Helens Corporations and Crosville, the service started in 1947 and its number was a Crosville one, which, because of the joint operators, remained unchanged when Crosville renumbered services into area groups with a letter prefix. When it commenced the service needed lowbridge buses and was the reason for Warrington's two lowbridge PD1s. *John Ryan*

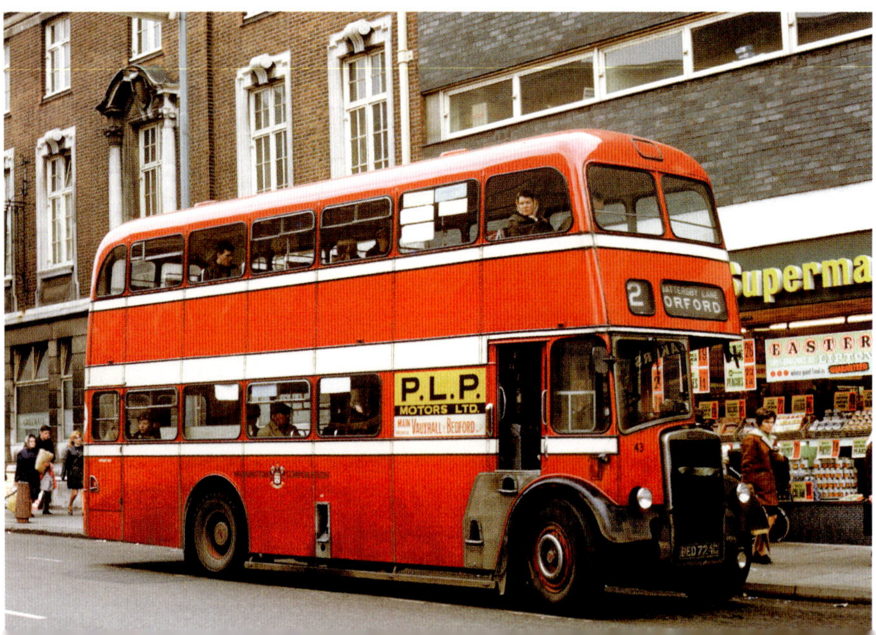

Nothing was done about widening Sankey Street and with no suitable alternative route for the services to Great Sankey and Penketh, twelve 7ft 6in-wide PD2 chassis were ordered from Leyland. Leyland no longer offered the width as a standard option and 41-52 were 'PD2/40 Special'. They entered service in mid-1965 but the need for their narrow width was removed early in 1966 when road works in the town enabled the narrow part of Sankey Street to become one-way. Number 43 is at the Buttermarket Street terminus by the Pelican Inn. The pub's owners, brewers Greenall Whitley, were an important employer in the town.
April 1968 *Roy Marshall*

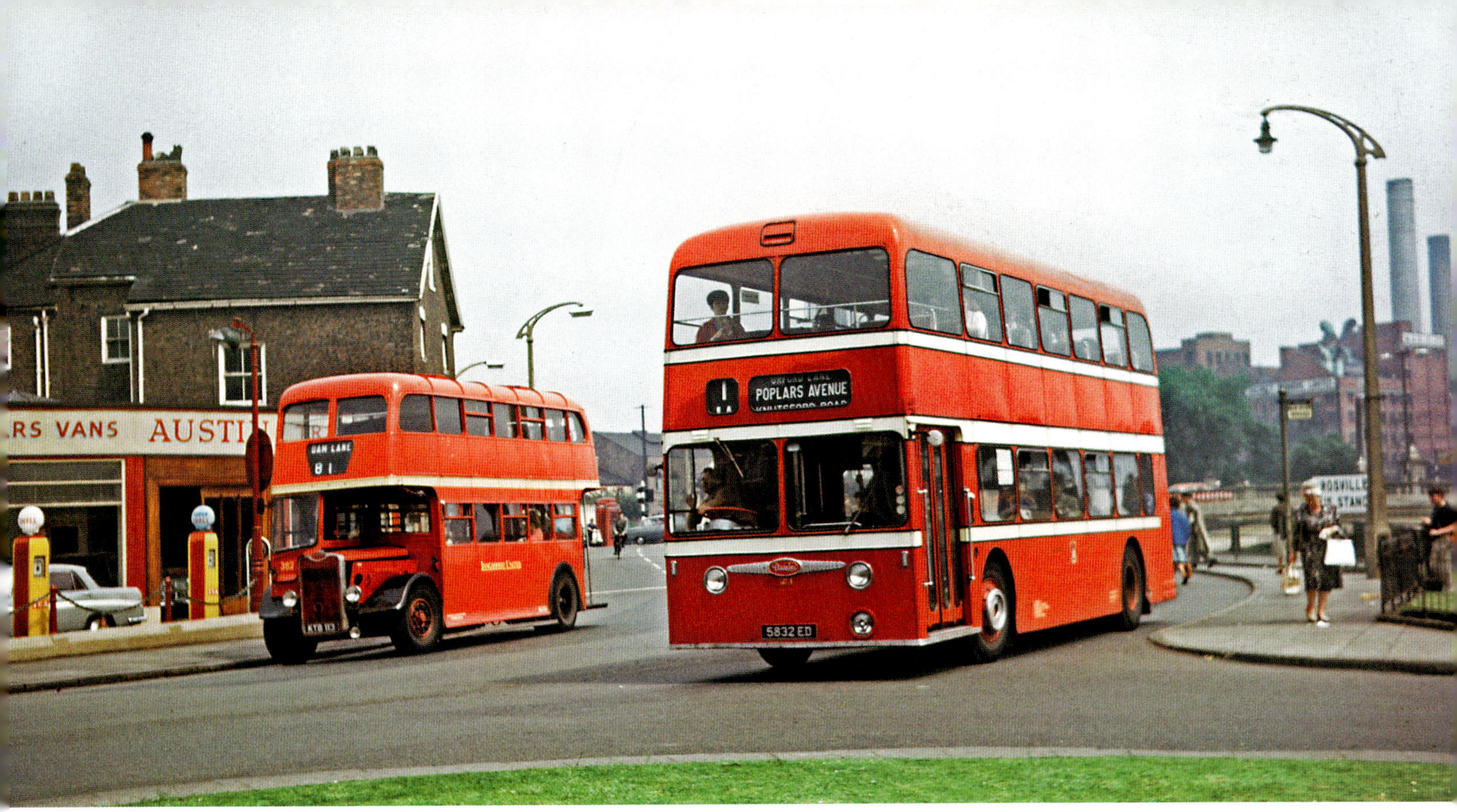

In between the two batches of PD2s there were nine Daimler Fleetlines with East Lancs bodies. Delivered in 1963, they were numbered 18-26. This is number 23 which had East Lancs body number 6000. The bus is stopped in the setting down lay bay at Bridge Foot and its driver is leaning out of his offside window to talk to the driver of Lancashire United Weymann-bodied Guy Arab 382 parked on the other side of the one-way road, waiting to take up service on joint service 81 to Dam Lane. May 1964 *Roy Marshall*

Along with the PD2 Specials came two more East Lancs-bodied Daimler Fleetlines, 27/28. Behind 28 at the Winwick Street terminus by the entrance to Central Station are PD2s 85 and 86, new in 1962, and a Crosville Lodekka. August 1968 *Roy Marshall*

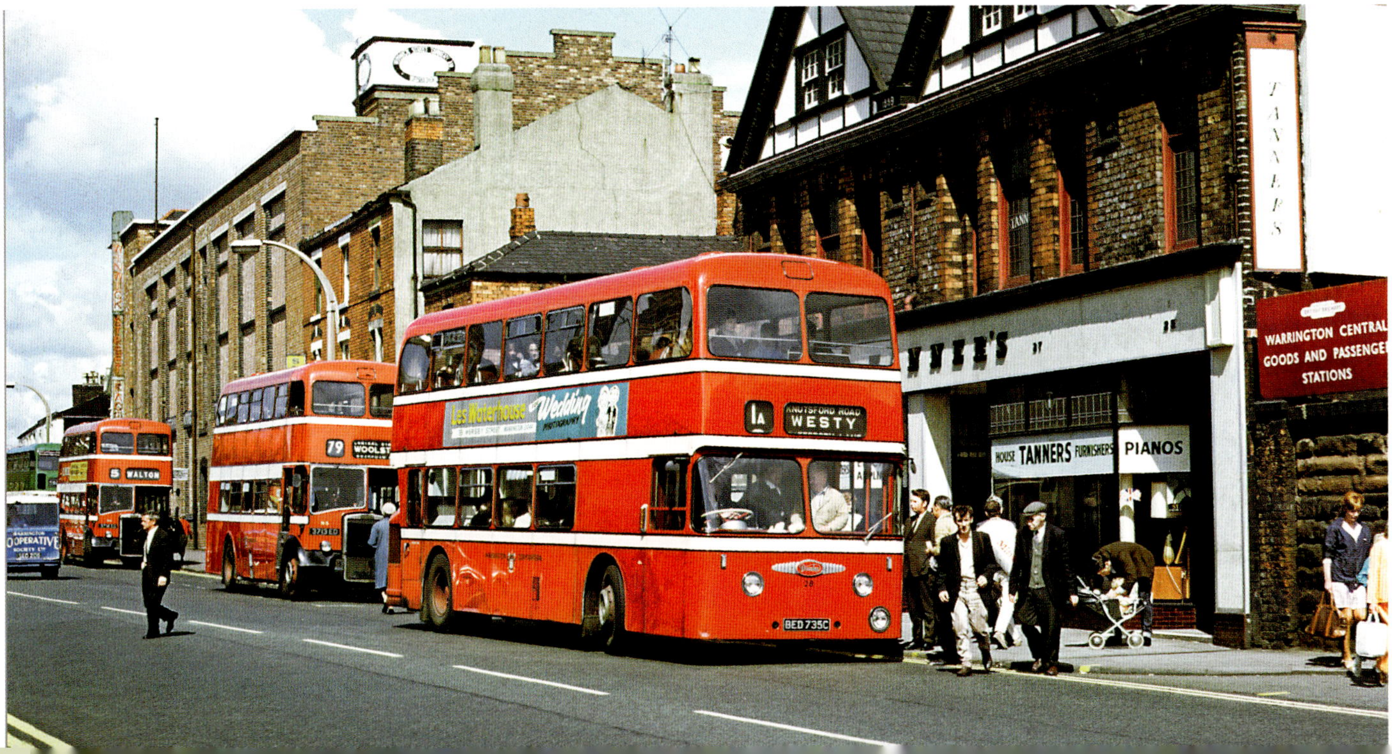

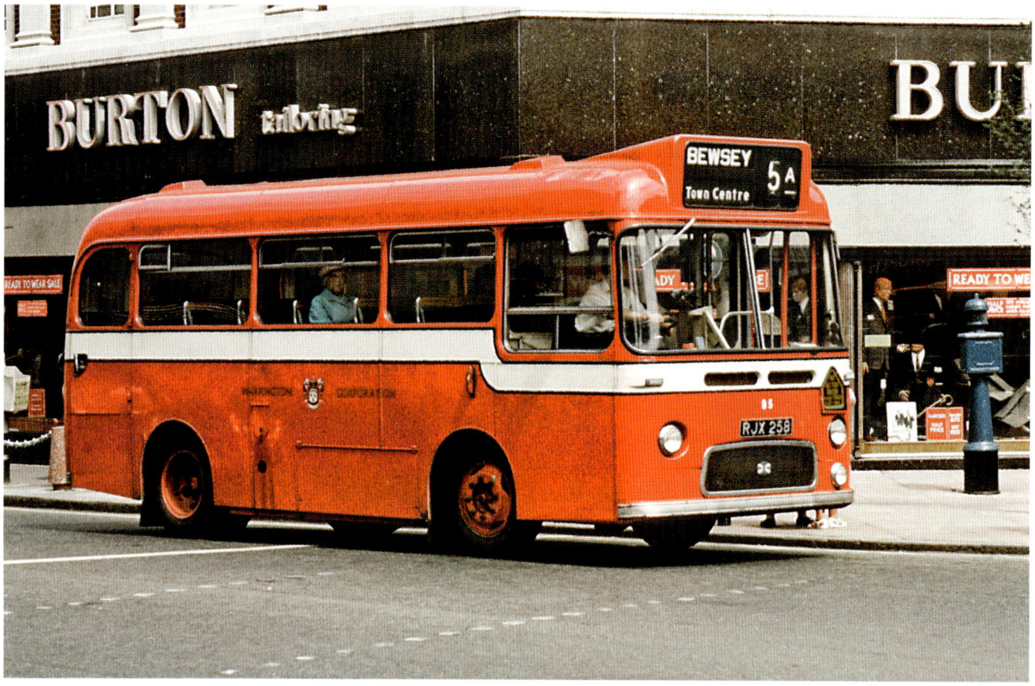

A somewhat curious choice to cover more of the one-man duties on service 5A, for which the Guy Arab had been converted, was this second-hand Weymann-bodied Albion Nimbus. It started life with Halifax in 1963, from which it was hired in December 1965. Purchased the following month, RJX 258 became fleet number 95. Sold to Ramsbottom UDC in December 1967, it passed with that fleet to the SELNEC PTE, becoming that PTE's only Albion. Here it is on the 5A at the junction of Buttermarket Street and Horsemarket Street in July 1967. *Roy Marshall*

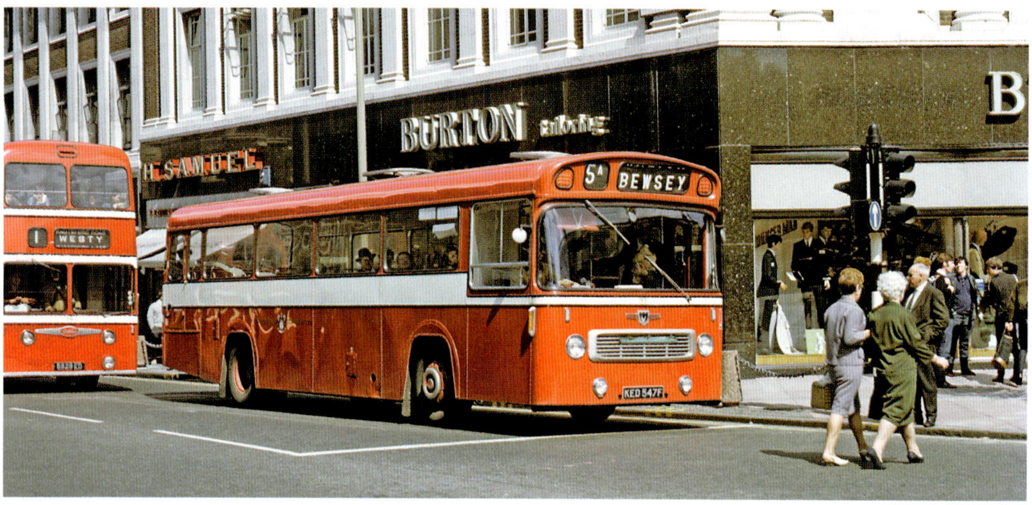

The little Albion was a stop-gap. A Leyland Panther Cub (East Lancs body as ever) had been ordered in April 1965 and three more in November of that year along with three Fleetlines that looked much the same as the previous ones. Panther Cub 90 entered service in May 1967 followed by numbers 91-93 in January 1968. Taken in April 1970, 93 is on the same service and at the same location as the Nimbus in the previous picture. *Geoffrey Morant*

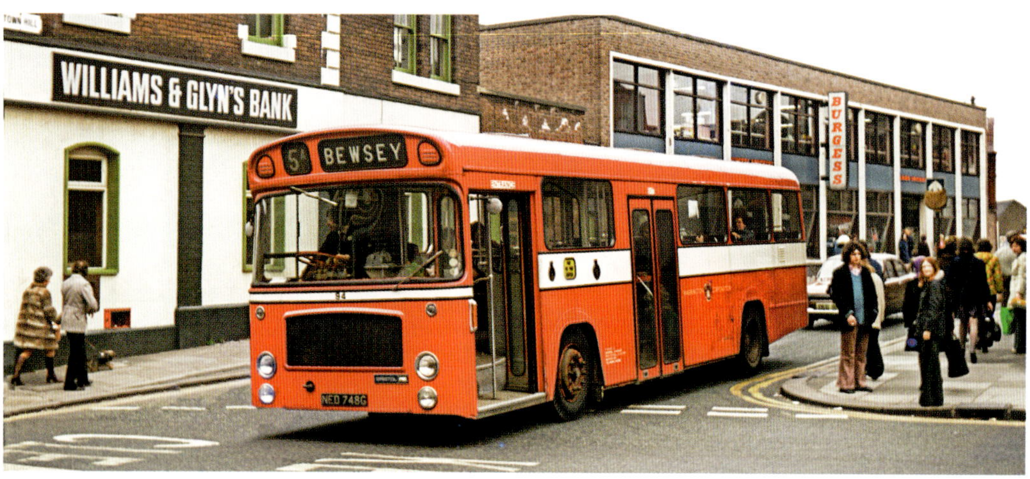

The Panther Cub was, perhaps, not Leyland's most successful model and for the rest of its single-deck purchases, Warrington chose the Bristol RE. The first two were the short wheelbase version of the RELL (later named the RESL) with Leyland-engines and 41-seat dual-door East Lancs bodies and they, too, went to work on the 5A. 94 turns out of Town Hill in April 1974, the month in which the town became part of the enlarged Municipal Borough of Warrington – and also part of the County of Cheshire. *Anthony Drury*

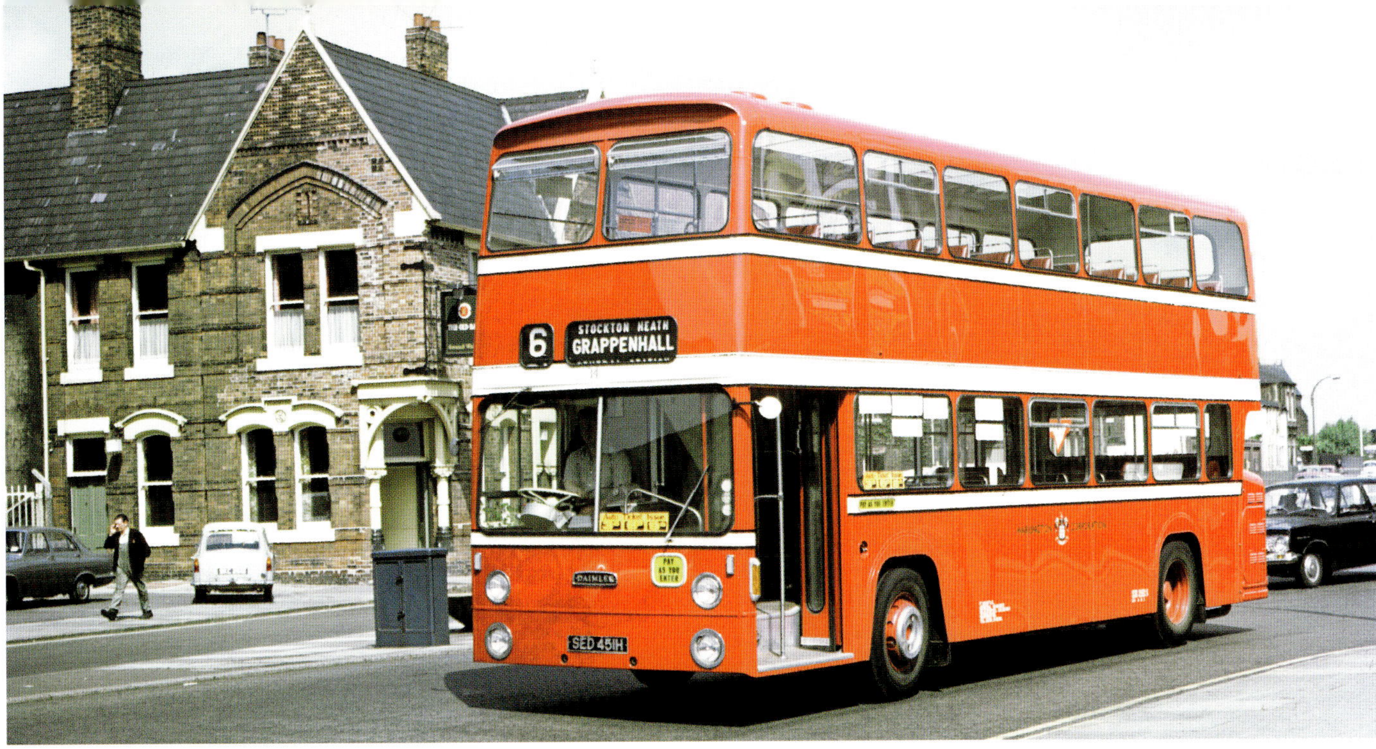

The next six Daimler Fleetlines, 32-37, new in March and April of 1970, were purpose-built for one-person operation. They had what might be described as a somewhat toned down version of Ralph Bennett's striking East Lancs body design for Bolton. A factor in this was Warrington's continuing with its existing livery at a time when most others were revising theirs – usually by adding more cream areas. Six similar ones (100-105) followed in 1973. At Bridge Foot, number 34 was only a few days old when Roy Marshall took this picture. *Roy Marshall*

As a result of the Easter Monday, 1970 fire which destroyed its Blackburn works, East Lancs was unable to fulfil the body contract for eight Bristol RESLs and the corporation had to find someone who could do the job – and quickly. Seddon's bodybuilding subsidiary, Pennine, got the job and the result was 53-60. *Geoffrey Morant*

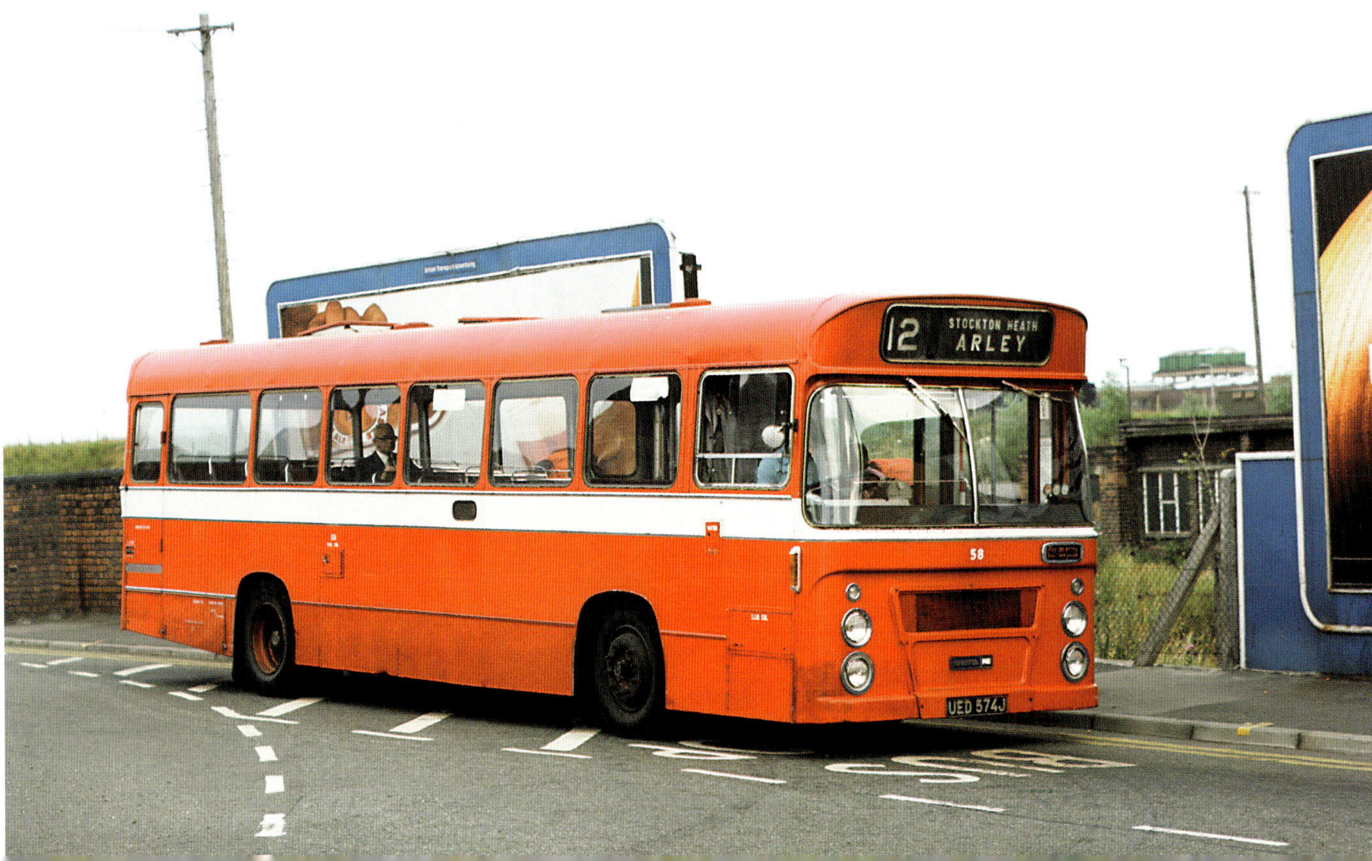

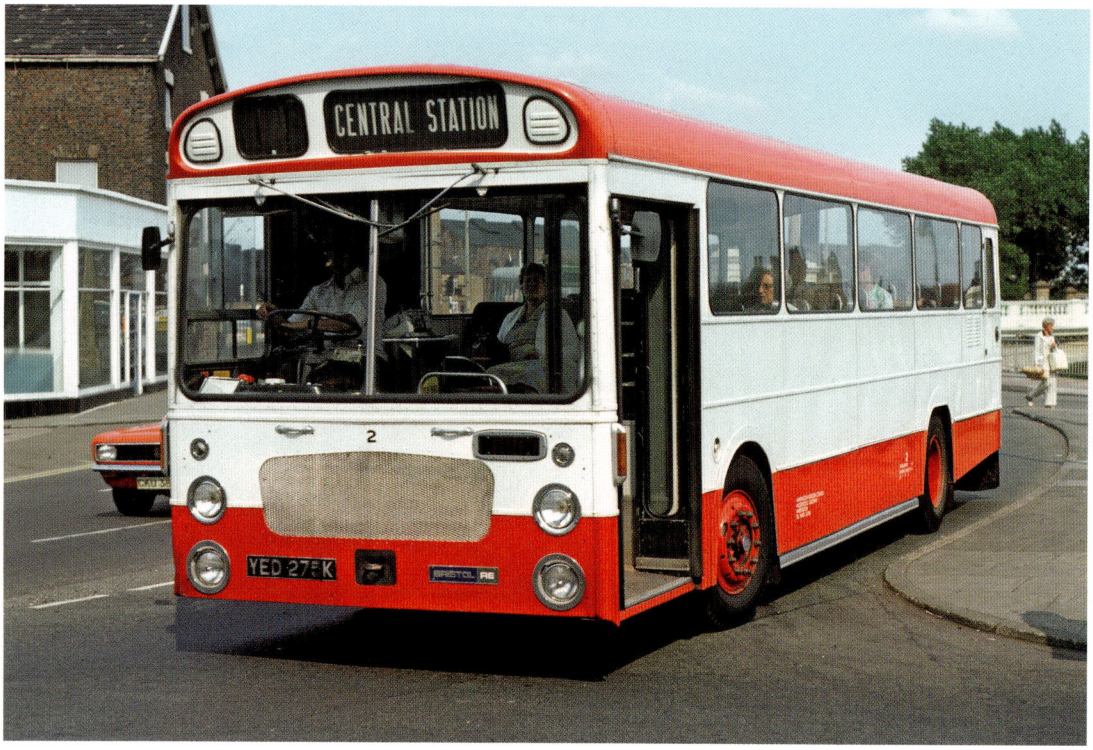

East Lancs was soon back in business with a rebuilt factory and bodied the corporation's next seven Bristol RESLs. Numbers 61-65 had dual entrance 40-seat bodies, whilst the other two, numbered 1-2 had more comfortable seats, single doors and a revised livery that was subsequently adopted for the Warrington Borough Transport fleet. They all entered service early in 1972. *Roy Marshall*

Any look at Warrington's buses would not be complete without pictures of the other operators which worked stage carriage services into the town. Naylor's Motor Service of Stockton Heath was joint operator on the service to Appleton and Arley, for which it had a Massey-bodied Guy Arab III. This picture shows NMB 314 leaving the Bridge Foot setting down lay bay on its inward journey on 30 May 1964 having just crossed over the River Mersey. Naylor's sold out their share of the service to the corporation in December 1964 – the deal included NMB 314 but Warrington did not operate it. *Roy Marshall*

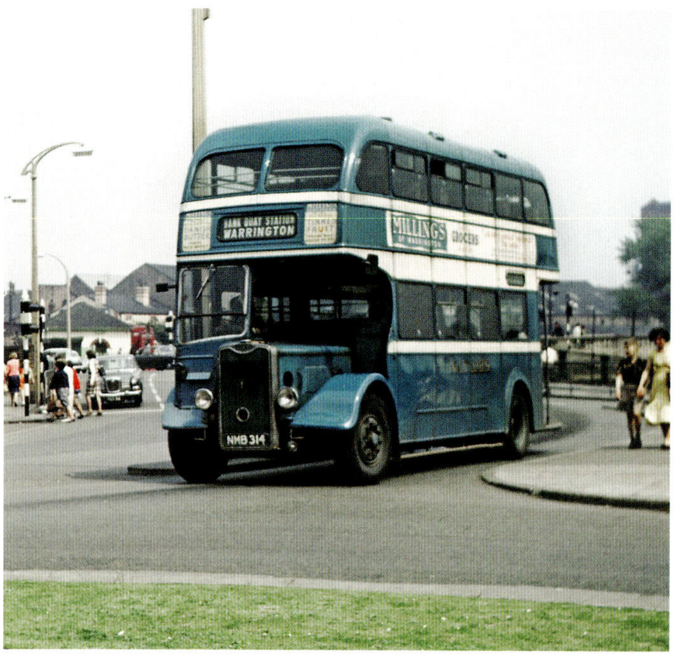

In addition to its services to Altrincham, Manchester, Flixton and the Northwich area, North Western worked local services 10 to Thelwall and 11 to Stretton jointly with the corporation. North Western had long had services numbered 10 and 11 in Manchester and it referred to the Warrington services as 10W and 11W, although latterly the actual buses usually showed simply 10 or 11. Relations with the corporation were harmonious and North Western's Warrington-based vehicles were kept in the corporation's bus garage. This picture shows Alexander-bodied Dennis Loline 874 at Bridge Foot. *Alan Murray-Rust*

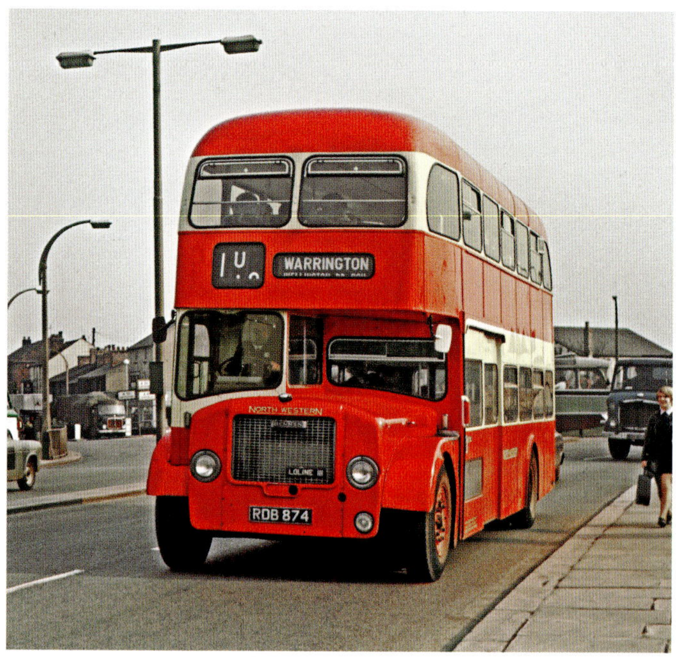

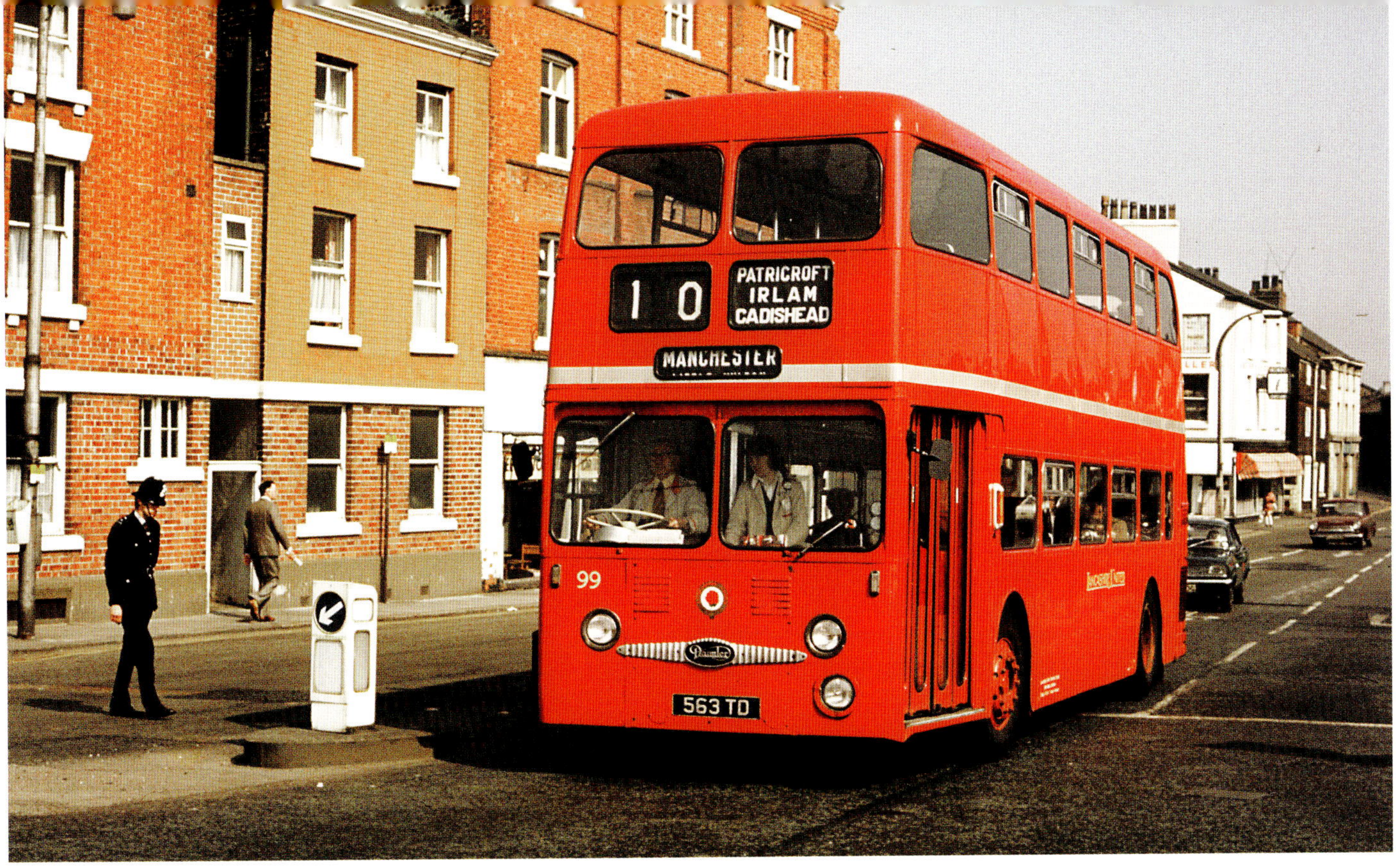

There was, however, another service 10 in the town and its number was a Salford one. Salford Corporation and LUT (but not Warrington) jointly worked the 10 service to Salford and Manchester. Lancashire United had a considerable presence in Warrington. In addition to local services 76-81 which were jointly operated with the corporation, LUT ran its own services to Ashton-in-Makerfield, Bolton, Leigh and Wigan. Jointly with Leigh Corporation (but, again, not Warrington) LUT worked the 46/47 to Leigh via Newchurch. It had a share in the (Ribble-numbered) 309/319/329/344 services to St Helens, Ormskirk and Southport, although these were usually worked by Ribble and St Helens – there are views in the St Helens and Ribble sections of this book. These two pictures show LUT Northern Counties-bodied Daimler Fleetline 99 in April 1974 leaving Warrington on the 10 and Leigh's East Lancs-bodied AEC Renown 15 departing on the 46 in 1969. *John Kaye, Alan Murray-Rust*

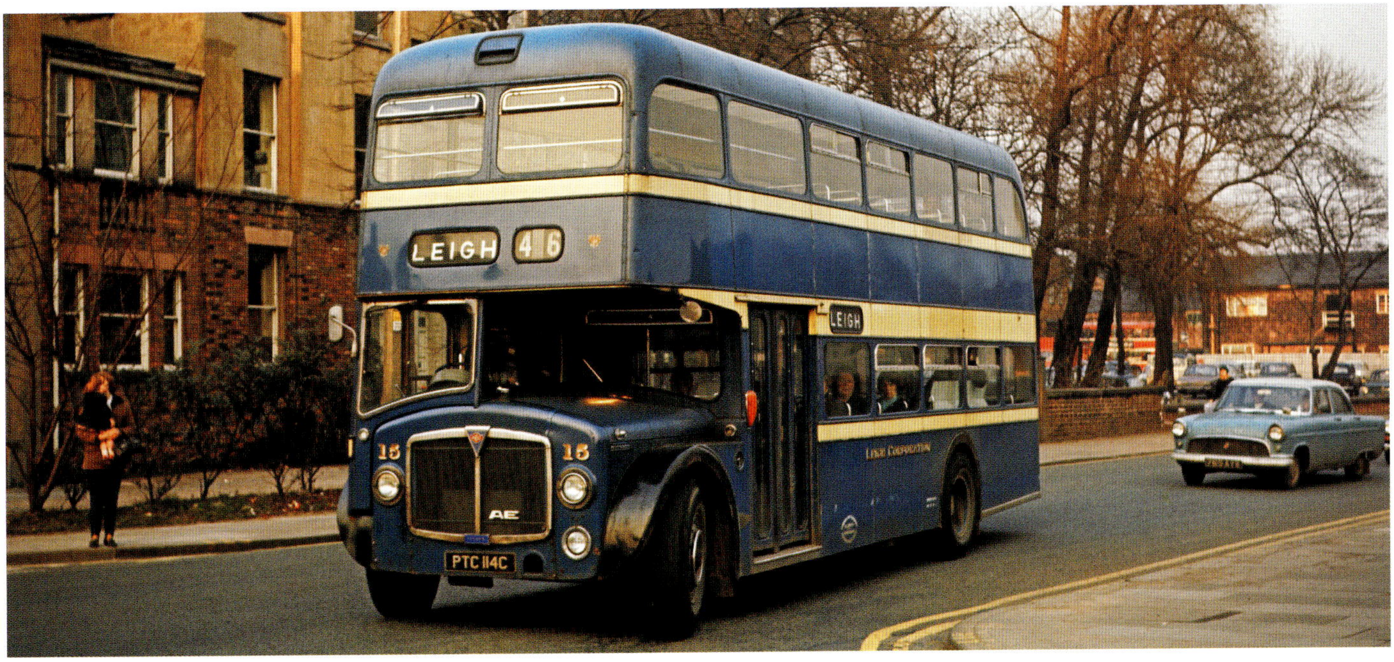

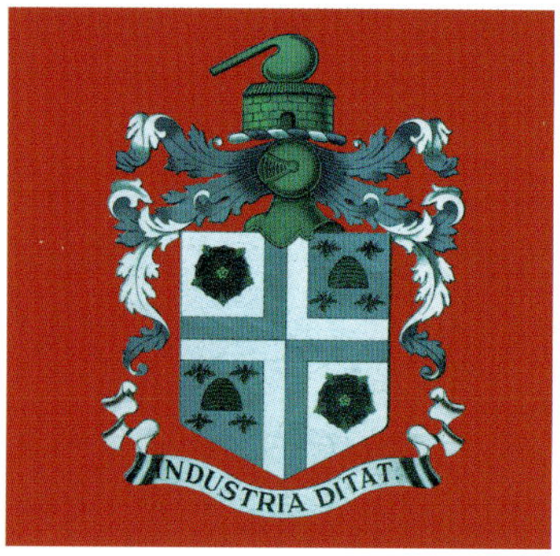

Widnes

For years Widnes was the centre of the country's chemical industry. The air and ground pollution caused by the chemical works along the banks of the River Mersey was by far the worst in the land and, until it was slowly and painfully cleaned and improved, Widnes was hardly an attractive place for its modest fleet of 40 buses.

Nevertheless its transport had claims to fame. Until 1961 the world famous Transporter Bridge provided the only vehicle and pedestrian link to Runcorn on the other side of the River Mersey and Manchester Ship Canal, clearance for ocean-going ships using the canal being the reason for this unusual type of bridge. Built in 1905 and the largest of its kind in the world, in the 1950s its 49,000 per year 3-minute journeys carried a total of 2 million pedestrians and 330,000 vehicles. Just after it was built, the corporation acquired its first buses – the four Commer double-deckers it bought in 1909 were claimed to be the first in the world to have enclosed top covers.

Although it had powers to operate anywhere, by and large Widnes' buses stayed within the town's boundaries, operating a neat and very comprehensive network of local services which served the town well. There were no service numbers but if there had, with all the minor route variations and combinations to serve individual roads, schools and works, there would have been more service numbers than there were buses in the fleet.

In 1961 the new Silver Jubilee Bridge replaced the Transporter, enabling Widnes buses to run to Runcorn. The 1974 local government reorganisation combined Widnes with Runcorn and other areas, and the new larger borough of Halton became part of the county of Cheshire. With a wider remit the transport undertaking flourished under the new title of Halton Borough Transport.

With construction of the new bridge (a small version of the more famous Sydney Harbour Bridge) well under way in the background, this is the Widnes side of the Transporter. Bound for Rainhill, one year-old East Lancs-bodied Leyland PD2/40 fleet number 28 and all-Leyland PD1 number 4 wait for foot passengers. A small queue of cars waits to draw on to the cradle, suspended from the dark-coloured trolley, the end of which can be seen just above the Car Park sign. The cream-painted winding house with its clock, the pub and newsagent's shop complete this atmospheric 1960 scene. *Geoffrey Morant*

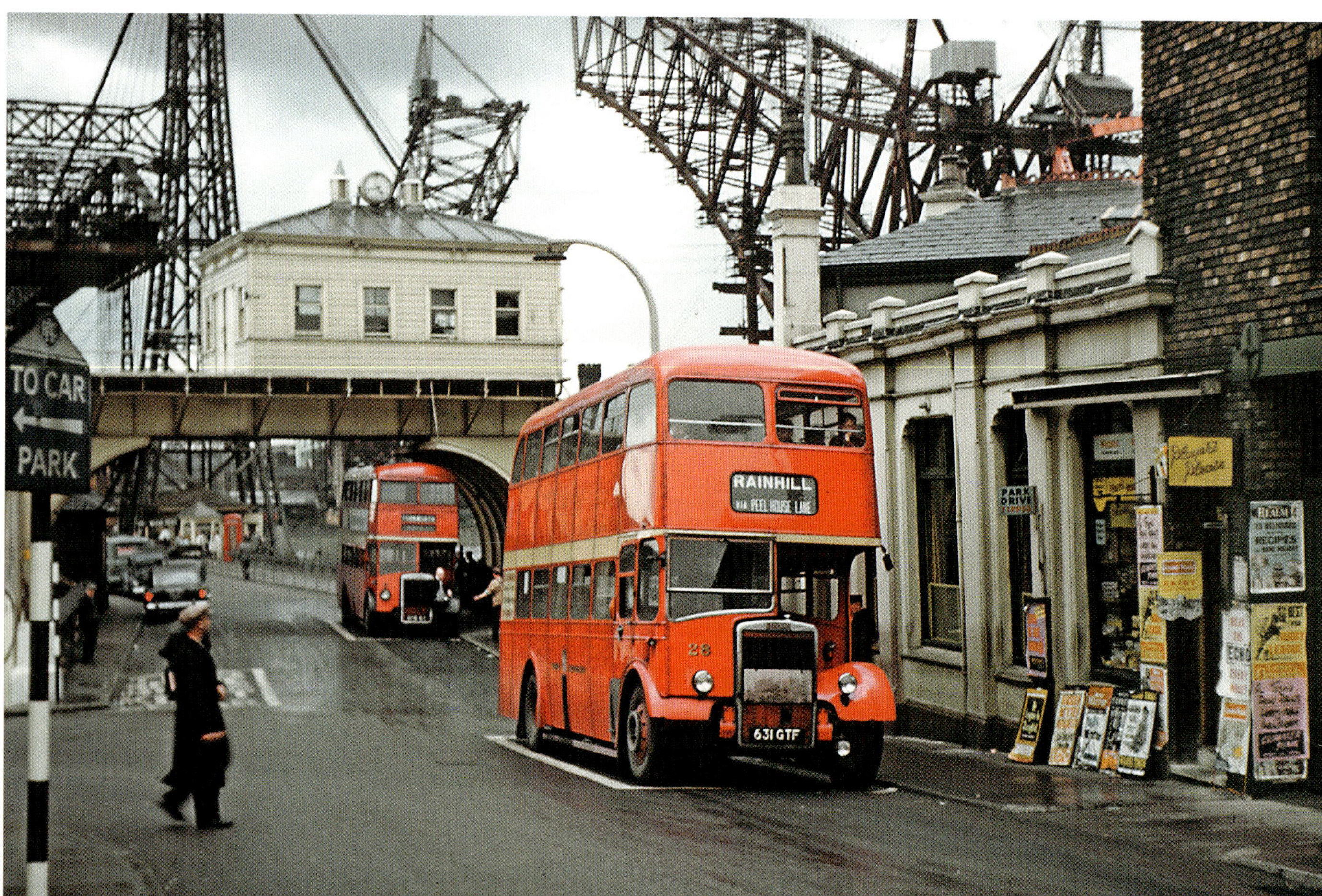

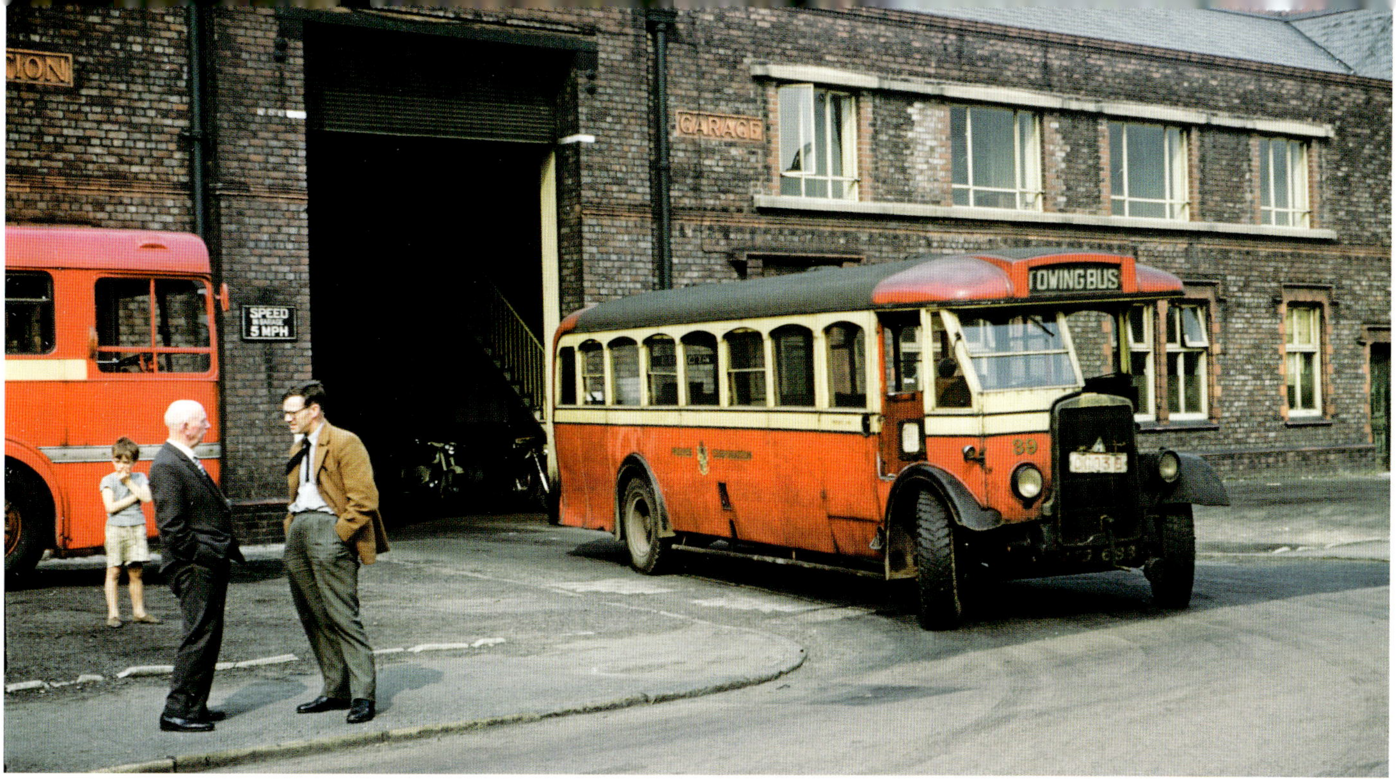

The dated style of the Massey body on 1935 Leyland Lion 39 made it look much older. Withdrawn from service in 1952, 39 was retained until 1969 as a towing vehicle. It saw little use as such but the Moor Lane garage staff were always willing to bring it out for a photograph. In this 1958 view it is in the second post-war livery – subsequently it was repainted in the brighter shade of red introduced in 1959 and seen here on the Leyland Royal Tiger single-decker the front of which is in the picture. *Michael Eyre*

Widnes' wartime vehicle allocation was twelve Daimlers. Fleet number 56 was one of three Daimler-engined CWD6s, 55-57, with highbridge Duple bodies delivered in 1945. The shade of red paint varied over the years and was also affected by the fumes from the chemical works and this picture shows the dark red livery used for a time after the war. The picture was taken in May 1950 and 56 still had its original wooden slatted seats on the upper deck. *C Carter*

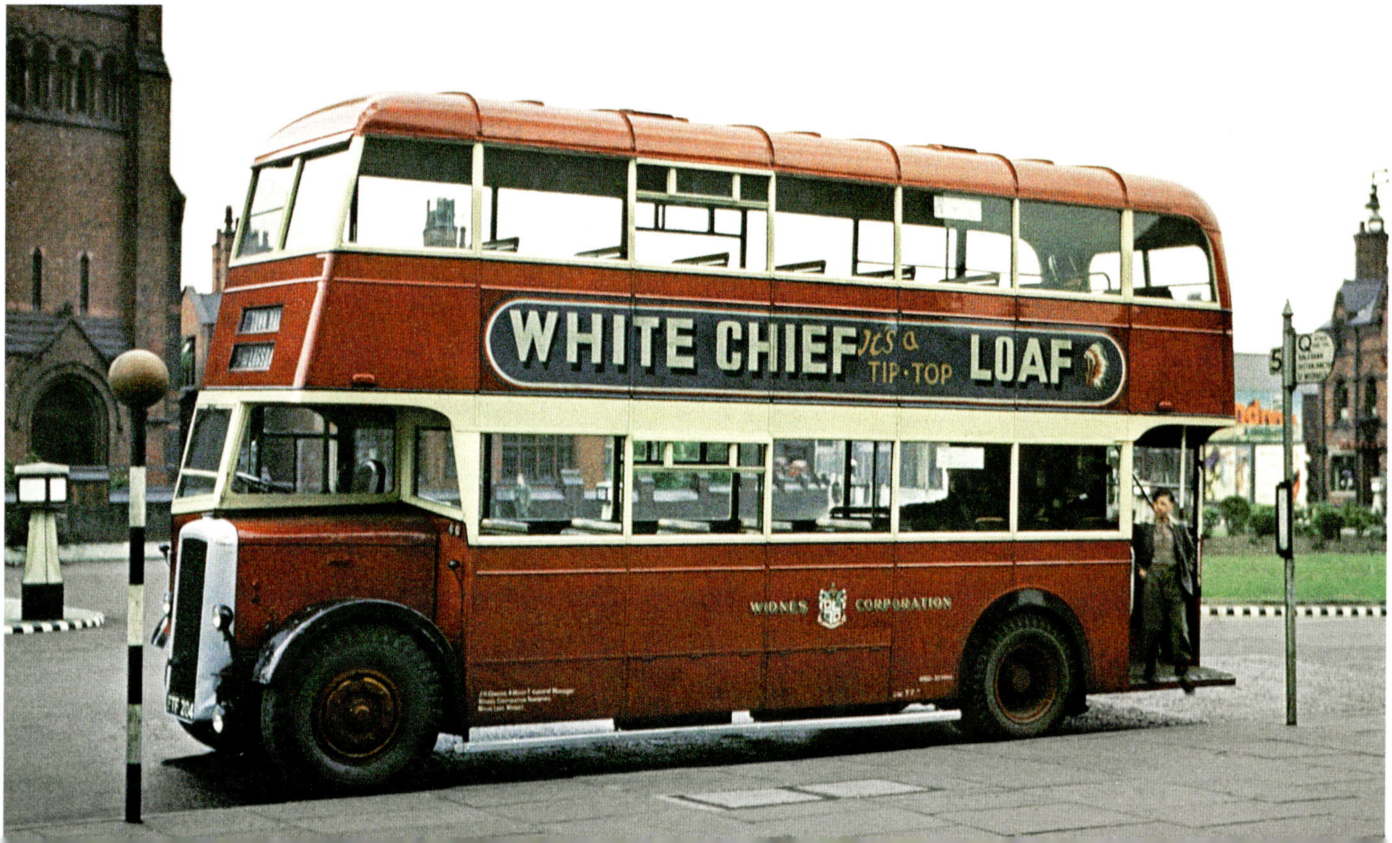

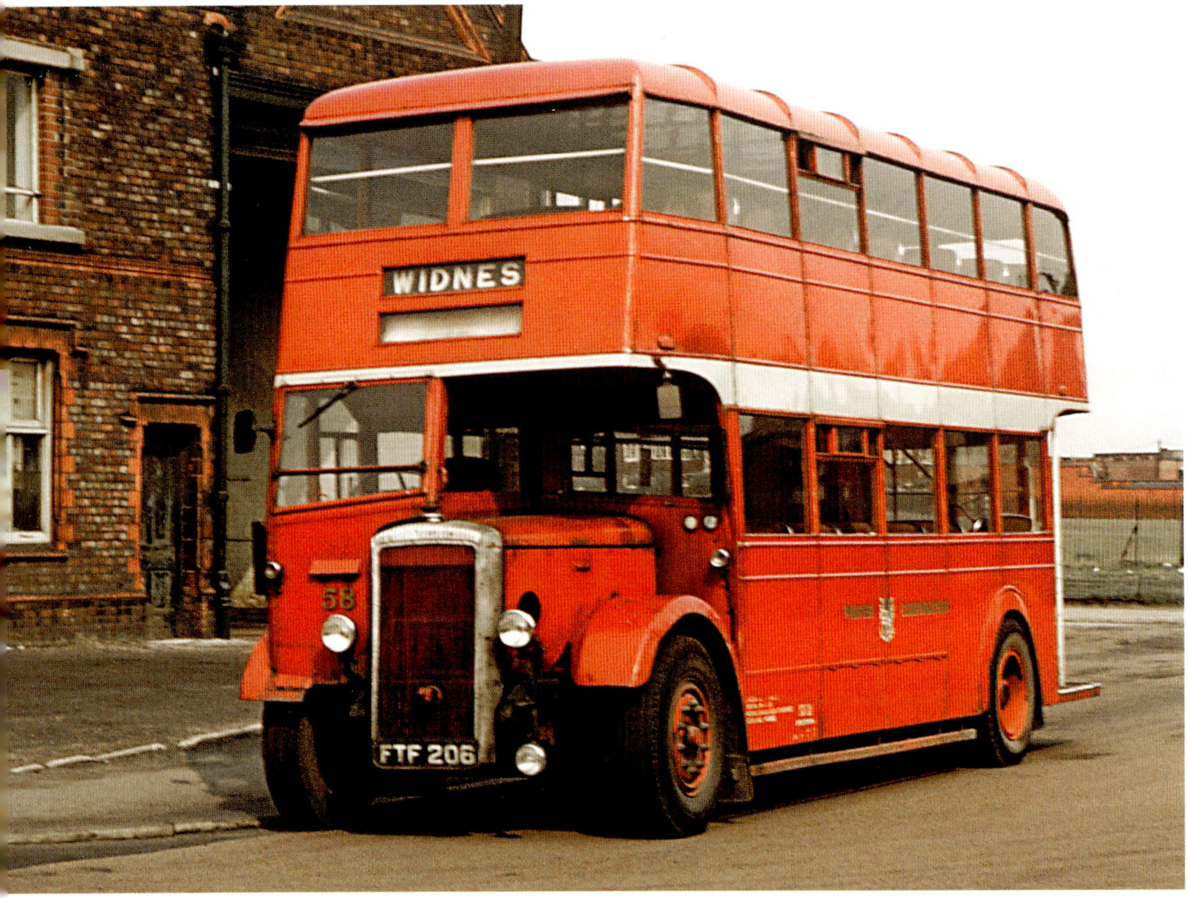

The other three 1945 Daimlers were CWA6s with Duple lowbridge bodies. Numbered 58-60 they had a remarkably long life, running until 1963/64. This 1962 picture, taken outside the garage in Moor Lane, shows 58 in the brighter red livery. It had been fitted with upholstered seats on both decks and had some rebuilding work on its body frame, albeit retaining all the original features including only one opening window on each side of each deck.
Michael Eyre

In 1954/55 five of the wartime Daimlers were rebodied by East Lancs – 49,51,53 and 60 with highbridge bodies whilst 59's new body was lowbridge. This is number 60 with its new body, parked at the town terminus in Victoria Road by St Paul's Parish Church, with a Leyland PD2 and an ex-London AEC at the stops in the background. Number 60 ran until 1968 – only four years longer than unrebodied 58 shown in the previous picture.
Bruce Jenkins

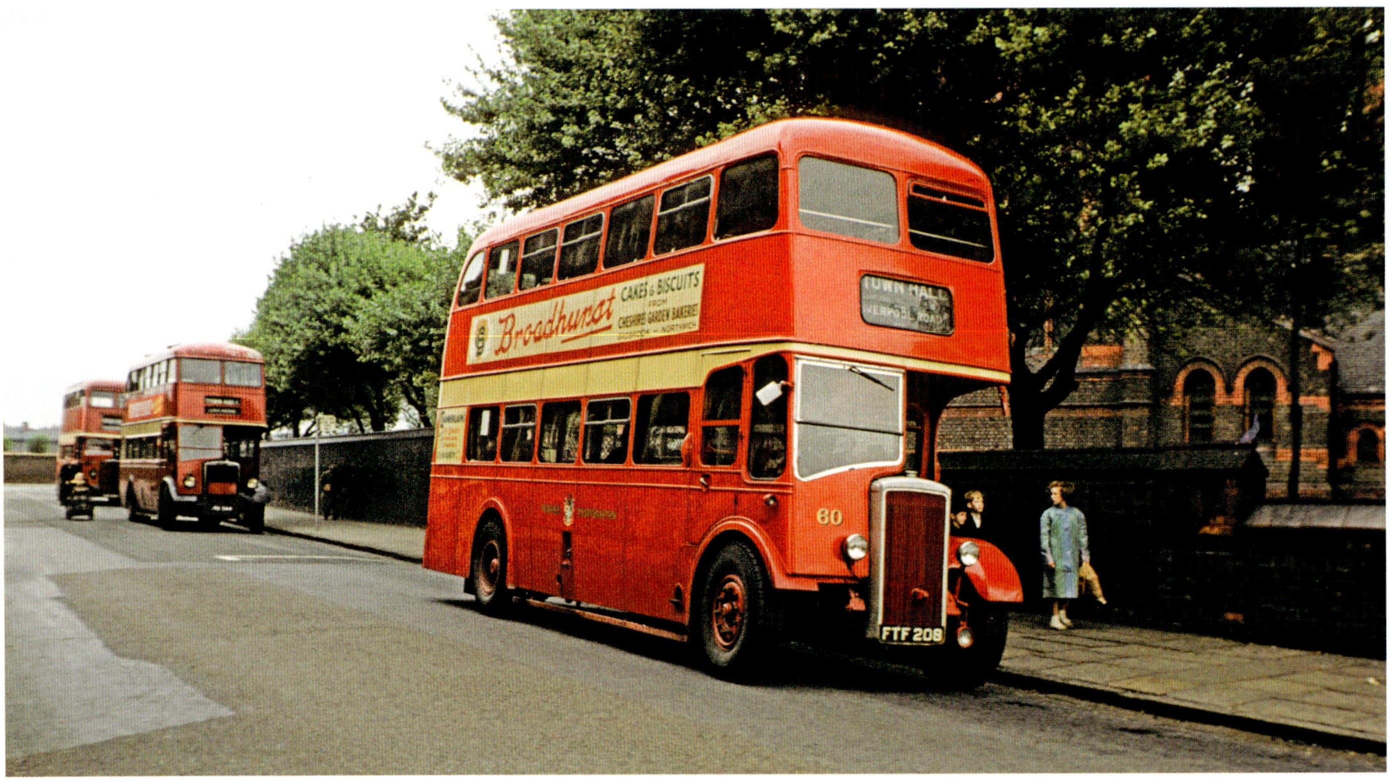

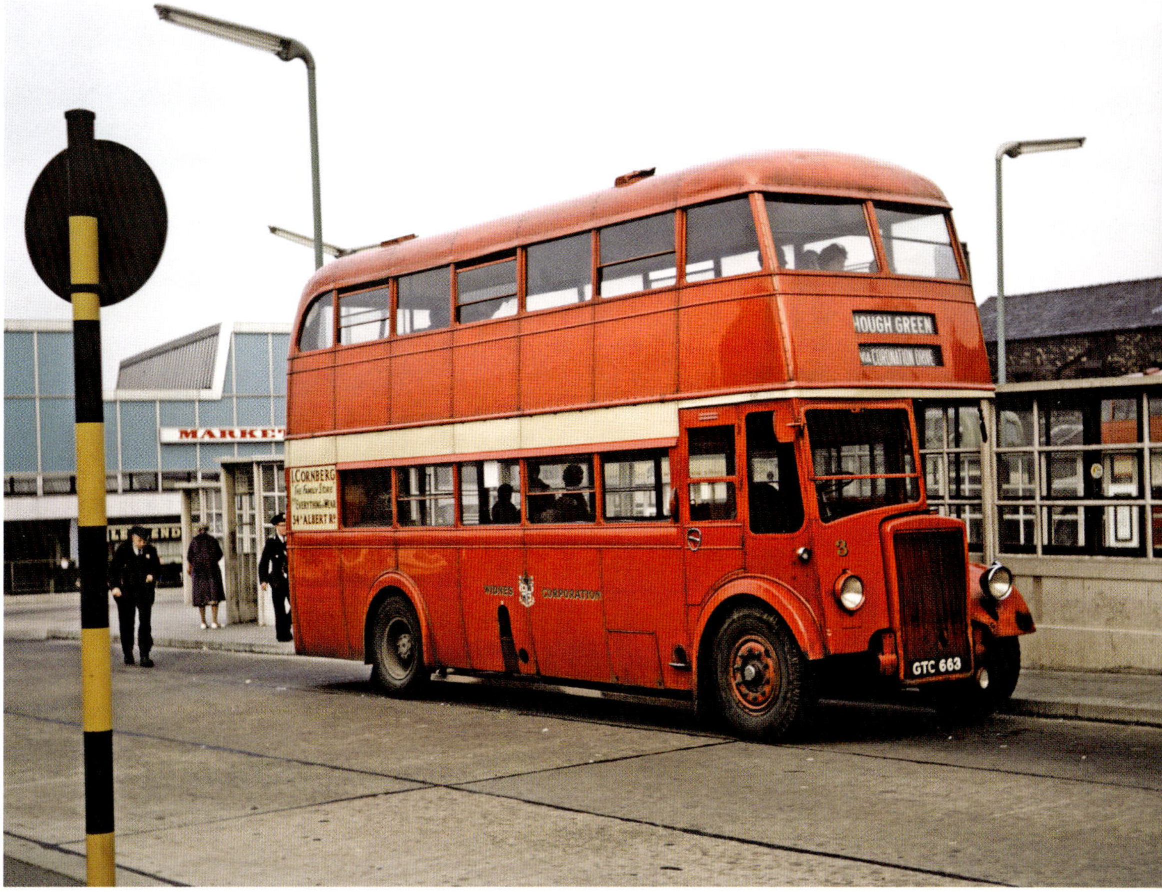

The war over, Widnes bought Leyland-bodied Leylands – two PD1s (1/2) in 1946 and four PD1As (3-6) in 1947. The corporation's operations changed markedly when the new bridge opened and its buses began to run across the county boundary into Runcorn. Crosville operated the services in Runcorn, and also services from Widnes to Liverpool. Widnes had a good relationship with the company and both extended services across the bridge, some jointly operated. This picture shows PD1 number 3 in Runcorn's High Street bus station on 7 October 1962. Widnes cared for its buses and got a particularly good service life from them – number 3 ran until 1967. *Roy Marshall*

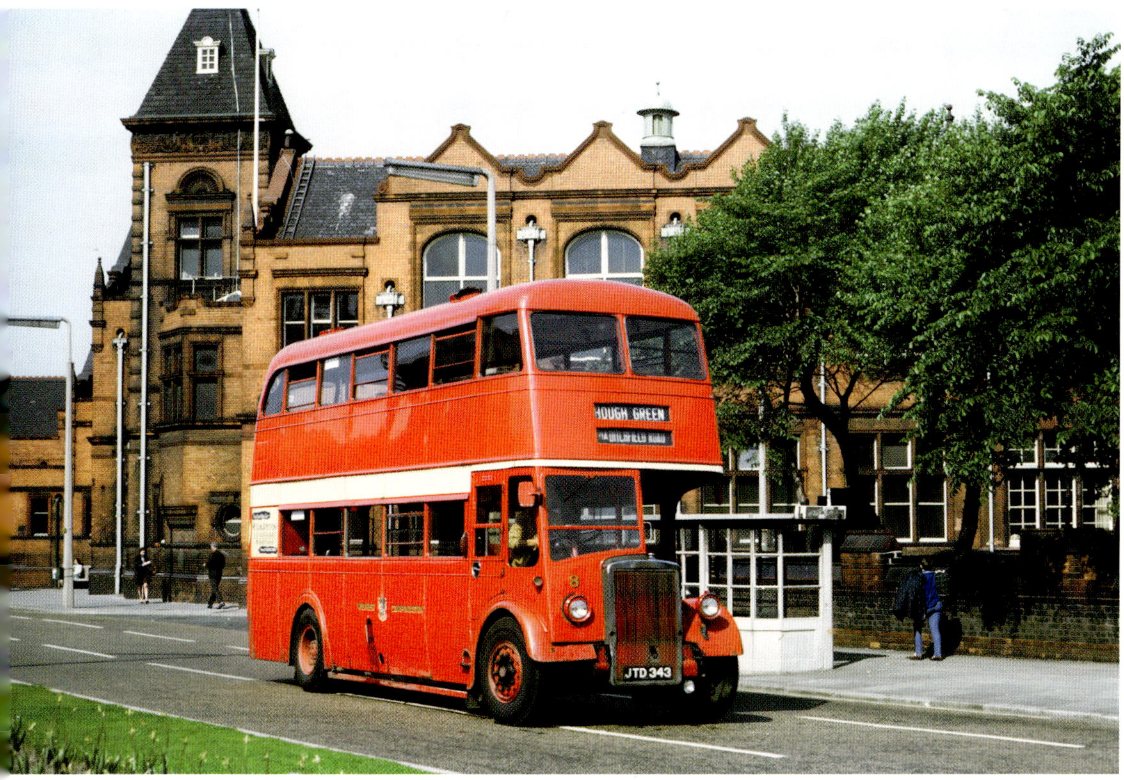

Within its compact operating area, Widnes' services were particularly comprehensive. No numbers were used, the intermediate blind sufficing to show the route. A look at the intermediate blinds on this, the previous and next pictures shows three of the two-mile long routes to the Hough Green estate.

Nine all-Leyland PD2/1s, 7-15, entered service in 1948/49/50. This June 1968 picture shows number 8 in Kingsway passing Widnes Technical College, bound for Hough Green via Ditchfield Road.
Roy Marshall

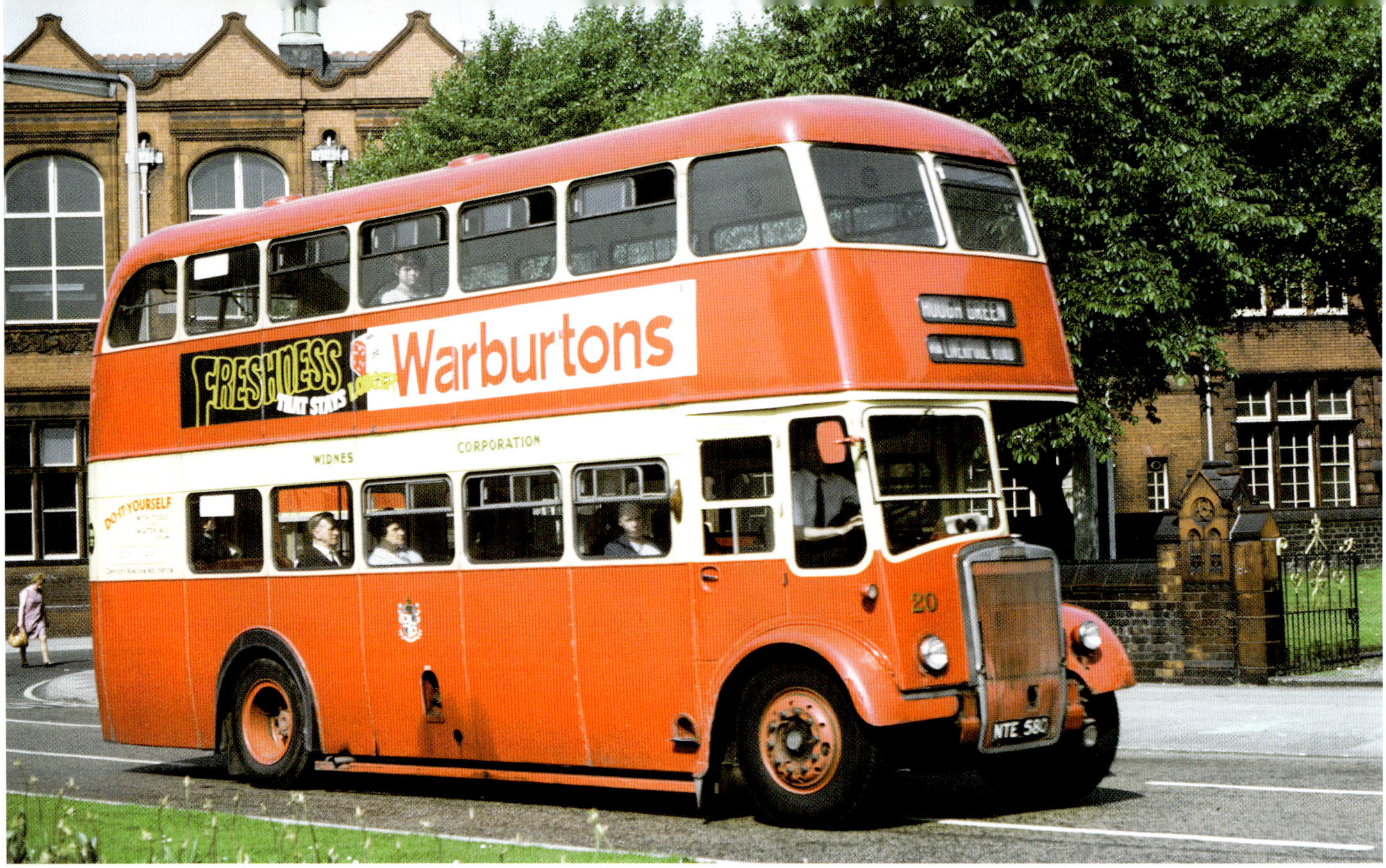

The livery was brightened in the mid-1960s by increasing the area of cream as here on Leyland-bodied PD2/12 20, one of four (16/17 and 20/21) new in 1951 and 1952. In this picture, taken outside the Technical College a few minutes after the previous picture, number 20 is working the next journey to Hough Green and will travel directly along the main road. *Roy Marshall*

New in 1952, numbers 18 and 19 were Leyland Royal Tigers with Leyland bodies. They were the first new single-deckers since Leyland Lions 38/39 of 1935 which they replaced – 39 becoming the department's towing vehicle shown in a previous picture. They were fitted for one-person operation in 1966. In June 1968, the driver of number 18 issues ticket from his TIM machine and it looks as if he will have a full load for the journey on the joint service to St Helens. The departure stands near the Town Hall were numbered and their numbers were shown in the timetable. The St Helens service departed from stand 4. *Roy Marshall*

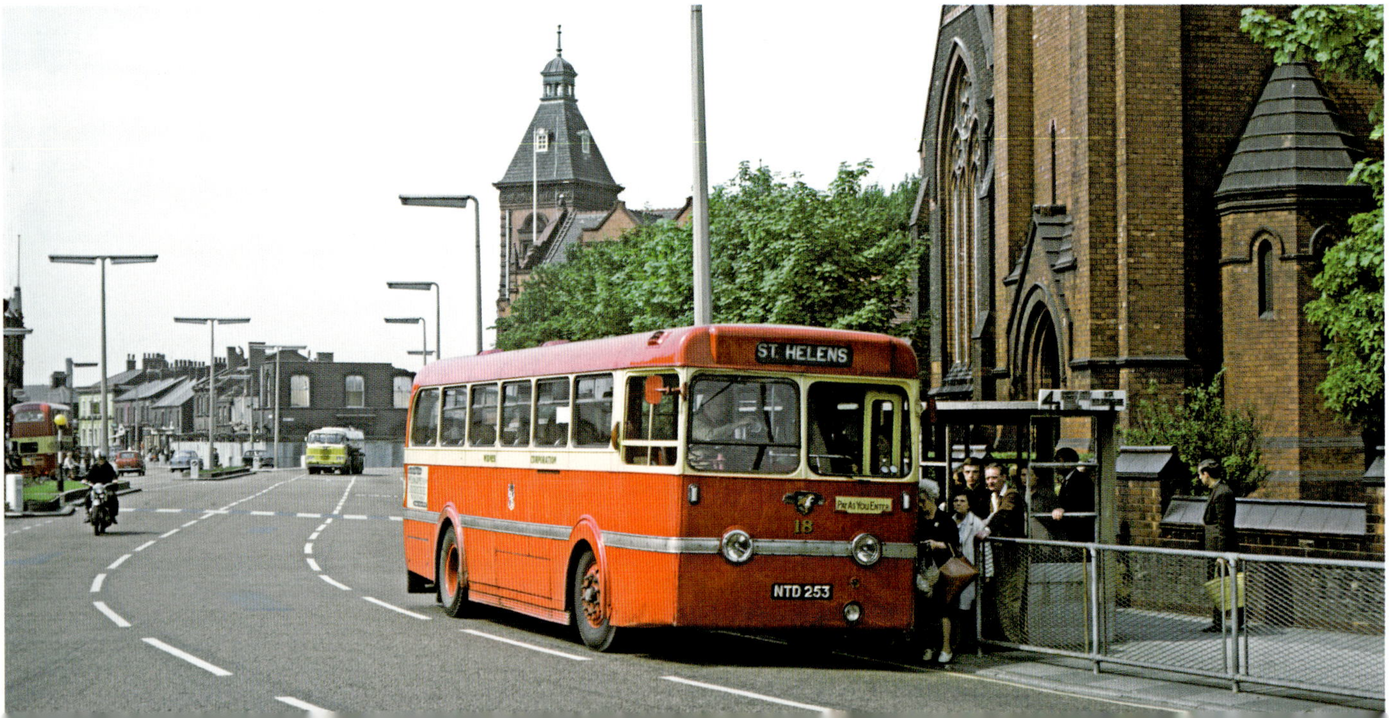

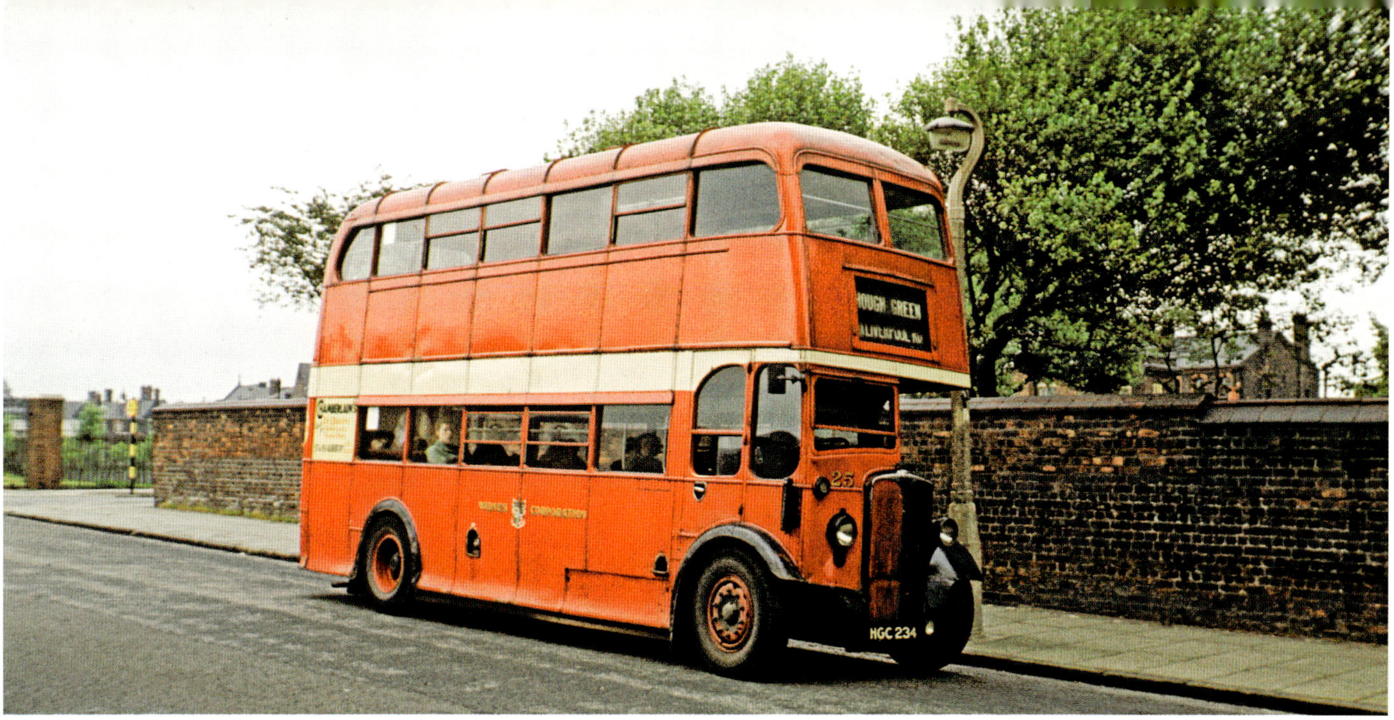

With new buses on long delivery and new housing developments to serve, four former London Transport Weymann-bodied AEC Regents were bought from Leeds dealer North's in August 1955. Quickly repainted into Widnes livery, they entered service that same month. The four had been new in 1946 as London Transport's STL 2682/3/97, 2701 and were the department's first and only AECs. Numbered 22-25 they were something of a stop-gap and were sold in 1960, 1961 and 1962. *Bruce Jenkins*

Leyland had ceased making bus bodies by the time more new double-deckers were needed and, in common with many Lancashire municipalities, Widnes went to East Lancashire Coachbuilders of Blackburn. Over the years 1957 to 1966 eighteen East Lancs-bodied Leyland PD2s joined the fleet. Numbered 26-43, they were bought in batches of two or three each year. Outside the garage in Moor Lane, in August 1967, this is number 34, one of two delivered in 1962. August 1967 *Roy Marshall*

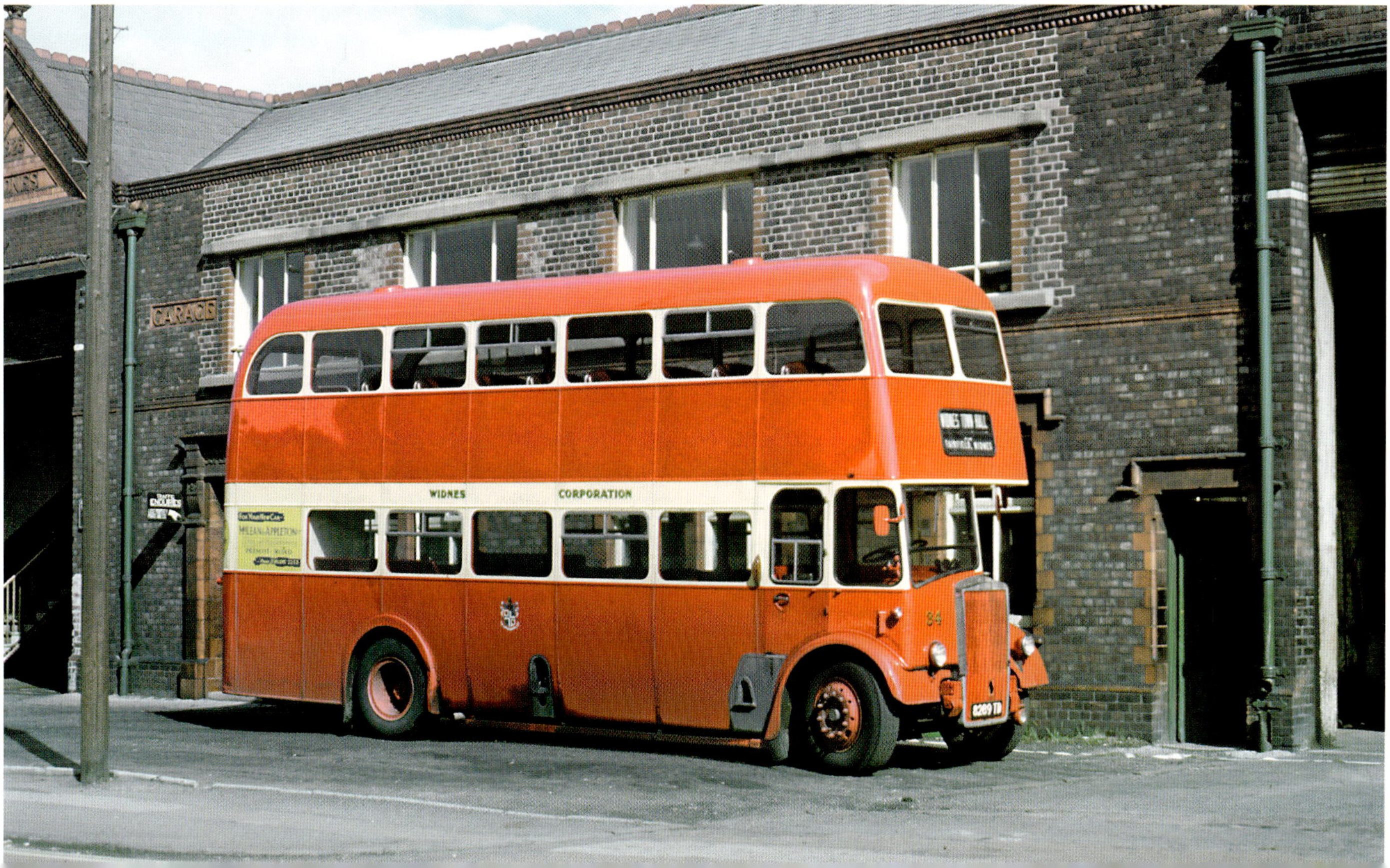

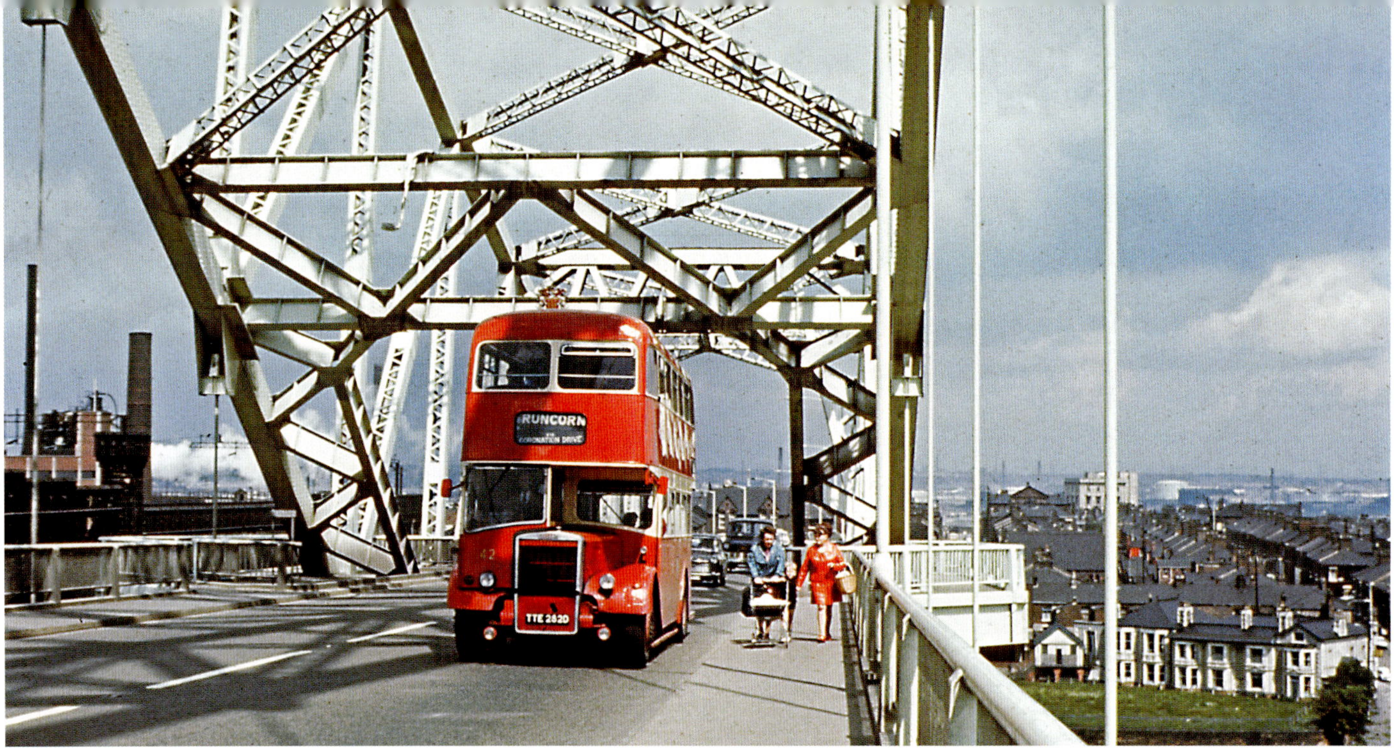

The opening of the Silver Jubilee Bridge in 1961 made a considerable difference to Widnes operations. On a bright sunny day, number 42 crosses the bridge bound for Runcorn. The picture was taken in 1966 and, as is evident on the left, the chemical works were still active although the long distance view shows that the air was clear. One of the stone pier towers and some of the ironwork of the fixed railway bridge of 1868 can just be seen on the extreme left. *Arnold Richardson*

In 1965 general manager John Craggs moved to Salford and the new manager was L T Quinn, previously deputy manager at Barrow. He changed vehicle policy to one-person operated dual-entrance single-deckers. The first were Leyland Leopards with East Lancs bodies. Numbered 44-50, three arrived in 1967 and two each in 1968 and 1969. The livery was also brightened as in this picture of number 49 passing the Central Library in Victoria Square. *Peter Jackson*

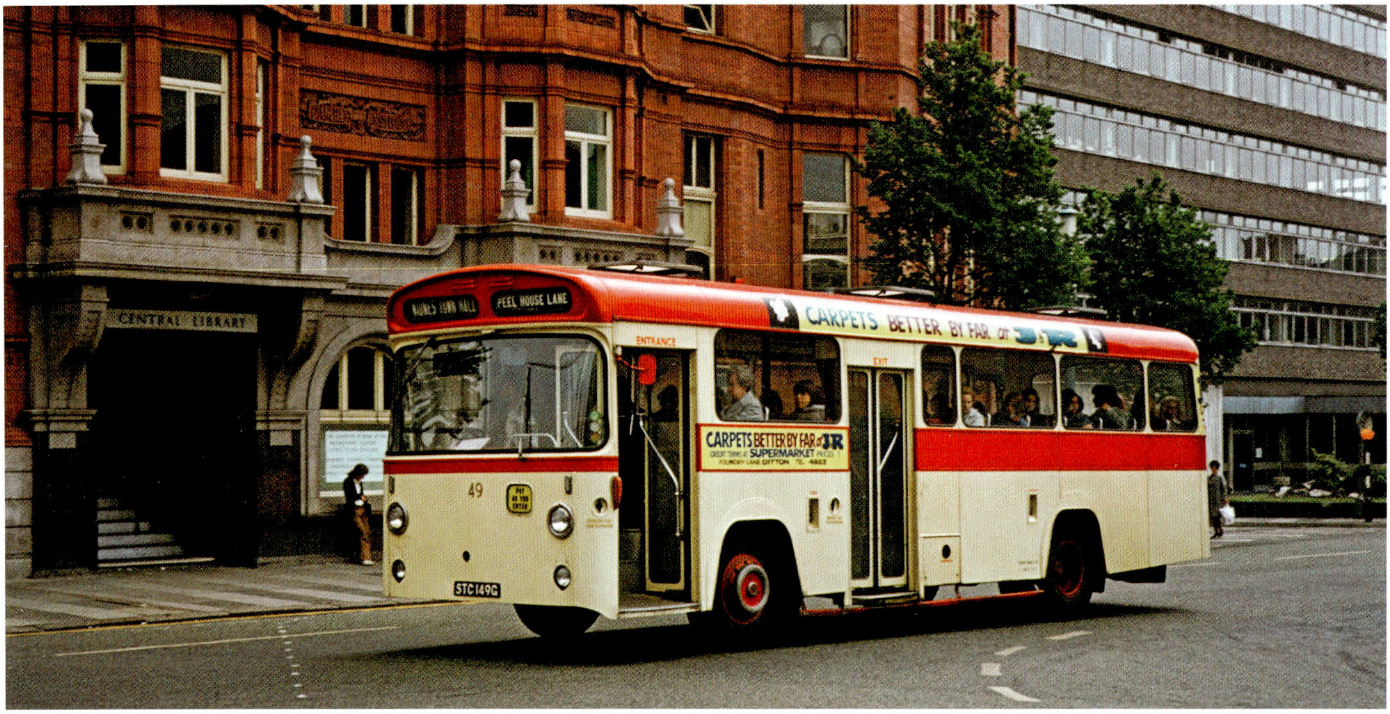

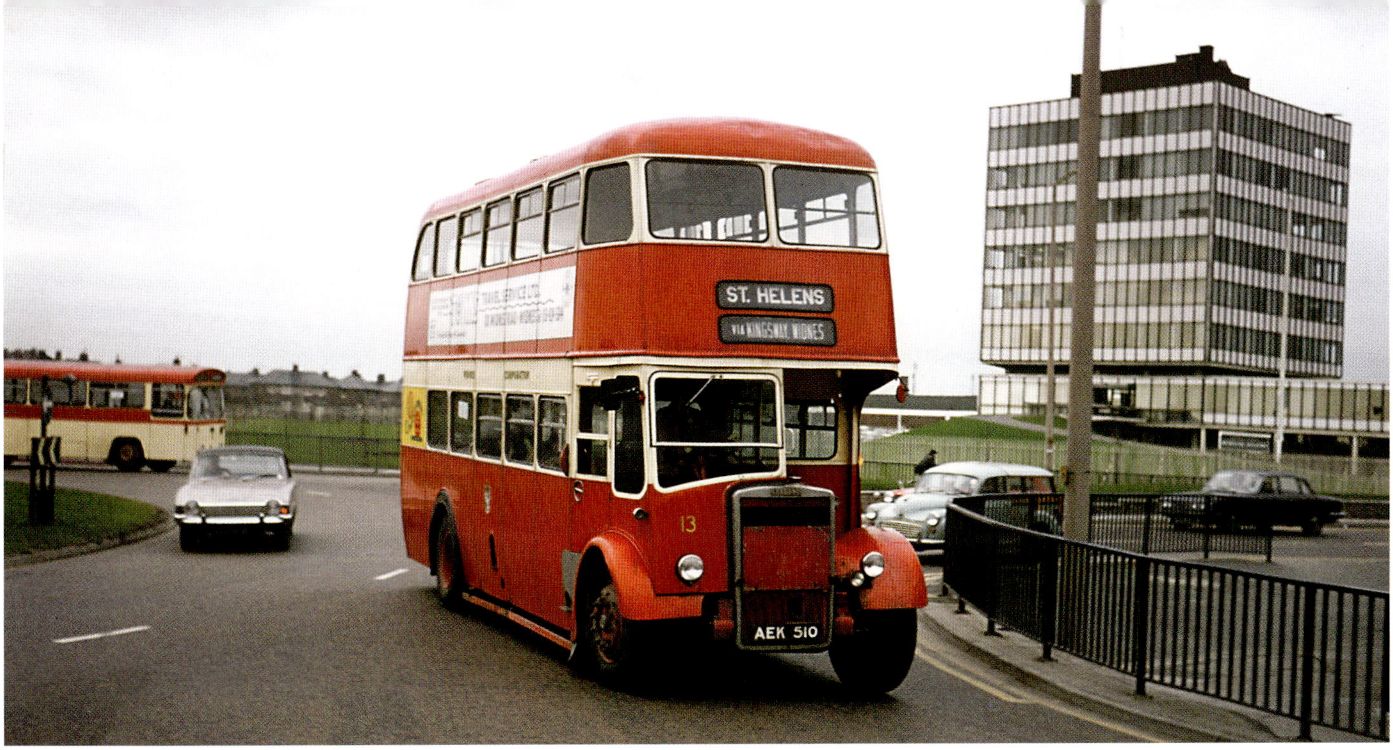

Second-hand vehicle purchases by municipal operators were rare in 1969 but Wigan Corporation was disposing of some Leyland-bodied PD2/12s new in 1953. They were in fine condition and it proved cost effective to buy some rather than overhaul Widnes own PD2s. Four were bought in 1969 and two more in 1970, their fleet numbers (22-25, 12-13) filling gaps in the fleet list. The St Helens service was one which was extended over the bridge to Runcorn whence number 13 has come in this March 1972 photograph. *Omnibus Society/Peter Henson*

In common with other local fleets, Widnes turned to Bristol for its final vehicle purchases which were eight Leyland-engined RESLs, as usual with East Lancs bodies, numbers 51-55 in 1971 and numbers 2-4 in 1972/3. This picture is of number 3 on one of the Crosville services extended jointly across the bridge into Widnes. Intermediate indicator boxes were altered to enable them to display the Crosville service numbers. June 1973 *Omnibus Society/Peter Henson*

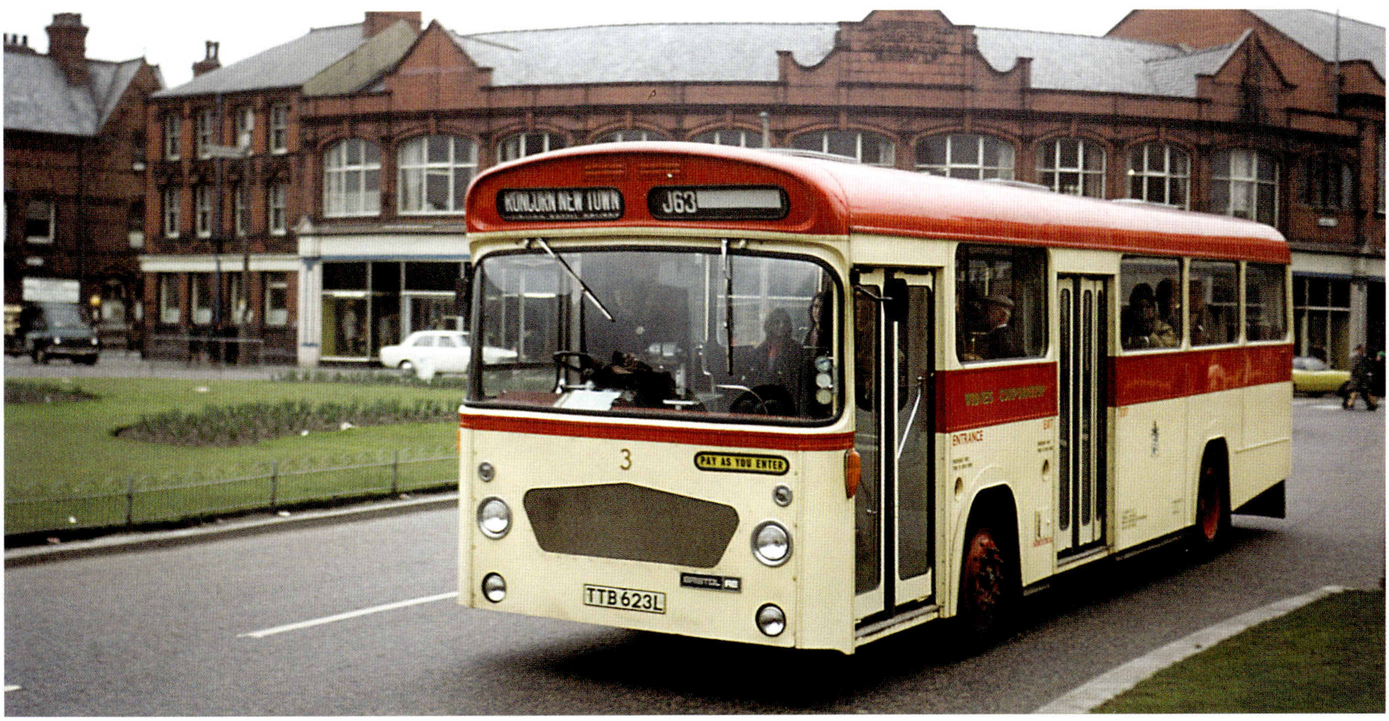

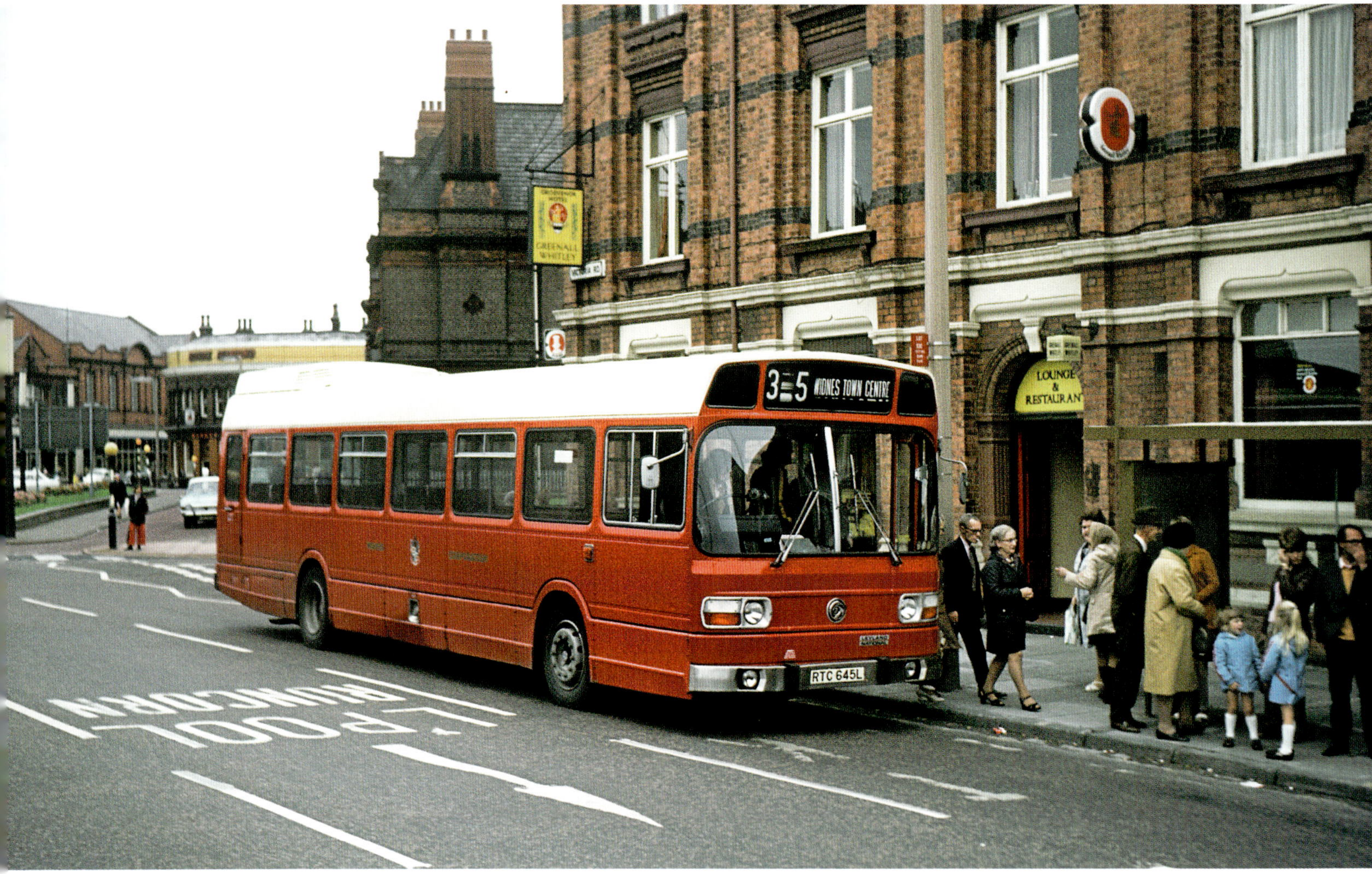

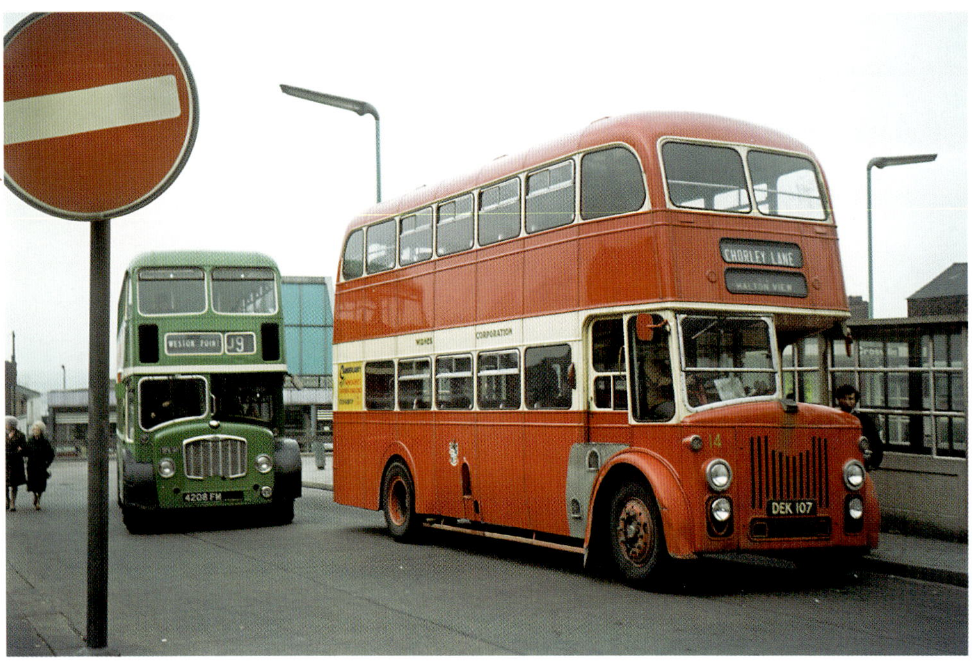

The bus numbered 1 was an early example of the Leyland National which entered service in August 1972. Leyland's policy for the National was that it was only offered finished in either plain white National Bus Company poppy red, leaf green, or London Transport red. Widnes chose London red, the nearest to its own livery, to which it added a white roof. It remained unique in respect of its livery although Widnes' successor, Halton, would buy many more Nationals. *Omnibus Society/Peter Henson*

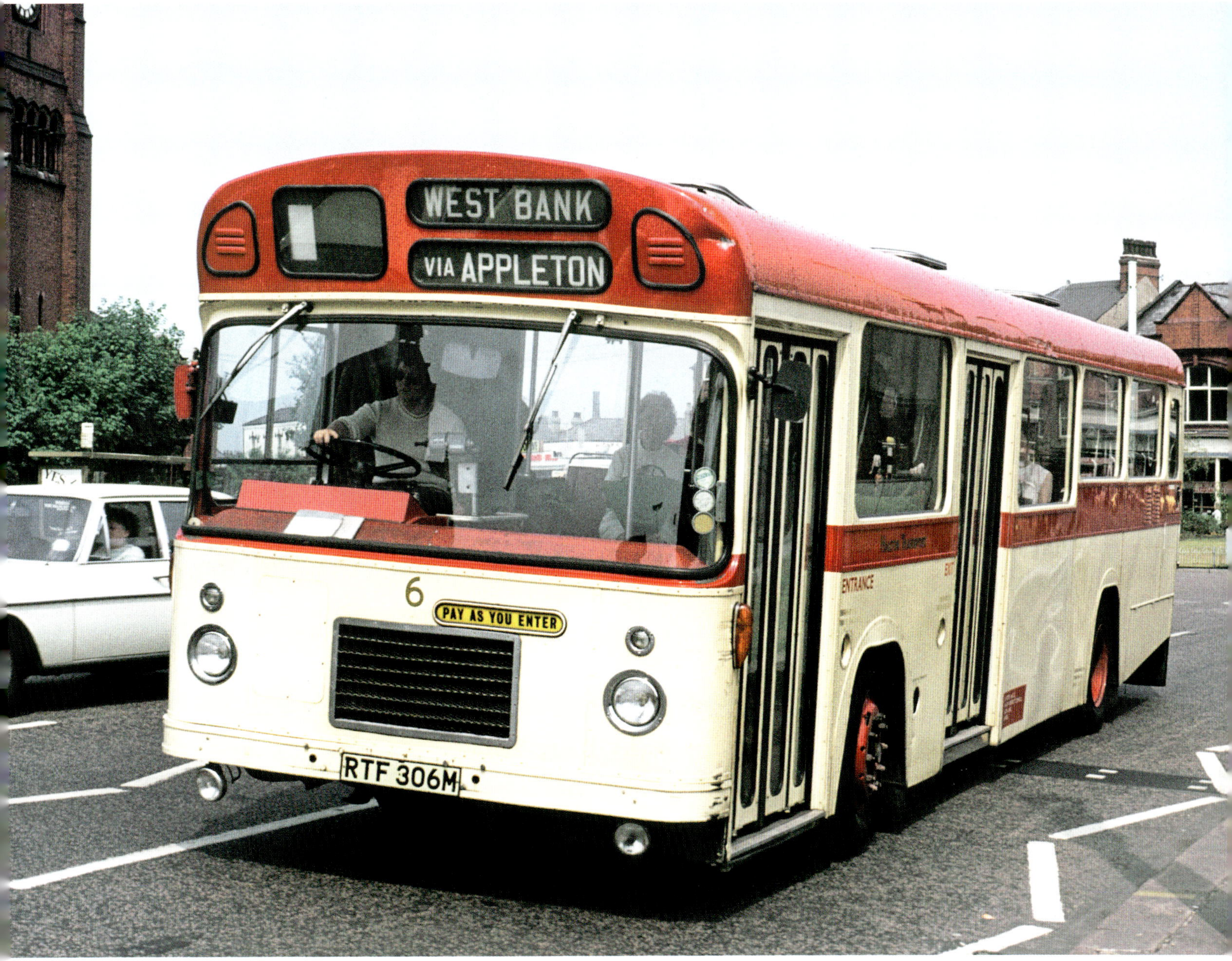

Three East Lancs-bodied 36ft-long Bristol RELLs (5-8) arrived four months before the local government revisions of April 1974 took Widnes into the new Municipal Borough of Halton. They were Widnes Corporation's last new buses and there are no good pictures of them in the short period before the changeover. This is number 6 with Halton in 1977; number blinds it might have but they were still not used for the local Widnes services. *Omnibus Society/Peter Henson*

Opposite Four more double-deckers were bought from Wigan in 1972 – this time they were Massey-bodied Leyland PD2/30s new in 1957/8 and again they filled gaps in the existing fleet numbers – 14,15,16,18. This picture shows number 14 in Runcorn bus station along with a Crosville Lodekka. The PD2 will cross the bridge but the Lodekka will not – it is going to Weston Point in Runcorn Docks. *Omnibus Society/Peter Henson*

Crosville

Based in Chester, Crosville's roots were in that city and the Wirral – its first service dated back to 1911 and ran from Chester to Ellesmere Port. The company expanded into Wales and, in the face of municipal opposition, into Liverpool, Widnes, Warrington and the Wirral. Crosville had some 230 buses on Merseyside with garages at Rock Ferry, Birkenhead (about 70 buses) and Heswall (30), and, across the Mersey, Liverpool (70), Runcorn (35) and Warrington (25). The services were its most lucrative and vital to the company's business. In contrast to Ribble, by and large Crosville avoided joint services and it had complex, usually hard fought, agreements with the municipalities within whose boundaries it operated.

From 1942 Crosville was a Tilling company, which meant that from 1946 almost all the new vehicles for its 1,000-plus fleet were standard Bristol/Eastern Coach Works ('ECW') vehicles. The company's history is well recorded in several volumes and the pictures in this book are a brief overview of its buses on Merseyside, beginning with pictures that set the scene on either side of the Mersey.

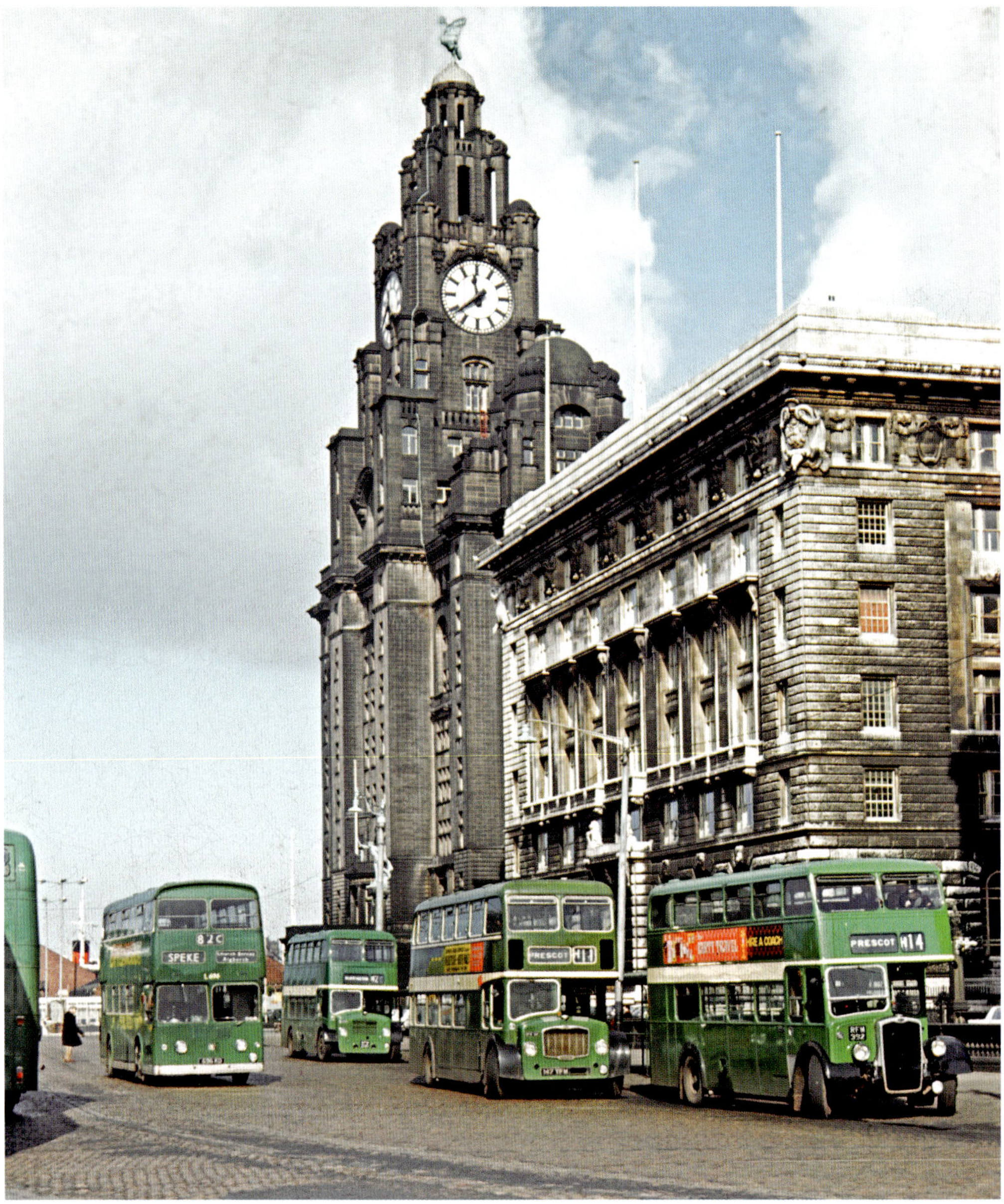

Dominated by the Liver, Cunard and (out of shot) Port of Liverpool Buildings, known as 'the Three Graces', the Pier Head was shared as a terminus by Liverpool, Crosville and Ribble. This is the Crosville terminus on 16 March 1965, with three generations of Bristol/ECW double-deckers. At the front is Bristol KSW DKB647 on the H14, one of the group of services to Prescot; behind with the distinctive grilles of its Cave-Brown-Cave heating system is FLF-type Bristol Lodekka DFB114 and third in line is earlier LD-type Lodekka DLG789. Crosville had no new rear-engined double deckers until 1974, in contrast to Liverpool Corporation whose Atlantean L696 is leaving Pier Head for Speke. *Bryan Pyne*

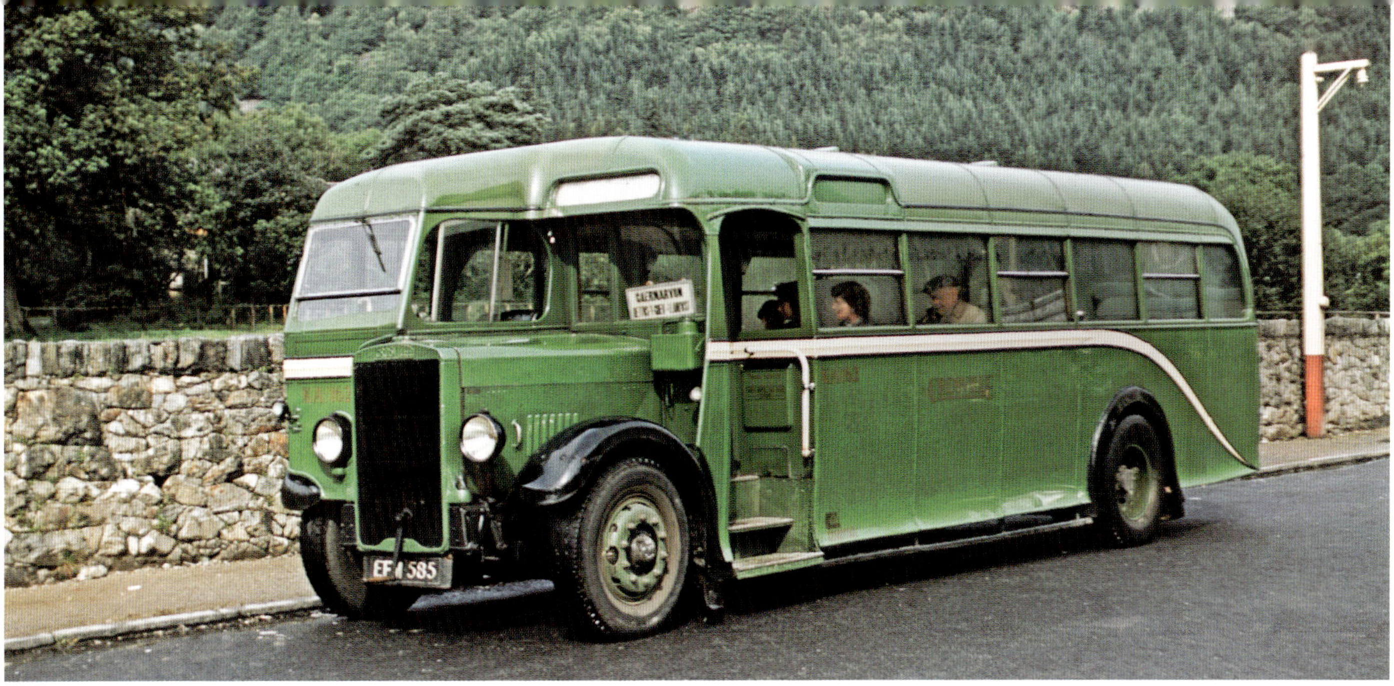

Before Crosville was moved into the Tilling group, it was a Leyland fleet and usually allocated its newest vehicles to Merseyside. Although not taken on Merseyside, these fairly rare colour pictures illustrate the type of Leyland that would have worked services in the 1940s and early 1950s. ECW-bodied Leyland TS8 KA162 was typical of Crosville's late 1930s purchases as was ECW-bodied Leyland TD5 M54 – lowbridge of course – and either type would as likely to be found in Warrington, Widnes or Woodside. For years Crosville used window cards ('widcards') to show the destination, instead of the more usual indicator and blinds. *Arnold Richardson*

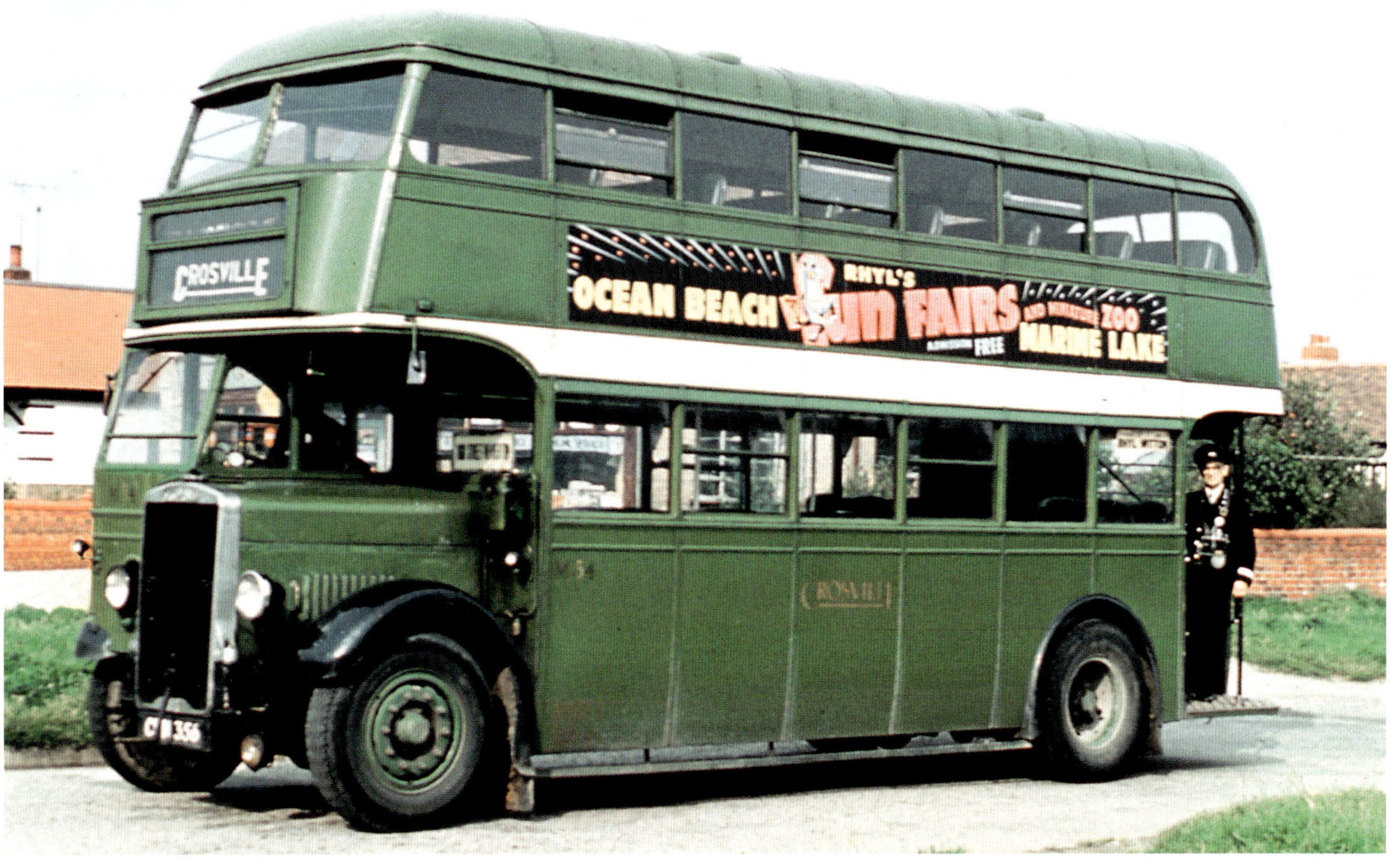

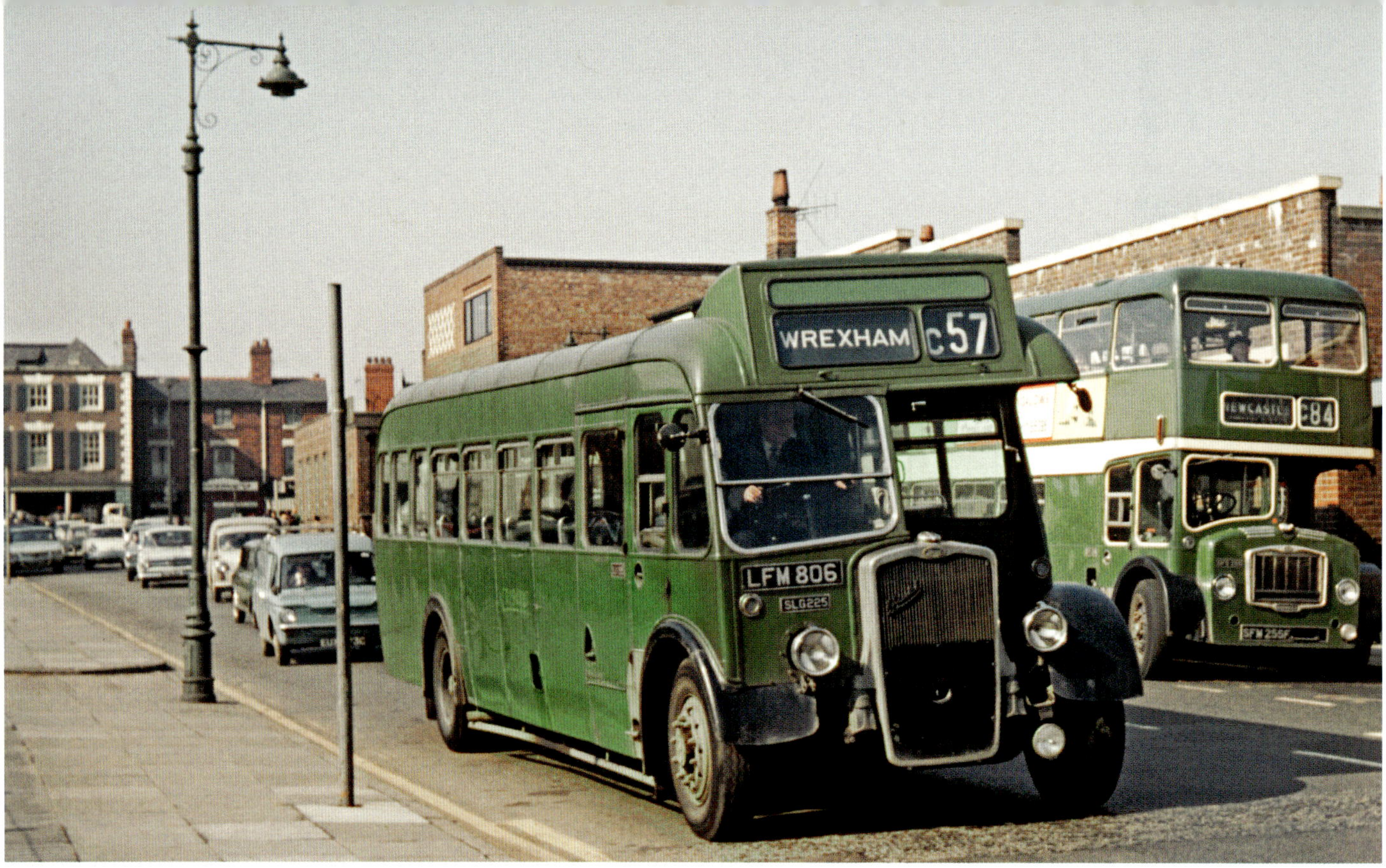

Delamere Street area was Crosville's principal terminus in Chester, with out of town services to all directions. In this late 1960s view, Bristol LWL6G SLG225 of 1951 is leaving for Wrexham, its ECW body looking drab in overall green. Crosville expected a long life from its buses and when SLG225 was withdrawn in 1970, it was one of the last half-cab single deckers in normal service within the National Bus Company. On the right on a C84 into Potteries territory at Newcastle-under-Lyme is one of Crosville's final batch of Bristol Lodekkas – FLF6G DFG255 new 1967. *Bill Ryan*

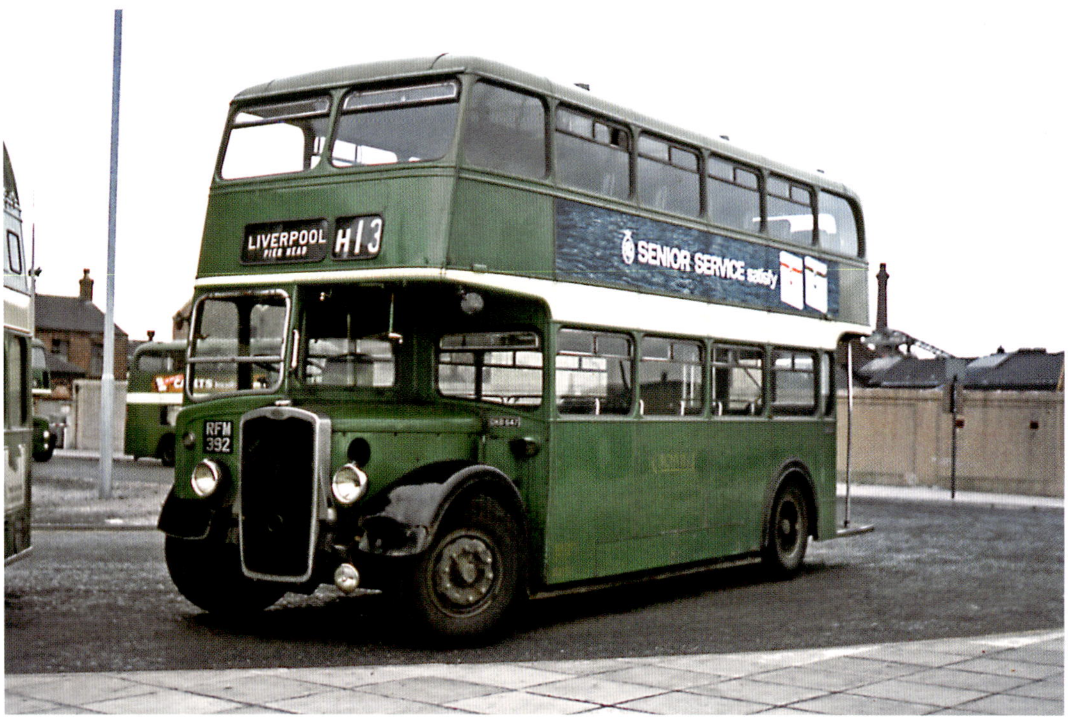

The busy services from Liverpool to the St Helens boundary at Prescot were an important source of income. Bristol-engined KSW fleet number DKB647 is in the lay bay at the Prescot terminus, along with a similar KSW and two Lodekkas. Crosville services had a letter prefixed separate number series for each operating area – C for Chester area, F for Birkenhead area, H for Liverpool/ Warrington, J for Runcorn, for example. *Arnold Richardson*

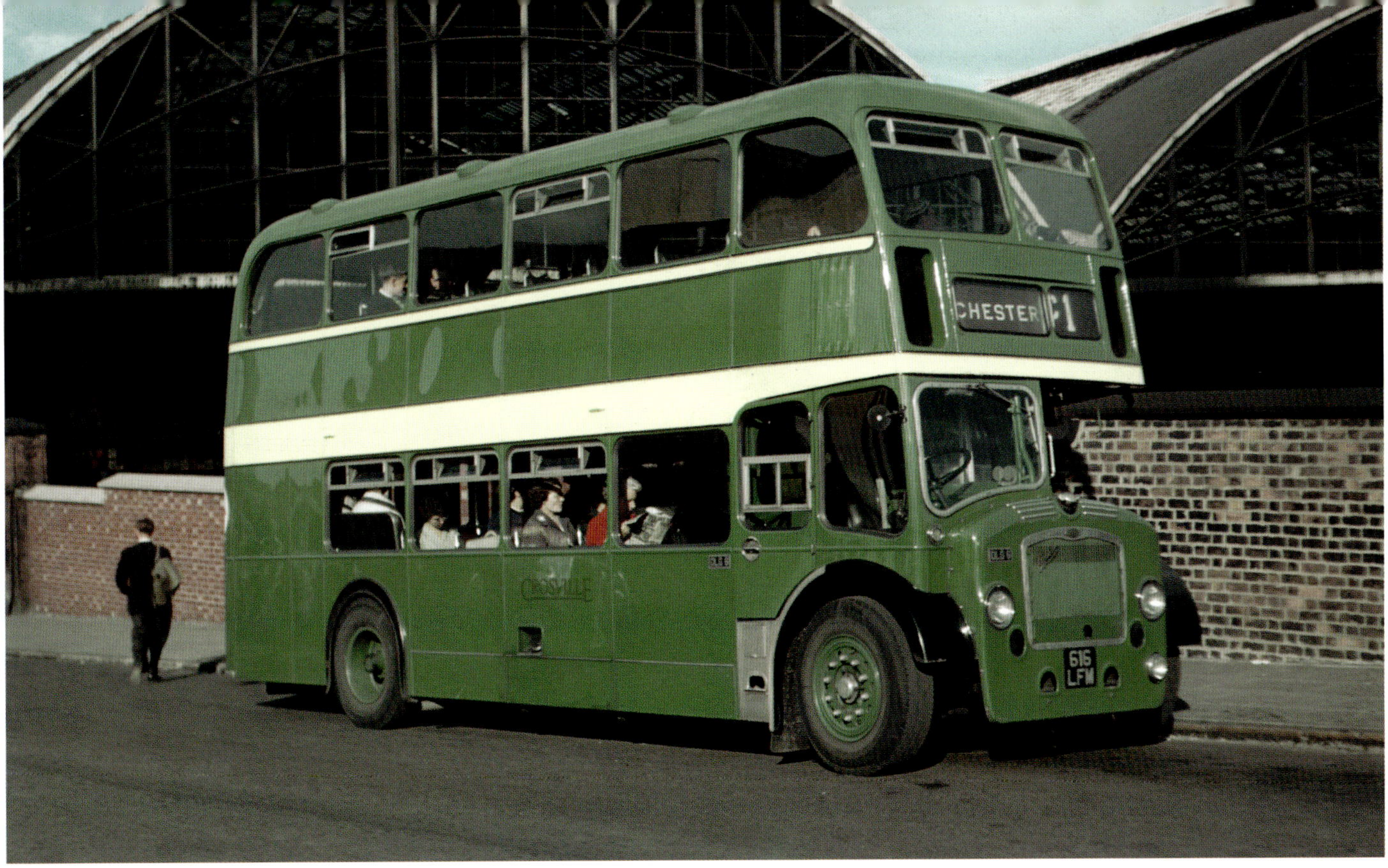

With the arched roofs of Woodside railway station as the backdrop, in April 1960 brand new Gardner-engined Bristol-ECW Lodekka DLG6 waits on the Woodside stands for departure time on the busy trunk C1 service to Chester. For years the Birkenhead – Ellesmere Port – Chester services accounted for one tenth the company's total revenue. *Geoffrey Morant*

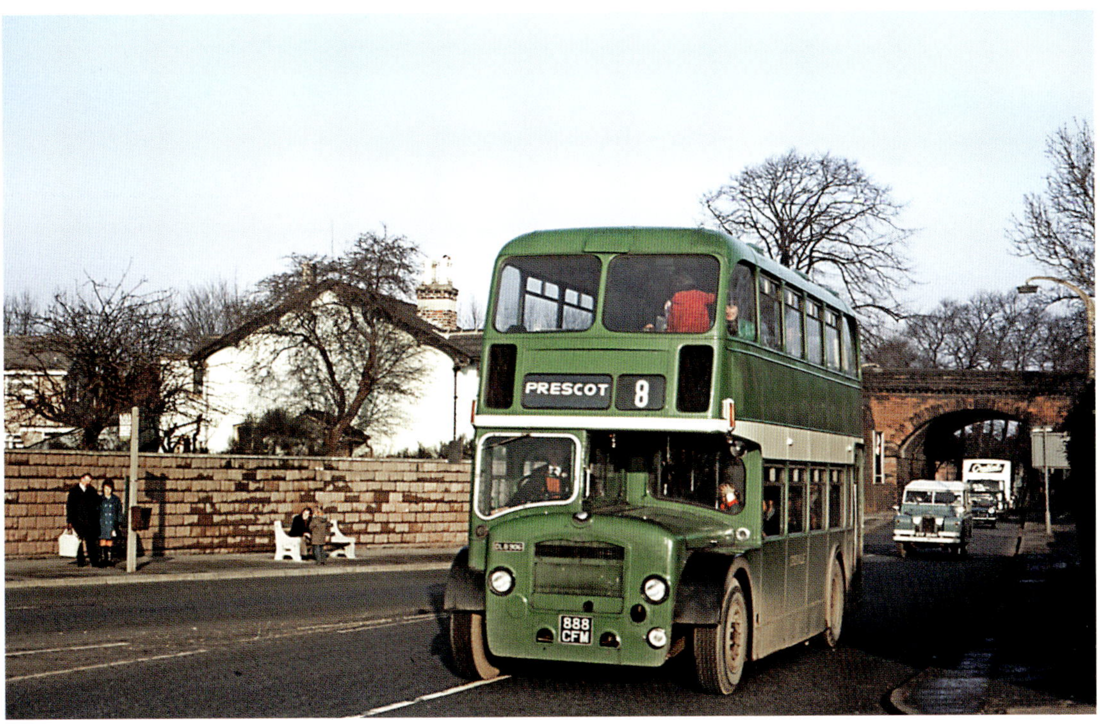

Crosville's services to Liverpool's eastern and southern suburbs were busy – for example, some seven buses an hour in each direction used Archway Road, Huyton, where the routes passed under this railway bridge near the station. With its H service prefix not set, LD6B Lodekka DLB906, new in 1958, is on the H8 from Liverpool to Prescot, where it will meet the equally busy St Helens Corporation services 7 and 8. *Peter Jackson*

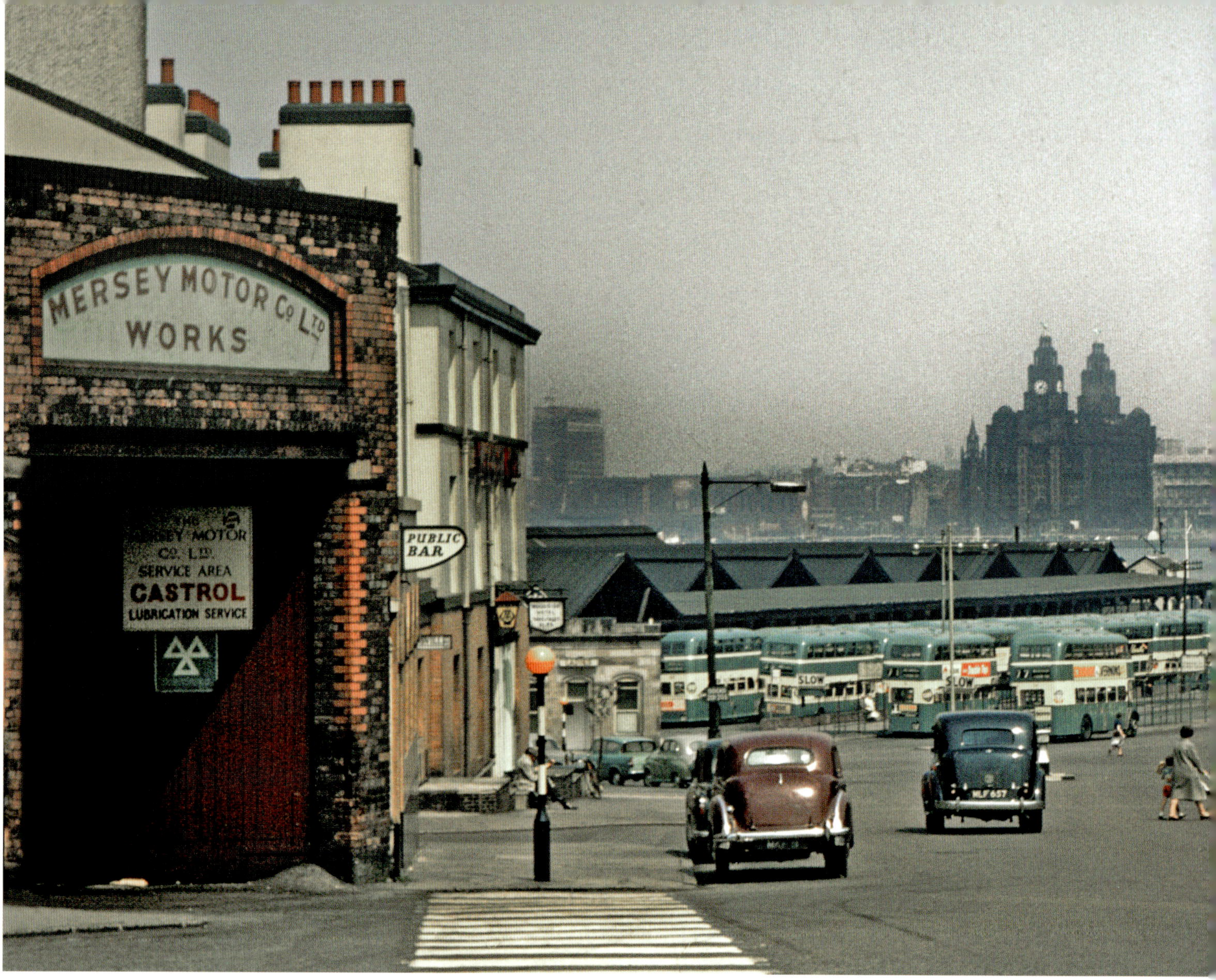

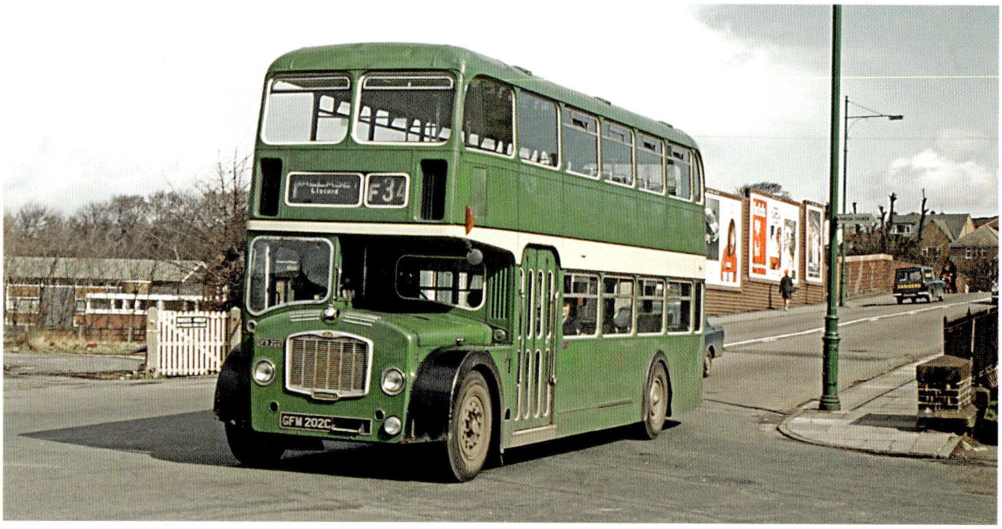

On the Wirral, West Kirby was the terminus of several Crosville services into the Birkenhead, Chester and Wallasey Corporations' operating areas. The F34 service followed a U-shaped route from Park Station, Birkenhead to Liscard Village, Wallasey via West Kirby, the journey taking 65 minutes. Although there was the rival electric train service to Birkenhead and thence through the rail tunnel under the Mersey into Liverpool, Crosville's buses usually had more passengers than 1965 ECW-bodied Bristol FLF DFB202 pictured approaching the centre of West Kirby. *Alan Mortimer*

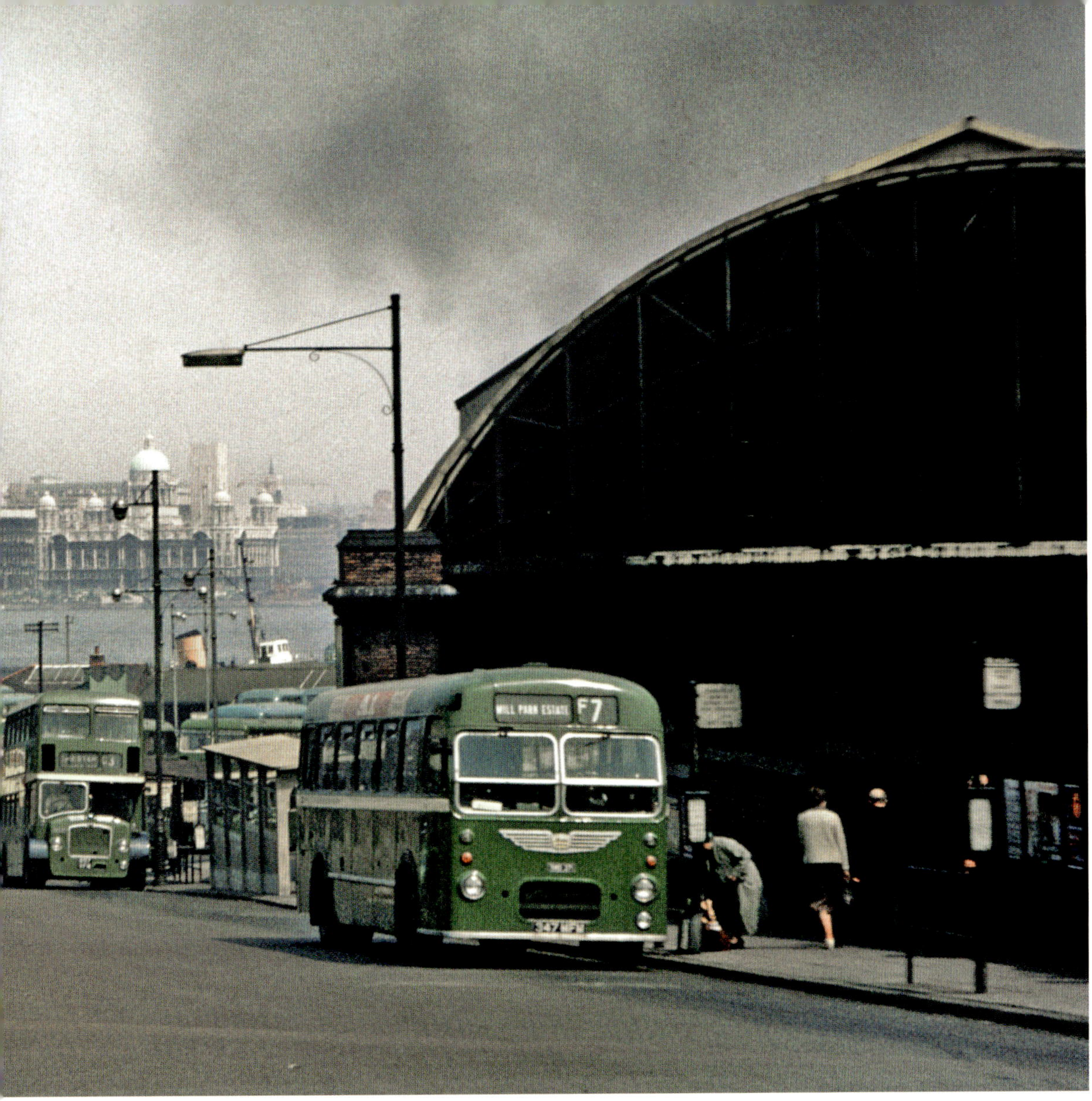

Nearest the camera in this 1964 picture of the Crosville stands at Birkenhead's Woodside terminus is SMG371, a 1960 Bristol/ECW MW6G on the hourly service to Mill Park Estate in Eastham. Behind is a Bristol Lodekka on one of the trunk Ellesmere Port – Chester services. Beyond are 31 Birkenhead buses, four more Crosvilles, the funnel of a Mersey tug boat and clouds of smoke from a steam locomotive in Woodside railway station. Across the Mersey, the Liver Building at Pier Head dominates the skyline. *G D Parry*

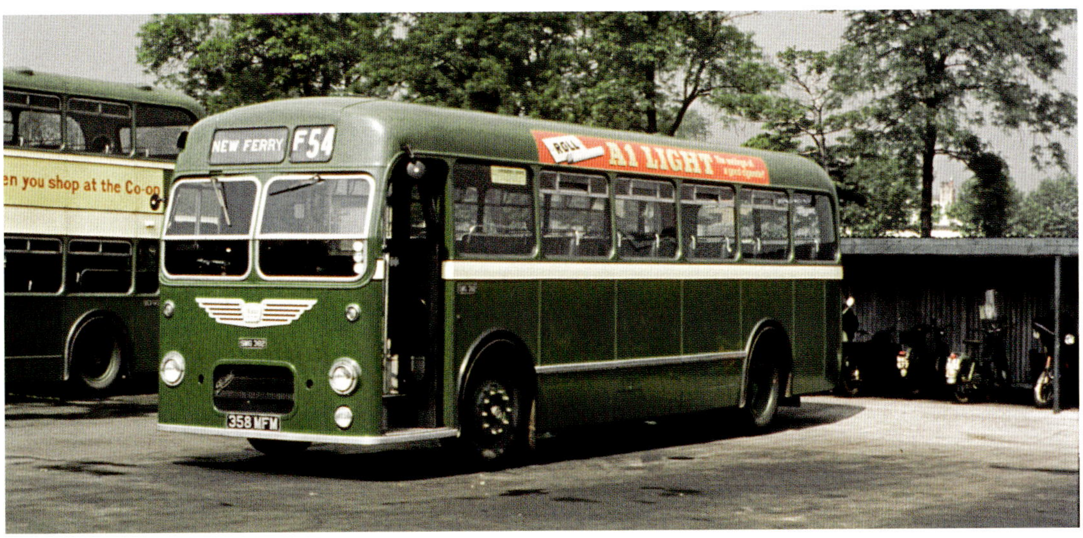

As familiar on the Wirral as the FLF Lodekkas were the Bristol/ECW Gardner-engined MWs. This is SMG382 (the letter code indicated S – single-deck bus, M – MW type, G – Gardner engine) in the garage yard at Rock Ferry, half way along the Mersey between Woodside and Port Sunlight it was, effectively, Crosville's Birkenhead garage.
Roy Marshall

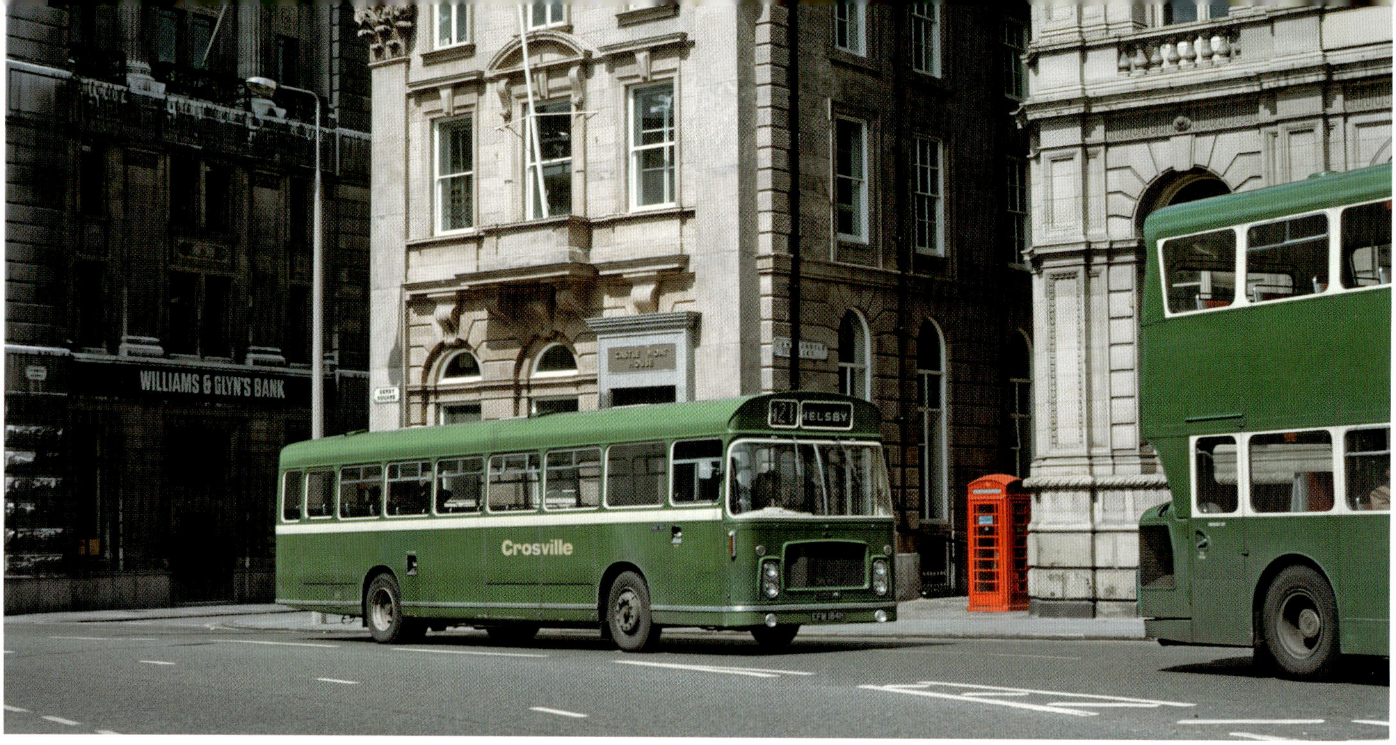

Crosville bought no new rear-engined double-deckers until 1974, preferring the large capacity 36ft-long Gardner-engined ECW-bodied Bristol RELL single-decker, some with dual doors and some with single doors. They ran on both sides of the Mersey and this is single door SRG184 following a Liverpool Atlantean on a quiet morning in Derby Square in the city. The journey on the H21 will first take it to Widnes and then over the bridge to Runcorn and finally back along the other side of the Mersey to Helsby. July 1973 *Roy Marshall*

Crosville's F18 and F19 services connected Woodside with the seaside village of Parkgate on the other side of the Wirral, the journey taking 39 minutes. Although the indicator blinds did not inform SRG66's passengers, most would know where it was going. *Arnold Richardson*

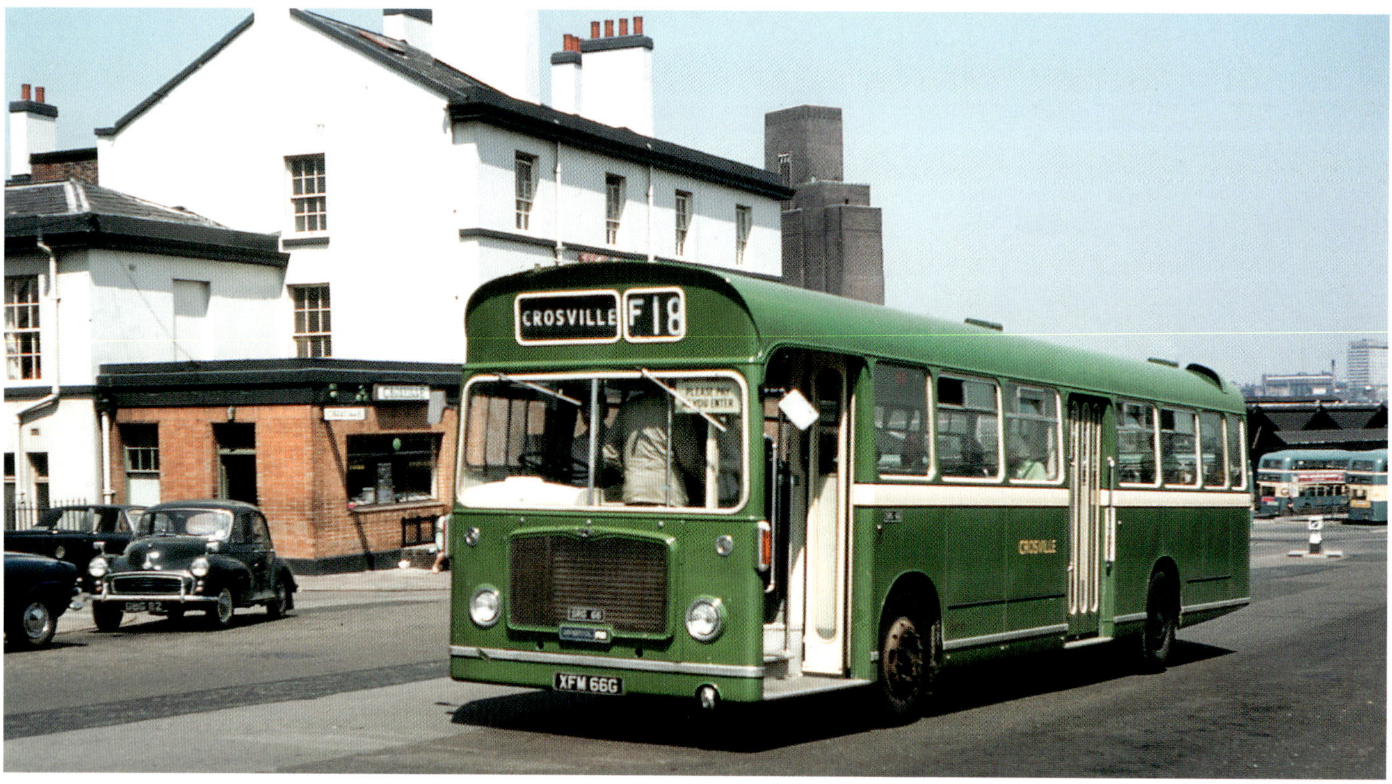

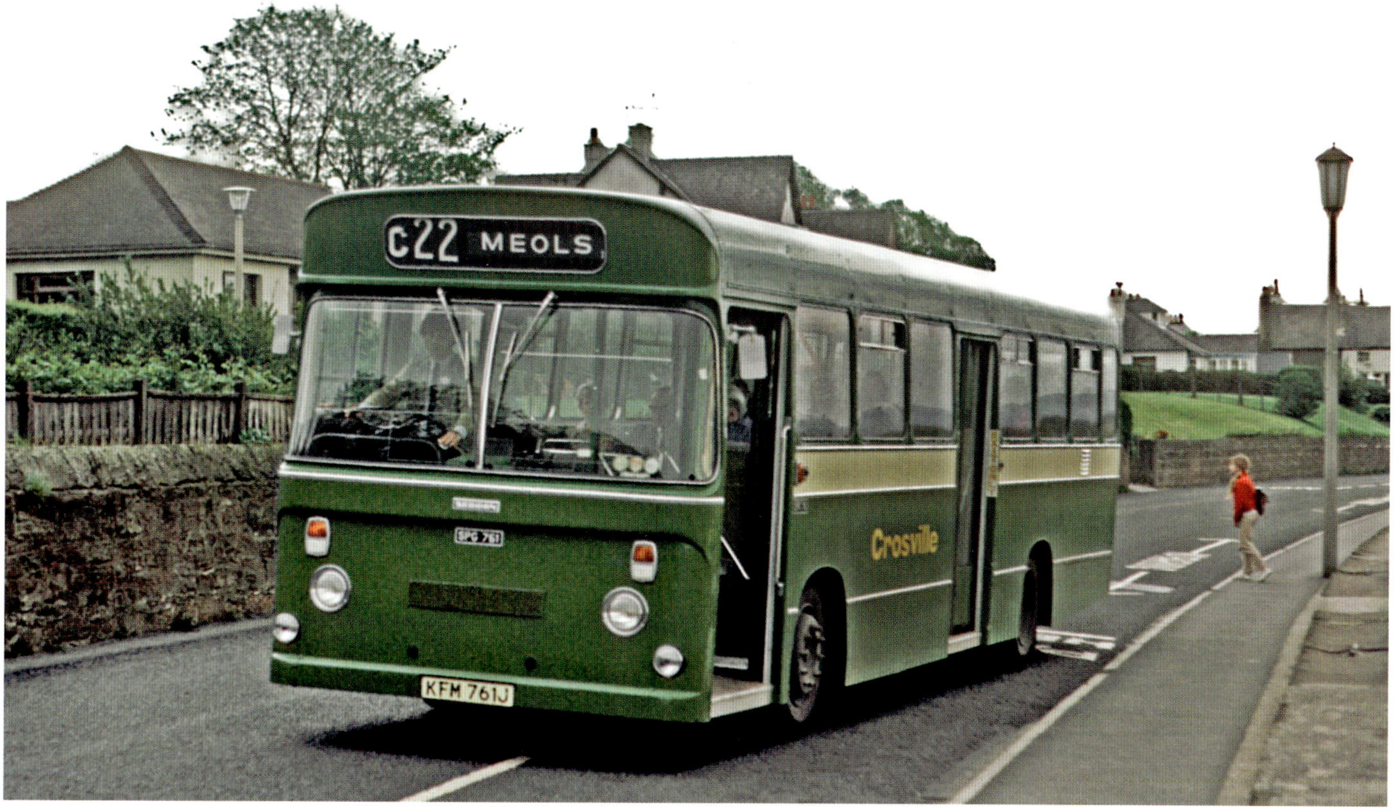

Crosville drew something of a short straw when delays in the supply of new vehicles caused the National Bus Company to order 100 of Seddon's RU and allocate them all to Crosville. The rear-engined RU had a Gardner engine but had had insufficient development and the problems they caused Crosville were made much worse by the Seddon bodies, which suffered from severe structural weaknesses and water leaks. This is SPG761 in May 1971 on the C22 which ran from Chester through Neston, Heswall, Thurstaston, West Kirby and Hoylake to Meols, serving the south west side of the Wirral peninsula. The picture shows it in Parkgate. *Roy Marshall*

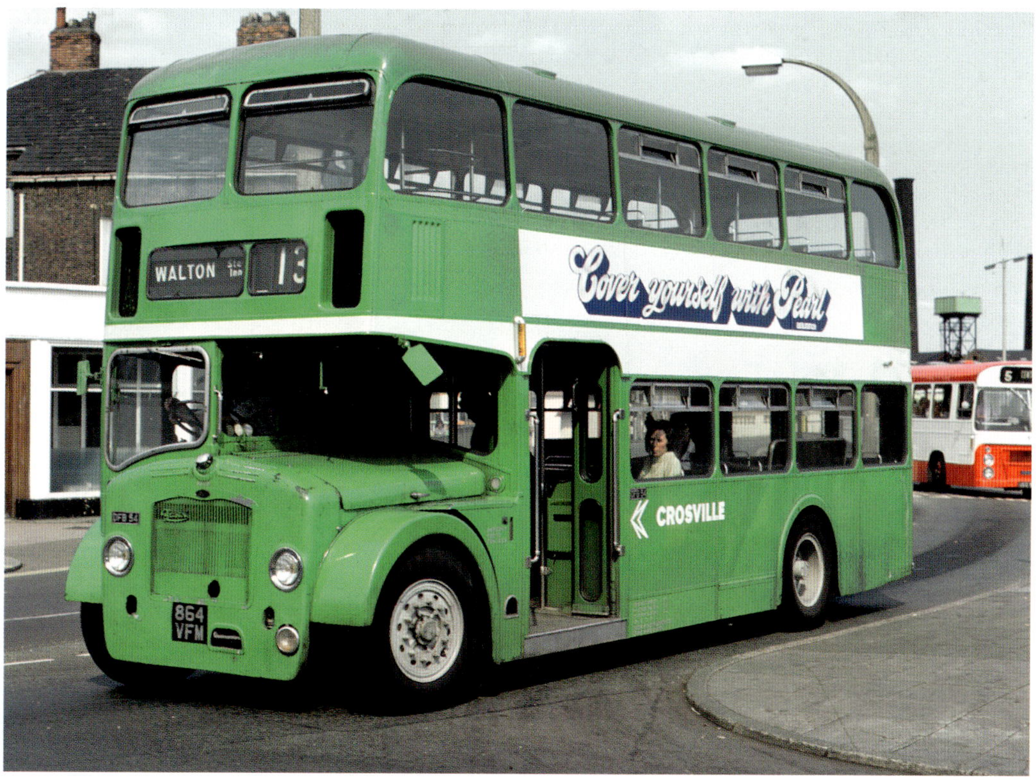

Crosville was joint operator with Warrington on services 13 to Walton and 14 to Stockton Heath – they were Warrington service numbers – and this is Bristol/ECW FSF6B Lodekka DFB54 inbound at Bridge Foot in 1973. The company's presence in Warrington increased when it took over North Western's Cheshire-area services when the latter company was split up by the Selnec PTE. This prompted Crosville to approach both Warrington and Widnes with an offer to take over the two corporation's transport operations. The proposals received short, sharp and very negative replies – an event which is the only justification for including a picture of a bus in the insipid National Bus Company leaf green livery. The rejections were well judged for, in their new post-1974 guises, the transport operations of Warrington and Widnes (as Halton) would flourish and long outlast Crosville. *Geoffrey Morant*

Ribble

Ribble had a major presence north of the Mersey. One quarter of Ribble's fleet of 1,100 was stationed at its garages at Aintree (around 80), Bootle (100), Liverpool (40), Southport (20), Ormskirk (20) and whilst some were coaches for long distance work, the majority by far were service buses. The busy Merseyside stage services, some joint with Liverpool, were Ribble's most lucrative and, when it came to vehicles, the buses that worked them were reliable and dependable Leyland PD2s and PD3s. During the period of this book few Ribble Atlanteans were allocated to Merseyside – and those that were there were used on the inter-town services.

The pictures in this section give an overview of Ribble's Merseyside fleet. A more detailed look at them and how Ribble came to have such a major presence is well documented elsewhere.

Ribble's post war double-decker fleet included 227 all-Leyland PD2/3s. Delivered in 1948/49/50 all but 42 had lowbridge bodies. The highbridge ones, 2618-2647/49-2660, were cancelled orders intended for Cape Town, South Africa. Known by the staff as 'Capetowns' almost all were allocated to Merseyside. This is 2650 in the forecourt of Aintree garage ready to take up service on the 59 from Old Roan, a district of Aintree, to Old Haymarket in the city. Ribble used much of the external advertising space on its buses to promote its own services. *Peter Whitworth*

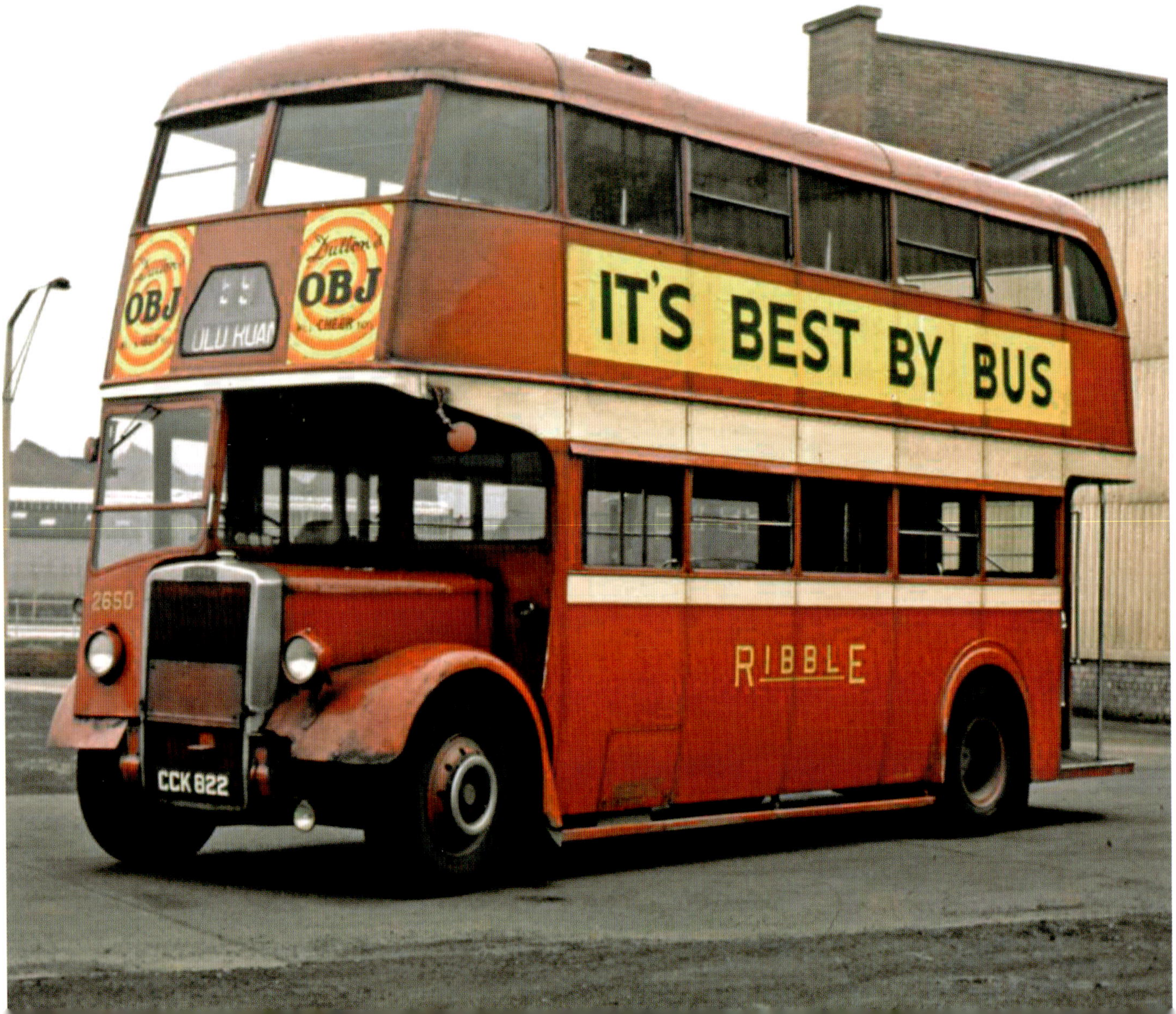

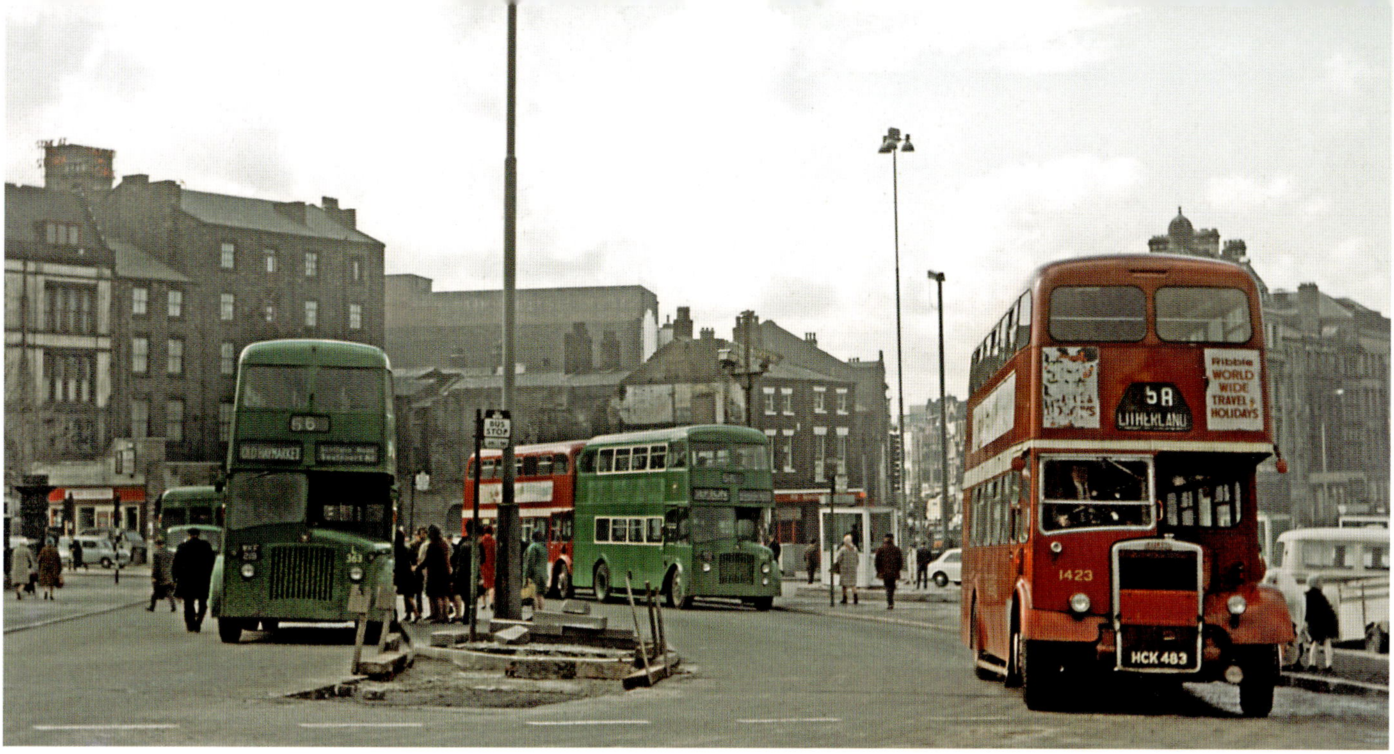

Leyland having given up building bus bodies, Ribble's next 120 PD2s, 1381-1500, were bodied by Metro Cammell (75) and Burlingham (45). All had highbridge bodies and many were allocated to Merseyside. Routes 48-59 (Liverpool series service numbers) were among those jointly operated with Liverpool Corporation and here, in the late 1960s, Ribble 1423 leaves Old Haymarket terminus in the city centre on a 58 for Litherland with Liverpool PD2s on the 56 to Sefton and another Ribble Metro Cammell PD2 behind. *Alan Murray Rust*

Whereas all the other joint services started from the city centre, service 52 ran roughly hourly on weekdays, more frequently on Saturdays, from the suburb of Walton through Aintree to a picturesque rural terminus at Sefton Church, with its mill and the lovely parish church of St Helen. The church originated around 1170 as the private chapel of the Molyneux family which owned large estates in Lancashire and is associated with much of Liverpool's history. Better known as the Earl of Sefton, the last Earl and his wife bequeathed Croxteth Hall to the city in 1972. *Alan Murray Rust*

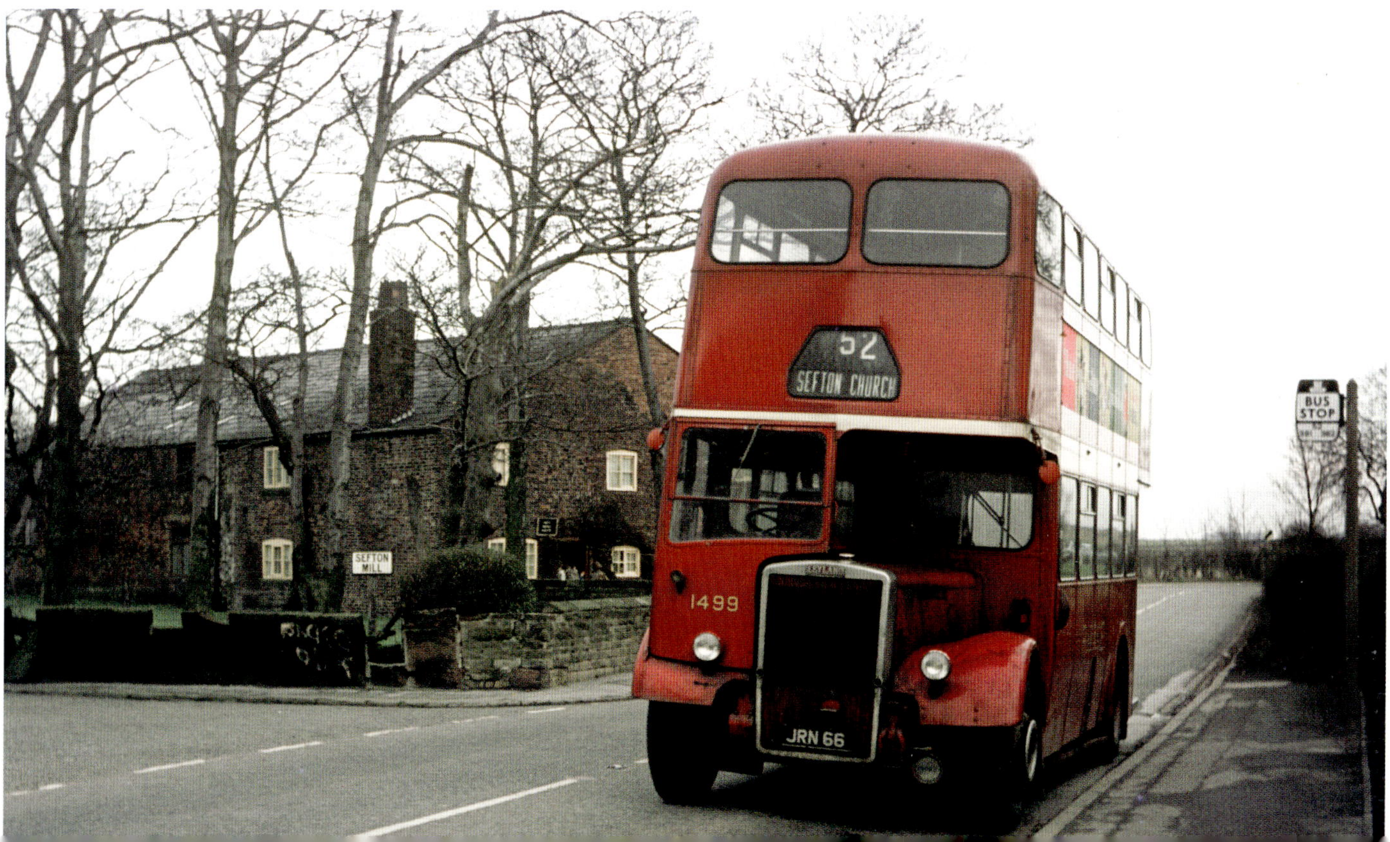

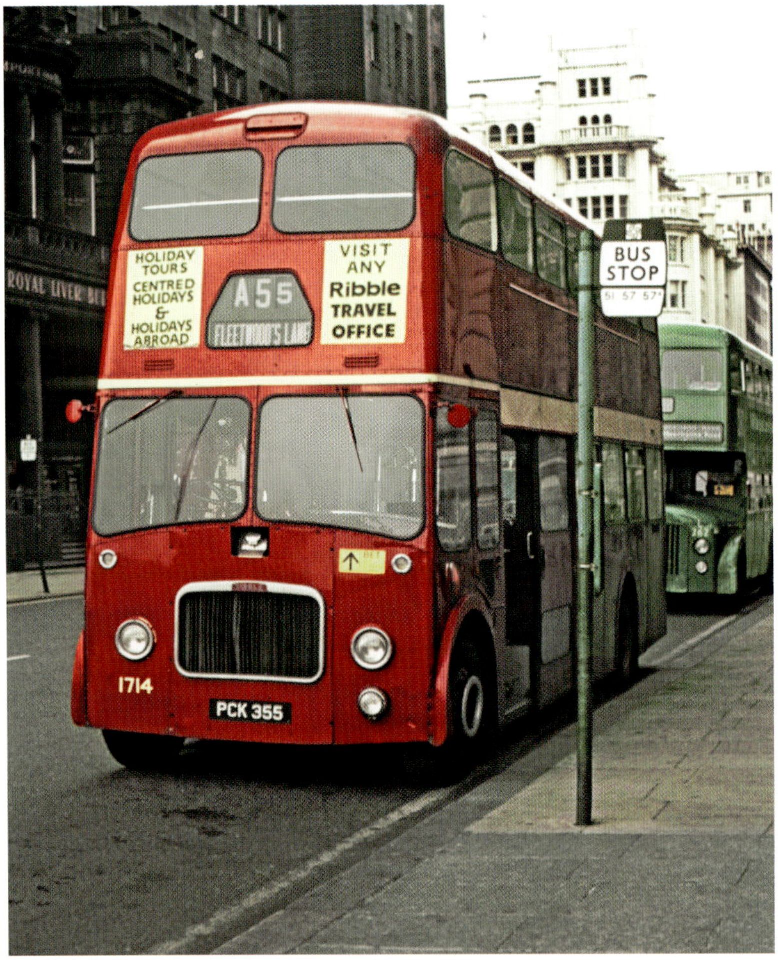

Left After the PD2s came Ribble's fine fleet of full-fronted, forward-entrance PD3s. Very much a trend setting design when they first appeared in 1957, they joined the PD2s as the mainstay of the Merseyside services. 1501-1605 were bodied by Burlingham and 1706-1850 by Metro Cammell. This picture is of 1714 at the Pier Head terminus where the 55 and others terminated on Saturday afternoons and Sundays. This bus is working what is properly a 55A but Ribble's third track blinds did not have 'A' on them and buses showed A55. *David Powell*

Right Ribble had its own bus station in Southport. Originally the Lord Street terminus of the Southport and Cheshire Lines Extension Railway, when the line closed in 1952, it was taken over by Ribble which converted it into a fine bus station. In August 1959 the crew of Ribble 1547, a Burlingham-bodied Leyland PD3/4, sit and read the paper during their break before they return to Liverpool. In the next bay, the driver of St Helens PD2 111, just arrived on the 309 from Warrington, stands waiting for his conductor who is inside the lower deck of the bus checking for any lost property. Ribble had good reason to be proud of its bus station with its arched glazed roof and hanging baskets. It closed in 1987 just after bus services were deregulated and a few years later Morrison's built a supermarket on the site, retaining the original frontage on to Lord Street – there is a picture of the imposing front of the building in the Southport part of this book. *Bruce Jenkins*

Ribble's Liverpool bus station was at the side of Lime Street railway station, on the corner of steeply graded Skelhorne Street and Bolton Street. The company's own local services in the area had an L-prefix and this picture shows eleven-year old 1586, one of the 105 PD3s with Burlingham bodies, coming in alongside Lime Street station on 29 November 1969 – two days before 'PTE Day'. Its destination is the same as the 55A in the previous picture but the L25 took a more roundabout journey through Ribble's territory of Bootle and Crosby. *Reg Wilson*

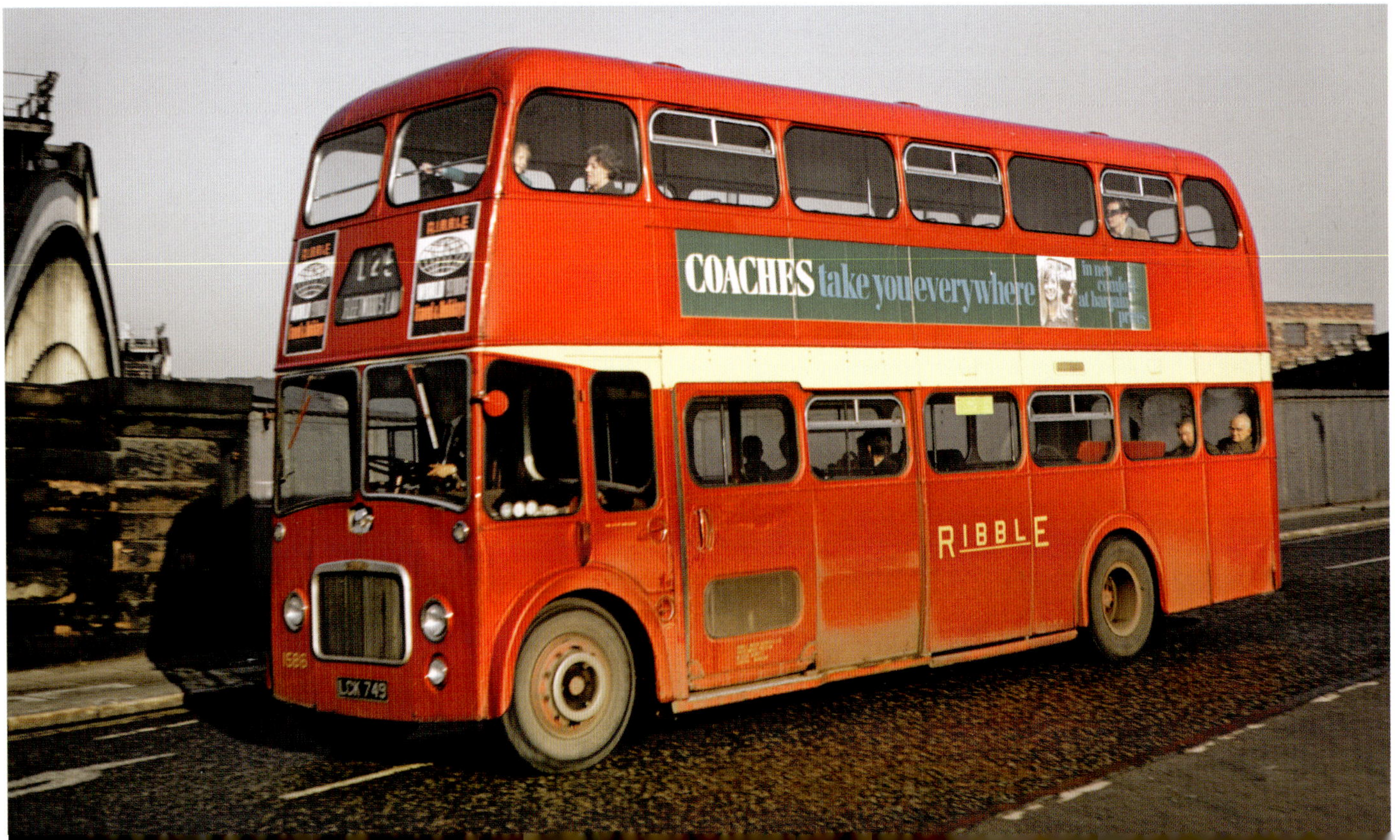

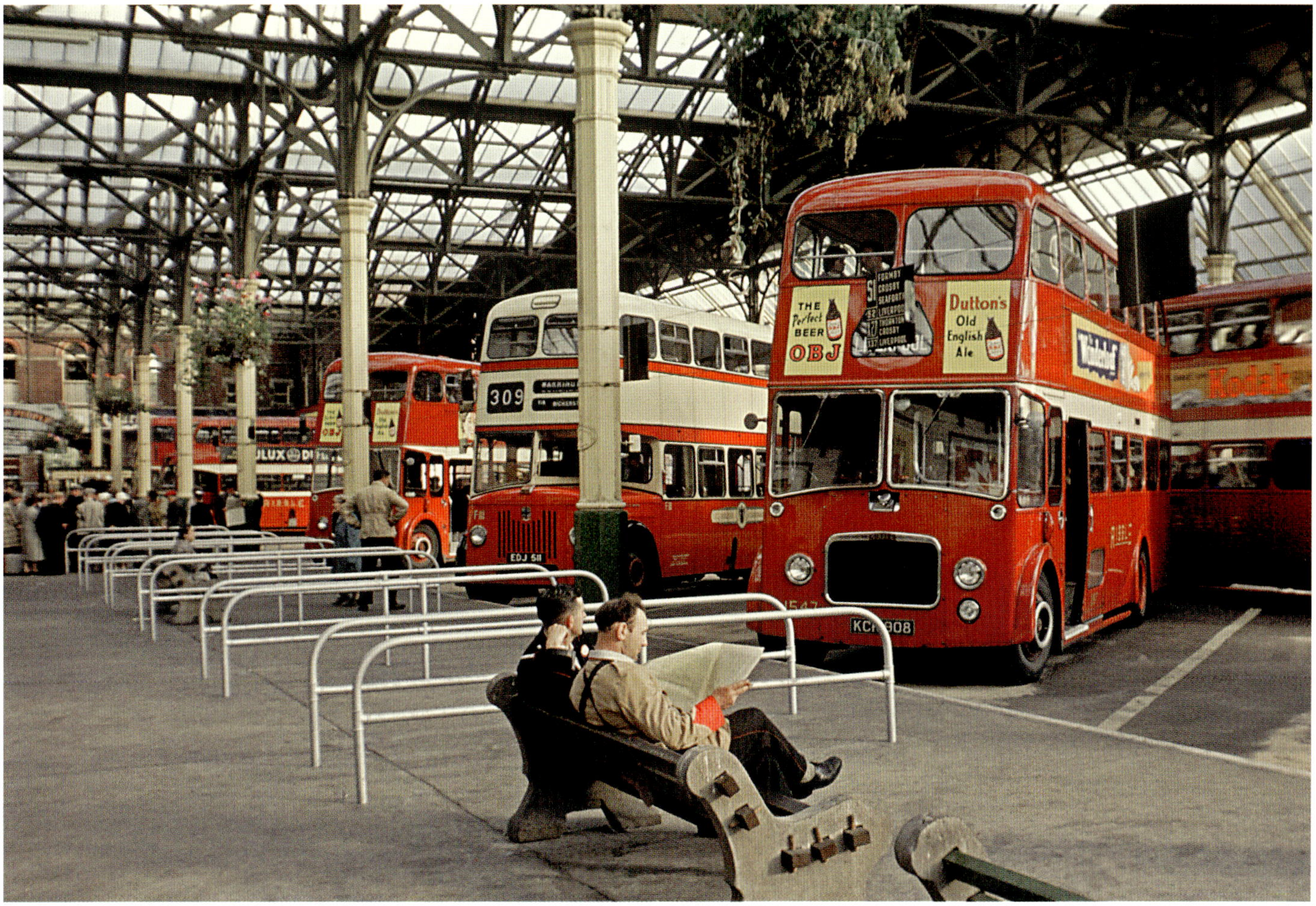

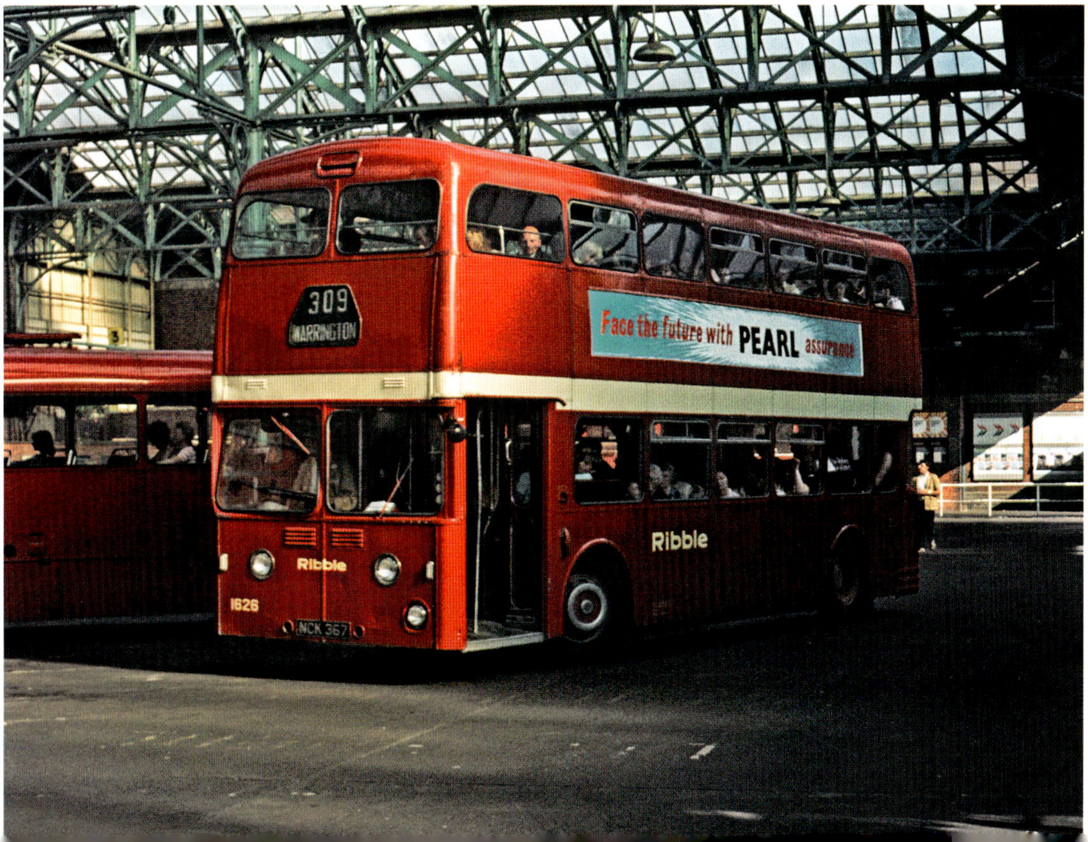

1606-1705 were Ribble's first Atlanteans. Not over reliable they were kept well away from the city services and the Liverpool allocation was two – both at Aintree. It was later doubled to four which produced some typical Scouse humour – *'We got 'em to cover breakdowns of the other two'*. They did appear on the inter-town services and in this picture at Lord Street bus station, Southport garage's 1626 reverses out of its stand for its journey to Warrington which would take ten minutes under two hours. Sunlight shines through the entrance to the bus station, made by opening up the side wall. This picture was taken in 1974 and, apart from repainting, the bus station was much the same as it had been in 1952. *David Powell*

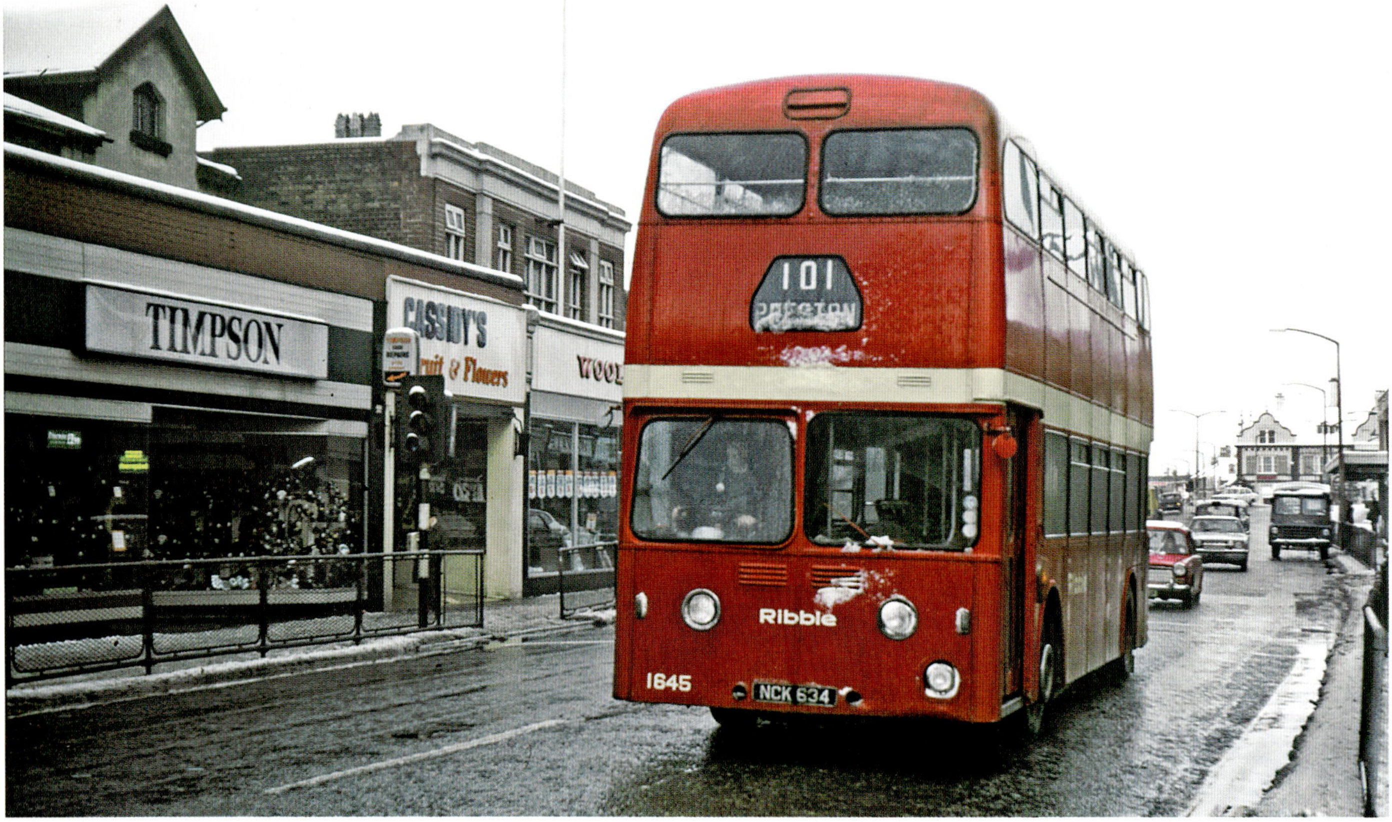

On a cold and snowy day it is perhaps not surprising that Ribble 1645 has very few passengers as it makes its way along the A59 (Rice Lane) in Walton on its journey from Liverpool to Preston via Ormskirk – most of which will be along the A59. *Richard Mellor*

Ribble still had a small need for low height vehicles and, unhappy with the reliability of the Atlanteans, bought sixteen Alexander-bodied Albion Lowlanders. In St Helens on 3rd April 1965 a brand new 1861 waits in Victoria Square outside the town hall for departure time on the 362 to Wigan. Jointly operated with St Helens and Wigan Corporations, the 362 was extended to Widnes on Sundays. Behind is St Helens PD2/22 87 and approaching in the distance is a Burlingham-bodied Ribble PD3. *John Kaye*

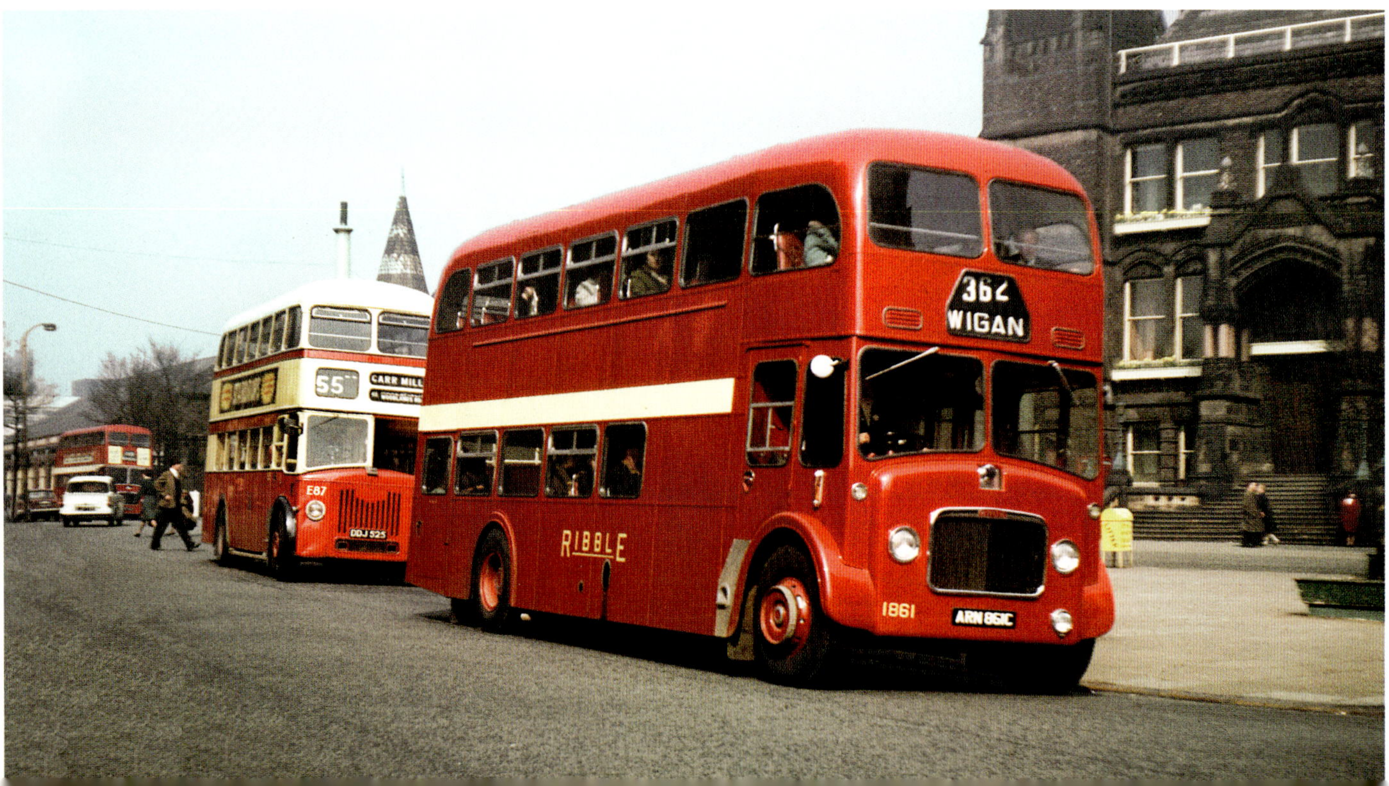

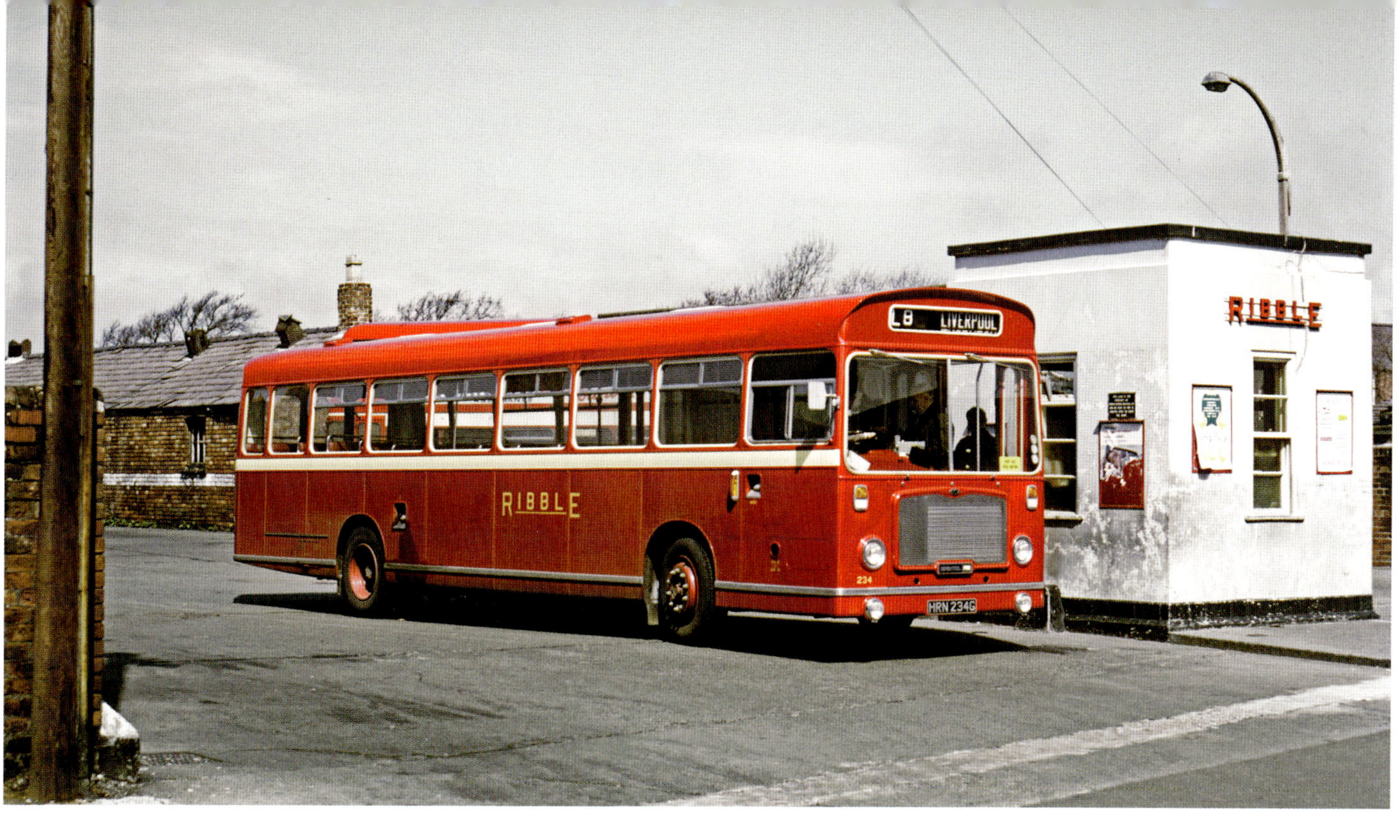

In 1969, 1970 and 1971 Ribble bought several batches of high capacity single-deckers for one man operation. They were Eastern Coach Works-bodied Bristol REs – something which did not go down well at Leyland although by then it owned Bristol. Even more irritating to the men of Leyland was that the second batch, 231-260, had Gardner engines. Bristol RELL6G 234 was brand new when photographed at Crosby bus station in April 1969. Bootle depot's allocation of them was primarily for the busy Crosby town circulars but as in this picture they were also used on services into the city. *Roy Marshall*

One-man high capacity single deckers might have arrived but into the 1970s the majority of Ribble's services into the city were still worked with reliable Leyland PD3s. In this picture with St George's Hall as the backdrop, Burlingham-bodied 1533 passes the entrance to Lime Street station, followed by one of the Liverpool Atlanteans converted to dual-door one-man and another Ribble Burlingham PD3. Two Metro Cammell-bodied PD3s are also in shot. *Ian Stewart*

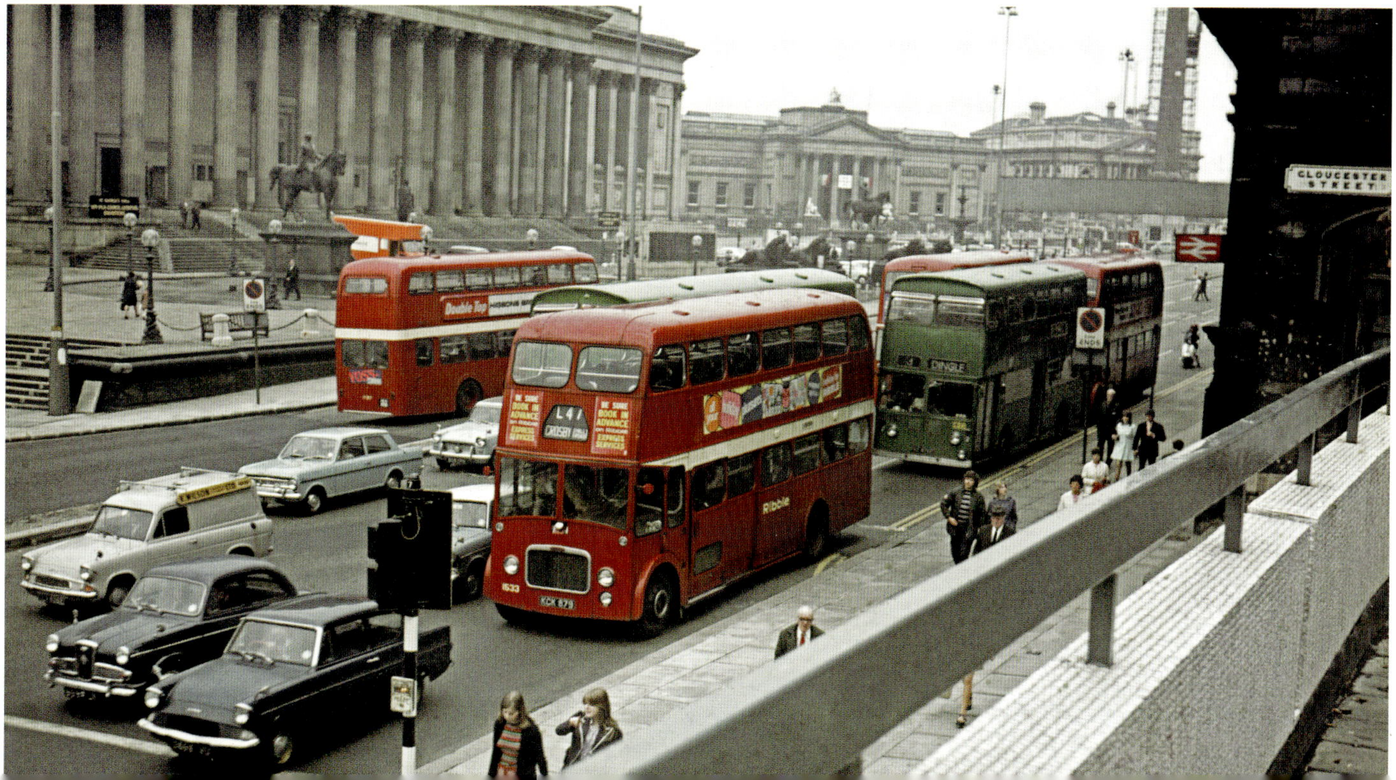

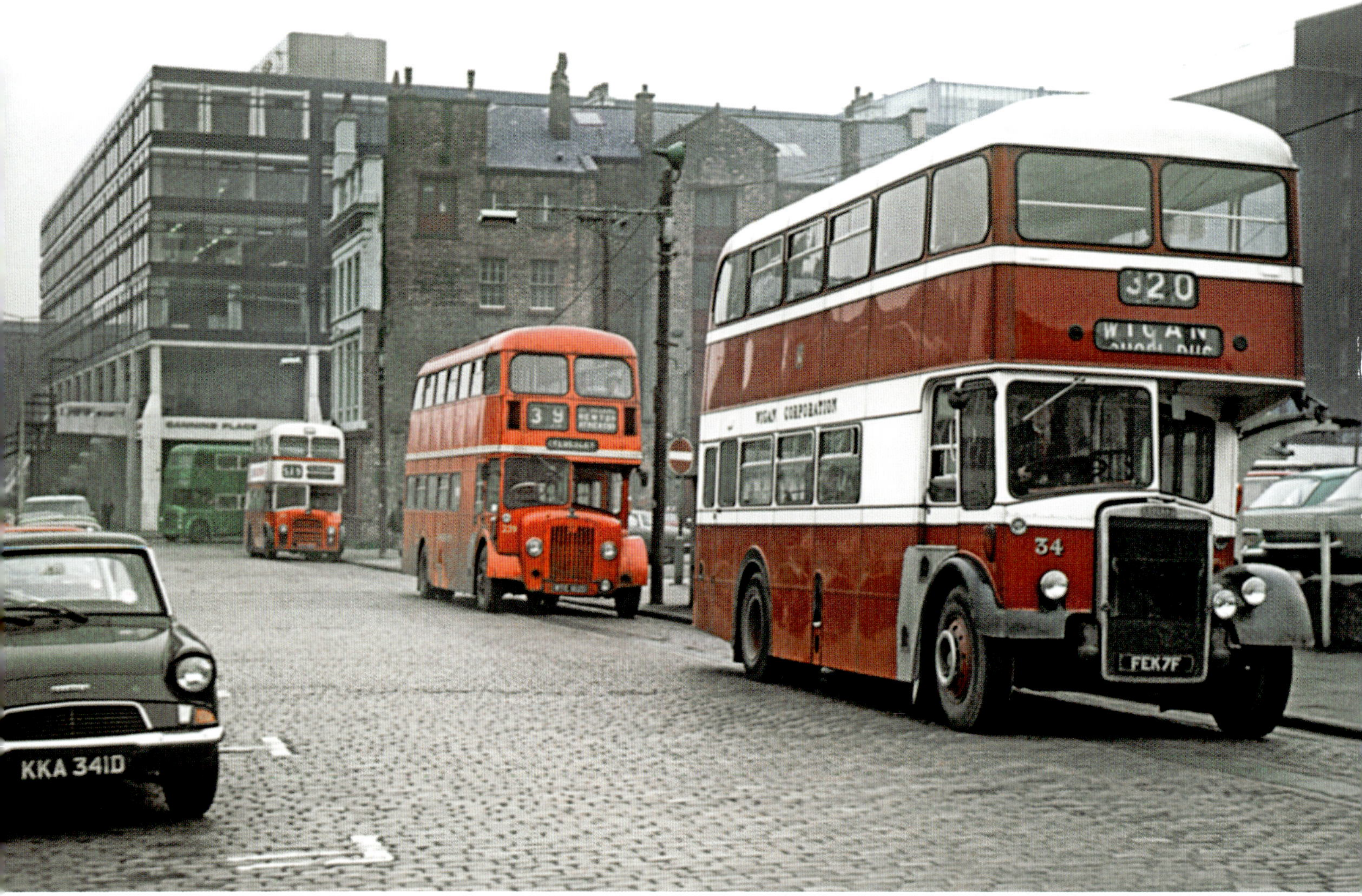

Wigan Corporation worked the 320 (Wigan – Liverpool) jointly with Ribble, St Helens and Lancashire United (LUT) – the latter having a small garage in the city for its express service vehicles. St Helens also came in on the 317, again jointly with Ribble. LUT worked the long stage service 39 to Manchester. A 2¼-hour journey, formally the 39 was joint with Salford, Leigh, St Helens and Ribble but solely operated by LUT. In this 1968 picture of South John Street are Wigan 34, a Massey-bodied Leyland PD2, LUT's Northern Counties-bodied Guy Arab 239, a St Helens East Lancs-bodied PD2 on the 317 – and a Halewood-built Ford Anglia car. *Online Transport Archive*